JETHRO TULL

JETHRO TULL

A History of the Band, 1968–2001

by SCOTT ALLEN NOLLEN

Foreword by Ian Anderson
Afterword by David Pegg
With the participation of
Glenn Cornick and Doane Perry

McFarland & Company, Inc., Publishers
Jefferson, North Carolina, and London

ALSO BY SCOTT ALLEN NOLLEN FROM MCFARLAND

The Boys: The Cinematic World of Laurel and Hardy (2001)

Robin Hood: A Cinematic History of the English Outlaw and His Scottish Counterparts (1999)

Sir Arthur Conan Doyle at the Cinema: A Critical Study of the Film Adaptations (1996)

Robert Louis Stevenson: Life, Literature and the Silver Screen (1994)

Boris Karloff: A Critical Account of His Screen, Stage, Radio, Television and Recording Work (1991)

Frontispiece: **Mayhem, maybe? The roguish Jethro Tull of 1971–1975: Martin Barre, John Evans, Jeffrey Hammond, Ian Anderson and Barrie Barlow. (Photograph courtesy of Ian Anderson.)**

Library of Congress Online Catalog data:

Nollen, Scott Allen.
    Jethro Tull : a history of the band, 1968–2001 / by Scott Allen
  Nollen ; foreword by Ian Anderson ; afterword by David Pegg ; with
  the participation of Glenn Cornick and Doane Perry.
      p.   cm.
    Includes bibliographical references, discographical references, and
  index.
    ISBN 0-7864-1101-5 (softcover binding : 50# alkaline paper) ∞
    1. Jethro Tull (Musical group).   2. Rock musicians—England—
  Biography.
  ML421.J5N+2001

                                           2001044978

British Library cataloguing data are available

Manufactured in the United States of America

Cover photograph: Andy Giddings, Ian Anderson, Martin Barre, Doane Perry and Dave Pegg pose to promote *Jethro Tull: 25th Anniversary,* 1993 *(Photograph by Martyn Goddard; courtesy of Ian Anderson)*

McFarland & Company, Inc., Publishers
  Box 611, Jefferson, North Carolina 28640
    www.mcfarlandpub.com

For Michelle
my Hunting Girl

TABLE OF CONTENTS

Foreword by Ian Anderson   1
Preface   3

Un-Easy Music: An Introduction   17
Becoming Jethro Tull   21
The Albums and Tours (1968–2001)   33
Conclusion   308

Afterword by David Pegg   313
Appendix A: The Members of Jethro Tull   315
Appendix B: Greatest Hits / "Best of" Releases   317
Appendix C: Song Copyright Information   323

Chapter Notes   327
Bibliography   339
Index   343

Ian Anderson, ca. 2000

FOREWORD
by Ian Anderson

Looking back over a 32-year career as one-legged flautist, singer, song-writer, strummer and dancing bear, I have to wonder sometimes if my sagging memory serves well enough to recall, with even part precision, the events, twists and turns, and countless personalities whose paths have crossed mine.

But with a little jogging and the anecdotal encouragement of other interested parties, I can usually mount a reasonably strong and continuous recollection of the Tull story so far.

The sampling of facts, thoughts and opinions expressed by various past band members in Scott Nollen's excellent book is sometimes at variance with my own version but, hey, the occasional contradictions, faint whiffs of scandal and clash of musical egos is about as close as the poor old Jethros are likely to get to a place in the hallowed drug-addled-near-death-experience backstage world of VH1's *Behind the Music* series.

So, read on, dear reader, and enjoy some of the elements and moments which have made up the history of Jethro Tull, as gathered and fine-tuned by Scott Nollen, whose previous authoritative works, together with his obvious "fan" status, provide the perfect credentials for a good curl-up on the sofa of dreams beside a warm winter fire with your favourite pussy by your side. (Pussy-cat that is, dog lovers.)

Ian Anderson
England, or thereabouts,
December 2000

PREFACE

"The Robin Hood of Highgate" is my earliest memory of hearing Jethro Tull. I was only eight in 1971, and I found this lyric fascinating as my 16-year-old sister wore out the grooves in her copy of *Aqualung* as it spun incessantly on the inexpensive fold-out, suitcase-style General Electric record player in our Harlan, Iowa, basement. Of course I wondered who "Cross-Eyed Mary" was, and I was puzzled even further the following year by the lyrics of *Thick as a Brick*, supposedly written by an eight-year-old, Gerald "Little Milton" Bostock. That full-size newspaper album cover was endlessly intriguing for a young lad, particularly after my sister's ex-husband had completed the crossword puzzle.

Increasingly bored with rock music, my tastes gravitated toward jazz and classical, with a growing interest in acoustic instruments as I entered my teen years. Every now and then, I'd find my sister's *Aqualung* record and give it a spin, being drawn to "Mother Goose" and "My God" because of their incorporation of medieval sounds. Following her departure from the parental nest in 1974, no new Tull albums entered our home until relatives bought me the *Too Old to Rock 'n' Roll: Too Young to Die!* album at Christmas 1976. At first I was disappointed, but eventually it grew on me: the songs were so utterly unlike anything else I'd ever heard.

The following spring brought forth a revelation, when the unadulterated British masterpiece *Songs from the Wood* set me on a path I am still traveling. Although I had been interested in Great Britain for a few years (mainly due to Sir Arthur Conan Doyle's *Sherlock Holmes* stories), hearing Tull's incredible blend of English and Scottish music with driving rock had such effects on me that I still find it difficult to describe. The next year's *Heavy Horses* allowed me to recapture the experience, and I spent an entire Sunday listening to the album incessantly until I was forced to

3

sleep. Now overwhelmingly fascinated with Celtic culture, I also completed my Tull record collection and branched out into the wonderful musical worlds of English folk-rockers Fairport Convention and Steeleye Span. Classical music still occupied a lot of my time, but Tull increasingly became the soundtrack of my life. I consistently was impressed by the content and poetry of Ian Anderson's songwriting, and equally by the band's seemingly effortless blending of engaging melodies, rhythmic invention, instrumental proficiency and all-around musical originality.

In November 1979, my friend Todd ("Dane") Jacobsen (a.k.a. "The Martin Barre of Council Bluffs") and I drove to Omaha, Nebraska, to see the Tull lineup many consider the best: Ian Anderson, Martin Barre, John Evans, David Palmer, Barrie Barlow and, on bass for a grand total of two weeks (due to the tragic illness of John Glascock), Dave Pegg, late of Fairport Convention, who just had played their "Farewell Concert" (but later would reconvene to great effect).

In 1982, I received a letter from my musical hero (and now successful fish farmer) Ian Anderson, to whom I'd written several times. He replied that he always was pleased to hear from a "fervent fan" and that he hoped the band would get close enough to Iowa for me to see them. (Jethro Tull has not played a concert in Iowa since April 18, 1979; according to Ian, other than Chicago and Kansas City, the Midwest includes few fans, and St. Paul [as you will read in an upcoming chapter] is just too cold.)

I didn't see a Tull concert again until 1989, in freezing Minnesota, but after some years of disappointment with electronically oriented albums and long gaps between releases, the band, with powerful Doane Perry on drums and Fairport's multi-instrumentalist Martin Allcock on keyboards and additional guitar, sounded as good as ever. And to top off a magnificent concert experience, I also won a tour contest dreamed up by Ian, who soon after sent me one of only 20 "Fish-o-Faxes," a custom salmon and Highland–cowhide wallet handmade at Strathaird, his farm on Scotland's Isle of Skye. (When tour manager Kenny Wylie phoned me from England, he couldn't believe two things: that it took 10 years for me to see Tull again, and how bloody cold it had been in St. Paul.) Ian also promised me free tickets and backstage passes to future Tull shows "whenever the band was in my area." Incredibly, the Fish-o-Fax arrived on my 27th birthday, on which I just had received a travel packet for a 10-day trip to Great Britain.

Through *A New Day*, the independent Jethro Tull information magazine, I learned that Dave Pegg was selling some of his custom-made musical instruments. As I was looking to buy a new bass guitar, I definitely was interested in getting one from the greatest folk-rock bassist of all

Dave Pegg (left) and the author outside "the Woodworm's Hilton," Oxfordshire, September 18, 1990. (Author's collection.)

time. The only major catch was that I had to fly to London and drive to a small village in Oxfordshire to collect it. (As well as raise plenty of "quid" beforehand.) As luck would have it, I was planning to land at Heathrow on September 18, 1990, the only day "Peggy" would be home that month (in between Tull tours).

After finding "the Woodworm's Hilton," Peggy's quaint 17th-century home (just down the street from the George, a lovely pub owned by one of his closest mates; the establishment was named, not to honor one of the Kings George, but the late guitarist Lowell George of the band Little Feat), I waited until his wife, Christine, chauffeured him into the driveway, and I was ushered past the recording studio and into the kitchen, where extremely hot tea was served. (Chris was quite surprised by my absolutely crude Yankee way of drinking it straight, *sans* milk and sugar.) By the time the day was over, I had purchased the handmade Scottish five-string bass Peggy played on *Rock Island* (and subsequent tour) and Fairport's *Red and*

Gold, observed him crawling around on my road map that he had spread out on the living room floor, watched the Tull "Kissing Willie" video with engineer Tim Matyear (the embarrassed Peggy had exited the room), eaten at the George (where the subject of writing a book first came up), heard many incredible stories and gotten into the shower with Dave (we were both fully dressed, as he showed me how to operate the English water system), who also (unintentionally) burned up my electric razor. "Just grow a beard," he advised. It was the beginning of a lovely friendship.

A little more than a year later, on November 24, 1991, I accepted Ian's offer of free tickets and backstage passes for a Tull concert at the Chicago Theatre. (Since I hadn't been working at my new full-time job for very long, I was forced to drive over and back—a round trip of more than 500 miles—in the same day.) Soon after I walked into the theater, about two hours before the concert, I was greeted by Peggy and Martin Allcock, who both were very happy to see a "White Bear" T-shirt (from a North Yorkshire brewpub and inn then owned by Neil Cutts, a friend of the Fairports) peeking out from under my sport jacket. Incredibly, both of them were bellied up to the bar, so I bought Peggy a beer as he pleasingly told me that he and his wife had enjoyed my 1989 book on Laurel and Hardy and that he wanted me to write "his life story." Of course, I accepted without hesitation.

When I asked Peggy if he cared to "have a couple" after the show, he replied, "I slept only three hours this morning, after ten pints of Guinness and three margaritas. And I was out the night before that, as well." He tried his best to convince me that he wasn't up to repeating it a third night.

After finding my seat, which of course was quite good, I was delighted to discover my name, along with those of the other 19 Fish-o-Fax winners, listed on page 12 of the official *Catfish Rising* tour program. Following the show, Peggy predictably had changed his mind about going out. Unfortunately, Ian had the flu, which he attributed, in part, to bad hotel air conditioning, so he wasn't in the best of spirits. Not wanting me to catch his "disease," he expressed concern when I tried to move his bottle of Beck's Dark out of the way as he signed some of my vintage Tull albums. We briefly discussed salmon, protectionist tariffs, the Fish-o-Fax and his tendency to tour during the worst of American winters, as his assistant Gerd Burkhardt stood by.

Disappointed that I didn't have more albums for him to sign, Peggy told me that Martin Barre was upstairs and that I should climb up to meet him. It seemed a bit intrusive barging in on Martin, his lovely wife, Julie, and two daughters who had flown in to visit, but he was quite polite and very reserved, so I had to coax him into discussing his prowess both as a guitarist and a marathon runner.

Back downstairs, the other Martin (a.k.a. "Maart") and I resumed our conversation about the wonderful White Bear, and he and Peggy, now fully energized, invited me to join them at a Rush Street watering hole known as Elliot's Nesst (named, of course, for the "untouchable" who hunted Al Capone). Doane Perry was even more quiet than Martin Barre; and Ian, preparing for his incognito method of exiting a building, waited for an early 1970s brown Chevy Nova to pull up outside the stage door. As he crouched down in the back seat, the rest of the band piled into the proverbial limousine and off they went to their hotel.

When I arrived at the Nesst, Peggy was playing Foosball and the perpetually smiling Maart, a great musician and an even nicer guy, was quaffing liter mugs of Heineken, which he was more than happy to provide for us all. Admitting that he used to drink a lot more, Peggy said he had cut down considerably, now choosing to mix one part white wine to three parts water while on stage. Just before I left for Iowa City, Midge Mathieson, one of the Tull roadies, pointed out that I could have traversed all of England from north to south in the same amount of time.

I next saw Tull during the "Light and Dark Tour" on October 10–11, 1992, when the band was playing a two-night gig at Chicago's Riviera nightclub. The first date was on Saturday evening, the 10th, after which I was supposed to meet Peggy at an Irish tavern for a party thrown by Dave's friend, contractor Brian O'Malley (who had been at the 1991 Chicago show but conspicuously absent from the Elliot's Nesst soiree). Led to believe it would be a private affair in the back room, my Tull compatriot Donald Craig Nance and I instead found wall-to-wall revelers yelling at the top of their lungs, gorging down bad snacks and slopping light beer from a keg. After forcing down some horrible food, Peggy, legendary Fairport drummer Dave Mattacks and O'Malley finally squeezed into the fray at about 11 P.M. I managed to drag Peggy into a somewhat less crowded corridor, where I finally met one of my biggest percussive influences, D. M., whose intense calm and quietness did not surprise me. Peggy was more subdued than usual, but we managed to cover several subjects between pints of Guinness and bad domestic beer.

About two hours later, Peggy, tired of the insane atmosphere of the tavern, left Mattacks to fend for himself and attempted to hail a taxi, to no avail. Offering the comfort of our car, I took a seat next to Peggy in the back, while our designated driver careened about the streets of Chicago. Peggy attempted to give directions to the hotel, but he couldn't remember where it was. He spent a great deal of time in my lap as some sharp corners were taken (including one straight onto Lakeshore Drive that nearly killed us all; needless to say, Tull would have been short one bass player for the following night's gig), but we all enjoyed a truly bizarre rendition of Bob Dylan's "Mr. Tambourine Man" harmonized by Peggy and Craig, who was riding shotgun in the front.

The next afternoon, we Iowegians walked along the Lake Michigan waterfront, spying boats, one rather large freighter, gulls, semi-aquatic dogs and Dave Pegg Rollerblading along the concrete pier. He asked me to join him, but, explaining that I had been run over while rollerskating as a child, I politely declined. (The previous day, Peggy reportedly had been reprimanded by Ian for falling over on the Riviera stage while 'blading.) Dave told us to join him for a pint at Elliot's Nesst after the concert, and then he mentioned that Martin Barre was messing about farther up the shore. Poor Martin, lost in deep concentration over a paperback, was nearly frightened to death as we approached him from the side. He didn't recognize me, so I reintroduced myself and mentioned that Craig, an excellent guitarist, had "worshipped at his shrine" for years. The eternally shy Martin didn't know what to think. He admitted that he disliked the Riviera, but he thought Chicago was a nice place to get out and about. (It is.) Interestingly, no one on the waterfront realized that two rock 'n' roll legends were in their midst.

The highlight of the post-concert get-together at the Nesst was a discussion with new keyboard player Andy Giddings, the first member of Tull who is my age (and has the same rapidly receding hairline), as well as being one of the nicest chaps I've ever met. He really impressed me as a live performer, and during the evening's two-hour concert, had wonderfully recreated the sounds of the original recordings. Andy also had added some jazzy passages to old Tull chestnuts, but, when I queried him about it, he replied, "I don't know a thing *about* jazz." Most satisfying was our agreement about the supremacy of the *Heavy Horses* album.

The following autumn, Tull were back in Chicago, again at a different venue, the new outdoor World Music Theater. On September 5, Peggy phoned to let me know that two backstage passes would be waiting at the box office the following Sunday. After the final encore of the revamped "Dharma for One," my friend Wade Slinde and I were escorted to the theater's open-air "holding area," where we spoke with Peggy, Andy and Doane. I told Doane that his "Dharma" drum solo nearly brought the outdoor roof down, and he replied that using the song as an encore nearly killed him each night. This backstage affair ended rather quickly, but with the aid of Peggy and the ubiquitous Brian O'Malley, we received directions to a motel (a far cry from the band's usual Chicago digs) in nearby Matteson.

Following a gas stop, Wade took a wrong turn onto a country road. Wheeling about, he floored it and sped toward a long-necked, slim-tailed, bright green *thing* that lounged in dead center of the lane. It would not be too exaggerated to admit that we rendered extinct the entire gecko population of Illinois. (I still wonder if some poor child had lost his pet, only to have it heinously beheaded by Mr. Slinde's sports car.)

With the road trip concluded, we discovered Peggy, Andy and Martin Barre enjoying a libation with Brian; David "the Irishman," a Dublin-born folk musician and real estate appraiser; a Kansas City couple who were friends of Peggy's; and some of the Tull crew. The ever-bashful Martin—looking somewhat out of place perched next to O'Malley with a vodka screwdriver in his hand—once again found my compliments embarrassing. For some reason, all who heard Wade's "lizard story" found it fairly hard to believe.

Wade spotted Ian (the erstwhile "Salamander" himself) nursing a cup of coffee at the bar, so I ventured over to interrupt his leisurely conversation with the faithful Gerd Burkhardt. Ian agreed to read my 1989 scholarly essay about his music (which formed this book's introduction), and when I told him that my interest in British history included the music of Jethro Tull, he replied, "*Recent* history, I hope."

Trying to settle a question that long had intrigued me, I asked Ian how, at the age of 46, he managed a nightly two-hour performance of singing, playing, leaping, running, dancing and all-around jestful insanity.

He replied, "I wrestle with Gerd every night. We go back to my room, cover ourselves with extra-virgin olive oil, and wrestle." Pausing only briefly, he added, "Are you available later tonight?"

Thinking it over, I joked, "Well, it's scary, but I *am* available."

Laughing heartily, Ian said, "That's a good one! It would be *scary!*" As for the usually stoic Burkhardt, he was doubled over, too.

As Ian asked me about my Fish-o-Fax, Gerd offered Wade a cookie. Attempting to join the conversation, he apologized for not being able to speak properly with food in his mouth.

"That's why we do it," said Ian slyly.

As the hour wore on, the bartender cut off the liquor supply, much to the chagrin of the Tull enclave (Ian and Martin already had retired for the evening). Not wanting to be bested, some of the gang purchased a dozen bottles of Beck's Dark and stashed them on a table in the lobby. Momentarily, Mrs. Kansas City excitedly announced that Peggy had agreed to sing a song; Andy was uncovering a baby grand piano in the hall.

Fighting off laughter, Peggy launched into "The Sailor's Alphabet" from the 1971 Fairport album *Babbacombe Lee* as Andy expertly plied the keys. But something had changed: the lyrics weren't quite the same. The song had become more accurate as far as befitting the sailor's trade—a wee bit more bawdy, to be sure. When the final choruses had ended in considerable mirth and bawdiness, I excitedly congratulated Andy. "That performance was far better than your version of the 'Locomotive Breath' introduction at the concert," I assured him.

"Why, thank you," Andy graciously replied, shaking my hand. As I attempted to photograph Peggy and Wade, the excited pianist jumped in front of my camera before retiring for a little bawdiness of his own.

When the Beck's was drained, everyone concluded that this state of affairs could not be tolerated. The Irishman phoned a cabby, and the rest elected the sober Wade as the other designated driver. While waiting for the cab, Brian and I warbled into a terrible a capella rendition of Fairport's "The Beggar's Song." Peggy pleaded for us to stop as we butchered the second verse.

The cabby finally pulled up, and we sped off for a lovely dive where etiquette-deprived locals imbibed until 4 A.M. Peggy, O'Malley and the Irishman piled into the cab, while Wade and I transported the partially anesthetized Kansas City couple.

Outside the dive, Peggy asked Wade and me to survey the joint, which we basically found to be a basement garage with flooded-out carpet and clientele to match, but the primitive redneck sounds of Lynyrd Skynyrd welcomed us like a less-than-royal fanfare.

As we bellied up to the bar, I realized that I'd forgotten to take off the backstage pass affixed to my sport jacket. Spying it, the shrewd bartender asked, "Oh, did you see Jethro Tull tonight?"

"Yeah," I replied, trying to ignore him, as Tull's bass player stood next to me. "How was it?" the barkeep insisted on knowing.

"It was *horrible!*" I said as I grabbed my beer. Peggy, his Birmingham accent going unnoticed by everyone behind the bar, was barely able to stifle a laugh.

Some strange things happened at that dive, which I'm certain is a fairly common occurrence. I never dreamed I'd share a conversation with a musical hero while standing in front of filthy floor urinals as the strains of Skynyrd's "That Smell" blasted in the background, nor hear him tell of the time his son threatened to kill him with an axe. ("But we're good mates now," he amended.) At one point, as I showed Peggy a photo from the 1979 *Stormwatch* tour booklet, he lamented his considerable hair loss. When I pointed out that I, too, being 15 years younger, had gone down that road, a charming photo, showing us (plus O'Malley, the Irishman and a descending Mr. Kansas City) with our heads together, was taken.

Mrs. K. C. still was able to maintain a coherent conversation, but her fun-loving husband was finding it difficult to form even the simplest words. Suddenly he pulled off his shirt and displayed his considerably hirsute torso to the crowd. Peggy, registering one of his unique, slightly scoffing facial expressions, thought this rather silly.

"I hope he doesn't take off his pants," I whispered to Mrs. K. C.

"You never know. He might," she replied.

But before he could contemplate (if such was possible at that point) dropping his drawers, the bartender requested, "Sir, you'll have to put your shirt back on." (We all assumed that this joint maintained a high degree of decorum.) Peggy and I attempted to instruct him as to which side of his shirt was right-side-out, but he was lucky to force it over his befuddled head.

At 4 A.M., the lights flickered on, making the dive look even worse. Back in our respective vehicles, we headed back to the motel, where Wade and I deposited Mrs. K. C. and her severely hiccoughing hubby, who continued to amuse Peggy. (Their flight to Kansas City was to depart O'Hare in less than three hours.)

Walking through the halls to Peggy's room, Wade, the Irishman and I witnessed Brian using Dave as a human wheelbarrow, with the latter "walking" with his hands and the former maneuvering his ankles. When Brian laughed loudly, Peggy warned him not to awaken the sleeping Ian, who was in the adjacent room. After we all engaged in some serious male bonding, Peggy offered his two beds to Brian and the Irishman, respectively, while he settled in to sleep on the floor, knowing the Tull flight to Denver was scheduled to depart a mere four and one-half hours later. At 5 A.M., I closed the door, and didn't see Peggy for another four and one-half *years*.

I next saw Tull on September 8, 1996, in Moline, Illinois, where I expected to suffer through an excruciating "revival" performance by Emerson, Lake and Palmer; but to my delight, Ian had decided that Tull should open the show, the first I had attended since Dave Pegg left the band during the summer of 1995. Unfortunately, Ian had moved since our last communication, and my request for passes had not reached him before the tour began.

All the performing members of Jethro Tull have been very busy over the past three decades, and Dave Pegg has been one of the busiest, having played bass with both Tull and Fairport alternately. After a Fairport "Acoustic" Convention concert in Chicago in March 1998, he told me why. (He had seemed reluctant to give the reason in writing or over the phone.)

"I'm an old man," he claimed. "I have to play old man's music." But his performance with a highly energized Fairport (including Simon Nicol, Ric Sanders and recent acquisition Chris Leslie, brilliant on fiddle and mandolin) belied his remarks.

On September 11, 1999, I again received two free tickets and backstage passes from Ian, who was so kind as to provide choice seats in the third row at Chicago's Auditorium Theatre, the best venue in which I ever have seen them perform. After I witnessed Tull at their absolute peak of perfection (Martin Barre sounded as good as he ever has in a live context), Ian's wife, Shona—whom I had never met—informed me that the guitarist had been seriously ill in the hospital until 3:30 that morning. What a trouper he had been during the two-hour concert, truly inspirational. (I later learned that he was suffering from a recurrent stomach ailment.) I also had the pleasure of finally meeting the friendly Kenny Wylie, who gave me some insights into touring and merchandising activities.

Ian was very receptive about this book, agreeing to read the manuscript and write the foreword, and was happy to accept a copy of my just-published volume, *Robin Hood: A Cinematic History of the English Outlaw and His Scottish Counterparts*—being particularly pleased to see that I had included the Scots contenders to the outlaw's mantle. He also—being a connoisseur of savagely hot peppers—received from me a bottle of the skull-keychain graced "After Death" habanero sauce, which I was certain he never had tried.

"Actually, I have a bottle of this in my refrigerator at home," he admitted.

"Well, now you have a back-up," I insisted. "You can share it with your bandmates." (I knew Doane Perry also tempts the very flames of Hell.)

"I'm not putting that in *my* suitcase," Shona informed Ian. "If it should explode, well…." (You see, I had piled so many gifts upon Ian that he couldn't accept anything from other fans. I am certain that Shona packed it well into the depths of *his* bag before they reached St. Louis.)

Ian and I discussed this book at some length, and he explained further the complex subject of rock 'n' roll merchandising, particularly why a volume such as this could never make a profit at concert venues. After every party—including the manufacturer, the distributor and the owners of the venue—takes a piece of the pie, little or nothing is left for the artist. (Hence the mass marketing of the T-shirt, "the only item that makes any money.")

Following my audience with Ian, I talked with Doane Perry, whom I hadn't met in person since 1993. He said he would be happy to join the book project and asked me to send him a batch of questions that he might be able to answer at some length.

Less than two months later, on November 3, I was back in Chicago, again to see Fairport at Fitzgerald's. The band was better than ever, with all the Fairports feeling well and being very sociable between sets and after the gig. The crowd was packed with Tull fans who had attended the September 11 show at the Auditorium—a few of them actually, shockingly, remembering me. Peggy had celebrated his 52nd birthday—aided by (of course) Brian O'Malley—the previous evening, so he was a bit dram-shy at the bar, repeatedly assuring me that he indeed would send a recording of his Tull reminiscences in time for this book's publication. (He also was pleased that I had dedicated my *Robin Hood* to him, making it clear that he planned to read it after he returned home to Oxfordshire.) Informing me that he would reminisce after the Yuletide holidays, he came through early, recording the tape just before Thanksgiving in St. Petersburg, Florida, after Fairport had played two gigs in Bermuda.

Just a few days prior to completing the manuscript, my mother and I, who first had heard those strains of "Aqualung" and "Cross-Eyed Mary" issuing from the basement way back in 1971, accepted another choice set of tickets from Ian, to see Tull at the Ravinia Festival in Highland Park, Illinois, on August 8, 2000. Following excellent sets by opening band the Young Dubliners and Tull, we ventured backstage to pick up Ian's proof-read version of the manuscript and to see the wonderful Doane Perry.

On our way in to talk to Ian, I finally was able to meet Peggy's successor, bassist Jonathan Noyce, a nice young chap indeed. I told him what a treat it was to hear him re-create Glenn Cornick's original "Bourée" solo of 1969, and an enormous smile lit up his face. (I soon learned that Jon is a good friend of Tull pioneer Cornick.)

During my chat with the fluted one (who again "shook hands" with his elbow to protect his wrist), I presented him with my yearly gift of habanero hot sauce—two bottles this time—and he was grateful that I had replenished his stock. "The Young Dubliners just finished off my last bottle," he said, also mentioning that he had (obviously) survived last year's gift of "After Death." As he handed back the corrected manuscript, which he had read while on the road, and talked about the content of the foreword he would write upon his return to England, I asked him what he thought of this entire undertaking.

"Very *interesting*...." he replied.

Back out in the visitors' area, my mother and I chatted with Martin Barre and Andy Giddings, whom I reminded of our previous get-togethers. He definitely had forgotten what I looked like, and when I talked of

The author (left) and Doane Perry, thrilled with his gift of habanero hot sauces, backstage at the Ravinia Pavilion, Highland Park, Illinois, August 8, 2000. (Photograph by Shirley A. Nollen; author's collection.)

our past sharing of a few bottles of Beck's, he replied, "Well, I don't really ever remember anything." Of course I expressed my admiration for his impressive buzz cut.

Doane was his always cheerful and friendly self, and, as we discussed his contributions to this book, I inspired him to share "The Donut Story" with other fans who were gathered 'round. (This infamous tale appears in the following pages.) I also gave him a gift of a double habanero onslaught, for which he was very appreciative. One of the bottles, a product of the "Mo' Hotta, Mo' Betta" line, delighted him.

After my mother and I had been thoroughly "Tulled," we exited the backstage gate and walked through acres of rubbish (the many thousands of fans had left the place looking like Woodstock) so I could phone a taxi. After two calls to the cab company and another to the hotel, whose staff refused to fetch us "after the desk closed," she and I were stranded after waiting nearly two hours, in the pitch dark, in Chicago, at 1:30 in the morning. Thank you, impressive hotel and taxi services. The real praise is due a certain young man named Justin who extricated us from that devastating dilemma.

On the evening of November 1, 2000, my wife, Michelle, and I caught another Fairport "Acoustic" show at Fitzgerald's. The Nicol-Pegg-Sanders-Leslie lineup was back in prime form, hanging about long enough to allow us to celebrate Peggy's 53rd birthday before they headed out for the next night's concert and party in Cincinnati. Dave was very anxious to see the published version of this book, and also reaffirmed that he still wished me to co-write his "memoirs."

When I told Peggy that his name would be on the cover of this book, he replied, "Finally ... I'm famous!" and again thanked me for dedicating *Robin Hood* to him, "my fine English friend."

Just before we left the pub, Peggy, ever-present pint in hand, gave Michelle specific orders to "take good care of me," serving up her first "rock-star" kiss. (I wasn't jealous, however; as usual, the male bonding was in full force.)

The album ratings in this book (based on a 1–5 point system) are not arbitrary, but based on my own assessments over the past three decades, combined with the views of longtime Tull fans, reviewers and music critics. Hopefully, the analyses of every song on all the albums provide sufficient explanations for these ratings.

First and foremost, I would like to thank Ian Anderson for becoming personally involved with this project. He not only proofread the entire manuscript during Tull's 2000 North American tour, but also wrote the foreword, provided many unpublished and rare photographs from his private collection, and granted permission to quote from his song lyrics. Additionally, he saw to it that this book was unencumbered by any lyrical or photographic copyright restrictions. In fact, Ian kindly honored each and every request I made over a ten-year period, always providing choice tickets and backstage passes at Tull concerts. But, most of all, I must express my gratitude for the three decades of musical joy he and the band have given me.

For their conversations over the years and assistance in completing this book, I would like to thank Martin Allcock, Shona Anderson, Martin Barre, Andy Giddings, Chris Leslie, Midge Mathieson, Dave Mattacks, Jonathan Noyce, Ric Sanders and Kenny Wylie.

Great appreciation goes to Glenn Cornick, a legendary bassist and terrific guy, who added so much material during the 11th hour, proofread the sections on the formative years of the band and provided photographs from his private archives.

A very special thank you goes to Doane Perry, a great drummer and a helpful collaborator, who provided hours of Tull reminiscences and proofread the portions of the manuscript covering his 16 years in the band. Amidst a frantic schedule, Doane made several suggestions that improved the book considerably, cheerfully contributing more time than he had to spare, including e-mailing from relatively remote parts of the globe.

Some Tull fans, from as far away as Turkey, also contributed to this book and its promotion: Raymond Benson, Rob Curtis, W. S. Gumby, Scott Huntley, Mark Louis, Aykut Oral, Amy Rosenblatt, Dag Sandbu and Jan Voorbij, webmaster of the excellent "Cup of Wonder" website. I also must thank David Rees and Martin Webb for their work on the fanzine *A New Day*, and for spending so much time searching for all things Tull. Their efforts have contributed to keeping the Tull flame alive.

Thanks also to the following individuals who either contributed to my research, helped take care of business, or played some sort of role in my three-decade fascination with Jethro Tull: Heather Bunting (Ian Anderson Group of Companies), Veronique Cordier, Andrew Godfrey (Chrysalis Music UK), Todd ("Dane") Jacobsen, Marilyn Klepacz (Ian Anderson Group of Companies), Tim Matyear, Donald Craig Nance, Harold Nollen, Michelle Nollen, Shirley Nollen, Debra Nollen-Richter, Keith Roberts (Young Dubliners), Brian O'Malley, Christine Pegg and Wade Slinde.

And last, but absolutely not least: thank you, Dave Pegg. "Cheers!"

Scott Allen Nollen
Los Angeles
Fall 2001

UN-EASY MUSIC:
AN INTRODUCTION

Historian G. E. Fussell has written that "the name of Jethro Tull figures in almost every textbook of economic and farming history from the most elementary schoolbook to the most advanced study."[1] Although the band was titled in 1968 "by accident," through the suggestion of a booking agent at London's Ellis-Wright management, the name actually reflects founder and frontman Ian Anderson's musical *oeuvre*.

Anderson consistently has denied that he is the author of "concept" albums (with the possible exceptions of *Thick as a Brick* [1972] and *A Passion Play* [1973]), but his thematics have remained fairly consistent since the release of *Aqualung* in 1971, a motif that addresses the way in which modern industrialized society has encroached upon and destroyed a more natural, organic way of life. This theme appears in several forms, but two major types of songs appear quite frequently throughout the Jethro Tull albums: one type poses industrialization and urbanism against nature, while the second suggests how sociocultural constructs (politics, religion, commercialism) restrict common sense and create both economic and intellectual poverty.

The incorporation of Celtic folk into Jethro Tull music, a fusion that reached its height with *Songs from the Wood* and *Heavy Horses* in 1977–78, but already can be heard in abundance on the second album, *Stand Up* (1969), provides a musical reinforcement of Anderson's lyrical thematics. His tendency to blend cutting-edge technology with traditional musical influences reflects his philosophical desire to maintain a simpler, more ecologically minded, lifestyle in a modern setting.

Moving into the English countryside in the mid–1970s and establishing a salmon farm on Scotland's Isle of Skye increased Anderson's appreciation for more traditional, organic themes. This change of lifestyle also created additional links with the historical Jethro Tull, who, born in 1674, lived in an England of less than six million inhabitants residing in tiny villages and on isolated farms. Wide sections of land—mountains, forests, and moors—still were untouched by human use and misuse. This past milieu, occurring prior to Great Britain's embrace of the Industrial Revolution during the 19th century, is reflected in a large amount of Jethro Tull music. This setting is recalled, not only in songs situated in the past, but also in those dealing with contemporary issues and events.

A second parallel is that the historical Tull also was a fully accomplished musician, spending his non-farming time at the organ (a quality Tull and Anderson both share with another farmer-composer-musician, the great Robert Burns [1759–96]). But, while Anderson chose to become a farmer, as well as a musician, Tull did not actively seek agriculture as a profession. "When I was young, my diversion was musick," he once said.[2]

A fascinating paradox exists in comparing the historical figure and Anderson's Jethro Tull music. A basic social criticism imbedded in the songs attacks how mechanization and industrialization have adversely affected the natural ecosystem, a development for which the historical Tull is partially responsible. Considered to be the "father" of modern farming methods, he invented the seed-drill, the first agricultural implement.

Songs from the Wood includes themes of celebration ("Songs from the Wood," "Ring Out, Solstice Bells," "The Whistler"), eroticism ("Hunting Girl," "Velvet Green") and ecology ("Jack in the Green"), all situated within a bygone, rustic milieu. "Jack in the Green" suggests the encroachment of urbanization into the natural world, but offers a glimmer of hope: "I saw some grass growing through the pavements today." The song proved a precursor to the overall theme of *Heavy Horses*, an album considered by many to be the epitome of the Jethro Tull experience. Beginning with a poetic and adventurous tribute to Anderson's cat ("And the Mouse Police Never Sleeps"), *Heavy Horses* includes nine explorations of the basic city-versus-country theme. Recalling "Jack in the Green," "Acres Wild" directly addresses the replacement of "wide open spaces" with "concrete." The title song is a majestic tribute to the plow horses of the British Isles, once an essential and powerful agricultural force rendered obsolete in the wake of mechanization.

Following in 1979, the haunting *Stormwatch* also focuses on the environment, particularly the damage wrought by petroleum and nuclear power in "North Sea Oil." Anderson's preference of nature over the "civilized" world is obvious on the album jacket's back cover depicting a gigantic, snarling polar bear stomping reactors into ice-covered terrain. Nearly a decade later, Anderson's concerns remained adamant, on *Crest of a Knave* (1987), an album that unbelievably earned the band a Grammy Award for the best hard rock/heavy metal album of 1988. A song that proved a well-received hit, "Farm on the Freeway," examines the governmental practice of paying off farmers to utilize the land for the extension of roadways. "Mountain Men," also recalling "Jack in the Green," depicts a nearly mythic existence in which Anderson yearns to return to a more organic past age.

The following year, Anderson's attack on modern values became obvious in "Part of the Machine," originally released as a single and included in its entirety on the *20 Years of Jethro Tull* box set, perhaps his most blatant criticism of society since his cynical portrait of organized religion on side two of *Aqualung* in 1971. Whether he has offered a thorough derision of modern society (the musically and intellectually dense *Thick as a Brick* and "Dark Ages" on *Stormwatch*, which parallels our era with the medieval period), or more specific subjects (imperialism, war, and impending Armageddon on *War Child* [1974]), Anderson has maintained this criticism as an essential aspect of his composition. Later albums include references to the depressed British economy ("Fallen on Hard Times" on *The Broadsword and the Beast* [1982]) and the ineffectual conservative approach of Margaret Thatcher ("Jump Start" on *Crest of a Knave*).

Anderson's populism is reflected in his many songs about the working class. At times, this "common man" theme is set in the past (the wandering musicians playing for Elizabethan nobility in "Minstrel in the Gallery" on *Minstrel in the Gallery* [1975]), but it also appears in modern settings in "Up to Me" on *Aqualung*, "A Stitch in Time" (a 1978 single) and "Steel Monkey" on *Crest of a Knave*.

"I don't think music should be easy to listen to," Anderson said in a July 1971 interview with *Rolling Stone*. "I think music of all kinds should require an effort from everyone involved. Both musicians and audience should be struggling toward something, even if it's not necessarily the same thing."[3] This attitude has helped Tull create music of a consistently unique quality: fresh, eclectic, and meticulously composed and performed. Avoiding the mainstream press and publicity, Anderson, unlike many "socially conscious" rock performers, considers his audience intelligent enough to understand his ideas without needing to be pushed in that direction, an aspect that induces the listener to become actively involved. Often, the "message" is in the originality of the music itself. Best-selling novelist and teacher Craig Thomas, in his 1993 essay celebrating the 25th anniversary of the band, suggested how Anderson, having created the character of "Tull," has used a complex fusion of styles and instruments to convey thought-provoking narrative content: "The persona speaks not simply with the lyrics he utters, but with the instrumentation and the musical elements he juggles, contrasts or amalgamates."[4]

Unlike most contemporary music, particularly that which is classified in the rock genre, the work of Jethro Tull is rarely simplistic, functioning on only one level. This feature is inherent in its eclectic nature, blending folk, classical, jazz and blues forms with rock, as well as in Anderson's lyrics, which often eschew didacticism for adventurous storytelling, as in the chilling yet soulful "Flying Dutchman" (on *Stormwatch*), which retells the tale of a "ghost ship" forced to sail against the wind until Judgment Day. Other songs, such as "Broadsword" and "Seal Driver" (on *The Broadsword and the Beast*) weave fantastic images of romantic days gone by. And, perhaps reflecting Anderson's tendency to merge "the old with the new," tracks such as "No Lullaby" (on *Heavy Horses*) and "Beastie" (on *The Broadsword and the Beast*) fuse subjects such as modern stress and psychological angst with images of legendary dragons and Scottish "beasties."

In his commemoration of the band's silver celebration in 1993, Chrysalis Music's Roy Eldridge wrote:

> The quality of originality is at its most obvious in Ian's music. Sure, its influences exist in the blues, rock, jazz and folk but he doesn't sample or steal: he draws from a variety of music that he listened or listens to and ends with a musical style that is sometimes diverse but ultimately his. The originality has been the big ingredient to a long career. Eccentric, possibly; idiosyncratic, probably; original, definitely.[5]

BECOMING JETHRO TULL

"Fortunate indeed the child who first sees the light of day in that romantic town," said the controversial industrialist and self-appointed philanthropist Andrew Carnegie, born in Dunfermline, Scotland, in 1835. In Fife, 17 miles north of Edinburgh on the north shore of the Firth of Forth, the town boasted an incredible history when Ian Scott Anderson was born there on August 10, 1947.

Dunfermline (meaning "the fortified tower by the winding stream"), first settled by the Picts, had become a residence of Scottish royalty by the middle of the 11th century, when Margaret, wife of King Malcolm III ("Canmore"), founded a Benedictine priory, further raised to abbey status by their son, David I, in 1128. However, the Normans soon obliterated the structure, raising their own nave, which survived for centuries to come.

Claims that Dunfermline was the medieval capital of Scotland have not been proved, but during the 16th century, the guest house of the abbey was transformed into a royal palace, where Charles I, the last monarch to be born in Scotland, arrived on November 19, 1600. Three years later, the "Union of the Crowns" between England and Scotland ended the royal connection with the town. By 1624, Dunfermline was nearly wiped out by a raging fire that left most of the inhabitants homeless.

By the 18th century, Dunfermline's fortunes again were on the rise, with coal mining and linen weaving leading the way to an economic prosperity that flowered during the coming years. In 1818, local developers began heavily to promote tourism after a dramatic discovery was made by historians claiming that the tomb and remains of Scotland's greatest monarch, King Robert the Bruce, had been found at Dunfermline Abbey (though Bruce's heart, contained in a special chest, had been buried at

Melrose Abbey, south of Edinburgh). The graves of seven other kings, four queens, five princes and two princesses also were revealed.

In 1848, when Andrew Carnegie was a mere 13, a decline in the hand-loom weaving trade led to his family's immigration to the United States, where he would make his fortune upon the backs of blue-collar men but give back to them, endowing libraries and scholarship funds for tax purposes and self-aggrandizement.

In 1903, Carnegie endowed a public library and baths, as well as deeding the historic Pittencrieff Estate as a public park to be used by the people of the town. He made it known that his intention was "to bring into the monotonous lives of the toiling masses of Dunfermline more of sweetness and light."[1]

Resembling a scaled-down version of Edinburgh across the Forth, Dunfermline featured a bustling High Street with curious Lowlanders venturing out to add some color to their humdrum lives. Those who veered into the recently splendored resting place of the Bruce of course felt considerably more reverent than the tourists who filed through. Wanting exercise, those seeking a look at Lowland braes could easily venture north to the commoner habitations at Cairney Hill or Limekilns.

During the 1920s, the collapse of the weaving industry and depletion of the coal mines led to a 6,000-person decrease in Dunfermline's population, leaving the town with 41,000 inhabitants. Following the hellish devastation of World War II, when young master Anderson made his worldly debut, the expansion of the incorporated Rosyth Naval dockyard and the development of the burgeoning electronics industry provided an opportunity for a lad inclined to the entertainment trade. On the legitimate musical scene, the establishment of Scotland's first full-time symphony orchestra occurred at this time.

Dunfermline's atmosphere was ripe for a child with a keen ear for music. During the first two decades of the 20th century, dedicated folk-music archivists like Gavin Greig and the Reverend James B. Duncan collected from the mists of obscurity hundreds of worthy traditional tunes and songs that subsequently would be arranged by Marjorie Kennedy-Fraser—versions played by the next two generations of Celtic traditionalists who spurred the full renaissance of Scottish and Irish music enjoyed the world over. As stated by the editors of *Collins Encyclopedia of Scotland*:

> Only in the late 20th century have the necessary institutional balance of social forces made possible the sustaining of a large body of professional musicians…. Some musicians are happy to cross the borders

between classical, folk, pop and jazz; others prefer to sustain the lines of traditional as they perceive them....[2]

Once embraced by music, Ian Anderson would exemplify this eclectic approach to creating his own unique niche, musically, expressively; but for now, he, like all young children, was guided by his parents, who attempted to give him a socially acceptable upbringing. In 1951, the family moved to Edinburgh, where the lad entered Roseburn Primary School two years later. He recalled:

> My family was not religious but they did encourage me to go to church and Sunday school as a child and ... although I tried it ... I didn't understand what was happening. And combined with the fact that I was a Scotsman; I had to wear a kilt to Sunday school which I consider rather indecent and still do, having rather thin legs and bony knees. I felt rather strongly against the whole idea.[3]

By 1955, Ian could not stand the fear tactics the church used to indoctrinate its parishioners. At age eight, he refused to attend any longer, creating an estrangement from his father that lasted for many years. A year earlier, city planners had resigned Edinburgh to a development plan that destroyed much of its historical heritage, a ruinous approach that reached its deleterious height during the late 1960s and early 1970s.

Ian acquired his first musical instrument, a plastic ukulele bearing a facsimile of Elvis Presley's autograph, in 1956. Each of the four nylon strings was a different color and would not stay in tune "for more than thirty seconds." "This wretched piece of tat was just about playable," he wrote.[4] Two years later, his father bought him a real guitar, a Spanish model the lad had viewed in an Edinburgh shop window. Described as "a ferocious beast," it set back the elder Anderson an entire £5.[5]

In 1959, Ian moved with his family to the northern English industrial town of Blackpool, where his parents ran a corner grocery and boarding house. At night, Mr. Anderson earned extra money as a watchman. Ian was enrolled at Blackpool Grammar School for Boys, where a "typical" headmaster taught "morally sound" Christian lessons, ideas he found difficult to grasp.

Of his earliest artistic roots, Ian admitted, "I like to think my parents really came from a musical son. If my parents had some music in them, it wasn't obvious to me or them. Maybe it skipped a generation."[6] Any interest in music was not the product of formal instruction, as it was for his brother, Robin, who became a successful ice skater and, later, manager of the Scottish Ballet. In 1971, Ian said:

I avoided piano lessons conscientiously as a child. I didn't want to become involved in something at that age that I didn't understand the worth of or the reason for. Most children when they're taught, and I use the word taught as opposed to encouraged, to play music ... do it rather to please their parents or to achieve some mastery over other children without any understanding of music.... I think it's easier to learn to play when you're older.... How can a child do anything other than parrot a piece of Tchaikovsky ... play it the way his music teacher tells him to play it. But how can he understand the emotions of a man many times older than him?[7]

Ian's first ambition to form a band struck him in 1963, when, fiddling about with his guitar, he asked his Blackpool schoolmates Jeffrey Hammond and John Evans if they also were interested. Hammond agreed to play bass, and Evans, who had been trained as a pianist by his mother, offered the use of the family living room in exchange for taking up the drum stool. An older boy called Hipgrave also joined in. Of his turning from further education to music, Anderson said:

I decided I wanted something more immediate in terms of doing something. So I decided to be a musician. I wasn't that keen on music really, I wasn't wild about it.... I started playing music when I was about 16, 17, and got into the origins of what was popular in the contemporary sense—the Beatles, the Stones, and all that. I got into the origins of their music, where they'd lifted it from—Howlin' Wolf, Muddy Waters, Sonny Boy Williamson and all the rest. I began to write music and developed a certain basic ability with instruments and a crude understanding of the musical vocabulary that one has to have in order to write or appreciate or simply understand music. No one ever taught me to read or write music or play an instrument, it was just the painful process of working it out yourself. How to make pleasing noises.[8]

Ian discovered he had innate musical ability, just as he would later realize his prodigious talents for other artistic and business endeavors. He explained further:

[N]obody can teach you to play music. They can teach you to make the noises at the right pitch and for the right duration, and they can teach you to produce a semblance of tone. But they can't teach you actually to play music, not in terms of music as a celebration, as an expression of life. No one can teach you that.[9]

Shifting his focus to singing, Anderson hired Michael Stephens, bass player for the popular local group the Atlantics, to handle the guitar work, and drummer Paul Jackman. With Evans switching to piano, they began to gig around the area as the Blades, named after a nightclub in Ian Fleming's 1955 James Bond novel *Moonraker*. Accepting the hefty compensation of £2, they played their first paying set at Blackpool's Holy Family Youth Club in late 1963. Commenting on what styles of music had influenced him, Anderson said:

> I suppose it was influenced by whatever I heard on the radio from the ages of 7 to 17, or whenever it was I started to write tunes. I think the only really clear-cut influence I had was the apparent simplicity, musically speaking, of Negro blues and, to some extent, the more popular big-band kind of numbers—Glenn Miller and that kind of thing—that I remember my father playing.[10]

Jeffrey Hammond recalled that the Blades offered "the first stumbling steps along the creative path ... together with many warm memories of friendships, youth clubs, utility vans, girlfriends, John's mother's home, the Top Ten Coffee Bar and innumerable gigs in dark, Satanic, northern mill towns."[11]

In early 1964, the band searched for a new drummer to replace Jackman, who had proved unsatisfactory. After one chap failed his audition due to his interest in the money he might earn, a 14-year-old Birmingham lad named Barrie Barlow rose to the fore. At this time, Ian graduated from the grammar school, having scored well on his exams "and ... due for a course as a teacher, lawyer or accountant ... one of those possessing a great moral fiber and suitably inclined to take his place in English society."[12] After working as a sales trainee at Lewis' Department Store that summer, he actually considered joining the Blackpool Police Force, but was dissuaded by an officer's suggestion that he first get a university education. So off Ian went to the Blackpool College of Art.

Michael Stephens left the Blades during the autumn of 1965, but two new musicians were added to bolster the sound: trumpeter-saxophonist Jim Doolin and tenor sax player Martin Skyrme. The name of the band changed, too: although Anderson still fronted, they now gigged as the John Evan Band. (The "s" in Evans was dropped for effect.) Anderson said, "John's mother gave us the money to buy a Hammond organ and a van. We had to call it the John Evan Band because we couldn't afford to pay her back. So she had some very limited glory, as opposed to financial reimbursement."[13]

Playing American blues and R&B material, the group went through more name and personnel changes. After a stint as the John Evan Big Band

Neil ("Chick Murray") Smith, Ian Anderson, Neil ("Ranger") Valentine (with saxophone), John Evans (seated), Barrie Barlow, Tony Wilkinson and Glenn Cornick pose in front of the Granada Television studio, London, May 23, 1967.

Sound, they became the John Evan Smash in 1967. After Stephens left, guitarists included former Atlantics fretman Chris Riley and Neil Smith; Hammond was superseded on bass by Bo Ward and Glenn Cornick; and drummer Ritchie Dharma briefly took over Barlow's drum chair. Also joining during this period were saxophone players Neil Valentine and Tony Wilkinson, on tenor and baritone, respectively.

Glenn Cornick (born Glenn Douglas Barnard) was a prodigiously talented member of the group. First playing guitar in 1962 at the age of 15, he switched to bass the following year. After gigging with some bands in his birthplace of Barrow-in-Furness, Cumbria (his parents' home was in

Rothesay on Scotland's Isle of Bute), he moved to Blackpool, where he played hotels and clubs with the Executives before joining the John Evan Band in 1966. Of his early influences, Cornick recalled:

> I originally used to listen to a lot of swing-blues stuff. And all the pop stuff that British people used to like: Buddy Holly, Cliff Richard and the Shadows. All British music comes from Cliff and the Shadows. That was the most universal thing. There isn't a bass player in Britain of my age who couldn't play every bloody Shadows song that ever was a hit. People might not admit it, but that was what they learned. And we were quite lucky, because Cliff Richard and the Shadows were incredibly good musicians—a rock 'n' roll band who, in 1960, knew how to use a diminished chord. And they didn't use it for show. They did it because it was the right thing to put in.
>
> You listen to the Ventures, and the Ventures are surf music. But the Shadows really had a depth to them that we didn't know they had. To us, they were just the coolest pop band that we had ever heard. So we had the advantage of listening to stuff that was actually very good.
>
> Other than that, when I was fifteen or so, I listened to blues. Early Muddy Waters and things like that. Country-blues stuff, not the B. B. King type of stuff. You wouldn't think that, at that period in small towns in Great Britain, you could go into record shops and buy that stuff, but you could. My first John Lee Hooker EP that I bought—up in a small town in the north of England—all these different American blues records. I don't know what led us to buy that stuff, but we did and thought, "Wow, this stuff is so cool!"
>
> I don't have any idea where my style came from. Part of it came from the fact that I didn't have a particularly good ear. Very often I actually had to sit down and work out things. And that's quite an advantage sometimes, because you don't play the obvious, cliché-type things.[14]

The Evan Band first took the stage at a Kirkham talent contest on March 5–6, 1966. After winning the competition, they were asked to return to the Elizabethan Club for two gigs on March 17–18. Following a performance at Warrington's Co-op Hall on April 23, Anderson received a bizarre nickname when a fan burst backstage to exclaim, "Man, you sound just like *Elvo!*" Having consciously adopted the John Mayall style of aping black American bluesmen (as did so many other British pop singers of the period), perhaps he failed to appreciate the comparison to Elvis Presley, but the moniker haunted him for some time. During the summer, the band played at several boat clubs in Nottingham, and on June 4, at the British Cellophane in Barrow, they opened for Herman's Hermits—an act they repeated later that month at Barrow's "99" club. On November 19, they opened for Pink Floyd at the Canterbury Technical College.

Gigging was now Ian's primary interest, as proven by his decision to drop out of art school:

> I studied painting for two years.... I moved away from painting because I wanted to do something that had a more immediate effect. I wanted to remove myself from the direct influence of tutors and teachers.... In being a rock musician, you're left totally to your own devices. Any talent or ability that emerges is something that comes from within you as you learn to do it, or as you're affected by things you hear or experience. It's not so much a matter of learning technique, but rather more a mental approach—learning the fine balance of achieving composition and harmony and balance and so on. There's the mathematical approach and the emotional approach, you know. You have to make those opposites work, perhaps against each other, to produce a joining together of the two forces. The process involves understanding your own emotions and the written word, neither of which I'm particularly good at, but am trying to learn about as time goes on.[15]

Now Anderson combined working at a newspaper stand with gigging and writing songs. On May 24, 1967, the John Evan Band received positive reviews after performing one of his originals, "Take the Easy Way," on Granada Television's *Firsttimers* talent program. In September, they made their first professional recordings at CBS Studios in London, where producer Derek Lawrence suggested that the band be renamed "Candy Coloured Rain." These demos for EMI included two covers—Ray Charles' "The Man with the Weird Beard" and Rex Garvin's "Sock It to 'Em, J. B."—and four Anderson originals: "You Got Me," "From 21 Subtract," "On the 7th Side of 9" and "Invasion of Privacy." (None of these recordings have survived.)

In November 1967, when the band members decided to move south to London in a real effort to earn some money, Anderson's father tossed him an old overcoat, saying, "You'd better take this. It's going to be a cold winter." Penniless, he adopted the oversized, somewhat ragged, dark coat as the main feature of his stage costume. Unwilling to take the gamble, Neil Smith quit, leaving the band without a guitarist; but luckily new managers Terry Ellis and Chris Wright suggested Mick Abrahams, an emerging blues player who had been playing with McGregor's Engine. Basing themselves in Luton, Abrahams' hometown, they replaced Barrie Barlow (who had sought out a "real" job in Blackpool) with McGregor drummer Clive Bunker. Glenn Cornick said:

> Barrie's ... not the kind of drummer I particularly enjoy playing

with. Clive is. Clive's great fun and dead solid. Probably nowhere as technical as Barrie.[16]

Then the band's name was discarded. Fed up with covering black blues material, and increasingly uncomfortable with Anderson's own vision for the group, Evans moved back home to resume his university studies. Tony Wilkinson stayed on a bit longer but soon left "Elvo," Abrahams, Cornick and Bunker to forge on as a starving four-piece blues-jazz outfit. At this point, their collective name changed more often than their repertoire, with booking personnel at the Ellis-Wright Agency (which became Chrysalis in late 1969) dreaming up new ones because, as Anderson perpetually has said, they "were so bad" that they could not score a second booking without changing their identity. "Ian Henderson's Bag o' Nails" led to "Bag o' Blues" and the unbelievably unbluesy "Navy Blue." To pay his rent, Anderson took a job vacuuming a cinema. "The other guys in the band at that time ... lived with their parents," he said. "I was the only one who was actually on my own."[17]

Chris Wright revealed the difficulties he and Terry Ellis faced in pitching their groups to club managers:

> We used to have games with artists ... they used to like to come in the office, and I'd say, "Get out of the office. I can't sell you to promoters if you're in the office." ... I think Ian hid under the desk, so that I wouldn't see him, so that ... we could get the bookings for them. His way of making sure that ... if there was a date going, that he got it.[18]

When the band finally were asked back to London's famous Marquee Club, they were performing as "Jethro Tull." Revealing that Dave Robson, the agent who chose the appellation, "had studied history at university," Anderson said, "Well, it was a sort of gritty, earthy kind of name, not something you get tired of like the Orange Bicycle or the Psychedelic Banana—you know, those groups who play backwards on records."[19]

Unfortunately, their initial recording as Jethro Tull was a fiasco. The track "Aeroplane" had been cowritten by Anderson and Cornick, who recalled, "We were up in Barrow, and we banged out some chords on the piano, and Ian put the vocals to it."[20] The name that appeared on the label, as released by MGM Records in February 1968, was "Jethro *Toe*"— not a mistake, as legend would have it—but a deliberate act. According to Cornick:

> That was that silly producer Derek Lawrence. He didn't like the name Jethro Tull; he knew what it was supposed to be, but he didn't

think it was cool enough. It wasn't a misprint.... Yet "Jethro Toe" sounds even less cool. I can remember fighting with him about the name.[21]

The fact that his name was listed as "Len Barnard" in the cowriters' credit, however, was a misprint. (Cornick had used his given name, Glenn Barnard, for a time.) Derek Lawrence later admitted that he was responsible, but thinking he had heard "Jethro Toe" over the phone, "didn't really want to change it. It was too late anyway ... because all the details had gone to MGM and it was all ready to go."[22] The B-side of "Aeroplane" featured an Abrahams song, "Sunshine Day."

During February, Tull played weekly gigs at the Marquee Club, and then landed a couple hotel club dates before returning for two more Marquee shows in late March and mid–April. This pattern continued throughout the year, but the band also managed to build a following substantial enough to command presence at larger venues, such as Hyde Park, where they again opened for Pink Floyd, on June 29.

At one April Marquee Club gig, Cornick celebrated his 21st birthday:

> We happened to be playing the Marquee Club, opening for the Who. Absolutely wonderful: John Entwhistle, after that night—I had beat-up, shitty old equipment—he was the one who said, "Here, Glenn. Call this bloke at a company called Hi-Watt. Tell Dave I told you to come on over." So I went over there and got equipment for absolute rock-bottom wholesale. Nobody was giving away stuff at that point.[23]

In Birmingham on August 4, Barrie Barlow was persuaded by John Evans to catch his old mates playing at Mothers, a local club:

> They turned up in this blue van to take us to the gig, and Ian came walking down the path; my Uncle Albert was in the front room and he looked out of the window and said, "What the *bloody hell* is that?" Because Ian at the time looked totally outrageous, because he was away from home and could do whatever he liked.... It was Mick, Clive, Ian and Glenn—and they were fabulous!... Each one of them was really strong in their own areas, as individual musicians and collectively. Ian playing harmonica ... and they were doing these blues things.... And of course the flute had never appeared with the John Evan Band ... because Ian then just played the guitar.[24]

Frustrated with his guitar playing, Anderson traded in his damaged Fender Stratocaster as down payment on a Shure Unidyne Three microphone and a Selmer Gold Seal flute, because the instrument seemed "different ... small, shiny and portable." (Cornick claimed that his cohort acquired the flute because a penniless chap in Blackpool gave it to him in lieu of cash.[25]) But working the instrument—which came "with no playing instructions"[26]—into a blues band was no easy task, as Anderson explained:

> [Management] wanted me to play rhythm piano at the back of the stage and let Mick Abrahams do all the singing. That was something I fought strongly against.... I wasn't a very good singer but he wasn't either. We used to do about half of it each. I mean that was almost like getting thrown out of the group. What it actually was was a polite invitation to leave. But I wasn't completely aware of that, I sort of hung in there and at a certain point in time some of the songs I had written and some of the things I was doing obviously became the feature of the group.[27]

Anderson had been impressed by the way African-American saxophonist Roland Kirk played flute on the 1965 album *I Talk with the Spirits*, a style attained by humming, or "singing," through the instrument. He later said:

> My biggest influence as a flute player is Eric Clapton. Clapton demonstrated to me, when I listened to his early guitar playing with John Mayall's Blues Breakers, that I was never going to be a great guitar player. I didn't want to be the second, third or tenth best behind Eric.
>
> When I took up flute, the logical thing was to refer, musically speaking, to somebody whom I revered for his rhythmic and melodic approach to music. So my flute playing was based on my interpretation of guitar lines, both in terms of riffs and improvisation around the blues scale. And I guess that's what made me a little different from other flute players who had been formally taught and played music based on scales.[28]

Taking this stylistic approach, Anderson was able successfully to blend the instrument into the fabric of rock 'n' roll.

The 1968 Sunbury Jazz and Blues Festival, staged in London's Kempton Park on August 11, allowed the band to make its mark on the British public. Anderson said:

> Then we played ... to about 80,000 people.... Having played to lots of little audiences in small clubs, it all anted up at the festival. All those people had seen us play at one time or another, and we were, even if I say it myself, the hit of the festival. The only other act that had a similar

reception at the three-day event was a surprise jam by Eric Clapton and Ginger Baker. But we received absolutely zero press coverage on that occasion for one simple reason: The press were all in the press tent drinking free beer. It's the gospel truth.[29]

At this point, the flute was only a small component in the Tull stage show, as Anderson focused heavily on vocals and harmonica while Abrahams offered up his blues guitar licks. Anderson described the way in which his "mad, flute-playing Fagin" character emerged:

> They [the press] thought that they noticed that I stood on one leg while playing, but I think that was a figment of their imagination. However, having been given that image, I thought I'd better live up to it, which made them and their photographers happy.[30]

THE ALBUMS AND TOURS (1968–2001)

This Was

October 1968 (U.K.) / February 1969 (U.S.)
Highest chart position: 10 (U.K.) / 62 (U.S.)
[Rating: 2.5]
Producers: Terry Ellis and Jethro Tull / Island 985 (mono) 985S (stereo)

Ian Anderson: vocals, flute, harmonica, piano, claghorn
Mick Abrahams: electric guitar, nine-string guitar
Glenn Cornick: bass guitar
Clive Bunker: drums, hooter, charm bracelet

Recorded at Sound Techniques, Chelsea, London, June 13–August 23, 1968
Recording engineer: Victor Gamm
Brass arrangement by David Palmer
Cover concept by Terry Ellis and Brian Ward
Photographs by Brian Ward

Tracks: My Sunday Feeling (Anderson)
       Someday the Sun Won't Shine for You (Anderson)
       Beggar's Farm (Abrahams-Anderson)
       Move on Alone (Abrahams)
       Serenade to a Cuckoo (Kirk)
       Dharma for One (Anderson-Bunker)
       It's Breaking Me Up (Anderson)
       Cat's Squirrel (trad., arr. Abrahams)
       A Song for Jeffrey (Anderson)
       Round (Anderson-Abrahams-Cornick-Bunker-Ellis)

Glenn Cornick commented on the genesis of the embryonic Tull album:

> There were all these different bands that were all successful, at least
> in Europe, that were all part of the same scene, working together. We all
> did go and support each other's gigs. We'd go to Nice gigs whenever
> they'd be playing, and they'd come and see us. We were all good friends
> with Spooky Tooth.
> And Spooky Tooth, after the first time we ever played with them,
> went to Island Records, their record company, and told them that they
> should sign us. There really was a closeness between all the bands.[1]

Before the album was recorded, Terry Ellis projected dates for the
band's first top 10 releases (single and LP) and initial trip to the United
States. He recalled, "What I recognized was that Ian had a very special
talent, and I talked to him in the very, very early days about himself, not
as a performer in a blues-pop group, but to think of himself as an enter-
tainer."[2]

Of his professional relationship with Ellis, Anderson later said:

> He was very important in the early days of the group.... He was, I
> suppose, very influential, because we ... grew up together, we developed
> our parallel interests and experiences in the music business together. But
> he wasn't actually ever the producer in creative terms. He was called the
> executive producer, which really means that he persuaded his bank man-
> ager to lend us the money to make the records. But he occasionally
> played tambourine and got in the way; and ... he was an emotional sort
> of spirit of assistance, rather than technically or musically of assistance.[3]

In May 1992, Anderson explained the title *This Was*:

> I felt that this kind of music would not be indicative of what we
> were going to play in the future, that it was just a starting point for
> introducing Jethro Tull to the public. And so it seems to me that, what-
> ever this album was going to be about, it would be more of an historical
> document in terms of showing the origins of Jethro Tull.... "This was
> Jethro Tull" as they used to be when they played at the Marquee Club,
> when they began playing together as a band.[4]

Years earlier, he had said:

> [A]t the time when I was of an age to be professional—and being pro-
> fessional meant earning a living—it was necessary to play some kind of
> music that was acceptable commercially in the club circuit in England

The original *This Was* Jethro Tull, from second left: Mick Abrahams, Ian Anderson, Clive Bunker and Glenn Cornick, 1968. Unidentified actor on the far left. (Photograph courtesy of Glenn Cornick.)

which was sort of a basic blues. We did all the Elmore James and Sonny Boy Williamson material revamped into a contemporary white English way.

There were two types of groups at that time; there were the blues groups and the progressive groups as they were called, Pink Floyd and the Nice, and we were sort of stuck somewhere between the two, really.[5]

Although Anderson revealed the "This Was" perspective in the liner notes, the jazz and blues elements give the album an improvisational edge that later, more polished efforts often lack. Craig Thomas noted that "the memorable 'Dharma for One' ... and 'It's Breaking Me Up' both aptly demonstrate the unique inner tension the band was capable of generating even in its first incarnation, with the heavy insistence of R&B set off against the jazz-inflected flute."[6]

At this time, Anderson began indicating his preference for more structured, competently performed music:

I like ... disciplined bands. When you listen to them you feel you're hearing the results of people having taken a lot of time and trouble to do a thing well, accurately, tastefully, thoughtfully. It's good to be given that sort of a pleasantly wrapped package.[7]

The Tracks of *This Was*

"My Sunday Feeling" provides an energetic opening for the album, with Abrahams and Cornick's bass riff echoed by Anderson's rhythmic flute and Bunker's jazzy (albeit somewhat sloppy) drumming. Though Anderson's faux-bluesman vocals are weak, the unique Tull sound already is taking root. Following the Mississippi Delta–meets–John Mayall "Some Day the Sun Won't Shine for You," "Beggar's Farm" returns the quartet to the solid band sound of the previous track, alternating between a moderate 4/4 groove and fast shuffle soloing by Abrahams and Anderson.

Abrahams' "Move on Alone," backed with dubbed-in David Palmer brass, is typical late–'60s R&B material, shorn of Anderson (making it sound more like Led Zeppelin than Jethro Tull); but the Roland Kirk instrumental "Serenade to a Cuckoo," the first tune Anderson learned, is a highlight. Here, after only playing a few months, Anderson demonstrates sensitivity, tonality (on a cheap flute) and improvisational ability. Though it had yet to acquire its minimalist lyrics, "Dharma for One," like "My Sunday Feeling," features the trademark Tull sound in its combination of jazz, blues, ethnic elements (Eastern Indian) and the bizarre "claghorn" (a saxophone-like instrument apparently invented by Jeffrey Hammond), but also includes the most extended studio jam session in the band's three-decade history. After Bunker bashes away (sometimes hitting the rims of his drums, as he also does on other tracks), Cornick and Abrahams get to prove their mettle, as well. Cornick said:

> It's just an excuse for a drum solo. Clive's drum solos were always funny, which is the one redeeming feature, because I hate drum solos. I hate bass solos. I mean, I hate any kind of extended solo. It's just showing off. It's never real music. Real music is a bunch of people playing together. Interacting, and *combined*, it's more than the individual things.[8]

Of course, no late–1960s, blues-based band could escape the studio without recording a slow 6/8 number: "It's Breaking Me Up" features Abrahams, on lead guitar, doubling the melody of Anderson's vocal. Though competent, the song offers no surprises, merely meandering along like another Led Zeppelin track (albeit without the passionate fire of the then-competent Jimmy Page).

As Anderson often remarked, public interest determined their repertoire at the time, and "'Cat's Squirrel' ... is [on the album] because people like it."[9] Again, the track is reminiscent of Led Zeppelin, but also of Jimi Hendrix and particularly Cream, reflecting Anderson's interest in the playing of Eric Clapton (but, at that time, what blues-rock musician, surely Mick Abrahams included, wasn't interested in "God?"). This was an instrumental track honed night after night in clubs, therefore offering little innovation but a certain degree of professionalism.

"A Song for Jeffrey," a tribute to Jeffrey Hammond, is a musical high point, its lyrics buried in the mix, sonically reflecting the "decrepit" look of the old geezers on the album's cover. Though its style bears similarities to "My Sunday Feeling" and "Beggar's Farm," the song features a very "woozy" groove and a unique ambiance that sets it apart from other Tull tracks and most blues material in general. The instrumental section is more jazz- than blues-oriented, a stylistic element reinforced by the brief final jam, "Round," a nice 3/4 piece that may leave the listener wanting more.

Anderson's desire to front his own band is readily apparent on *This Was*, which demonstrates a clear difference between his material and that of Mick Abrahams: one artist's desire to create original music versus another who was content to carry on (*à la* John Mayall, Led Zeppelin, Cream, Fleetwood Mac and others) the English style of aping (perhaps "modernizing") the work of African-American bluesmen. Even at this early point in the band's existence, Anderson was trying to establish an individual style. "A Song for Jeffrey" was released as a single, backed with "One for John Gee," Abrahams' tribute to the manager of the Marquee Club who had asked them back for another gig. Gee recalled, "It was a very jazz-orientated group, which I liked. And ... we put them in here on Friday evenings, and they built up a tremendous following."[10] While playing the club circuit, they also recorded versions of "A Song for Jeffrey," "Stormy Monday Blues" and "Love Story," a new single, for broadcast on BBC radio.

Glenn Cornick commented about the overall musical style of *This Was*:

> It was a fake blues album, because we made it for the blues scene. If you didn't play blues songs, you didn't *play*. It was a commercial decision to become a blues band. Realistically, it was, "If we want to get successful, what do we have to do?" We'd all listen to some blues, but I don't think for any of us, it was a big thrill, other than Mick Abrahams, who won't approach anything that is not blues. As he still says, "If it's not blues, it's shit."[11]

The First Tour

Glenn Cornick spoke of an interesting visitor to early Tull gigs:

> I remember, back when the Beatles used to come and see us. We
> didn't know them well, but I know Paul McCartney came several times
> to see us at different places. And he'd stand in the background, and
> somebody would say, "Oh, Paul is out there, watching you guys."[12]

Not long after *This Was* was released, Abrahams left the band. Anderson recalled:

> There were very bad problems between Mick Abrahams and Glenn
> Cornick. They didn't like each other. There were problems that arose in
> the band in terms of Mick's commitment. He didn't want to travel
> through other countries, and he gave us an ultimatum and said, "I will
> only play three nights a week!" The rest of us just found that impossible.
> We wanted to play every night. We wanted to be successful! So we found
> it impossible to continue with Mick under those circumstances, which
> put me in the situation of then having to write all the music and come
> up with new ideas.[13]

Guitarist Tony Iommi's band Earth (later known as Black Sabbath)
were sharing the stage the night of Abrahams' final Tull gig. Iommi later
said, "[Tull] were passing each other notes on stage—Mick was giving Ian
notes saying, 'I'm leaving' and so on! They asked me that night if I'd be
interested in the job."[14]

About Abrahams' departure, Glenn Cornick said:

> We drove him home, parked the van outside his house, threw all his
> equipment in the street and said, "You're fired." In the three months or
> so before that happened, Ian was living in North London, I was living in
> South London, and Mick and Clive were living in Luton. Mick had the
> van most of the time. We'd go up and play a gig in ... Newcastle-upon-
> Tyne ... get back to Mick's home at three in the morning—and Mick
> would drive Ian and me to Luton station to wait in the freezing cold for
> the seven o'clock train back to London. We really appreciated that!...
> There was loads of stuff like that. I built up a grudge against Mick, and
> really didn't have any time for him.[15]

Soon after, Tony Iommi received a telephone call asking him to audition in London. After seeing so many people, including Davy O'List of
the Nice, in line to play, he became nervous and tried to leave, but was

asked not to return to Birmingham until he had tried out. After a "jam with Clive, Glenn and Ian," he went home "and got the call to say [he'd] got the job."[16] When rehearsing with Tull, Iommi, who had to report at 9 A.M. each day, "really felt bad about leaving Earth" and brought along his old bandmate, drummer Tony "Geezer" Butler. After a few days, the guitarist told Anderson that he was too uneasy to continue:

Ian Anderson on stage at the Marquee Club, London, 1968. (Photograph courtesy of Glenn Cornick.)

I was so used to hanging around with everyone, but the Tull lads seemed to be separate in some ways.... Clive and Glenn would be together, but Ian would be sitting at another table, and it seemed alien to me. The first time we went to eat, I went and sat at a table with Ian, thinking we were all together, but apparently not! I don't like situations like that. If it's going to be a band, it's got to be a band together.... I said I wanted to leave. [Ian] suggested I give it a bit more time, but I explained that I just didn't feel comfortable, and that I didn't think things were going to work with me.[17]

What Iommi didn't realize was that Anderson, in order to steer the course of Jethro Tull, preferred to isolate himself from others when not practicing or performing. Clive Bunker later remarked:

In the three years I was with the band, he certainly went into himself more, which is understandable really. I would hate to have been in his position where he was the front man, the key man. All of the pressures of the band were on him, because he wrote all the stuff. On a tour he'd be the one that would supposedly go to bed early, but in fact he would go back to his hotel to start writing so that we would have a store of stuff ready for when we got back.[18]

Per Anderson's request, Iommi agreed to stay in the band until December 12, for an appearance on the television show *The Rolling Stones' Rock 'n' Roll Circus*, in which the Stones, the Who, Eric Clapton, Taj Mahal and John Lennon and Yoko Ono also would play live or pantomime to a pre-recorded backing track. Tull contributed a mimed version of "A Song for Jeffrey," which Anderson actually sang live; but the film was held back because Mick Jagger was not satisfied with his group's performance.

How did Tull, such a neophyte band, get booked on this program? Glenn Cornick said:

> Charlie Watts used to go around and see who was out there playing. He'd seen us. We'd started having a bit of a name by then, but *only just*. The album was only just out. So we weren't *completely* unknown, but certainly not a household name. And I always thought Mick Jagger kept track of the business that was going on, but it was actually Charlie. I'd never met him before we did the show.[19]

While waiting to perform on the *Circus*, Cornick witnessed his father going off with none other than legendarily crazed Who drummer Keith Moon:

> Keith Moon was marvelous. Completely out of control. Every story you've heard about him is probably a little *less* than the truth. My dad was with me, and he disappeared with Keith for two or three hours, and wouldn't tell me what happened! You know, "We were just hanging out for a while." I mean, I have no clue.[20]

Once again, Anderson had to audition guitarists. Following a thumbs down from Mick Taylor (who opted for John Mayall's Blues Breakers and then the Rolling Stones), he was keen to locate Martin Barre, a Birmingham musician who had been scared to try out when he first saw the advertisement. Born in Kings Heath on November 17, 1946, Barre had done well academically at Yarwood Primary, Kings Norton Grammar School and Tudor Grange Grammar. At the age of 15, he cut his first demo recording with a local group, the Dwellers, and soon moved on to the Moonrakers, a band that covered material by the Ventures and the Beatles. In 1968, having studied architecture at Birmingham's Hall Green College and Lanchester University in Coventry, Barre was set for a professional career but realized that music interested him more.

During a London gig with Gethsemane, in which he played guitar, tenor saxophone and flute, Barre had been approached by Terry Ellis, who asked him to drop by the Tull audition. The members of Tull had heard him play when Gethsemane had opened for one of their gigs, but what they had experienced on that evening had nothing in common with the sounds that emanated from his guitar at the audition. In a room literally packed with guitarists, many of whom were cut after only 10 seconds of blues soloing, Barre, who had thrilled to their set at the Sunbury Festival, was so terrified that his fretwork degenerated into rubbish. But he liked the band so much that he later phoned Anderson, who, although having made a decision, asked him to report for a private jam session. Barre arrived with his guitar, but no amplifier, this time making it impossible for Anderson to hear his strummings over the sound of his heavy breathing. Admiring his perseverance, the band gave him another legitimate audition at a pub in North London, where, winning the job, he was told that rehearsals would begin in a Soho basement just after Christmas.

Following much frantic practicing over a two-day stretch, learning Abrahams' old numbers as well as some new material, Barre proved a wise choice when he was unleashed on fans at the Penzance Wintergardens on December 30. Five additional English gigs were followed by two in Scandinavia, where they shared the same bill with Jimi Hendrix. "Imagine being a guitarist in that situation," commented Barre. "It's possible that I was so nervous that I stopped worrying about what I was doing, and just got on with it through sheer terror."[21] Of the legendary Hendrix, Glenn Cornick said:

> I can't say that I knew him closely and personally, but I talked to
> him quite a few times. At one time there was some talk about me doing
> some recording with him, but it never happened. It would have been fun
> to have done it.
>
> He was with it most of the time. Really much more than people
> have heard. You get this crap about, "Well, he was loaded all the time."
> The truth is, he was a really nice guy, and he was really together most of
> the time. You know, people want to hear that he was an asshole who was
> on drugs all the time.[22]

Of his guitarist mate, Mr. Barre, Cornick later revealed:

> Martin's a good guy. He's a really great guy. It's lovely to see him

whenever I get a chance to see a Tull tour. He is fun to watch. When he joined the band, he wasn't really that great as a guitar player, but I honestly can't imagine it having worked with anybody else.[23]

On January 24 and 25, 1969, Tull played their first U.S. dates at New York's Fillmore East, in support of Blood, Sweat and Tears, and then shared the stage with Led Zeppelin, Vanilla Fudge and other bands at ballrooms and clubs. They also headlined at some smaller clubs, building a fan base as they headed toward San Francisco and the Fillmore West, before returning to the East Coast and then back to England during the second week of April.

While playing at the Boston Tea Party February 13–15, Anderson wrote the song "Living in the Past" in a Holiday Inn hotel room. After finishing a gig at the State University of New York in Stony Brook the next day, the band recorded the backing tracks at the Vantone Studio, which was operated by Frankie Valli of the Four Seasons, in nearby West Orange, New Jersey. Glenn Cornick recalled:

> Martin could not get the chords right, all the way through the song. So on the released version there's actually still one wrong chord in it. Martin will tell you which one! It was really funny, 'cause we brought in people from the New York Symphony Orchestra to do all the "da da da da" stuff, and these blokes, supposedly the best players around, couldn't read in 5/4 time. I mean, Stravinsky is in the weirdest time signatures and they could have played that, but 5/4 time, no way! So if you listen closely to "Living in the Past," all the strings are in time, but they don't play with any rhythm. But it sounds great on the record, because we all played it with the accents.[24]

Perhaps giving Barre a 5/4 jazz number as his recording "initiation" was a bit cruel, but the song grooves along with such ease (thanks in no small part to Bunker's improved drumming) that few listeners will notice that "wrong chord." Anderson recorded the slick vocals at Western Recorders in Los Angeles during their March 13–16 stint at the Fillmore West. A brief song dealing with a retreat from unpleasant current events, it sums up Anderson's view of the hippy movement in the line "Now there's revolution, but they don't know what they're fighting." Cornick said, "Ian was always a little above all of that, I think. More than anything, that's what it was."[25]

Following a series of dates in England and Ireland, Tull returned to the U.S. in mid–1969 for two solid months of appearances, primarily at huge festivals. Cornick remembered the experience as being "bloody depressing":

We did some good gigs; but we'd show up … supposed to be on at seven o'clock at night, and they'd be running eight hours late, so we'd be told to go and take a rest and come back in the middle of the night. I remember playing outside Toronto and going on at four o'clock in the morning. It was bloody cold at night, and my fingers were dropping off as I tried to play. We were in New York when the Woodstock Festival was going on, and we were invited to play at Woodstock. Ten Years After were up there, so we called them up and said, "What's it like up there?" and they said, "It's pissing down with rain. It's out of control. It's one of the worst fucking gigs you've ever seen!" So we decided not to go. Probably not one of the better moves we ever made."[26]

Though they had received an invitation while playing a Central Park show on July 28—Tull were at the Fillmore West in San Francisco on August 14, the day before Woodstock began, and already had gigs scheduled in San Antonio and Houston. Cornick added, "Houston was just a last minute fill-in gig at a small club and Woodstock was August 15, 16 and 17. We could have played Saturday or Sunday."[27]

One enormous event, however, was well worthwhile, as Cornick described:

> The Newport Jazz Festival [held in early July] was a good one. I remember playing on the same bill as Roland Kirk, who Ian was always accused of copying. Roland Kirk was really thrilled to meet us, and pleased that Ian was doing all that stuff because it had made Roland Kirk famous! We had a good time with him. The Newport Jazz Festival was interesting because it was the first year they'd had any sort of rock 'n' roll on, so we were breaking new ground there.[28]

Anderson, however, felt uncomfortable playing on the same stage with jazz greats Woody Herman and Ray Charles, until he realized that the open-minded audience also enjoyed their own jazz and blues influenced material, as well as that of Jeff Beck, Led Zeppelin and Blood, Sweat and Tears.

Stand Up

September 1969
Highest chart position: 1 (U.K.) / 20 (U.S.)
[Rating: 4]

Producers: Terry Ellis and Ian Anderson / Island ILPS 9103
All songs written by Ian Anderson (except where indicated)

Ian Anderson: vocals, flute, acoustic guitar, Hammond organ, piano, mandolin, balalaika, harmonica
Martin Barre: electric guitar, flute
Glenn Cornick: bass guitar
Clive Bunker: drums and percussion

Recorded at Morgan Studio, London, spring-summer 1969
Recording engineer: Andy Johns
Strings arranged and conducted by David Palmer
Cover concept by Terry Ellis and John Williams
Cover printed from woodcuts by Jimmy Grashow

Tracks: A New Day Yesterday
          Jeffrey Goes to Leicester Square
          Bourée (J. S. Bach)
          Back to the Family
          Look into the Sun
          Nothing Is Easy
          Fat Man
          We Used to Know
          Reasons for Waiting
          For a Thousand Mothers

Beginning in mid–August 1969, Tull took a five-week respite from touring. With new material written and honed during scores of gigs, they returned to England to complete the recording of *Stand Up*, which was released in late September. Wanting to add another strong element to the blues basis of the band, Anderson began working ethnic folk elements into his songs, experimenting "with exotic instruments ... mandolins, balalaikas, whistles, saxophones, all kinds of things."[29] He and Martin Barre also wanted to create an unusual sound for the electric guitar:

> [W]e were trying to get the same quality in the guitar sound as the shift you get with a Lesley cabinet for a Hammond organ. We tried playing the guitar through the Lesley but that didn't work. We wanted a real shift across the stereo. So the engineer, Andy Johns, the brother of producer Glyn Johns, had this idea of moving the mike around whilst Martin was playing. He got a very expensive Neuman 67 and was swinging it on the end of its lead around the studio over quite a big area. We were doing it live and it was an amazing sound which we used on "A New Day Yesterday."[30]

Martin Barre said:

> *Stand Up* was the first real album I had ever made. A lot of the
> songs were written by Ian on guitar, so I just played his parts pretty
> much, since they were written before I joined. But that format would
> change a lot as the band developed through the years.[31]

Of Barre's contributions and the style of the album, Cornick explained:

> You think of *Stand Up*, and you think, "Who else would have fit in
> there?" Mick Taylor would have held us back into more of that blues
> style that we were unconsciously escaping from. There was never a point
> at which we said, "Oh, we're not going to be a blues band." You don't
> think of it in that way. You're not thinking, "How does it compare?" A
> lot of people said, "Oh, they've sold out. They're not playing blues any-
> more."
>
> We sat down and said, "Did we stop playing blues?" We hadn't
> noticed that we had. We hadn't realized how much we'd changed. You
> don't just sit down and scrap everything you've ever done and start
> afresh. When you're out there playing, you have a new song, so you add
> that to the set. If it works, you keep it. If it doesn't, you dump it. And, as
> we put in new songs, I suppose we were changing. But, step by step,
> obviously the change from Mick to Martin made a big difference. We
> weren't consciously turning our back on what we'd done before, and we
> weren't even sure where we were going. You don't sit down and say,
> "Well, we'll be a blues band with a little pop influence and a little folk
> influence here." You do what material you do, and from that, you become
> what you become.
>
> It's not usually a conscious decision, unless you're talking about the
> crap that's going around now, where people sit down and plan a band
> together where they get four of the best looking guys they can find. That
> is not creating music.[32]

To enhance the scope of some tracks, they sought out orchestral
arranger David Palmer, who already had provided arrangements for *This
Was* and "A Christmas Song," the first piece Anderson wrote after Abrahams left the band. While in the British Army, Palmer had studied at
Kneller Hall, the Royal Military School of Music. After doing his bit for
queen and country, he majored in composition at the Royal Academy of
Music, winning the Eric Coates Prize during his graduation year. Palmer
later recalled:

> I started as a film music writer as a ghost writer, and during that
> time I was in London when Jethro Tull came into the studio to make

The *Stand Up* band: Clive Bunker, Glenn Cornick, Martin Barre and Ian Anderson, 1969. (Photograph courtesy of Glenn Cornick.)

> their first album, and Ian Anderson and Terry Ellis ... asked the studio engineers if they could recommend a musician that had an affinity with rock music, understood the whole business of writing music down and using other musicians.... That is how I started with Ian....[33]

Terry Ellis conceived the album's title and legendary packaging, featuring a cut-out of the band that popped up when the gatefold jacket was opened. Of the album's status in the Tull catalog, Anderson claimed:

> I don't necessarily think that *Stand Up* ... is a great album, beautifully played with terrific songs on it. In many ways the songs are naive, simple, a little self-conscious in some ways. They're not by any means, I feel, my best songs, particularly lyrically. But it was a pretty good album by the standards of 1969, and at least it was interesting and pretty original.[34]

Cornick claimed, "The whole of *Stand Up* is about Ian's relationship with his parents.... If you ever did a psychological profile of Ian, his family and his religious upbringing would be an important part of it."[35]

The Tracks of *Stand Up*

"A New Day Yesterday" immediately introduces the band's heavier sound, due to Barre's style and multi-tracked guitar parts. (Morgan Studio offered 8-track facilities, while *This Was* had been recorded on a 4-track at Sound Techniques.) Anderson's leadership is apparent from the first verse and chorus, which concludes, "It was a new day yesterday, but it's an *old* day now." Literally from his initial moment as a serious songwriter, though only 21, he already was focusing on the past and aging. Although a blues number, the lyrics are atypical of the African-American style, and more like a classic torch song: The narrator, having found a wonderful woman, sees her only once before losing her. In the opening verse, their walk "through the trees" (an environment that would become integral in Anderson's songs) provides a pleasant and positive image that soon is undercut by loss. Musically, the lyrics are masterfully supported by an ominous undertone created by Cornick's bass and Barre's single-note riff track (which is separate from his chord track). The song also contains Anderson's first real flute break, though he had contributed brief solo spots to *This Was*.

"Jeffrey Goes to Leicester Square" moves the album from blues to ethnic folk, here the Indian style previously hinted at in "Dharma for One," but traditional rather than an electric jam. As he had done on "A New Day Yesterday," Anderson electronically processed the sound of the main rhythm instrument, in this case a three-string balalaika, giving the track a strange ambiance. Apparently another tribute to Jeffrey Hammond, it deals with a "bright city woman" whom the narrator considers a very stuffed shirt, providing the first social criticism song to be released by the band. ("A Christmas Song" had been written but would not be issued until 1972.)

Though he was credited for writing J. S. Bach's "Bourée," Anderson later claimed that he agreed to it because, in 1969, no blues-rock band could get away with playing classical music.[36] Originally the fifth movement of Bach's Suite in E Minor for Lute, this particular bourrée, written during the composer's Weimar period (1708–1717), has become one of his most famous, due in part to Tull's cool jazz arrangement featuring Anderson on double-tracked flutes, one performing the melody and the other an obligato, as well as a swinging solo break in the middle—an achievement for a young man who had been playing the instrument for only a year. And Cornick, given his own spot, shines on one of the greatest bass solos in rock history. He later revealed:

The bad news about the solo, although it sounds great on the record, is that it was probably the worst recording session we ever did in our lives. We recorded it in Olympic Studios in London, not far from where I lived. And we had such a terrible time working in there that we walked out after several hours in the studio, thinking that we had nothing—that the whole session was trash. That whole track of "Bourée" was snipped together from different takes. The bass solo is the beginning and end of a much longer solo. It was much improved by taking out all the stuff in the middle. Just the very first melodic part was a piece that I had worked out. Other than that, it was just winging it.[37]

"Bourée" was the first Tull recording clearly to indicate Anderson's interest in music from earlier historical periods, here a folk and courtly dance form from 17th- and 18th-century France. He revealed that he first heard it "repeated over and over from the bed-sit below mine in Kentish Town where an English student was attempting to learn classical guitar in his spare time."[38]

"Back to the Family" provides lyrical and musical counterpoint and confusion, the narrator contemplating whether or not he should give up a life on his own to return home, as the band alternates between a slow, bluesy groove in the verses and loud, driving rock in the choruses. It is a song written by a young man who recently has struck out to find his own fortune, one that is stylistically foreshadowed here: not only is the unique Tull sound becoming more recognizable, but so is Anderson's workaholic tendency, in the lyric "doing nothing is bothering me."

That trademark sound is developed further in "Look into the Sun," the first Tull song to open with Anderson's acoustic guitar (eventually it includes some electric wah-wah soloing by Barre). Beginning as a lament for a failed relationship, the three-verse ballad progressively gains a little more hope, its fourth chorus ending on a positive note:

> So when you look into the sun
> and see the words you could have sung
> It's not too late; only begun
> Look into the sun.

"Nothing Is Easy" returns to a mix of jazz and blues, sounding a bit like "My Sunday Feeling" during the opening riff, played in unison by Anderson's flute and Barre's guitar. Again beefing up the sound with two separate tracks, Barre also takes some solo spots, trading them with Anderson during an extended instrumental section and then joining him for a furious jam at the conclusion. Lyrically, Anderson himself is the narrator, telling his listeners to "just give us a play" if life is getting them down. When he sings "Your fingers may freeze, worse things happen at sea, there's good times to be had," he *really* is being upbeat, a point of view only occasionally expressed in Tull music.

"Fat Man" not only brings back the Indian element of "Jeffrey Goes to Leicester Square," but is also the first Tull song to incorporate a "medieval" mandolin sound. Though the Beatles previously had used an Eastern instrument like the sitar to add a cosmopolitan ingredient to a particular song (with other bands, of course, quickly jumping on the bandwagon), here Tull manage to create a truly ancient ambiance that has not become as dated.

One of the most underrated Tull songs, the 6/8 blues "We Used to Know," weaves another tale of a man looking at his past, speaking of the "bad *old* days" and having "fears of dying, getting *old*." At this point, Anderson could have had no idea that he would be with Jethro Tull three decades later, nor that the band even would last longer than most others currently performing. By already pretending to be old (on the *This Was* cover; in the *Stand Up* lyrics), did he attempt to "defeat" aging or to ignore the changes that it inevitably brings? Whatever his reasons, the lyrical lament of "We Used to Know" gets a passionate shot in the arm when Barre rips into one of the best solos of his career, concluding the song with a blistering build up that peaks with a wailing note he repeats three times—a style of "straight" blues playing to which he rarely would return. "Reasons for Waiting" is the type of tender love ballad very atypical in Anderson's *oeuvre*, and the first issued Tull song that features him almost exclusively. Playing acoustic guitar, flute and Hammond organ as well as singing, he is joined by Barre on a second flute part and a lovely Palmer string arrangement.

A "Dharma"–like track that would not be out of place on *This Was*, "For a Thousand Mothers" closes off the album with bluesy but solidly driving rock. However, this song, Anderson's declaration of independence from his parents, is far more polished and rhythmically tight than anything on the earlier album. Like other songs on *Stand Up*, it ends with an extended jam, the final moments including a flute "flurry" that would become one of Anderson's indelible trademarks. Glenn Cornick remembered, "Ian just came along with an E-minor chord, but it's my riff."[39]

The *Stand Up* Tour

Stand Up was on the margins of the folk-rock genesis that began in England during 1969. At the same time that the Tull album hit number one on the British charts, Fairport Convention's *Unhalfbricking* stood at number 11. The latter band's legendary *Liege and Lief* climbed the charts soon after. Three decades later, Glenn Cornick observed:

> The big difference between being a musician now and being a musician then is that stuff hadn't been categorized, because nobody had done most of it before. You think of Fairport Convention. They couldn't go and listen to all the folk-rock clichés, because nobody really had played folk-rock before. But they weren't consciously breaking new ground. I'm sure they didn't sit down and say, "Oh, yeah. Here we go. We're going to invent folk-rock. Boy, are we going to do something." They were writing the songs and playing in the style they were all comfortable playing in. And it became something.[40]

The *Stand Up* tour officially began at Newcastle's City Hall on September 25, 1969, and then moved on to Edinburgh, Dublin (where Anderson's overcoat reputedly was stolen by fans), Belfast, and back down to London before hitting other cities in England, the Netherlands, Belgium and France. Then Tull were off for their third tour of the U.S., where during another duo of dates at the Fillmore East, Anderson received the incredible news:

> I think it was Loew's Midtown Manhattan Hotel when Joe Cocker, who was on tour at the same time, came into breakfast one morning and said, "Oh, congratulations. I have just heard on a phone call that your album has gone to number one in the English chart." I remember I was having scrambled eggs and bacon and whole-wheat toast and orange juice and some coffee....[41]

Glenn Cornick recalled the unbelievable clientele at the Loew's Midtown:

> There were sixteen English bands in the hotel at the same time. There was Tull, there was the Who, there was Led Zeppelin, Savoy Brown, Free and Spooky Tooth. One bomb, and you could have blown up almost the entire British music scene. Can you imagine how wild and strange that was, being in one hotel, and everybody you knew from Britain was there? And that was not uncommon. It was a very, very strange and funny scene.[42]

Released only in Britain, the "Living in the Past" single also climbed the charts in late 1969, reaching number three and securing the band a spot on the popular *Top of the Pops* television show. Two follow-up singles,

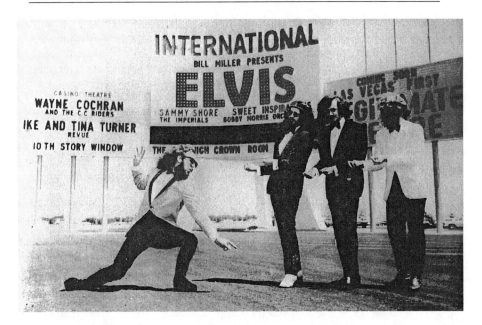

"Elvo" strikes a pose in Las Vegas during the 1969 *Stand Up* tour. (Photograph courtesy of Glenn Cornick.)

"Sweet Dream" and "Witch's Promise" (backed by "Teacher"), respectively reached number nine and number four on the British charts.

Glenn Cornick revealed his general impression of touring that year:

> I was twenty-two years old. I was running around America. Everybody loved us. I mean, what more could you ask for? I could never understand why the other guys in the band didn't enjoy it nearly as much as I did. I think that's why I gained the reputation for being the "playboy" of the band, which actually in so many ways isn't true. I think, more than anything, just the fact that I got a real kick out of being out there.
>
> It doesn't relate at all to the music. It's just the social aspect of being out on the road. It was great fun to be out on the road. I couldn't think of anything that would be more fun to do with my life when I was twenty-one or twenty-two years old than racing around America, meeting all these great people. It was thrilling to do it. Everybody else would sit in the hotel, watching *The Joey Bishop Show*, wishing they were home.[43]

Cornick's unique image also appeared at this time:

> Trademarks happen. They're not things that you plan on happening. I came over to the States, and I don't know what I looked like at that

time. I certainly didn't have any plans on looking like anything specific. I guess my hair grew and my girlfriend at the time gave me a headband. And that became the image that I developed. She became my first wife, Judy [Wong]. It's funny, from one small thing, you go step by step from that. I turned into this raging hippy that I appeared to be—being only a hippy in the British sense.

It was really interesting for us, because, coming over during the period that we did, when, for the United States, the youth were in the midst of the Vietnam War. We were very aware of how much the hippy movement was a real deep-seated social movement here. You went back to England and the hippy movement was a fashion statement, because we didn't have the social trauma, like in the States.

I can understand why people might want to raise a lot of hell, because chances are that next month you could be off to Vietnam—and being shot at and napalmed. It really does affect the way you look at life. Whereas, for us, we'd come over and see these people, and they'd say, "Nice to see you," and, for all we knew, they were shipped off. We saw a lot of people get shipped out. I knew people who got shipped out, people who died over there.

So we were on the fringes of it, but it didn't directly impinge upon us the way it did on American kids. And we got back to England and, you know, "Hippies are great fun. Smoke dope and wear headbands." That was what the hippy movement was in England.[44]

Benefit

April 1970
Highest chart position: 3 (U.K.) / 11 (U.S.)
[Rating: 4]
Producer: Ian Anderson / Island ILPS 9123
All songs written by Ian Anderson

Ian Anderson: vocals, flute, acoustic and electric guitars
Martin Barre: acoustic and electric guitars
Glenn Cornick: bass guitar
Clive Bunker: drums, percussion
John Evans: piano, Hammond organ

Recorded at Morgan Studio, London, winter 1970
Recording engineer: Robin Black
Executive producer: Terry Ellis
Cover design by Terry Ellis and Ruan O'Lochlainn

Photography by Ruan O'Lochlainn
Graphic presentation by Ken Reilly

Tracks: With You There to Help Me
           Nothing to Say
           Son
           For Michael Collins, Jeffrey and Me
           To Cry You a Song
           A Time for Everything?
           Teacher (U.S. version) / Alive and Well and Living In (U.K. version)
           Inside
           Play in Time
           Sossity: You're a Woman

Following a break for the 1969-70 holiday season, Tull regrouped for a brief tour of Denmark, Finland, Sweden and Germany before flying to Los Angeles to appear on the television show *The Switched-On Symphony* with the Nice, Santana and the L.A. Philharmonic. Though the band played "Bourée" with the orchestra, Anderson turned down conductor Zubin Mehta's request that they join in for an all-out jam at the end. Anderson said:

> I don't know if there was a moral to be put over by bringing rock and the classics together in the program, but if there was, it certainly was not to be served best by each of the units compromising their own standards to find a very low musical common denominator purely for the sake of playing together.[45]

Following one more German gig, Tull spent two months recording their third album, *Benefit*, and preparing for a lengthy spring-summer tour of the U.S. Although Anderson had written a number of very riff-oriented songs during the previous tour, he also continued to practice his acoustic guitar skills and asked old mate John Evans, who now was doing well at the Chelsea College of Science, to contribute his musicianship on piano and Hammond organ. A versatile player rather than an individual stylist, Evans was easily able to fit into the musical context of the band, lessening the responsibilities placed on Martin Barre.

Glenn Cornick recalled the *Benefit* recording sessions:

> On *Stand Up*, there tended to be more actual and complete songs, so you actually knew what you were recording. When it got to *Benefit*, it tended to be just backing tracks. You never knew where you were supposed to fit in the song, because you didn't know where the vocals were.

The *Benefit* lineup: John Evans, Ian Anderson, Martin Barre, Clive Bunker and Glenn Cornick, 1970. (Photograph courtesy of Glenn Cornick.)

That became difficult, although most of *Benefit* turned out wonderfully. One of my favorites was "Inside," one in which I knew where the vocals were. If I didn't know where the vocals were, I could never have played that, because I wouldn't know where I would be stepping on the verses. But most of *Benefit* was just, you didn't know what it was or where it was from.

Usually Ian would come with a guitar and play the changes, a chord sequence and a bit of rhythm, without so much as a vocal pattern. Sometimes he would have riffs. Some of the riffs are his, but a lot of the other riffs aren't.[46]

The Tracks of *Benefit*

Following the success of *Stand Up*, Anderson's dominance began to be reflected on the album jackets, and *Benefit*—though the band members fumbled about with confusing arrangements—features "Songs written by Ian Anderson" listed above the other credits on the back cover. Sonically superior to the previous album, *Benefit* features a more mature Tull, balancing melodic acoustic material with a much heavier ensemble style—a blend that anticipates the future evolution of the band. This fusion is apparent in "With You There to Help Me," another song about individual expression, in which a strumming acoustic guitar is mixed into the solid wall of sound contributed by Barre, Cornick and Bunker. The track was inspired by Jennie Franks, a young secretary at Chrysalis publishing, whom Anderson had fallen in love with.

"Nothing to Say," which criticizes those who use social causes for their own ends, begins as a march, then segues into an impassioned double-time ballad, becoming pseudo-symphonic on the choruses driven by Barre's rhythm and lead guitar parts; while "Inside," a celebration of hearth and home (a favorite subject of Scots songwriters), is a folk-oriented flute-and-electric mandolin number anchored by Cornick's jazzy bass. ("Jeffrey" makes his third appearance in an Anderson title or lyric in the latter song.)

"Son," another song inspired by Anderson's estrangement from his father, opens with a musical vengeance, the heaviest rock yet waged by the band, leading to the bitter lyric, "'Permission to breathe, Sir.' Don't talk like that. I'm your old man." A lyrical lead guitar passage by Barre fades out, making way for Anderson's flamenco-style acoustic work, accompanied by Evans and then the return of Barre, before the entire band kicks back into the original heavy rock riff. (Although the entire album anticipates *Aqualung*, this song particularly does, its musical style and biting, cynical content sounding like an earlier version of "Hymn 43.")

Jeffrey Hammond's last title appearance occurs in "For Michael Collins, Jeffrey and Me," a folk-oriented song, featuring a beautiful melody and lyrics, that bursts into powerful choruses enhanced by Barre's lead work. The aforementioned Collins is not the famous Irish revolutionary, but one of the three astronauts who manned the Apollo 11 space flight to the moon in 1969. Here Anderson sympathizes with Collins, who had to stay behind in the mother ship while Neil Armstrong and Buzz Aldrin received the glory for actually walking on the moon. It is perhaps the album's masterpiece and certainly one of Anderson's greatest songs. Glenn Cornick explained:

> "Michael Collins, Jeffrey and Me": We had no idea what this was. We just knew there was a backing track, and there were some odd little timing things in it, but didn't know what they referred to. It's a wonderful song and it came out nicely, but I think that could have been two or three times as good if we really had known what we were doing. If we had it to the point where we could actually rehearse it as a song, as opposed to just a bunch of chords and a vague tempo.[47]

The classic "To Cry You a Song," which opened the second side of the original LP, sounds like a blues-rock number written during the Middle Ages, with Barre's single-note riffing during the verses leading up to driving choruses. The greatly improved Clive Bunker stands out on this track. Years after recording it, Anderson thought that the lyrics were blatantly naive:

> "Flying so high" ... would you believe ... it never occurred to me that this might be taken as a reference to drugs, but people back then thought I was a serious druggie. And I don't think anybody believed me when I said that I didn't take drugs—I really didn't. And haven't. So to me it was like a really very naive and silly thing to have written, something that was actually an aeroplane song, singing about being away on tour or something, about some girlfriend I had at the time. But how many people will have heard that and thought, "Hey, man, cool, peace?" So that's an example of very, very bad lyric writing, because I created something which was almost bound to be misunderstood. And yet it didn't occur to me what I was saying. I wasn't really that familiar with the vernacular of my contemporaries.[48]

In his 1993 essay on Anderson's songwriting, Judson C. Caswell observed:

> [His] attitude toward drugs and alcohol acted to distance him from his audiences and from his contemporaries. He felt as if he grew up in a generation that he didn't belong to. Unable to express the sentiments overtly without ostracizing much of his audience, his opinions toward drugs were "bottled up" and arose as bitterness and anger in his music toward the general culture of the times.[49]

Many years after his *Benefit* experience, Martin Barre elaborated on the subject of drug use:

> When we went to America in the early '70s, it was a drug cult. We always made it very clear that not only were we anti-drugs, but that we didn't like people coming to our concerts and taking drugs. You can get people dying—one night we came off stage and somebody on drugs had stuck a carving knife in and killed himself.
> It's terrible, people are killing themselves because of you. There is a responsibility if you are involved in the media, and you take that very seriously.... Take some bands—it doesn't matter what their music is like, whether you hate or like it—they are encouraging the drug culture. They go out of their way to be outrageous ... they aren't keeping it quiet by

doing it in hotel rooms, they do it out in the open and want the audience to take up their ideas as part of being a fan....[50]

Glenn Cornick offered an additional view on the band's response to drug use:

> We weren't involved in the drug culture. I'm not saying that nobody in the band ever smoked any dope, because I know that some, including me, did occasionally. But we were certainly not a "dope band," like the American bands. The American bands were stoned *all the time.* That's the big difference between British bands and American bands. American bands were always stoned. British bands were often drunk.
>
> But drugs were never a part of Jethro Tull. While Ian never took drugs, why did he go on stage and pretend to be a druggie? And he did. He made jokes about it in such a way that implied that he was using. He actually made comments and gestures that really did sell the idea that he was doing drugs.[51]

"A Time for Everything?" combining the favorite Tull elements of chamber music and driving rock, is another of Anderson's "old man" songs: Here the narrator is 50, his life over, realizing that he has run out of time. "Teacher," on the other hand, tells the tale of a young man who quickly becomes disillusioned with formal education, realizing that what he is being taught is not necessarily true. Anderson's voice is at its best on the latter track (recorded exclusively for the U.S. LP), and the fusion of the flute with Barre's single-note riff creates a chanting, "ancient" blues ambience that recalls the introduction of "To Cry You a Song." Glenn Cornick revealed how this track came about:

> "Teacher" was a throwaway song for us. I don't think anybody in the band ever liked it. It was the B-side of a British forty-five. Ian wrote it as a B-side: "Better write something, get it off." And it was never taken any more seriously than that, until American Reprise said, "Well, we want something that's more like a rock 'n' roll song to put on the radio." I suspect it was them who picked the song. We completely re-recorded it. The album version is a totally different recording. It's rearranged, and the British version doesn't have flute in it. And the main reason we had to re-record it was that they needed something that was a pop song that featured the flute. And so we did it and said, "Fair enough," and put it on the *Benefit* album. We didn't think it was as good a track as "Alive and Well and Living In," the track that was taken off the album. We much preferred the English version of the album but, I suppose, looking back at it over the years, on the oldies stations in L.A., "Teacher" is played

almost every day. You won't find it popular in Europe. "Living in the Past" would be the one people know in Britain or anywhere in Europe.[52]

"Play in Time" begins with a Celtic-style melodic riff played in unison by Anderson and Barre (a sound the Irish band Horslips appropriated soon after), then segues into driving R&B featuring excellent Hammond organ work by Evans. After a bizarre instrumental section, which incorporates Barre's guitar played backwards on the tape, this "tartan psychedelia" ends with a reprise of the unison flute-and-guitar riff and a fade out on the R&B section. The musical alternation and confusion certainly reflects Anderson's lyric, "Blues were my favorite colour, 'til I looked around and found another song that I felt like singing," indicating his move away from the music of African-Americans to that of his own homeland.

Concluding the album, "Sossity: You're a Woman," yet another expression of individuality, contains some of the best music ever written by Anderson, whose unique guitar technique really begins to shine. Except for Evans' Hammond, the instrumentation is entirely acoustic, with Anderson and Barre both playing the guitar parts. Again, Anderson's voice is in top expressive form, and his flute counter melody, as well as his tambourine playing, created the most medieval-sounding Tull song to date. ("Sossity" resulted from a particularly fertile period of his writing for acoustic guitar, as the subsequent releases of *Aqualung* and *Living in the Past* would prove.)

While other band members could confer with Anderson on the musical arrangements, they might not have any idea what the songs were about. Twenty-two years after *Benefit* was released, Anderson claimed:

> The title "Sossity" was a pun on the word "society," but Martin Barre didn't know that. He thought Sossity was a girl's name. He actually had a boat which he called *Sossity*. Afterwards, when I'd heard he'd named his boat this and beautifully painted the name on it, I said, "Martin, that was just a joke about society!" So he sold the boat![53]

Glenn Cornick named *Benefit* as his favorite Tull album, "without question. There's some great songs on there, and a much greater variety than on *Stand Up*. A lot of it is about [Anderson's wife] Jennie, of course, rather than Ian's family."[54] Cornick also shared his views on why he and Anderson eventually "grew apart":

> I've always felt it was because of his upbringing. Ian's parents didn't approve of the way he looked and behaved after he got famous, and his

father would not walk down the street with him because he looked so weird. Ian didn't want his parents ever to come to see him play, but my mother used to sneak Ian's mother into the back of gigs to see him. And even though Ian claimed to be an atheist or agnostic, he retained that streak of Scottish Presbyterian Puritanism in him. He was very offended when we toured the States when I was off chasing girls. I mean, I was twenty-one years old, and there was more available than anyone could handle in a hundred years, so I took advantage. But Ian never liked that.[55]

The *Benefit* Tour

Having played on the album, John Evans now was needed to complete the new Tull sound in a live context. While rehearsing in Germany, Anderson phoned to request that he become a full-time member of the band. Initially reluctant to abandon his studies, Evans was persuaded by his Chelsea tutor to "do it for a couple of years, make some money and invest it or buy a house, and come back and get your degree."[56] With the keyboard player on board, Tull opened the U.S. *Benefit* tour at Denver's Mammoth Gardens on April 17–18, 1970 (where the young man on drugs killed himself),[57] and continued, save for a three-week break in June, until August 16.

On May 23, they played a triple bill with John Sebastian and Clouds at the Fillmore East. After hearing the set, which included "Nothing Is Easy," an early version of "My God," "With You There to Help Me," "We Used to Know" and an extended version of "Dharma for One," one critic wrote:

> Almost every day someone is coming up with some new sort of gimmick. A few of them work and others don't. Not knowing a darn thing about a complicated instrument such as the flute, and after a year and a half of producing unbelievably good music with it, it is a definite gimmick that works. So it is with Ian Anderson and Jethro Tull. Outrageous show-stopper that he is, adorned in a checked maxi Edwardian coat with Robin Hood boots and a big mop of Brillo hair, Ian is the driving force in this group's many albums. I was surprised that he did allot an unusual amount of freedom to his other musicians.[58]

Returning to England, they took a five-week gigging hiatus, but made an appearance at the monumental Isle of Wight festival on August 30. Sharing the stage with Jimi Hendrix, the Who, Kris Kristofferson and many others, they played to a drunken and drugged audience of a half million who, as portrayed by a famous documentary film, turned their "peace and love" message into one of indifference, vulgarity and violence. (As shown in the film, Anderson attempts to talk some sense into the few who apparently are listening.) Glenn Cornick remembered it as "the best festival I was ever involved in. Out of this world. All the horizons were people. That film is crap. There was just a little aggravation, as always."[59] The festival was followed by more English dates, a jaunt to Paris and another tour of the States in October and November.

On November 4, a "night off," as described by Anderson, the band played a Carnegie Hall benefit for New York's Phoenix House drug rehabilitation center. In the entire history of that esteemed auditorium named after Andrew of Dunfermline, only one other rock band had been allowed to play there: the Beatles in 1964. The following day's reviews focused on Anderson's insane stage antics more so than on the music, which ranged from high-energy versions of "Nothing Is Easy," "With You There to Help Me," "A Song for Jeffrey" and "To Cry You a Song" to extended improvisational renditions of "Dharma for One" and "We Used to Know." Introducing the early version of "My God," Anderson said they had tried to record it, but "it turned out shitty … but it will be on the next album." (Considering its bluesy roughness and harsher lyrics than in the later *Aqualung* version, as well as the snorting and honking flute solo Anderson played at this point, his comments are understandable.)

John Evans fared well during his 11 minutes in the spotlight, combining variations on Beethoven's Sonata Number 8 in C-Flat, Opus 13 ("Pathétique") and Rachmaninov's Prelude in G-Sharp Minor, Opus 3, Number 2, with sundry classical, jazz and R&B elements, calling it "By Kind Permission Of." At midpoint, he and Anderson segued into a lovely piano and flute duet that eventually returned to Beethoven before the entire band kicked in for a bluesy jam. Bunker, too, was able to stretch out, again on "Dharma," which now included Anderson's Buddhist lyrics. Barre added extra drive to Mick Abrahams' old rhythm guitar part, and the band chanted along and played various percussion instruments during a break before Bunker launched into his solo, culminating with a masterful single-stroke roll and two runs across his tom-toms before they all exploded into a furious ending.

Announcing that his mum liked "Sossity: You're a Woman" because "it has a nice tune," he and Evans (playing the flute part on the organ) combined a condensed version with "Reasons for Waiting" (on which Evans approximated both the flute and string parts on the keys). Ending the show, the band began "We Used to Know," with Barre soaring into a superb solo, but then shifted into a Cream-style jam, leaving the guitarist alone to play a noisy mélange that went on too long before "For a Thousand Mothers" reared its head. (Though someone in the audience kept calling out, "For Michael Collins, Jeffrey and Me," the song, never a live selection, had not been included on the set list.) After the show, Anderson and Jennie, who recently had married him at the registry office in Watford, England, were introduced to the Duke and Duchess of Bedford.

In New York, the band were preparing to fly back to London to begin working on the next album and plan another tour. Just as Anderson, Barre and Bunker gave their tickets to Terry Ellis, the calm manager asked Cornick to join him in the John F. Kennedy Airport coffee shop. The bassist subsequently explained:

> The guys got on the plane, and Terry told me, "Well, Ian doesn't want to work with you anymore. We've canceled your plane ticket and you're on the flight tomorrow." So they could jump on the plane without having to see me. It leaves a very bad taste in my mouth after all these years. That was a very unpleasant way of doing things. I bore a very heavy grudge for a long time, but now, it's bloody thirty years later. Who gives a shit? It takes so much more effort to maintain a grudge than it does to say, "Oh, well. What the hell. Live and learn."[60]

As to the musical capabilities of the band, Cornick said, "We weren't knowledgeable musicians. None of us really had any great knowledge of music. We were all winging it. It was like, 'What can we try? Will this work?'"[61] As consolation, Terry Ellis subsequently signed Cornick's new band, Wild Turkey, to the Chrysalis label.

Cornick added:

> I couldn't have stayed in the band that much longer, because I don't think I would have worked for *Thick as a Brick*. It's a good record, and there are some things on *Thick as a Brick* that I really like. But I wouldn't have fit into that format. I'm not a circus performer. I'm pretty sure that, if I'd stayed around, at that point I'd have been out on the street anyway.
>
> Having to learn and play all that stuff exactly note for note every night would have driven me up the wall. I don't know. Never having done it, maybe I would have gotten a kick out of it. But, it seems to me, I probably wouldn't have. I probably could have worked through *Aqualung*, but after that I'm sure I would have started to feel really strange about the whole thing.
>
> Jeffrey was probably great for that. Jeffrey is, in a certain way, a comic. He's a great bloke. I always liked Jeffrey a lot.[62]

Not only did Cornick become a casualty of Tull's touring, but the entire band had experienced a rough time financially. Commenting on the first two years on the American road, Anderson explained:

> We did a thirteen week tour the first time where we lost a lot of money and the second time we did a lot of dates supporting Led Zeppelin as the opening act. We just about broke even on that tour and on the third tour, the last tour in '69, we came in and did some shows sort of on our own really—small theatres and things. We made a little bit back on that. And then in '70 we actually began to co-host shows with groups like Mountain and that sort of thing, middling name groups where it was a toss-up as to who went on first.[63]

Aqualung

April 1971
Highest chart position: 4 (U.K.) / 7 (U.S.)
[Rating: 5]
Producer: Ian Anderson / Island ILPS 9145
All songs written by Ian Anderson (except where indicated)

Ian Anderson: vocals, flute, acoustic and electric guitars, percussion
Martin Barre: electric guitar, descant recorder
John Evans: piano, Hammond organ, mellotron
Jeffrey Hammond: bass guitar, alto recorder, vocals
Clive Bunker: drums, percussion

Recorded at Island Studios, Basing Street, London, late 1970
Recording engineer: John Burns
Orchestra arranged and conducted by David Palmer
Executive producer: Terry Ellis
Paintings by Burton Silverman

Tracks: Aqualung (Ian Anderson–Jennie Anderson)
　　　　Cross-Eyed Mary
　　　　Cheap Day Return
　　　　Mother Goose
　　　　Wond'ring Aloud
　　　　Up to Me
　　　　My God
　　　　Hymn 43
　　　　Slipstream

Locomotive Breath
Wind Up

Long considered to be Tull's first "concept album," *Aqualung* may be half a concept album, since only side two of the original record (or the second half of the CD) explores a thematic motif, that of organized religion. Fast becoming the Bertrand Russell of early 1970s contemporary music, Anderson, in five separate songs, tore into the bigotry and closed-mindedness of those who he believed had no grasp of true spirituality.

With Glenn Cornick out of the band, Anderson brought in his old mate Jeffrey Hammond to take over the bassist duties. Hammond had graduated from art school and was having difficulties making a living as a painter. When Anderson allowed him to move into his house to decorate it, he first observed Tull at work—including the recording of the single "The Witch's Promise"—and then was asked to join when Cornick was axed. Hammond said:

> I was very fortunate to be in the right place at the right time, and to have the old boy network working in my favor. It was a really tremendous opportunity and exceptionally exciting. So as soon as they came back from the tour we started recording the album *Aqualung* and getting ready to tour again.[64]

Prior to his abrupt departure, Cornick had worked on several songs intended for the album:

> I was on four of the original takes of *Aqualung*, only one of which ever came out, which was "Wond'ring Again," the original version of "Wond'ring Aloud." There's a version somewhere of "My God," which is a very, very good version which hasn't been released. I'm not quite sure why. Ian changed all the words around. We played that for almost a year while I was still in the band, so it was a song that I was very familiar with, and we did a really good job on it. There's a couple other songs, and I don't even know what they were, that were recorded. A lot of the stuff we did were just backing tracks.[65]

In 1992, Anderson said:

> *Aqualung* is obviously seen by many people as being the seminal Jethro Tull album in many ways. They are right in the sense that it is the album that has continued to bring Jethro Tull to the attention of more people than any other. *Aqualung* was released at a time when Jethro Tull was just becoming popular in America and had already become popular

in most European countries. So although it wasn't hugely successful in the year of its release it has continued to sell consistently since then.[66]

Indeed, *Aqualung* has continued to sell so well that it earns the most royalties of any album in the Tull back catalog, a windfall made possible by the band's performances of "Aqualung" and "Locomotive Breath" at nearly every concert since 1971, and frequent inclusions of "Cross-Eyed Mary" and "My God" at live shows.

The genesis of the album occurred after Jennie Anderson returned home with some photographs she had taken of unfortunates and homeless people on London's Thames embankment. One old man in tattered clothing fascinated her and Ian, sparking the idea of the album's cover and title song, the first two verses of which were cowritten by Jennie. Ian, however, would come to regret some of the associations the idea created:

> [T]his particular guy ... had a defiance and nobility about him, and indeed, so much better it would have been to have used her photograph with the guy's permission instead of that, I think, really not very attractive or well executed painting on the front cover.... I've never really liked the *Aqualung* cover, although a lot of people think it's terrific. I didn't like the fact that it was made to look like me.... Terry Ellis was wanting this to be a character: It could be like me, or it could be somebody else. And I said, "Hey, look, this is going to get dangerous ... we don't want to start getting anybody thinking: 'Wait a minute. Ian Anderson is looking like this character of whom he says on the album cover something about God being within all men, even within *Aqualung* ... therefore Ian Anderson thinks he's God'!" I said, "Terry ... just make it look like some old guy!" But I got talked into this. I've always regretted letting it be that way.[67]

The "not very attractive" painting was done by Burton Silverman, a New York artist who had contributed to *Esquire* and *Newsweek*.

Prior to beginning the recording sessions in December 1970, Anderson had considered bringing in someone else to produce a Tull album. He revealed:

> I went to see George Martin ... famous for the Beatles albums, and asked him to help us, or at least to give me some advice about production, because I was finding it a little bit overwhelming. But he gave me the advice ... that since I was doing okay, that I should carry on and get stuck into it....[68]

Although he had contributed a good measure of acoustic guitar work to *Stand Up*, *Benefit* and a few singles, Anderson really began to develop a distinctive style on *Aqualung*. He later explained where his English influences originated:

> Back around 1968, '69, there were a few guys who were part of the "contemporary folk" scene—Pentangle's John Renbourn and Bert Jansch, Richard Thompson of Fairport Convention—and were certainly not traditional English folk players. Although some of their techniques were traditional folk, they seemed to be doing something different: singing very personalized songs that, seemingly, did not have a great deal to do with the American tradition. Seeing people like that gave me the confidence to try and strum a few chords and sing.... I would try and find the little things I could play with my limited technique—something that would relate to the melody, or harmonize with the melody, or produce a little turnaround. Some little embellishments that would be relative to the song. They became very much a piece of the song, part of the arrangement.[69]

At this point in his musical development, he continued to disassociate himself from blues and jazz music, claiming, "Really what I am is a folksinger and that's the honest truth, more than anything else, inasmuch as what I'm singing about is the folk music of today."[70]

Glenn Cornick observed:

> During the time I was with Tull, I listened to a lot of Pentangle. And we used to work with them quite frequently. And I also listened to Roy Harper a lot. I mean, that's where Ian invented himself from. Ian's voice and guitar playing is taken directly from Roy Harper. It is so close—even Roy Harper's mannerisms—it's amazing how closely they are in style. Not the *songs*, just the vocal style and the guitar style.[71]

In his July 22, 1971, review of *Aqualung*, *Rolling Stone*'s Ben Gurson criticized Anderson for taking his subject matter too seriously and singing it with melodrama and theatricality, yet found much to admire in the music:

> Tull is one of our most serious and intelligent groups, and Anderson's choice of subject for *Aqualung* ... is witness to that. Further, Tull has a musical sophistication to match its thematic ambitions. Where *This Was*, their first album, was aimless and disorganized, *Stand Up*, with its dabbling in ethnic and classical forms, was eclectic in the best sense. Out of that experimentation was forged in *Benefit* a sound which finally provided the band with a concrete identity.... Once a group has arrived at a coherent style, the next logical step is a concept album, and it is on

the shoals of concepts that many a band runs aground. Often such albums lack the hint of self-irony, which is basic to great rock and roll, and therefore come off sounding pompous.[72]

The Tracks of *Aqualung*

The first half of the album (subtitled "Aqualung") is a bona fide masterpiece blending folk, blues, psychedelia, theater, classical and medieval music with hard rock. The first six notes of "Aqualung"—one of the most legendary introductions in the history of rock—open the song like a symphony and clearly demonstrate Anderson's interest in Beethoven. The most intricate piece of music that he yet had produced, it has several distinct movements that elicit different emotions from the listener. The menacing opening and heavy power-chord verses underscore the initial description of the Aqualung character, who is pedophilic, dirty and dripping snot—disgusting, to say the least. But when the second "movement," or acoustic section, begins—with Anderson strumming his guitar as he sings one of his finest melodies—the listener hears the homeless man as a sympathetic, pitiful character: "an old man wandering lonely, taking time the only way he knows" and with a "leg hurting bad, as he bends to pick a dog-end."

During the second acoustic verse, having been joined by Hammond, Bunker and Evans, Anderson includes the album's first reference to organized religion, initially referring to the Salvation Army and then paraphrasing a line from the introduction of Robert Burns' poem "The Holy Fair," which is noted by the poet as being quoted from "Hypocrisy à la mode": "Feeling alone, the army's up the road, salvation à la mode and a cup of tea."

Beginning the third "movement," the band adds some potent kicks as Anderson tells of Aqualung's most harrowing experience—"Do you still remember December's foggy freeze—when the ice that clings onto your beard in screaming agony?"—and then breaks for Barre to enter with the most memorable solo he ever would play, a stunning, melodic passage that builds from the first note to the last. Since that 1970 session, he undoubtedly has taken that ride more often than any other, yet has improvised upon it as much as possible. Twenty years after he laid down the original version, he said:

> The only thing I can remember about cutting the solo is that Led Zeppelin was recording next door, and as I was playing it, Jimmy Page

walked into the control room and waved to me. How I didn't stop playing I don't know, but I carried on somehow. Still, I had no idea when I
did it that it would become such a popular solo. When I cut solos in
those early days, it was always sort of a fun thing to do, very carefree.
Clive Bunker and Glenn Cornick would be in the control room yelling,
"Yeah, go for it, just cut loose," but later we got a bit more constricted,
and there was less improvisation in the music.[73]

After Barre soars over the band's up-tempo movement, the song
dynamically drops back into a quiet folk mode, featuring only Anderson,
repeating the second half of the third verse—"Aqualung my friend—don't
you start away uneasy, you poor old sod, you see, it's only me"—before the
ominous opening notes and power chords return to remind us that the
pathetic man is indeed viewed as disgusting, not by the narrator, but by
society. The song then ends with some excellent Bunker drum fills and
the most famous example of the Martin Barre "power slide" (here an E-
flat quickly strummed just before sliding his left hand down the guitar
neck).

Though a much more straightforward blues-rock song, "Cross-Eyed
Mary" also opens with a seedy atmosphere, a dark and brooding tone
established by the tight 4/4 pulse of Hammond and Bunker, over which
Barre lays some eerie chords. This effective introduction creates the image
of a John walking down a street in search of a whore even before the song
crescendos into the nasty, steamy blues riff that, like its counterpart in
"Aqualung," underscores the vivid and vulgar description of a "low-life"
character: here a teenage prostitute who services old geezers and is taken
to school by the "jack-knife barber," presumably after receiving a back-
alley abortion.

The lightsome acoustic piece "Cheap Day Return" is an autobiographical song in which Anderson expresses the emotions he experienced
while trying to get back to London via the Glasgow train to visit his ailing father. In fact, having had a rather unhappy relationship with his dad,
he feared he might not be able to reach the hospital before the old man
passed away: "The anticipation of that occurred to me ... on Preston plat-
form, waiting for the train back down south."[74] The subtlety of John
Evans' accordion and David Palmer's orchestral arrangement beautifully
background this first "solo" Anderson work ever released.

Anderson's classic acoustic sound really emerges on "Mother Goose,"
which, aside from Barre's inevitable power chords, is nearly a straight
medieval piece, driven by Bunker's traditional-style percussion and lent
an ancient ambience by the recorder work of Barre and Hammond (who

also sings harmony vocals). (The "whistling" sound of the recorders as the track fades out anticipates a passage in 1973's *A Passion Play*.) Based on people he had observed in Hampstead, the song borrows from Robert Louis Stevenson's *Treasure Island* when the narrator calls himself "Long John Silver" (earlier he instead calls himself "a schoolboy," also suggesting Stevenson's stories, which often feature young male protagonists). But apparently Anderson's fellow Edinburghian had no influence on "Mother Goose." Later writing that he had "never read any of the works of R. L. Stevenson,"[75] he instead viewed the song as being full of "craziness":

[A] ... surrealistic pastiche with summery motives, things in or around Hampstead Heath, strange characters, a little like nursery rhyme characters, but not about any one specific thing. It was just a place where I used to occasionally go and walk alone on Sundays when I first went to London and started playing; the biggest park near where I lived. And there were always all kinds of weird people there—still are. I was probably one of them at the time.[76]

Ben Gurson observed:

"Mother Goose" is the kind of song that Anderson writes best. As in "Sossity" on *Benefit*, he uncannily captures the feel of a real Elizabethan madrigal (a consort of recorders here helps it get across). It's a song about a Hampstead fair, and is filled with descriptive detail which is at once archaic and up to date. Lyrics and melody mutually accomplish the same purpose, for both express the continuity of English life.[77]

An Anderson solo masterpiece that lends some welcome light to a series of dark songs, "Wond'ring Aloud," like "Cheap Day Return," begins with voice and acoustic guitar, then adds Evans (on piano) and a Palmer string arrangement. Addressing the fact that each person is responsible for his or her own behavior and morality, he masterfully blends a specific character's experience with a universal philosophical stance:

Wond'ring aloud—how we feel today.
Last night sipped the sunset—my hand in her hair.
We are our own saviors as we start both our hearts
beating life into each other.
Wond'ring aloud—will the years treat us well.
As she floats in the kitchen, I'm tasting the smell
of toast as the butter runs.
Then she comes, spilling crumbs on the bed,

and I shake my head.
And it's only the giving that makes you what you are.

"Up to Me" is the album's strangest song, a mixture of psychedelic blues (Barre using a wah-wah pedal) and medieval-sounding acoustic verses highlighted by flute and percussion (sleigh bells can be heard during the bridge). Opening with a bit of crazed laughter suggesting Bedlam or a similar locale, it returns the focus of the album's first half to struggling characters, this time the narrator himself being "a common working man."

The material on the album's second half resulted from Anderson's personal observations about organized religion, not from any deliberate bookish study. In July 1971, he revealed:

> Several months ago in Rome when I was talking to some Roman Catholics about religion, in particular their own, it became rather obvious to me through our mutual discussion that their religion was something they adhered to through fear. Although they were no longer involved in the direct application of the principles of their faith they refused to renounce it. A couple of them admitted to it being through fear, fear of eternal damnation, fear of all the things they were told were going to happen if you don't do things the right way. "Your religion is the only true religion and everyone else is wrong" sort of thing.
>
> I really believe that fear in respect to religion is very powerful, possibly the most powerful part, fear of the unknown, fear of death and most of all the fear of not being able to understand oneself, not being able to come to grips with oneself in terms of objective analysis. In these terms the East is so far ahead of us because that's what they do teach, to come to grips with oneself.[78]

Here, Anderson proves that he came to the same conclusion as did Freud and Russell (in *The Future of an Illusion* and *Why I Am Not a Christian*, respectively) without reading any of their famous works—an observation powerfully expressed in "My God," a song that he had been working on (and playing live) for some time. In another interview at the time, he recalled his fear-filled childhood experiences with religion:

> To me, it's a terrible chance to take—to expose a child to religion in such a way as he may be contaminated by the fear aspect of it, as opposed to the idea of love, the idea of coexistence. I think religion is something better entered into as one reaches an age of greater awareness and experience.[79]

The second half of the album is thematically heavier than the first—indicating the harsher, unrelentingly cynical viewpoints expressed therein—though it also incorporates the same range of musical styles. "My God" is an excellent example of what Ben Gurson praised as "the fine musicianship and often brilliant structural organization of the songs." And although he faulted the album for being "depressingly anticlimactic," due to Anderson's "misplaced emotion," he was impressed by the blending of musicality and message on this track:

> The nub of the issue is Christian hypocrisy, how people manipulate notions of God for their own ends. There is some rather obvious talk of plastic crucifixes, Blakean allusions to locking "Him in His golden cage," and invective; "The bloody church of England/In chains of history/ Requests your earthy presence at/The vicarage for tea." Beneath the accusatory tone is a moving musical theme. Again, the structure is constantly shifting. There are stately hymnal changes, a jazzy flute break, a pomp-and-circumstantial motif which, when inverted, assumes a more chromatic, modern queasiness. The gamut of religious experience is encompassed in this song.[80]

Opening with an emotive solo acoustic guitar passage—blending classical elegance with blues passion—Anderson is joined by Evans' piano before he begins his sneering vocals. After singing of God being entrapped by human dogma, his lyric, "So lean upon him gently and don't call on him to save" prefaces a *sturm-und-drang* explosion of the band that again suggests the influence of Beethoven. Following a full verse, an instrumental break offers some expressive, wailing soloing from Barre before the band punctuates an Anderson flute passage that leads into a multi-tracked sonic collage of flute and "sacred"-style chanting. With this spiritual fervency ended, the bluesy riff again returns on flute and piano, and just after Anderson sings, "And the graven image, you—know—who—with His plastic crucifix!" the entire band again explodes like an ancient Teutonic force. Recalling the instrumental break, the song then fades out on a flute note underscored by chanting.

A song that criticizes the sectarian and selfish use of the Jesus icon, "Hymn 43" begins by satirizing "The Lord's Prayer": "Oh Father high in heaven—smile down upon your son"; but it also (as in the second verse) allows Anderson to exercise his disgust with more specific unpleasantries carried out by crusading Christians:

And the unsung Western hero,
killed an Indian or three,

and then he made his name in Hollywood
to set the white man free.
Oh Jesus save me!

Like "Son" on *Benefit,* the song begins with a hard-rock vengeance, fore-shadowing the anger soon to be demonstrated by the narrator. Barre plays his rhythm guitar part with absolute viciousness, using the string-scraping effect he would employ in many later Tull tracks. In fact, "Hymn 43" was the heaviest "straight" rock cut the band had performed up to that time (and its near-"metal" sound would not be exceeded until the release of *Minstrel in the Gallery* four years later).

The soothing "Slipstream," opening with Anderson's voice, then acoustic guitar, and soon joined by a Palmer string arrangement, provides a welcome respite to the blatant power of the previous two tracks. But lyrically pulling no punches, it deals with those who believe they can buy their way to heaven, while having no grasp of true spirituality—a view musically echoed by Palmer's violins, which bow uneasily back and forth as the song fades out.

Another legendary track, "Locomotive Breath," which would become a tour de force encore number at concerts, was actually patched together in the studio. Before any other band members became involved, Anderson played bass drum and hi-hat cymbal to produce a 4:30 drum track, over which Bunker later overdubbed tom-toms and cymbals, and also played the famous "locomotive" scraping sound with the electric rhythm guitar (the same effect Barre used on "Hymn 43"). Though Anderson had arranged so much of the song, Evans created the superb piano prologue, beginning in classical mode and smoothly segueing into jazz, over which Barre added some blues licks. An electric guitar crescendo opens the intro-duction to the first verse, the string scraping accompanying the lyric, "In the shuffling madness of the locomotive breath," which begins this tale about predestination, a Presbyterian concept Anderson was taught as a child in Edinburgh, and the endless conflict between religious and secu-lar beliefs. (The lyric "Old Charlie stole the handle, and the train won't stop going, no way to slow down" suggests how the evolutionary theory of Charles Darwin has challenged the traditional theories of creation.) A second rhythm guitar part, sounding like a wailing string arrangement, is an early example of the "orchestral" style Barre would continuously develop over the years.

Opening with bucolic piano, then very quiet acoustic guitar and vocals, the quasi-theatrical "Wind Up" is Anderson's personal declaration of spiritual belief, telling of his parents' and headmaster's attempted indoc-trination of him, and his own discovery:

> And I asked this God a question and by way of firm reply
> He said—I'm not the kind you have to wind up on Sundays.

Just after the lyric, "Well you can excommunicate me on my way to Sunday school and have all the bishops harmonize these lines," the band kicks in with a vengeance, Barre adding a separate harmony rhythm part as Anderson sings, "How do you dare to tell me that I'm my father's son," and truly driving his cohorts like the metaphorical train of the previous song during "when that was just an accident of birth" and through Anderson's confident assertion that his individual path is richer than that of those who "lick the boots of death born out of fear." Barre plays an excellent solo akin to his "Aqualung" effort as the band continues to rock furiously, and then the solo piano returns for a reprise of the initial verse, which eventually is backed by the entire band, who ultimately disappear, leaving Anderson alone to strum his acoustic guitar and repeat:

> I don't believe you: you had the whole damn thing all wrong—
> He's not the kind you have to wind up on Sundays.

"Hymn 43," backed with "Mother Goose," was released as a single, the first Tull 45 to become available in the U.S. ("Living in the Past" was held back until the following year.)

The *Aqualung* Tour

Jeffrey Hammond recalled some aspects of the *Aqualung* tour:

> I remember going around buying some unusual stage gear, flying goggles and so on. I very clearly remember the first concert I played in Odense in Denmark. It was a long time since I'd been onstage anywhere and I hadn't realized how hot it was, and I was wearing these goggles which just steamed up halfway through the first song. I couldn't see a thing! It was very much a case of in at the deep end.[81]

January dates in Scandinavia, Austria, Germany, Switzerland and Italy were followed by a month in Britain before they once again invaded the U.S., touring from April 1 until the end of May, when Clive Bunker decided to quit. A drummer more interested in feel than technique and polish, he was bothered by the increasing complexity of the music, so he made the decision to marry and move to a farm outside Luton, where he set up a dog kennel business. He also invested some of his hard-earned

Tull money in a local engineering firm, but occasionally accepted offers to record or perform live with various musicians, including Mick Abrahams (in Blodwyn Pig), Robin Trower (in Jude) and Manfred Mann.

Barrie Barlow, having combined a dead-end day job with gigging around the Birmingham area, had given up on "all the aspirations [he'd] had about being a professional musician," but literally was accosted by an inebriated John Evans, who, just having returned from the tour, drove across a neighboring lawn and flew into the house where Barrie and some friends had gathered to watch a championship soccer game.[82] Having heard *This Was* only, Barrie had to buy the other albums and begin to practice for his audition:

> Requiem [a band he currently drummed with] were rehearsing at that time in a children's home in St. Annes, and the equipment was all set up there, so Ian and John came up. Ian and I just had a jam together to start with, and it was great, because Ian is a great rhythm player, really good to play with. And then we did "To Cry You a Song"...[83]

Barrie quit his job and joined Tull at Sound Techniques in May 1971 to record a few tracks for an EP, including "Life Is a Long Song," "Up the 'Pool," "Dr. Bogenbroom," "For Later" and "Nursie," nearly reuniting one of the incarnations of the John Evan Band (only Barre had not been a member). (Anderson believed that record companies were bilking the public with single releases, so he made certain that his band offered more music for their fans' money.) A new U.S. tour opened on June 9 at the Salt Palace in Salt Lake City, followed by an even bigger show at Red Rocks in Denver, where there were not enough seats for the 12,000 people who arrived. Barrie (who was dubbed "Barrie*more*" by Anderson) remembered:

> [R]iots—and that was my second gig! They were dropping tear gas.... Those hippy girls, all smoking dope. A great cloud of dope, tear-gas everywhere, people turning over police cars and setting fire to them ... it was a bit heavy! I did this drum solo, and I was so nervous I got off the kit and started to do a tap dance, just to make it a little different![84]

A short time after the incident, Anderson said:

> Well, that was largely a riotous affair occurring at the back of the amphitheater, a thousand or so people trying to bust in with various weapons of war at their sides. At first the police wouldn't let us go on. It took hours of patient explaining that if we didn't get up on stage, there was a

large chance that there might be 10,000 people rioting, instead of 1000.... But we, as well as the audience, were just sort of victims, innocent bystanders. It was like a war going on outside. The CS gas drifted through—it was very uncomfortable, you know, seeing babies being carried out unconscious from the stuff. I think we all felt the sooner we got out of there and got on with the playing, the sooner the situation might resolve itself. So we just went on and were as boring as we could possibly be and hoped everybody'd go to sleep.[85]

As a result of this incident—vehicles were destroyed, 20 people were arrested and another 28 were hospitalized—Red Rocks was declared off limits to rock bands for the next two decades.

Of his initial experience with the band, Barlow added:

When I first joined Tull it was really happy. It was like being in the John Evan Band: John was there, Ian was there, Jeffrey ... and it still had that sort of schoolboy humor. Just being together ... it was like a family. And we were earning! It was great. If all you have ever wanted to do is earn a living playing music, and you are doing it with your friends ... it was heaven....[86]

In July, the band received an additional publicity boost when Anderson appeared on the cover of *Rolling Stone* magazine, having consented to a rare, in-depth interview with Grover Lewis, who well described his subject's on-stage look as "nothing if not tatty piss-elegant in skin-tight yellow breeks, a brocade sash that serves as a kind of codpiece, medieval-style boots, and a long plaid jerkin-coat."[87] Lewis also leveled high praise on the band: "[I]t's abundantly clear that Jethro Tull is hardly your household variety British rock-and-roll band on tour. In energy, invention, and performance, the group is more like a natural force, a wind or a river."[88] Attempting to squeeze in their two cents, John Evans told Lewis, "I listen to Tchaikovsky. I like melodies," while the eclectic Hammond admitted to liking Captain Beefheart, Prokofiev, Delius and Frank Sinatra.[89]

Referring to his maniacal stage persona, Anderson said:

When I first tried doing things in terms of leaping around or "looking good," management put the pressure on me to develop into being a sort of character actor. So, for a while, I attempted to be a weirdo, sort of strange and good to look at. But it didn't work.

Still, there came a point when I started doing it just for myself, and it gradually evolved into being, for me, at any rate, a true physical expression of the music we play. I have a brother [who was an ice skater].

I imagine there must be some form of physical expression that runs in my family.

Actually, a lot of what I do on stage is a caricature of what I think people see me as. Never is it very much a sexual thing. It's my own way of taking the mickey out of what I do. To be able to put the whole "rock-star figure" into perspective, you've got to be able to stand back and laugh at yourself, which is what I do from time to time. Hamming it up.[90]

A second U.S. tour opened in St. Petersburg, Florida, on October 15 and then moved all over the East, twice hitting New York's Madison Square Garden. At this point, the band, earning $15,000 to $30,000 per gig, traveled in an old turbo-prop aircraft and Cadillac limousines driven by chauffeurs who called each of them "Sir"—quite a step up for a bunch of blokes who, just a few years earlier, were a ragged blues group in a van. Tickets for the gigs sold for $5.50.

At one show, promoters refused to set up chairs on the floor, which would have prevented them from packing in as many young ticket buyers as possible. When the local police chief feared a riot, Terry Ellis assured him that Anderson could handle anything that happened: "They don't trust uniforms. The only person they trust is Ian. And if he tells them to cool down, they'll cool down."[91]

Anderson, alone on stage, opened the 90-minute shows with "My God," which always shook the walls as the band kicked in and the lights went up. At the sound check for the November 18 Madison Square Garden concert that closed the tour, New York Knicks star and future New Jersey senator Bill Bradley wandered into the arena, asking, "Do you think they'd mind if I watched? I really like their music." [92]

Living in the Past

June 1972 (U.K.) / October 1972 (U.S.)
Highest chart position: 8 (U.K.) / 3 (U.S.)
[Rating: 4]
Producers: Ian Anderson and Terry Ellis / Chrysalis CJT1
All songs written by Ian Anderson (except where indicated)

Ian Anderson: vocals, flute, acoustic guitar, mandolin, balalaika, Hammond organ, harmonica, tin whistle
Mick Abrahams: electric guitar

Martin Barre: electric and acoustic guitars, vocals
Glenn Cornick: bass guitar, Hammond organ
Jeffrey Hammond: bass guitar
John Evans: piano, Hammond organ, mellotron, celeste, harpsichord, vocals
Clive Bunker: drums, percussion, glockenspiel, vocals
Barrie Barlow: drums and percussion

Recorded at Sound Techniques, London; Morgan Studio, London; Vantone
   Studio, West Orange, N.J.; Western Recorders, Los Angeles, Calif.;
   Carnegie Hall, New York, N.Y.; Island Studio, London
Recording engineers: Victor Gamm, Andy Johns, John Wood, Robin Black,
   John Burns
Remixed at Morgan Studio, London, by Robin Black
Remixing supervised by Ian Anderson
Strings arranged and conducted by David Palmer, Lou Toby
Photographs by Sam Emerson and Tony Loew, Brian Ward, Ed Caraeff, Ruan
   O'Lochlainn, Jackie O'Lochlainn, Michael Graber

Tracks: A Song for Jeffrey
           Love Story
           A Christmas Song
           Living in the Past
           Driving Song
           Bourée (J. S. Bach)
           Sweet Dream
           Singing All Day
           Teacher
           Witch's Promise
           Inside
           Alive and Well and Living In
           Just Trying to Be
           By Kind Permission Of (Evans)
           Dharma for One (Anderson-Bunker)
           Wond'ring Again
           Hymn 43
           Locomotive Breath
           Life Is a Long Song
           Up the 'Pool
           Dr. Bogenbroom
           For Later
           Nursie

   Though *Living in the Past* is a compilation of songs, none of which
were recorded specifically for the new release, only eight had appeared on

previous albums (and "Dharma for One" as included here was expanded from the original *This Was* version and taped live at Carnegie Hall). Of the tracks that had been issued as singles, only "Hymn 43" had appeared in the U.S., making "Love Story," "Sweet Dream" and "Witch's Promise" as new to American fans as the 11 that either had been included only on European EPs or never released in any form. After the commercial successes of *Aqualung* and *Thick as a Brick* (discussed below), an increased interest in Tull led Chrysalis to release this previously recorded material in a deluxe package featuring a color photo booklet and informative liner notes.

After the now-primitive "A Song for Jeffrey" opens the album, the sound of the band improves greatly on "Love Story," recorded at Morgan Studio in November 1968 and marking the last track on which Mick Abrahams played. Anderson's unmistakable electric mandolin and flute stylings provide an introduction to this odd song about a love interest who apparently isn't pleasing her man very much. Though Abrahams handles the electric rhythm guitar part, the sound that developed with Barre on *Stand Up* is already in evidence, suggesting Anderson's overriding influence.

Also recorded in November 1968, "A Christmas Song" immediately took Tull in the direction of traditional English folk music, an element that would become even more prominent in years to come. (Anderson actually incorporated the first three lines of the carol "Once in Royal David's City," the lyrics of which were written by Cecil Frances Alexander in 1848.) However, here he inverts the caroling tradition: Rather than offering a Solstice celebration focusing on the sharing of peace and plenty, he condemns those whose greed prevents them from doing so:

How can you laugh when your own mother is hungry?
And how can you smile when your reasons for smiling are wrong?

Anderson's dual mandolin parts and tin whistle are brilliantly supported by his own jiggy bass line and marching snare technique (the liner notes in the album are incorrect in their respective crediting of Cornick and Bunker). The only non–Anderson component is David Palmer's lovely chamber string arrangement (the first he wrote for a Tull recording).

"Living in the Past" (also issued as a single in the U.S., where it climbed to number 11 in the charts) is followed by "Driving Song," a grungy blues number about the grind of life on the road, cut at Los Angeles' Western Recorders during the *Stand Up* tour in March 1969. Like Abrahams' playing on "It's Breaking Me Up," here Barre's lead part matches

the melody of Anderson's vocal, and he unleashes some Clapton-style soloing on his Gibson Les Paul before trading blues licks with the flute at the
end.

"Bourée" is followed by "Sweet Dream," an excellent, primarily
acoustic song opening ominously with 12-string flamenco stylings and an
effective David Palmer brass arrangement. A descending single-note electric guitar riff by Barre underscores Anderson's lyrics, beckoning his
intended companion to escape parental clutches for "all the things you
want to be." A bridge section crescendos into a driving chorus, advising:

> Get out and get what you can
> while your mummy's at home sleeping.
> No time to understand
> 'cause they lost what they thought they were keeping.

A repeat of the verse-bridge-chorus structure follows before Barre pushes
the band along with an intense solo, leading them back to the bridge-
chorus sections.

Cut at Morgan Studio in September 1969, the laid-back jazz number "Singing All Day" provides a nice counterpoint to "Sweet Dream,"
opening with Anderson on Hammond organ, Cornick laying down a nice
bass line, and Bunker playing lightly with brushes. A song about an unat-
tainable woman, it features the improvisational quality—particularly in
the rhythm playing of Barre and the flute soloing of Anderson (who also
plays balalaika)—that makes *Stand Up* and portions of *This Was* so unique
in the Tull catalog.

The British version of "Teacher," a different arrangement than the
one on *Benefit*, is followed by "The Witch's Promise," a 3/4 song, recorded
at Morgan Studio in December 1969, that is a virtual blueprint for later
Anderson efforts that cloak a modern sensibility within the mask of
medievalism. Here an unappreciative woman destroys her relationship, but
the tale is told in the form of a timeless fable about a witch, given brilliant musical support by a lovely melody introduced by an Anderson flute
"flurry." Barre handles the acoustic guitar work this time, with Evans on
piano and mellotron (rather than using a Palmer string arrangement),
Cornick playing a masterful bass part, and Bunker adding some nice Mid-
dle-Ages cymbal work.

Benefit's "Inside" is followed by "Alive and Well and Living In,"
recorded at Morgan in January 1970 (and included only on the British version of *Benefit*). A jazzy piano introduction gains a Latin percussion feel
and a medieval-style melody backgrounded by another of Barre's ominous

undercurrents. A very pleasant flute part is matched by some nice acoustic soloing, uncredited but apparently by Barre.

A beautiful acoustic song recorded at Morgan in June 1970, "Just Trying to Be," an Anderson "solo" piece, was a forerunner to its brethren on *Aqualung*. Opening with acoustic guitar and Evans on celeste, it eventually includes Anderson harmonizing with himself on a haunting chorus that concludes with another statement of individuality:

> And they can't see that we're just trying to be
> and not what we seem.

Disc two of the original album opens with two tracks from the 1970 Carnegie Hall concert, "By Kind Permission Of" and "Dharma for One," before moving on to "Wond'ring Again," an ageless Anderson masterpiece about the destruction of the environment, also cut at Morgan that June. Following an acoustic guitar introduction, Bunker joins in on glockenspiel, leading the full band into the chilling apocalyptic lyric:

> There's the stillness of death on a deathly unliving sea,
> and the motor car magical world long since ceased to be
> when the Eve-bitten apple returned to destroy the tree.

Recorded a few months before the official *Aqualung* sessions, the song features similarly cynical but insightful views, the bridge lyric, "The natural resources are dwindling and no one grows old, and those with no homes to go to, please dig yourself holes," leading to a reprise of "Wond'ring Aloud" (which presents the upbeat side of the same coin). As Anderson plays those familiar chords (first accompanied only by Evans and then the entire band), he gently sings what may be his greatest verse, a beautiful poetical passage with Stevensonian imagery:

> We wandered through quiet lands, felt the first breath of snow,
> searched for the last pigeon, slate grey I've been told.
> Stumbled on a daffodil which she crushed in the rush, heard it sigh,
> and left it to die.
> At once felt remorse and were touched by the loss of our own,
> held its poor broken head in her hands,
> dropped soft tears in the snow,
> and it's only the taking that makes you what you are.

But Anderson, returning to his "Aloud" version, concludes the song on a note of hope:

> Wond'ring aloud, will a son one day be born
> to share in our infancy
> in the child's path we've worn.
> In the aging seclusion of this earth that our birth did surprise,
> we'll open his eyes.

"Hymn 43" and "Locomotive Breath" are followed by five tracks the band cut at Sound Techniques in May 1971, just after Barrie Barlow joined. At this point, all traces of the early blues influence had disappeared, and Anderson's folky acoustic playing had become a driving force in the overall sound. The very pleasant "Life Is a Long Song" begins with a Scottish-style solo introduction by Anderson, who sings of bringing "good cheer" to one who is feeling down. Barre (on lead acoustic guitar) and Evans join in on the second verse, while Hammond's bass and Barlow's drums are kept buried in the mix (finally coming to the fore during the fourth time through, a flute solo). As bright as the song is, however, Anderson must ground his listener in reality, concluding, "But the tune ends too soon for us all." (In 1988, Barlow's busy drumming was brought up to a level with the other instruments for the song's inclusion on the *20 Years of Jethro Tull* box set.)

An "ode" to the band's hometown, "Up the 'Pool" is another highlight, featuring Anderson on acoustic guitar and violin backed with a potent pulse by Hammond and Barlow (on bass drum). Filled with detailed, descriptive imagery, the song, particularly the chorus, literally allows the listener to experience the Blackpool beach on a weekend day, when tourists from the south and midlands of England go "up the 'Pool from down the smoke below":

> There'll be buckets, spades and bingo, cockles, mussels, rainy days,
> seaweed and sand castles, icy waves.
> Deck chairs, rubber dinghies, old vests, braces dangling down,
> sun-tanned stranded starfish in a daze.

The full band kicks in on the choruses and then joins in on a gang vocal during a repeat of the first verse. Several familiar sites are mentioned: the Golden Mile, the Iron Tower (which tops a zoo and ballroom) and Edward Pier, amidst all the typical attractions intended to soak vacationers (casinos, amusements, fish and chip stands). Anderson ends the song after a final chorus, singing, "Oh, Blackpool. Oh, Blackpool," and adding a final acoustic riff and chord that add a distinct atmosphere of ambiguity, noting his love-hate relationship with the locale.

"Dr. Bogenbroom" is a prime example of the direction in which the

Tull sound was heading in 1971, opening with the ominous overtones of *Aqualung* material, yet remaining primarily acoustic, here blending Evans' harpsichord and Hammond's bass with Anderson's unmistakable guitar technique. As the musical atmosphere is created, the initial lyric, "Well, I've one foot in the graveyard and the other on the bus" suggests that the track could be part of a soundtrack for a twisted Charles Dickens film adaptation starring Christopher Lee in the title role. Featuring choruses driven by Anderson's acoustic rhythm guitar, the song also includes an electric solo by Barre during an instrumental section concluding with Evans' double-tracked piano and harpsichord. (While "Life Is a Long Song" anticipates the sound and content of 1977's *Songs from the Wood*, this track points the way to the next Tull record, *Thick as a Brick*.)

After three matchless folk-rock songs, the band shifts gears into jazz-rock fusion mode on the instrumental "For Later," introduced by Evans' Hammond organ. Recalling their early days, but with greater precision and finesse, they move the tune along at a nice clip, breaking briefly for some Barre wah-wahs, Bunker bongos and an Anderson flute "squeal" before kicking back into high flight. Though the cut includes some fine flute soloing, it is little more than album filler, the band jamming for a few minutes.

"Nursie," on the other hand, is another acoustic masterpiece, performed solo by Anderson on a single guitar, with his voice in top form. Having witnessed his father suffer through a serious illness, he wrote:

> Tip-toes in silence 'round my bed
> and quiets the raindrops overhead.
> With her everlasting smile
> she stills my fever for a while.
> Oh, nursie dear,
> I'm glad you're here
> to brush away my pain.

Living in the Past also allowed Anderson financially to pay tribute to his parents. Following excellent sales of the album, he purchased a new home for them, ending the estrangement that had lasted for several years.

Thick as a Brick

10 March 1972 (U.K.) / 10 May 1972 (U.S.)
Highest chart position: 5 (U.K.) / 1 (U.S.)
[Rating: 4.5]

Producer: Ian Anderson / Chrysalis CHR 1003
Written by Ian Anderson

Ian Anderson: vocals, flute, acoustic guitar, violin, saxophone, trumpet
Martin Barre: electric guitar, lute
John Evans: piano, Hammond organ, harpsichord
Jeffrey Hammond: bass guitar, vocals
Barrie Barlow: drums, percussion, tympani

Executive producer: Terry Ellis
Recorded in London, December 1971
Strings arranged and conducted by David Palmer
Cover concept by Roy Eldridge
Cover material written by Ian Anderson, Jeffrey Hammond and John Evans

Tracks: Thick as a Brick (A side)
           Thick as a Brick (B side)

Once again, Tull produced a new album in the weeks surrounding Christmas. For rehearsal purposes, they rented the Rolling Stones' basement studio in the East London district of Bermondsey, where Anderson hoped to try something completely different. Recalling the "nerve-wracking experience" of recording earlier projects, he now was pleased to have extra breathing room:

> The first album on which we were able to experiment a bit more was *Thick as a Brick*. We did about two or three weeks of arranging and rehearsing with the band, the recording of the backing tracks probably took two to three weeks, and I would imagine that additional overdubs and mixing took another two or three weeks. So we had a bit more time to explore things.[93]

Noting that others had viewed *Aqualung* as a concept album, Anderson thought the band should make such a work as a follow-up, although the lyrics did not begin as a grand theme:

> It wasn't a conception really, just the act of writing a song thinking about what might have been, what I began life as being, what kind of childhood images moved me—dealt with in a very oblique fashion, because I'm not setting out to create a threadbare tale of emotional woe or to even delineate emotional happenings. I'm just creating a background lyrical summation of a lot of things I feel about being a contemporary child in this age and the problems that one has—the problems of being precocious beyond one's age or having interests beyond one's age,

and to some extent being ruled in a kind of heavy-handed, unexplained fashion by ... father figures....[94]

Many years later, he added:

> The whole thing was really over the top. It wasn't done to make fun of our audience, it was done with a sense of fun that we wanted our audience to share with us. Lyrically it's okay, but it's supposed to be done by this young boy, this precocious kid. And the whole album cover and everything about it was all done to make it pretty obvious that it was a joke. But of course, some people still thought that there was a Gerald Bostock who really did write all this.... So it was done humorously, warmly, but it was meant to be a little bit of a satire about the whole idea of grand "rock band concept albums."[95]

Martin Barre later revealed some of the impetus behind the band's compositional approach:

> I like to think of myself as an open-minded musician, so I didn't mind if our music became more arranged and clever, like playing over bars of fifteen or playing in 11/8 or 7/4 time. Nobody gives a damn about such nonsense these days, but back then it was done all the time. And I think we really did it to show off and be clever, nothing more. Ian wrote the guitar riff to "Aqualung," because that's the whole song, but from *Thick as a Brick* onwards, we were all writing and arranging our own parts on the records. The way we wrote music was never conventional, either, so instead of me playing chords for a whole song, I would do riffs, melody lines and chords all in one song, apart from the solo. Over the years, we've always tried to be ourselves and not follow other bands.[96]

Thick as a Brick was rehearsed in sequence, day by day, as the band members developed the music. Barre described the process:

> [O]n a Friday we'd finish off with a sort of soft acoustic thing, and then Saturday morning Ian would turn up and say, "Right, we'll go into a guitar solo here, and a riff," or whatever, or "We'll change the key from E-flat to B-flat." And it was fun because you never really knew where things were gonna go. It was recorded that way as well—in sequence, on the same piece of tape.[97]

Barre also noted the inferiority of the rehearsal venue and dining accommodations:

> We went down to this disgusting, smelly, dark, dirty basement ... filthy, just a dreadful place, where we sort of shut ourselves away all day

learning music. So really, something good had to come out of it, because
it was just such a dreadful place.... My biggest memory of learning it
was going down to the café for lunch ... Rosie's Café ... it was down the
road in this place near Bermondsey. It was dreadful food: sort of pie,
chips, mushy peas, pie and custard served by this gross, huge woman who
had a mustache and a beard, and whose hygiene was definitely question-
able.... And it was always incredibly hot in there. Everybody smoked.
All the windows were steamed up. I can always picture being in that café
as part of the rehearsals....[98]

It was at this point in the evolution of the band that Barre necessarily had to develop the ability to play rhythm and lead guitar simultaneously. Glenn Cornick observed, "That's because of the way the band
is—because of his role in the band. He has to fit in between and around
things, between when Ian is playing guitar and what everybody else is
doing." [99]

The sections of music were recorded in a fairly spontaneous manner,
some captured on the first take. As well as his usual flute, Anderson overdubbed several additional instruments, including saxophone, trumpet and
violin, which he later described as emitting a "dreadful, squawking, awful
noise" while in his hands.[100]

Roy Eldridge recalled the idea behind the album's legendary cover,
which took longer to produce than the recording itself:

> I'd moved from music journalism at this time to accept the shilling
> offered by Chrysalis founders Terry Ellis and Chris Wright and act as a
> press officer for the growing roster of artists on the label. Due to my
> newspaper background, I was drafted in to coordinate the packaging of
> the next Tull album ... the design of which was based on an old fash-
> ioned local broadsheet newspaper.
>   This was a monumental package which demanded a phenomenal
> amount of Ian's, John's and Jeffrey's time. Their input and commitment
> were vital, as everything had to be written, down to the small ads, all of
> which had a relevance to Ian's concept for the album. The "St. Cleve
> Chronicle" was released in February '72, having demanded 24-hour days
> from everyone concerned.[101]

Craig Thomas argued that *Brick* is not really a cohesive concept album
(a work whose musical and lyrical content consistently focuses on a central theme), but a 45-minute "song suite" that extends the eclectic exper-
iments the band had performed on *Benefit* and at the Carnegie Hall
concert:

This further widening of musical horizons, and the extended length of songs, can be found on ... *Living in the Past*, where in "By Kind Permission Of" and "Dharma for One" we find Beethoven, jazz, Gershwin, Debussy and the blues, among other elements, mostly appropriated by piano, organ and flute.[102]

The Sides of *Thick as a Brick*

Thick as a Brick truly is a musical smorgasbord comprising elements from the medieval, classical, folk, jazz, theatrical and rock 'n' roll genres. A more intense and expanded work springing from the style developed on *Living in the Past*'s folk-rock songs, it is highly structured in classical fashion, but also features each band member's musical contributions and improvisational soloing at various times. Although eschewing the heavy rock style of *Aqualung*, it actually includes far more startling tempo and dynamic changes, particularly when Anderson's bucolic acoustic guitar passages, combined with lilting melodies, are offset by the entire band bursting in at very fast tempi. Rather than deriving its strength from the heavy power chords of Barre, as on *Benefit* and *Aqualung*, here the band operates more as an ensemble unit, featuring Barre's inventive riffs, solos and "orchestral" double-tracking, and Evans' heady Hammond work.

The "message" of *Thick as a Brick* is delivered by Anderson in the first four lines of the song. Opening with "Really don't mind if you sit this one out. My word's but a whisper, your deafness a shout," the narrator indicates that he has reached a point where attempts to educate the closedminded are futile. "I may make you feel, but I can't make you think" then reinforces the first two lines and can be read in at least two different ways: that such statements can arouse emotions but not reasoning; and that music also can have this effect. This quatrain then concludes with the harsher and (for 1972) quasi-pornographic "Your sperm's in the gutter. Your love's in the sink." Incorporating a slang term popular in northern England during his youth, Anderson follows with "So you ride yourselves over the fields, and you make all your animal deals, and your wise men don't know how it feels to be *thick as a brick*." This introduction, with the soft, lilting music offset by the cold lyrics, immediately establishes a dramatic counterpoint represented in a number of ways during the 45-minute piece.

The initial "movement" shifts between the acoustic guitar and the driving ensemble work, highlighted by a furious solo from Barre, before culminating with a thunderous minor chord reminiscent of Beethoven. Truly startling, this musical transition perfectly reinforces the previous description of the narrator's loss of individual identity:

> And the love that I feel is so far away:
> I'm a bad dream that I just had today
> and you shake your head and say it's a shame.

A second movement now begins, with Anderson combining another folk melody with the memorable tale of "the Poet and the Painter," one of the album's finest passages. Anderson, Barre and Barlow all are featured in solo spots, with Evans and Hammond collaborating impressively. The first verse of this section is an Anderson masterwork:

> The Poet and the Painter casting shadows on the water
> as the sun plays on the infantry returning from the sea.
> The doer and the thinker: no allowance for the other
> as the failing light illuminates the mercenary's creed.
> The home fire burning: the kettle almost boiling
> but the master of the house is far away.
> The horses stamping, their warm breath clouding
> in the sharp and frosty morning of the day.
> And the poet lifts his pen while the soldier sheaths his sword.
> And the youngest of the family is moving with authority.
> Building castles by the sea, he dares the tardy tide to wash them all aside.

Not only are these lines a clever metaphor for a young man's attempt to challenge the status quo, but the sheer imagery they create is unforgettable. Like "Wond'ring Again" on *Living in the Past*, this verse is reminiscent of the vivid and socially perceptive poetry of Robert Louis Stevenson.

The third movement opens with Evans' most famous, eccentric organ riff and a woozy violin part by Anderson. Split by a quasi-classical instrumental passage, two verses describing the inevitable "selling out" of the individual to society's institutions are backgrounded by this uncomfortable atmosphere, a blend of musical styles best described as medieval jazz-rock fusion.

Part one (side A of the original LP) ends with a fourth movement combining Evans' organ riff with flamenco flourishes from Anderson's guitar, Barlow on glockenspiel and an anthem-like, Renaissance-style brass arrangement. Some studio-generated "wind" accompanies a plodding *sturm-und-drang* dirge as the music fades out.

Part two opens with the dirge-like march, which is suddenly overtaken by a hellishly driving reprise of an instrumental passage heard early in part one. Barlow takes an extended solo break, including some 1970s bombast on tympani, before the entire band, led by Evans, savagely erupts.

A cacophonous intermezzo, blending several disjointed musical passages with a bizarre narration by Jeffrey Hammond (the band's old school-mate, Hipgrave, is mentioned), and a brief return to part one's opening verse are followed by the album's second acoustic masterpiece. "Sacred"–style chanting leads to a beautiful melody and impressive chord changes given additional emphasis by Evans on harpsichord. Again, Anderson's lyrics, suggesting that the "thinking man" has become, not a new hope, but only a different representative of the same old establishment, are exceptional:

> The poet and the wise man stand behind the gun,
> and signal for the crack of dawn.
> Light the sun. Light the sun.
> Do you believe in the day?
> Do you? Believe in the day!
> The Dawn Creation of the Kings has begun.
> Soft Venus (lonely maiden) brings the ageless one.
> Do you believe in the day?
> The fading hero has returned to the night
> and fully pregnant with the day,
> wise men endorse the poet's sight.
> Do you believe in the day?
> Do you? Believe in the day!

(Here the imagery and florid language suggest the poetry, not of Stevenson, but of Edgar Allan Poe.) From this point until the finale, the various elements of medieval music, jazz and rock are enveloped in an overwhelmingly English classical influence suggesting Barre's interest in the work of Edward Elgar. His anthem-like lead guitar parts provide a pleasurable musical counter to Anderson's relentless tale of history inevitably repeating itself: humankind's inability to overcome the dogmatic thinking that continually leads to disaster. The piece ends as it begins, reassuring its listeners that they forever will be trapped in society's vicious circle:

> So you ride yourselves over the fields
> and you make all your animal deals
> and your wise men don't know how it feels
> to be thick as a brick.

Rolling Stone's Ben Gurson again found much to praise about the band's musical adventurousness, this time giving Anderson more credit for creating such a grand project:

Besides lyricist and impersonator, Anderson is also composer, arranger,
singer, flutist, acoustic guitarist, violinist, saxophonist, trumpeter, satirist
and overall conceptualizer. His adeptness at most of these functions, in
particular, his ability to balance and fuse them, has created one of rock's
most sophisticated and ground-breaking products.[103]

Gurson's perceptive comments about the innovative musical aspects
of the album yield perhaps the best review Tull ever received:

What marks this album as a significant departure from other Jethro Tull
work, and rock in general, is the organization of all its music into one
continuous track. Albums like *Sgt. Pepper* or *Tommy* were complete enti-
ties in themselves, but still chose to use songs as their basic components.
While sections of *Thick as a Brick* are melodically distinct, they all inher-
ently relate to each other.... The lyrics, clever and dense as they are, are
chiefly valuable as a premise for the music.
    Since *Stand Up*, Jethro Tull's music has always had a chamber music
feel to it; here, the structure, too, of classical music is more closely followed.... The playing, not surprisingly, is tight as a drum. ...Whether or
not *Thick as a Brick* is an isolated experiment, it is nice to know that
someone in rock has ambitions beyond the four or five minute conven-
tional track, and has the intelligence to carry out his intentions, in all
their intricacy, with considerable grace.[104]

The *Thick as a Brick* Tour

The completion of the *Brick* recording was followed by a January–
March 1972 tour of Europe, including a series of dates in Scandinavia and
the U.K., before another grueling, three-month tour of North America
was undertaken. According to Anderson, the tour took place at a time
when theatricality became an element in live rock 'n' roll performances:

Perhaps it was at that point—the beginning of people getting away
from going on stage and playing an hour of music in jeans and T-shirts,
which tended to have been the way things were. Suddenly there was
something that was a little more theatrical and organized. By the standards of a U2 concert or a Michael Jackson concert or a Madonna concert, it would be incredibly tame theatrically. But, by the standards of
back then, it must have been quite an unusual thing. Quite a lot of effort
would appear to have gone into it, and a lot of detail would have com-
municated itself to the audience if they were in the right mood.... It was
the beginning of Monty Python's success in the U.S.A., for example. The

Americans were just beginning to cotton onto the surreal and absurd and quite often challenging humor ... and were very open to these sort of new ideas. Alice Cooper at the time was ... chopping his head off in a guillotine on stage every night, whereas ... my approach was a little more gentle, with rather elegant tights and a natty codpiece.[105]

But as Tull's music increasingly became less dependent on heavy riffs, more complex and much quieter in its inclusion of folk, jazz and classical elements, Anderson began to experience a great deal of frustration when playing live:

The difficulty ... was trying to play the acoustic music we didn't have to play when we were doing the heavy rock music of the *Aqualung* album. The audience was just about able to cope with the acoustic section in "Aqualung," or in "Wind Up" or "My God," knowing that they were going to get the big rock 'n' roll riff any minute. With *Thick as a Brick* suddenly there was a lot more music that was really stretched out. The audiences, particularly in America, were not sympathetic to the concert atmosphere that it was necessary to maintain: that they had to be quiet in the quiet places, and could react and jump up and down in the loud bits.[106]

Barre admitted:

We were petrified by the thought of playing it live. The first time we played the whole thing live was a terrifying experience; there is so much to remember, so many odd time signatures, 7/4s and 6/8s ... it was all done on adrenaline. It's amazing what fear can do![107]

Anderson added:

[The tour] began with ... a pretty disastrous concert.... It was a nightmare ... we sort of just about managed to scrape through it, and it was a very nerve-wracking moment, because then we were going on to a major tour.... It was a pretty scary opening night.[108]

Among the acts opening for Tull were Captain Beefhart and His Magic Band, Gentle Giant, Glenn Cornick's Wild Turkey, and the Eagles, another folk-rock oriented group soon to establish great success. Following the Eagles' set, the road crew, in the guise of foreign spies, crept onto the stage to remove their gear and set up the Tull show. After 30 minutes, more "spies" appeared, one of them removing his hat to release an enormous mane of hair. A spotlight proved that he was, of course, Ian

Anderson. To give themselves a break between the two lengthy *Brick* "sides," the band incorporated an interval of comedy skits based on articles in the album's newspaper. Concluding the nearly 90-minute set, Anderson wryly announced, "And now for our second number...."

On May 1 in New Orleans, Anderson wrote a piece that paired the band members with a 50-piece orchestra. (Though the work was recorded, it has not been released.) Longtime Tull fan Mark Louis attended the June 18 concert at the Memorial Auditorium in Dallas:

> It was one of the best shows I have ever witnessed. And, I do mean show because it contained great entertainment, fine music, peculiar British wit, and the band made the audience feel part of the party.[109]

In mid–July, Tull played concerts in New Zealand, Australia and Japan, the first time they traveled to the Orient. Following a three-month hiatus, they once again set out for the U.S., for six weeks of gigs ending at Madison Square Garden on November 13.

The Tull lineup of 1971–1975, enjoying a bit of 18th-century roguishness: John Evans, Barrie Barlow, Martin Barre, Jeffrey Hammond and Ian Anderson. (Photograph courtesy of Ian Anderson.)

A Passion Play

6 July 1973 (U.K.) / 23 July 1973 (U.S.)
Highest chart position: 13 (U.K.) / 1 (U.S.)
[Rating: 3.5]
Producer: Ian Anderson / Chrysalis 1040
Written by Ian Anderson (except "The Story of the Hare Who Lost
His Spectacles," by Jeffrey Hammond, John Evans and Ian Anderson)

Ian Anderson: vocals, flute, acoustic guitar, soprano and sopranino saxophones
Martin Barre: electric guitar
Jeffrey Hammond: bass guitar, vocals
John Evans: piano, Hammond organ, synthesizers, speech
Barrie Barlow: drums, tympani, glockenspiel, marimba

Recorded at Morgan Studios, London, March 1973
Orchestra arranged and conducted by David Palmer
Program design by Jennifer Ann and Geoffrey Dowlatshahi
Photographs by Brian Ward

Tracks: A Passion Play [including "The Story of the Hare Who Lost His
Spectacles"] (side A)
A Passion Play [including "The Story of the Hare Who Lost His
Spectacles"] (side B)

Sections titled for the 24-karat gold CD release, 17 March 1998
(Mobile Fidelity Sound Lab UDCD 720):
Lifebeats
Prelude
The Silver Cord
Re-Assuring Tune
Memory Bank
Best Friends
Critique Oblique
Forest Dance #1
The Story of the Hare Who Lost His Spectacles
Forest Dance #2
The Foot of Our Stairs
Overseer Overture
Flight from Lucifer
10:08 from Paddington
Magus Perde
Epilogue

The enormous commercial success of *Thick as a Brick* induced Anderson to write a serious concept album as a follow-up:

> I guess we all collectively fell into a trap of thinking, "Oh, shit, maybe we should do this kind of thing again and instead of being silly about it, maybe we should take it seriously." And I think that was a problem with *Passion Play* for me personally…. It didn't have the humor or the warmth that *Thick as a Brick* did.[110]

The project began while Anderson was holed up in a small apartment in Switzerland, where he had exiled himself to escape an 83 percent British income tax, writing bits of music on his Martin acoustic guitar. After Christmas, he was joined for rehearsals by the rest of the band in a stark building just outside Montreux, which they eventually abandoned for the Chateau d'Herouville near Paris to record the *Brick* "sequel." The chateau studio, which Anderson described as "rotten" and having "awful food" (Barre claimed the cook served baked sparrows), previously had provided a similar haven for Cat Stevens and Elton John. Having applied for citizenship in Switzerland (where the tax was only 20 percent), they remained at Herouville (which Anderson later would dub the "Chateau D'Isaster") for several weeks, recording an entire album's worth of material that eventually was abandoned. Anderson explained:

> [F]or those with families or even girl friends, it was proving to be a very difficult time emotionally, and it was really taking its toll on the band as a playing ensemble, but as individuals more pertinently … at least two guys in the band said, "Look, sorry, but we can't do this. We have to go. We must leave. We don't want to break up the group but we just can't remain away from our homes, the places we were brought up. The money isn't important. We just have to go home." And so it was a question of either we all went back or the band would have literally broken in half at that time. So I threw in the towel with the "go homes" and everybody agreed that's what we should do. And that all took place within twenty-four hours after getting a phone call to say that our papers had come through to become residents of Switzerland … and we had worked for a year to get those residency papers.[111]

Jeffrey Hammond remembered:

> What … I remember liking is … that when we were recording at the Chateau studios we had a lot of free time when the equipment was set up, and we could go and mess about and do stupid things, which I think can be quite a rewarding thing to do, although maybe from Ian's

point of view that wasn't the case. It was the kind of thing that really excited me, and it probably wasn't good for Jethro Tull, it was getting away from what the group is, and from what Ian wanted to do. And generally Ian does what he wants to do, which is fair enough because he is in charge of the whole show.[112]

During the 17 days that remained before they began the next tour, Anderson wrote new material and *A Passion Play* was recorded. Of the released version, Hammond said:

> *Thick as a Brick* had been quite a departure from what had gone before, and it is always difficult to follow something like that. I know a lot of people thought what came after that, namely *A Passion Play*, struggled to keep up with it. I did not see that myself, but I think maybe things did get out of line where I felt one had to do more and more of it, and it became almost manic in a way…. I probably wasn't a very good influence after that, in the sense that perhaps those kind of things got too important in relation to the music. Eventually of course they dropped away quite naturally, but it did take time.[113]

Hammond also made a salient point about the nature of concept albums and Tull's relationship with the genre:

> I know there were at that time a lot of so-called "concept albums," but I think in many cases people did them purely for the sake of doing them, but I think in the case of both those Jethro Tull albums there was nothing of that idiom about them at all, but rather it was the kind of music that the group, really as a group rather than just Ian taking too firm a hand, produced quite genuinely and naturally. I don't mean to say that each member wrote some of the music, but the band as a whole developed the music in a genuine sense of togetherness which wasn't always evident at other times….[114]

As a follow-up to the *Thick as a Brick* newspaper, Anderson designed a bogus play program picturing the band members in featured roles. Naming himself "Mark Ridley," he noted that the actor's West End debut was "as 'Elvoe' in Ron Read's social critique *The Demo*."

Having been Tull-friendly since the release of *Stand Up*, *Rolling Stone* now could not endorse their extravagant extra-rock pretensions. In his August 30, 1973, review, Stephen Holden identified "*A Passion Play* [as] the artiest artifact yet to issue from the maddeningly eccentric mind of Ian Anderson … a pop potpourri of *Paradise Lost* and *Winnie the Pooh*, among many other literary resources, not to mention a vast array of musical ideas derivative of influences as far-flung as Purcell, flamenco and modern jazz."[115] Then he dissected its jumbled content:

> Viewed as a recorded oratorio, or as a prolonged "single," or as any in-between hybrid, *A Passion Play* strangles under the tonnage of its preten-sions—a jumble of anarchic, childishly precocious gestures that are intellectually and emotionally faithless to any idea other than their own esoteric non-logic.... The scenario roughly parallels the Passion of Christ.... Ronnie Pilgrim, a supercilious atheist, describes his own funeral, then goes through purgatory, part of which is a movie rerun of his life ... a descent into hell ... followed by a resurrection into the drawing room of a Magus Perde. I leave it for the devout Tull freak to argue the details.... In tone, it is the ultimate exaggeration of self-indul-gent English whimsy, an intellectual tease inflated with portent but devoid of wonder....[116]

Holden did echo his *Rolling Stone* predecessor Ben Gurson in praising the musical aspect of the album, though he also believed the performance was not enough to prevent the work from collapsing under its own weight:

> The Jethro Tull band ... is truly virtuosic in the manner of a polished chamber ensemble. The high points are those interludes that feature Anderson's extraordinary flute playing, some of it seemingly multi-tracked. Two short pastoral sections that precede and follow the abom-inable "pooh perplex" ["The Story of the Hare Who Lost His Spectacles"] are especially lovely. The overall impact of this music, how-ever, is very slight. Not a single leitmotif sticks in the mind.... Finally, one leaves *A Passion Play* with the feeling of having been subjected to 45 minutes of vapid twittering and futzing about, all play and no pas-sion....[117]

The Sides of *A Passion Play*

Those who dislike *A Passion Play* find "The Story of the Hare" the most obnoxious creation in the entire Tull canon. And the fact that this short tale was split over the original album's two sides made its inclusion even more unwelcome. Even the most diehard Tull fans have been driven to distraction by it. Here cowriter and narrator Jeffrey Hammond's self-confessed "bad influence" can be heard (and seen, in the film that was shown on the tour and subsequently made available on the *25 Years of Jethro Tull* video in 1993).

The album opens with an electronic approximation of wind, harking back to *Thick as a Brick* before the band introduces a driving classical-style passage that ends as a door slams. In fine voice, a pseudo-operatic Anderson enters singing some of his most beautiful melodies as the listener learns that the dead narrator is speaking from beyond the grave. Following a key change, the music alternates between full-ensemble instrumentals and verses featuring Anderson's voice and Evans' masterful piano. Barre also adds a pleasing element with very tasteful electric guitar work.

The structure of the album is far more classical than that of *Thick as a Brick*, which primarily blends folk-rock and jazz. Nearly 12 minutes into the piece, Anderson's flute finally rises to the fore and the classic Tull sound emerges as the band is driven by Barre's trademark string scraping during a reworking of a section from the Chateau d'Herouville sessions (later titled "Critique Oblique"). Anderson's eccentric humor reaches its apex at this point, shortly before the absurd Monty Python–meets–Lewis Carroll "Hare" tale begins. (A bit of Gershwin-style piano from Evans almost rescues it at one point.)

Early in part two (side B of the original LP), after the hare finally takes his leave, Hammond's pulsing bass and Anderson and Barre's lovely Spanish guitars take the *Play* into a much more pleasing direction. An impressive acoustic verse followed by an extended instrumental section (highlighting Evans on the newly fashionable synthesizer) then lapses into a musically absurd percussion passage. A reference to the "maypole and dance" foreshadows a Scottish-sounding march section and a lovely, bucolic acoustic guitar section during which the listener is nearly lulled off before Barre literally explodes with a startling electric chord progression (an effect recalling a similar change in dynamics in Tchaikovsky's Sixth Symphony, the "Pathétique").

The final portion of *Play* is the best overall, similar to *Thick as a Brick* and not nearly as disjointed and bizarre as earlier sections. This more accessible material rocks along steadily until Anderson's saxophone makes another appearance. A reprise of the "Fulham Road" lyric that opens the album then leads to a climactic gasp of Evans' keyboards and a meandering finale as the piece fades out.

While some Tull fans revere *A Passion Play* as the band's best work, others consider it a flawed album. Listening to it back-to-back with *Thick as a Brick* provides evidence for the latter opinion. While the earlier album was innovative and musically and lyrically satisfying, *Play* became an effort both to recreate the success of *Brick* and to fashion an even more unusual work. Though some fans, like W. S. Gumby, have stated that "the story ... ties things together,"[118] the content is a maddening jumble of references gleaned from the Bible and classical literature, including Dante's

Inferno. (The title itself, of course, refers to the popular German passion plays depicting the life and crucifixion of Jesus Christ. J. S. Bach's *St. John Passion* and *St. Matthew Passion* are two famous musical examples, consisting of recitatives, arias and polyphonic choir compositions.) Portions of the album are quite breathtaking, but as a whole it suffers from an overwrought theatricality.

The *Passion Play* Tour

The *Passion Play* tour, the first half of which was a performance of the entire album, began before it was released. Opening at Frankfurt's Festhalle on February 2, 1973, the band played a series of shows in Germany, Switzerland, Sweden and Austria before embarking on another mammoth North American tour spanning nine months. Only two English dates, at London's Wembley Stadium on June 22 and 23, were worked into the schedule.

Many critics savaged the band, prompting Terry Ellis to make a comment that they would cease playing live. On Saturday, September 29, at the Boston Tea Gardens, they closed the tour, and 10 months would pass before an audience saw them again. Jeffrey Hammond recalled:

> That was the most catastrophic thing [Ellis] could say, and I just did not understand it. It was completely beyond me ... there was no truth in the "Tull Quit" story, and for whatever reason it was put out, it certainly backfired and did the group no good at all. I remember people [in the band] being furious about it.[119]

Many Tull fans loved the *Passion Play* concerts, which were among the most elaborate ever staged by a rock band. Seeing "The Hare," as well as the legendarily bashful Martin Barre, who considered the material a tremendous challenge to play live, cavorting about with Jeffrey Hammond, was unforgettable. Anderson explained:

> I think it was difficult actually, not because it was so difficult to play. It was just difficult to remember it all because you didn't have any let-up. It was just so intense and you really had to at all times have your wits about you just knowing what was coming next.... It's the mental side of it ... the actual feat of memory just to recall thousands of notes in the right order. And all of this done without the aid of music manuscript or too much in the way of any kind of prompts. You've got to know it.[120]

Mark Louis, who attended the July 16 show at the Tarrant County Convention Center in Fort Worth, Texas, recalled:

This concert had a distinctively updated sound, with splashes of synthesizer added to the mix. It also used early multimedia technology to great effect.... In my opinion, *A Passion Play*, both the album and tour, were not nearly as satisfying, artistically or musically, as *Thick as a Brick*. Nevertheless, it was good entertainment which far exceeded most of the 1973 rock or pop music and was unmatched by other groups who attempted these monster epics.[121]

War Child

26 October 1974 (U.K.) / 14 October 1974 (U.S.)
Highest chart position: 14 (U.K.) / 2 (U.S.)
[Rating: 4]
Producer: Ian Anderson / Chrysalis 1067
All songs written by Ian Anderson

Ian Anderson: vocals, flute, acoustic guitar, alto, soprano and sopranino saxophones
Martin Barre: electric and Spanish guitars
Jeffrey Hammond: bass guitar and string bass
John Evans: piano, Hammond organ, synthesizers and piano accordion
Barrie Barlow: drums, glockenspiel, marimba and percussion

Recorded at Morgan Studios, London, spring 1974 (except "Skating Away" and "Only Solitaire," originally recorded at the Chateau d'Herouville, Switzerland, summer 1972)
Recording engineer: Robin Black
Strings arranged and conducted by David Palmer
Philamusica of London led by Patrick Halling
Executive producer: Terry Ellis

Tracks: War Child
Queen and Country
Ladies
Back-Door Angels
Sea Lion
Skating Away (on the Thin Ice of the New Day)
Bungle in the Jungle
Only Solitaire
The Third Hoorah
Two Fingers

After the backlash against *A Passion Play*, Anderson held a press conference at Montreux, during which he chided critics who had not spent enough time listening to the album—publicity that could not have done the band much good. Moving on to another unusual and ambitious project, he focused on producing *War Child*, the title of which was inspired by a Roy Harper song, as a film with an accompanying orchestral soundtrack. David Palmer, who had contributed to all the previous Tull albums, now was enlisted as Anderson's collaborator. Palmer later recalled:

> We recorded a lot of music. Martin Barre wrote a little acoustic guitar piece, which we developed into something much larger. There was one particular piece that Ian wrote, called "Waltz of the Angels," I think, that was really very good. He played it on the guitar, and it was almost like Benjamin Britten or Tchaikovsky. It was a very, very good piece of music. We had a tape of that but sent the only copy to London Weekend Television because they wanted some music for a series they were planning.[122]

Anderson and Palmer met with Sir Frederick Ashton, who liked the music and agreed to create the choreography, and Monty Python's John Cleese, who was hired as "humor adviser." However, after Bryan Forbes signed on as director, and typical film financing problems reared their heads (the money men feared the uncommercial nature of a plot focused on the "afterlife" of a young girl killed in an accident), the project became so delayed that Anderson could not allow the band to suffer an extended hiatus. Very disappointed, he then adapted the concept to the separate song format, still titling the album *War Child*:

> I enjoyed playing fairly simple, shortish pieces of music—a sort of renewing thing, another cycle. It was an enjoyable album to make, a very easy album to make. It had a good vibe to it.... For us, it was absolutely the right thing to do at the time, because that was the mood.[123]

While developing *War Child*, Anderson also accepted his first production project outside Jethro Tull, that of guiding the expanded Steeleye Span in the recording of their *Now We Are Six* album. Energized by the drumming of new member Nigel Pegrum, Maddy Prior and company served up a selection of excellent British folk-rock, including "Thomas the Rhymer," a song that tells the tale of the legendary Scots poet-seer. (Exceptions are two bizarre novelty tracks on which David Bowie played saxophone.) Anderson also mixed the album, which hit number 13 in the English charts shortly after its March 1974 release. Span, named after a character in a medieval play, had opened for Tull and would have a marked effect on Anderson's future songwriting.

The Tracks of *War Child*

Most of the material for *War Child*, which follows *A Passion Play* in dealing with issues of life and death and moral relativity, was written during the second half of the elaborate *Passion* tour. In general, it carries on the indictment of hypocritical society explored on the three previous albums. The title track, which opens the album, introduces the motif of chaos that permeates all the songs, whose narrative (and sometimes musical) confusion encompasses themes of behavioral ambiguity, interpersonal argumentation and out-and-out war. An air raid siren fades in while a complacent couple sits at breakfast, the man declining "another cup of tea" because he'll "be late for the office." As Anderson's *Passion Play* alto sax reemerges, the maintenance of the modern capitalist status quo takes precedence even over an impending (presumably nuclear) enemy attack.

The second song, "Queen and Country," is a hard-hitting condemnation of British imperialism mixing driving hard rock with a Russian ethnic component, as John Evans' accordion and David Palmer's strings accompany Anderson's portrait of Royal Navy seamen who sail away to exploit foreign cultures for the benefit of nobility back home:

> They build schools and they build factories
> with the spoils of battles won
> And we remain their pretty sailor boys
> Hold our heads up to the gun.

Anderson's references to sailors plundering "gold and ivory, rings of diamonds, strings of pearls" harks back to Queen Elizabeth I's employment of both Royal Navy officers and privateers (the "Sea Hawks") to raid the ships and bases of the powerful Spanish Armada, but the Russian element and the focus on more modern "schools" and "factories" suggests that little has changed since the Elizabethan era. (Some historians have argued that civilization has yet to emerge from the Dark Ages, a subject Anderson addresses on a later album, *Stormwatch*.) And as Tull fan Jeroen Louis has suggested,

> There seems to be a little parallel between these sailors and a band on
> the road. "It's been this way for five long years, since we signed our souls
> away." When Ian wrote this song Jethro Tull had been touring for about

five years. "Schools and factories" were being built with their tax money, while the band were abroad for Queen and country. As many other fellow rock stars they were advised to live in exile and settle on the continent to avoid the British taxman. Eventually they missed their Mum's jam sarnies so dearly that they ran back to Mother England, even if it meant they had to break off their recordings in the "Chateau D'Isaster." This took place shortly before the *War Child* project, so I thought there might be a little link here.[124]

"Ladies" portrays the females who honor the "solitary soldiers" who uphold the Empire. A classic Anderson bucolic introduction combining acoustic guitars and flute eventually metamorphoses into a somewhat cacophonous clash of electric guitar and alto sax, the latter squawking into Robert Burns' "Auld Lang Syne," Anderson's only musical reference to Scotland's bard. (There are two lyrical borrowings from Burns: previously on *Aqualung*, and later on *Heavy Horses*.)

A folk-blues number that explodes into an extended Barre solo section, "Back-Door Angels" is another of Anderson's statements about dogmatic thought. Like *Aqualung*'s second half, *War Child*'s remaining songs criticize closed-mindedness in general and religious parochialism in particular:

> Why do the faithful have such a will to believe in something?
> And call it the name they choose, having chosen nothing.

For a brief few bars, the song regresses to the synth-heavy sound of *A Passion Play* but soon breaks free into Barre's furious soloing, which is highlighted by expertly executed pregnant pauses, the entire band thundering back in perfect unison after each break.

Opening with a driving, Beethoven-like classical interval, "Sea Lion" is a favorite of Tull fans. Anderson described his inspiration for the song:

> "Sea Lion" is slightly ecological in content, probably influenced through being brought up in ... Blackpool, where the sea was dirty gray, largely because of the dumping of all the town's sewage a very short distance off the shore. As an adolescent, a teenager, I used to go there when there was a big storm and the waves and great clouds of spray came crashing. We used to dodge the waves coming over the promenade there. Little did we know then that what we were dodging was every kind of variation of *E. coli* bacteria known to man....[125]

In a broader sense, the song uses the tale of the circus Sea Lion as a metaphor for the uncertainty, chaos and often utter helplessness of humanity and the repression the individual encounters at the hands of the establishment. The bridge, featuring a march tempo and Scottish-tinged melodies that anticipate "The Third Hoorah," returns to the original verse structure, during which "this Passion Play" is mentioned, the first of *War Child*'s two references to the earlier album.

One of Anderson's all-time eclectic masterpieces, "Skating Away (on the Thin Ice of the New Day)" is a truly diverse amalgam of English, Russian and Indian musical components. The first verse—

> Meanwhile back in the year One, when you belonged to no-one
> You didn't stand a chance son, if your pants were undone
> 'cause you were bred for humanity and sold to society
> One day you'll wake up in the present day
> A million generations removed from expectations
> of being who you really want to be

—leads to the chorus—

> Skating away
> Skating away
> Skating away on the thin ice of the new day—

as Barre's sitar-like acoustic guitar riff and Barlow's tabla-style percussion accompany these lines embodying the struggle for freedom from repression. The following verse also refers to the previous album:

> And as you cross the wilderness, spinning in your emptiness
> you feel you have to pray
> Looking for a sign that the Universal Mind
> has written you into the Passion Play.

This content is not surprising, however, since the song was recorded during the Chateau d'Herouville sessions, and was re-mixed and overdubbed for *War Child*.

The next track, "Bungle in the Jungle," an atypically commercial track that became an FM-radio staple for many years, also rips into the notion of an almighty higher power who lords it over his subjects. Here human existence is metaphorically described as an endless greedy game played by members of the animal kingdom for the amusement of their creator:

> The rivers are full of crocodile nasties
> and He who made kittens put snakes in the grass

He's a lover of life, but a player of pawns
Yes, the King on his sunset lies waiting for dawn
to light up his jungle as play is resumed
The monkeys seem willing to strike up the tune.

Of the subject matter in "Bungle in the Jungle," Anderson commented:

> We're all animals, competing-aggressive, out to win at the expense
> of others. And we have our codes, our rules and laws that we've invented
> which are convenient within the context that we operate. At this point in
> history the rules are one way. They change throughout the ages. But if
> aggression and competition is what everybody wants to do then I'll go
> along with it.[126]

"Only Solitaire" (another track recorded at d'Herouville) is an Anderson solo acoustic attack on critics who had lambasted him in the past. First brashly spinning mesmerizing "quotes" from his detractors, he then, with priceless wit, turns to answer them:

> And every night his act's the same
> And so it must be a game of chess he's playing
> "But you're wrong, Steve. You see, it's only solitaire."

Anderson had planned to integrate the Highland bagpipes somewhere on the album and, after hearing a young piper playing outside a London department store near the Chrysalis office, hired him and two others to lend a martial Scottish sound to "The Third Hoorah," the first of his songs to outwardly reflect the musical heritage of his homeland. Two years later, he attempted to explain the appeal of the pipes and his tendency to blend traditional elements into his own compositions:

> It's more than a liking for the instrument. It's a response to the
> music—that droning quality—Celtic music. It's something special. One
> can't really pin down what. It has to be some kind of a folk memory.[127]

Reprising the lyrics of the opening track, the narrator again encourages the "War Child" to "dance the days and nights away," here emphasizing the inevitability of a person morally "selling out" in order to survive in modern society. Having played like an entire orchestral percussion section during his years with Tull, Barrie Barlow, who adds some remarkable snare work to Barre's brilliant, Celtic-tinged electric guitar, revealed the rationale behind his approach, which he later viewed as rhythmically excessive:

When we did *War Child* there were massive spaces in the backing track, and I'm thinking, "What is happening here? Better fill this bit, it's boring"... But then we hear it, and there's vocals on it and all manner of things and I would never have played those things had I known. And it is hard to work like that, without the whole song in mind.[128]

Originally recorded as "Lick Your Fingers Clean" during the *Aqualung* sessions in 1970, "Two Fingers" addresses the events of Judgment Day. Perhaps the initial verse, written at the same time as "My God" and "Hymn 43," is the most utterly cynical thing Anderson ever penned, a pessimistic view of society's past and future:

I'll see you at the Weighing-In
When your life's sum-total's made
And you set your wealth in goodly deeds
Against the sins you've laid
And you place your final burden
On your hard-pressed next of kin
Send the chamber-pot back down the line
To be filled-up again.

Here flamenco-style acoustic guitar and tambourine are joined by Barre's power chords and Anderson's grating soprano saxophone that blends well with the rudeness of the electric guitar. When Anderson sings, "You really should make a deal...." his phrasing and inflections are reminiscent of the stinging sneer of Roger Daltrey when performing the lyrics of Pete Townshend.

On the album cover, Anderson unveiled his infamous Elizabethan minstrel's costume, complete with knee boots and silver codpiece. Increasingly criticized for this "outlandish" look, he included it as a visual extension of the English elements in the band's music. Drawing on the work of folklorist A. L. Lloyd, Judson Caswell wrote:

The figure of the minstrel as he is commonly shown is misleading. The languid lute-player in ... *Swan Lake* ... was not the representative of his craft in the fourteenth century; rather we should think of the sly jester of, say, Shakespeare plays, sardonic, irreverent, plebeian-oriented, outrageously subversive.[129]

Caswell pointed out that Anderson's stage costume also reinforced the lyrical content of songs on *War Child* (as well as future Tull projects), an attitude fostered by the press reaction to *A Passion Play*:

The lyrics on this album not only present the oblique cultural criticisms of the laughing jester, but there also is the first evidence of [his] bemoaning of the lack of a sense of history and place in the modern world.... First off, in the song "Back-Door Angels" he offers the proposition, "Think I'll sit down and invent some fool—some grand court jester." This is the first verbalization of that particular image, though that has been the approximate content of his stage performance all along. He describes his persona through the eyes of a rock critic in the song "Only Solitaire." This song not only clearly defines him in court jester terms, it also serves to show his sense of isolation from the rock music world, particularly when he poses the question, of himself, "Well, who the hell can he be when he's never had V.D., and he doesn't even sit on toilet seats?" These are his perceptions of the prerequisites for belonging to a rock culture, and hence he is not interested in being a part.[130]

Upon the release of *War Child*, journalist Steve Gaines called Anderson a "brilliant, sensitive and confusing artist ... the best avant-gardist in the music business."[131]

The *War Child* Tour

Ending their "retirement" on July 25, 1974, Tull toured Australia, New Zealand, Japan, mainland Europe and Britain, with two U.S. dates at Detroit's Cobo Hall thrown in for good measure, finishing in Copenhagen on Thursday, December 5. Jeffrey Hammond also unleashed his most memorable attire, the black-and-white striped "zebra suit" accompanied by similarly decorated gear: hat band, bass guitar and stand-up double bass. Hammond remembered his experiences with the female orchestral musicians who played on the album and tour:

I particularly liked the string section we used, and they were a nice complement to the live shows as well. I don't think they enjoyed it quite so much though, because they were generally seated next to my bass speakers and were continually asking for the volume to be turned down: It used to make them bounce up and down on their seats and I think they were probably stone deaf by the end of the tour![132]

Although the orchestral soundtrack had been scrapped, the inclusion of classical music in the *War Child* experience did include a chamber-style piece called "Pan Dance," which Anderson wrote to accompany a dance troupe called Pan's People, who demonstrated their terpsichorean skills at the November 14–17 London Rainbow shows.

After the holidays, the band hit the road again, opening in the American South on January 17, 1975, for a series of 44 dates ending at the Boston Gardens two months later. On March 30, they were in Berlin to inaugurate the European leg of the tour, which ended in Zurich on April 20, when they planned to record a new album. But April Fool's Day brought bad tidings for Anderson, when, at Kiel's Ostseehalle, he badly twisted an ankle and had to perform some of the remaining dates confined to a wheelchair. A more pleasant experience for the mad minstrel was the development of a personal relationship with Shona Learoyd, the lovely young woman who had been working as his personal assistant, appearing on stage each night to give him his guitars. (She appears on the *War Child* back cover in the guise of a circus ringmistress.)

Minstrel in the Gallery

5 September 1975 (U.K.) / 8 September 1975 (U.S.)
Highest chart position: 20 (U.K.) / 7 (U.S.)
[Rating: 4.5]
Producer: Ian Anderson / Chrysalis 1082
All songs written by Ian Anderson

Ian Anderson: vocals, flute, acoustic guitar
Martin Barre: electric guitar
Jeffrey Hammond: bass guitar, string bass
John Evans: piano, Hammond organ
Barrie Barlow: drums, percussion

Recorded at Radio Monte Carlo with the Maison Rouge Mobile Studio, April 1975
Recording engineer: Robin Black
Strings arranged and conducted by David Palmer
Violins: Patrick Halling (leader), Elizabeth Edwards, Rita Eddows, Bridget Procter
Cello: Katherine Thulborn
Cover artwork by R. Kriss and J. Garnett, based on a print by Joseph Nash
Photographs by Brian Ward

Tracks: Minstrel in the Gallery
Cold Wind to Valhalla
Black Satin Dancer
Requiem

One White Duck/0^{10}=Nothing at All
Baker St. Muse
I. Pig Me and the Whore
II. Nice Little Tune
III. Crash Barrier Waltzer
IV. Mother England Reverie
Grace

Minstrel in the Gallery was recorded with the band's new mobile studio in Monte Carlo, France, during the spring of 1975, a period during
which Anderson claimed the band was creating too much of a "party
atmosphere."[133] The 24-track recording gear, housed in a truck, was parked
outside the local radio station while they rehearsed. They then performed
the takes in an actual gallery (pictured on the record's back cover), literally
becoming the plural form of the album's title character. Again forced to
eat bad food (Anderson claimed it was horse), they astonished passersby
by riding mopeds from the hotel to the studio and "poisoneria."[134]

At the time *Minstrel* was made, Anderson described the process of
making an album and how he felt about the completed music:

> After all the actual recording is finished you have to mix it, play the
> tapes to cut it, listen to tape lacquers and cut it again, and make changes
> and cut it again, and finally make test pressings—it drags it out. So it
> doesn't get finished really for quite awhile after the music's finished; when
> it's actually ready to go it's nothing to do with me anymore. It's already
> with them [the public], I mean they can do what they like with it. They
> pay $6 for the privilege ... Unless I continue to play the songs onstage, if
> they're those kind of songs that continue with me in a personal way by
> playing them as part of the show every night. Then I feel closer, perhaps,
> to the music. Not the album per se, but the music itself.[135]

He also discussed his current tastes in music:

> [Jazz] had a sort of passing interest for me.... I'm interested in music in
> general and I've listened to all sorts of music a little bit, but I've never
> been moved by anything on a continuing basis, other than a very limited
> selection of some Negro blues, which I find is still as moving to me as it
> ever was. And I find that some of the indigenous folk forms of England
> and Scotland also continue to move me.... I certainly don't want to be a
> student of that kind of music.... It's something that I have only a passing
> awareness of. Since I was brought up in Edinburgh, Scotland, and I
> heard the bagpipes from an early age, it's a sound that rings in my ears.
> It becomes almost a folk memory of certain sounds and relationships of
> notes—a motive stirring of the blood. [136]

But what of other popular rock bands of the time? Of Led Zeppelin, he said:

> I think they're one of the best rock and roll groups there are; I think musically they're very good and I think what they represent in terms of the rock group idiom is very accurate. They're a very accurate portrayal … they epitomize, if you like, the English hard rock thing better than the Stones probably and better than the Who. I mean, they're arrogant and they all play with some sort of conviction, but as to whether what they do is worth anything in the long run then history will, as usual, retrospectively decide. I don't know, I don't understand it; maybe there's more to it than meets the eye. I think about that a lot actually. I think there's maybe more to a lot of things I don't understand. Maybe it's because they're so simple, they're so good. But I write really simple songs too. I've written some really simple ones, really crystal clear. But they seem to have a lot more in them than other people's very simple songs. There's a few of them on the new album, there's always bits of them on all albums. "Wond'ring Aloud" was a simple song, a very simple sentiment and quite an accurate one as well.[137]

Later commenting on *Minstrel in the Gallery*, Anderson lamented:

> Technically, it was a very good album, one of our better ones. We managed to get a great sound, having had the luxury of being able to set up the studio the way we wanted it.... Musically there is some pretty good stuff on it, but I think the band was suffering.... Jeffrey Hammond was a great guy, a great bass player, in the context of what he did, but he wasn't a real musician's musician. He just didn't know much about music. John Evans was really going off the boil. He had lost interest in rock music and was only playing Beethoven stuff endlessly on the piano. He was also drinking far too much.... Barrie Barlow is a bit of a dissident type who was always picking fights and arguments. And the band, although it was playing reasonably well, just lacked real harmony.[138]

In his own defense, Barlow claimed, "I became a sort of spokesman for the group whenever we were unhappy about something. They would all come to me to moan about this and that, and I always ended up having to confront Ian."[139]

The Tracks of *Minstrel in the Gallery*

Even more than *Aqualung, Minstrel in the Gallery* features the starkest Tull contrast between acoustic folk music and blistering hard rock. In particular, the title track ties together the Elizabethan era with modern references in the lyrics: first we hear a dialogue between members of the minstrel troupe (Anderson playing two characters) and then a voice (David Palmer's) announcing their forthcoming performance to the "lord and lady"; but soon we hear references to "TV documentary makers." The Renaissance element is musically reinforced by the introduction blending acoustic guitars and flute, which then starkly but smoothly segues into the modern rock section, allowing Martin Barre to sink his teeth into a masterful solo combining classical-style structures with his trademark blend of bluesy riffs and bone-crunching power chords. When Anderson's vocals return, reprising the verses from the acoustic portion, the hardest driving sound in the history of Tull proves that this song was truly a landmark in the band's output.

"Cold Wind to Valhalla" features one of the best Tull introductions ever, the combination of acoustic guitar, ethnic percussion and flute creating an atmosphere that suggests a freezing gale lashing across ice-laden lands. This instrumental passage demonstrates how Anderson, like a talented classical or film composer, knows how musically to punctuate the thematic material of a piece. Again, Anderson spins a tale of bygone days—a poetical evocation of the Norse legends—yet includes a reference to modern society, at one point perceptively stating, "We're getting a bit short on heroes lately."

Opening with flute and electric guitar, "Black Satin Dancer" features a quasi-operatic vocal by Anderson (who again composed some wonderful, moving melodies). His romantic, at times erotic, lyrics are beautifully backed by Barre; and here, again, the guitarist exhibits a vast array of styles, merging classical, blues and rock. Barrie Barlow also turns in a fine performance, here and on the rest of the album contributing some of his most intricate and polished playing to date.

"Requiem" is a near-solo Anderson piece, with only Jeffrey Hammond's acoustic bass and David Palmer's strings backing the acoustic guitar and voice. It is a beautiful song about loss and the emotional frustration and pain connected with a failed relationship, in this case with his wife Jennie, whom he recently had divorced. Perhaps, at this time, he was thoroughly disenchanted with women. First he sings,

> Well, my lady told me, "Stay."
> I looked aside and walked away along the Strand.

And in closing the song,

> Well, I saw a bird today.
> I looked aside and walked away along the Strand.

Perhaps the prettiest and most comforting of all his "solo" performances, "One White Duck/0^{10}=Nothing at All" is another acoustic piece
minimally supported by Hammond and Palmer. This song also is an introspective commentary on his broken marriage, with the narrator wandering about the streets, having no real direction in his life. Tull fan Neil R.
Thomason has noted:

> A traditional wall ornament in northern England is/was a set of
> three porcelain flying ducks, each smaller than the last. They tend to sig-
> nify a well-established, settled household. If only one remains, "one
> white duck on your wall," the suggestion is that the household or mar-
> riage has broken up....[140]

The lengthy suite "Baker St. Muse" has been described as a mini–
Thick as a Brick, but resembles its predecessor only in structure. This
omnibus song weaves a tale about a single evening's experience on London's famous Baker Street, thus differing greatly from *Brick*'s generalized
view of modern society. Creating imagery that would not have disgraced
Robert Louis Stevenson, Anderson blends lovely melodies and accomplished poetry into a superbly self-contained piece of music that, in some
ways, is superior to its sometimes shambling forerunner. Devoid of the
pretension of *Brick* and *A Passion Play*, this song sounds much more immediate, both in terms of content and musical performance.

Four specific vignettes are included in the suite: "Pig Me and the
Whore," recalling the seediness of street life earlier explored on *Aqualung*;
"Nice Little Tune," a lilting bridge to "Crash Barrier Waltzer," a critique
on society's disregard for the homeless; and "Mother England Reverie,"
another of Anderson's most exquisite compositions. Opening this fourth
section, he makes another direct jab at the press: "I have no time for *Time*
magazine or *Rolling Stone*." The listener easily can understand Anderson's
later comments about the album being "too introspective": Here again the
lyrics are highly autobiographical. As the tempo picks up, a brilliant verse
emerges:

> There was a little boy stood on a burning log,
> rubbing his hands with glee
> He said, "Oh, Mother England, did you light my smile:
> or did you light this fire under me?
> One day I'll be a minstrel in the gallery.
> And paint you a picture of the queen.
> And if sometimes I sing to a cynical degree—
> it's just the nonsense that it seems."

Although he eventually became uncomfortable with *Minstrel*, Anderson named the brief piece "Grace" as a favorite:

> I literally woke up one morning and looked out the window and just sang words that perfectly evoked for me a feeling, and put it to sort of a quartet arrangement for strings. For me it evoked something that I think countless people will sort of share in and understand. The only twist is in the words:
> "Hello, sun,
> Hello, bird,
> Hello, my lady,
> Hello, breakfast,"
> and the next line: "May I buy you again tomorrow?"
> And "May I buy you" is so ambiguous, whether it applies merely to the $2.50 breakfast at the airport or the whole thing. I mean, we pay for all this in one way or another. That ambiguity is a consciously put-in thing, but it's not something that anybody will really pick up on, though some people obviously will. The last line doesn't even need to be there for most people. It's there as an extra twist, an amusement. It's there if you happen to feel, like I do, a certain cynicism about all your pleasures in life. Because I wake up some mornings and the sun is shining and the birds are twittering and I feel like going out and strangling the little bastards.[141]

Though "Grace" is one of several pieces that does not feature the entire band, nothing on the album is strictly solo Ian Anderson, as Hammond and Palmer are always there to support his unique acoustic guitar stylings. While these pieces demonstrate Anderson's need to express himself as an individual, the remainder of *Minstrel* includes the band working together splendidly, playing with a sense of near-desperation no doubt created by the circumstances under which the album was recorded. This element gives Tull a somewhat less polished presentation, but the performance still features the same intricate arrangements, here made more impressive by spontaneous playing.

The title track was released in abbreviated form (sans Anderson's acoustic introduction and Barre's savage solo) as a single, backed with "Summerday Sands," which was left off the album (but finally reissued on the 1988 *20 Years* box set).

The *Minstrel in the Gallery* Tour

With the album completed, the band played a few German and French dates in late June and early July 1975 before beginning the obligatory tour of North America, opening in Vancouver on July 24 and ending in Athens, Georgia, on November 22. Following the October 27 concert at the Milwaukee Arena, journalist Dominic Jacques wrote:

> Anderson is a sorcerer, whirling, twirling and bounding across the stage. As he performs, a giant rabbit casually walks past him. Nothing unusual. No need to be alarmed. Giant rabbits show up at rock concerts all the time…. Tull's theatrics work well because the band doesn't fall into the trap of taking itself too seriously. There is no pretense here. Anderson has been called "the original madman" and "the fool to this band of tarot card musicians." In a profession full of fools and madmen, he is the real thing.[142]

Playing mid-sized venues, how were Tull stacking up financially against other rock bands? Anderson admitted:

> I don't know if we can afford to do these gigs again. See, I've always worked on the philosophy that we can go out and gross about two or three million dollars on a seven-week tour if we play football stadiums and outdoor shows and concentrate on all the major markets and none of the smaller ones. We can do a very big gross, the same as Zeppelin and the Stones do. But I never thought that I'd be justified then in writing *musician* on my passport where it says occupation, which is what I am, that's what I do. And if we were to go out and play football stadiums and not play the smaller halls, even though there might be 5, 6, 7,000 people who want to come and see the group, we would be much better off. We could lie low most of the year, lay off most of the crew, but then it would have to say on my passport *entrepreneur*, not *musician*. If you're a musician and going to play to people at all, you've got an obligation to go wherever people are, and not just do it wherever the money is right.[143]

After the tour, Jeffrey Hammond decided it was time to depart for more creative pastures. During a band meeting, after playing with them for five years, he merely stated his intentions, totally out of the blue:

> I wanted to be able to express myself, and I couldn't do it musically … it became very frustrating…. I had to make the decision, and it was an awful business because I had to do it in a rather blunt way … Ian is a very persuasive person and I suppose I was rather concerned that I might be persuaded to carry on longer than I wanted to…. And anyway, they were much better musically when I left.[144]

The Elizabethan elements on *Minstrel in the Gallery* were indicative of the direction in which Anderson's songwriting would continue to travel in ensuing years. At the end of the tour, he described the musical growth he had experienced since the early days of the band:

> I had no awareness or tolerance for classical music or folk music or anything of that sort, which really are the roots of our [British] music. I mean they're the roots of my music now, oddly enough, because I've come to realize the importance of the indigenous music of my particular part of the world.
>
> That is and will be what I am ... the traditional music forms, not Negro blues anymore. That's something peculiarly African and Southern states American. I have to deny now to myself the importance of anything that originates from the United States....
>
> And I also have to attempt to recognize the extent to which I'm moved or manipulated by whatever it is that's come out of Western Europe since music began as we know it. So now I would say I'm a British musician. But I also now recognize classical music when I hear it. I consider myself much closer emotionally and experience-wise to the Beethovens and the Chopins and even the Debussys, than to Muddy Waters or Howlin' Wolf or any of those guys, whom I still love. Most of all J. B. Lenoir, who died a few years ago, who was positively the finest.[145]

In describing the obscure Lenoir, whom he saw perform once, Anderson revealed his own self-critical side:

> If there's anything like 100-percent pure emotion and sincerity, then it came from that guy, because he never made a penny in his life. He hardly even made any records. What he did was totally unfettered by anything remotely resembling success.... He had none of the problems that I would have if I wanted to sing music in that kind of a way and total responsibility for my emotional sincerity, which I can't do because of all the trappings of sitting ... in the Beverly Wilshire. I have to admit that a certain percentage of what I do is actually living a lie. He didn't have to do that, so he could put everything into one distinct and narrow channel.... Unfortunately nobody really recognized him before or, seemingly, since his death. But he was a beautiful singer and a beautiful player. To me he really said everything there was to be said about that kind of music. It was the pure plea, the desperate cry, not for self-pity, but in a proud, human way.... He was a proud and pure voice, and desperate with it. Desperate—that's the thing ... which I can only listen to, I can't participate. Because I'm not that desperate anymore. I never have been. I only starved for a fortnight. That's all I did. People talk about paying their dues, but I only starved for a fortnight.[146]

Too Old to Rock 'n' Roll:
Too Young to Die!

23 April 1976 (U.K.) / 17 May 1976 (U.S.)
Highest chart position: 25 (U.K.) / 14 (U.S.)
[Rating: 4]
Producer: Ian Anderson / Chrysalis 1111
All songs written by Ian Anderson

Ian Anderson: vocals, flute, acoustic and electric guitars, harmonica, percussion
Martin Barre: electric and acoustic guitars
John Evans: piano
John Glascock: bass guitar, vocals
Barrie Barlow: drums and percussion
David Palmer: saxophone, Vako Orchestron, string arrangements
Maddy Prior and Angela Allen: backing vocals

Recorded at Radio Monte Carlo with the Maison Rouge Mobile Studio,
    December 1975
Recording engineers: Robin Black, Trevor White and Peter Smith
Sleeve design and illustrations by Michael Farrell and David Gibbons

Tracks: Quizz Kid
        Crazed Institution
        Salamander
        Taxi Grab
        From a Dead Beat to an Old Greaser
        Bad-Eyed and Loveless
        Big Dipper
        Too Old to Rock 'n' Roll: Too Young to Die
        Pied Piper
        The Chequered Flag (Dead or Alive)

While on a Christmas holiday in Switzerland during December 1975, Anderson once again decided to take Tull in another direction. After messing about with a few songs, he wrote a number called "Too Old to Rock 'n' Roll," which he then played for David Palmer. Soon an isolated song became a concept, a projected musical for the stage. Initially Anderson intended to represent archetypes from several walks of life but eventually narrowed down the plot to feature only an aging rock star. Focusing on the cyclic nature of fashion, he wanted to stress that a once-popular artist can remain true to his vision if only he waits long enough for his style to come around again—a concept that is explored with a great deal of complexity, as Anderson paints his old rocker "Ray Lomas" as a character both to be pitied and ridiculed.

After Barre, Barlow, Evans and new bassist John Glascock convened in Brussels to work up the material, the band realized that producing it for someone else (Adam Faith, in this case) might not work, and another album with separate songs was recorded instead. Prior to joining the band, Glascock, an Islington native who hailed from a musical family, had played on eight albums with various groups, most recently the flamenco-rock band Carmen, who had opened for Tull on the *War Child* tour. Though left-handed, he amazingly played with his right, using a pick.

Long before the album was released, Anderson poised himself for the inevitable press reaction that he was actually Ray Lomas. He said:

> The title openly invites all sorts of attacks on the music contained therein and I really don't mind because it was going to happen anyway. The first two or three interviews I did ... in Spain were the first ones I'd done ... and the second or third, if not the first question, was: Are you too old to rock 'n' roll?[147]

Forever plagued by those who assumed that the title song was autobiographical, he later recalled:

> *Too Old to Rock 'n' Roll* had the light, the humor and the warmth that wasn't there on the preceding album, and it's a slightly easier album to get into, to enjoy and to function within, although it's a bit quirky rock 'n' roll. Stylistically it's not a very satisfying album for me, it's a bit too pop-rock. It doesn't have enough of the basic kind of blues or R&B type of thing for me. Things like "Taxi Grab" were okay, first time for a long time that I played harmonica, for example. Things like "Salamander." Those were the nice bits of it.[148]

Anderson was a mere 28 when the album was released. He explained:

> It [my attitude] is actually the antithesis of "Too Old to Rock 'n' Roll." The "Too Old" song was actually spawned in a moment of depression. At one point on an American tour I'd been really down after a duff gig that was probably my fault and I thought: "I'm really past all this. Why should I be traveling another 500 miles to another town? Let me off at the roundabout." Whereas "The Chequered Flag" is lyrically more like "Bungle in the Jungle." It's accepting the hardness of life, and saying, "Well it's hell. But it's all worth it, getting out there and doing it."[149]

Interestingly, the album's cover and interior comic strip—telling the tale of the rocker's fall from grace, motorcycle accident and eventual comeback—depict Ray Lomas looking exactly like Anderson. (All the characters shown on Tull album covers bear a striking resemblance to him.)

To "repay" Anderson for producing their 1974 *Now We Are Six* album, Steeleye Span's Maddy Prior sang backing vocals on the title track, while Angela Allen lent her voice to "Crazed Institution." Not only did he perform his usual arranging and conducting duties, but David Palmer also played the Vako Orchestron synthesizer and "late-night" saxophone solo on "From a Dead Beat to an Old Greaser."

When the album was released, Anderson made a highly perceptive comment about the role of music in human endeavor:

> [T]he origin of music seems to lie in the emotional response to things ... spiritual, whether it was merely dancing around the bonfire acknowledging the gods on high, some sort of deity, for the rains and the harvest, the birth of a new child, or expressing sorrow or joy, someone dying. It's an emotional response. We all have the need for emotional expression some way.[150]

The Tracks of *Too Old to Rock 'n' Roll: Too Young to Die!*

From its first strummed chord, *Too Old to Rock 'n' Roll* proves a radical departure from all preceding Tull albums. No two Tull albums sound alike, but this effort—with its pop-rock style and subject matter—really surprised fans, who recently had enjoyed the thunderous hard rock of *Minstrel in the Gallery.* "Quizz Kid" opens the album, its straight-ahead rock and roll tone providing an effective score for Anderson's critique of the television game shows that were enormously popular during the late 1960s and early 1970s. Ray Lomas' successful appearance on one of these shows illustrates the fact that any manipulated "dunce" can appear a "quizz kid ... a whizz kid" in front of the lazy masses who waste their time in front of the idiot box. At one point, Anderson recalls a line from *War Child*'s "Queen and Country" when he refers to the contestant's appearance in front of a TV camera as "hold[ing] your head up to the gun." Musically more upbeat than the songs on the previous album, "Quizz Kid" features some nice interplay between Barre's lead guitar and Anderson's flute.

"Crazed Institution" is extremely quirky, but sounds more like vintage

Tull, particularly the acoustic-based material from 1970-71. Anderson's criticism of pop culture reaches its apex in this song, when he suggests how media "stars" begin to accept the worship of their fans. The egotism of modern pop icons, particularly rock stars, is given a good thrashing when he incorporates some striking Christ imagery:

> And you can ring a crown of roses 'round your cranium,
> Live and die upon your cross of platinum.
> Join the crazed institution of the stars.
> Be the man that you think you really are.

When this chorus is repeated, the last line is altered to "Be the man that you know you really are," thus depicting the superstar as coming to believe all the hype surrounding his success.

"Salamander" is a little acoustic masterpiece, a medieval-tinged blues that harks back to *Minstrel* (particularly the opening of "Cold Wind to Valhalla") and anticipates the material on the next album, *Songs from the Wood*. Another of Anderson's songs about streetwalkers, it grooves along steamily yet intimately as Ray Lomas propositions Salamander: "Burn for me, and I'll burn for you." Barre's bluesy acoustic lead work and the tambourine are a perfect accompaniment to Anderson's vocals and rhythm guitar.

Moving away from the rural, ancient sound of "Salamander," the gritty urban blues of "Taxi Grab," features Barre on slide guitar and Anderson on harmonica (his first use of the instrument since *Stand Up*), and depicts Lomas' successful conquest in the back seat of a cab. An outstanding instrumental bridge shifts from Barre's trademark multi-track leads (with his Gibson tone at its finest) to a seductive acoustic slide guitar passage. Ending with a brief blues instrumental, this song benefits from one of the best grooves created by the band since the first three albums (undoubtedly aided by the superb bass work of John Glascock, meshing seamlessly with Barlow's precision percussion).

A truly funereal lament, "From a Dead Beat to an Old Greaser" is Anderson's critique of the 1950s anti-establishment "beat generation." The "old greaser" Ray Lomas, after a conversation with an obsolete "dead beat"—who speaks of "tired young sax players ... sharing wet dreams of Charlie Parker, Jack Kerouac, René Magritte, to name a few of the heroes who were too wise for their own good—left the young brood to go on living without them"—he realizes the danger of "living in the past." (Here Anderson lists Parker, a musician; Kerouac, a poet; and Magritte, a painter. Shades of *Thick as a Brick*?) Turning the tables, speaking "To a dead beat from an old greaser," Ray informs the old beatnik:

Think you must have me all wrong.
I didn't care, friend. I wasn't there, friend.
If it's the price of a pint you want, ask me again.

Musically reinforcing the song's references to "tired young sax players" and Charlie Parker, David Palmer adds a soothing, spare saxophone solo.

The acoustic "Bad-Eyed and Loveless," the most straightforward blues song Tull had performed since the *This Was* days, is a none-too-subtle evocation of an aging man's unfulfilled sex fantasy; while "Big Dipper," a driving, funky blues, recalls the days when Ray Lomas (naming himself after the rollercoaster on the Blackpool beach) had plenty of birds and sought to "go big-dipping daily."

The title song dramatizes Lomas' motorcycle crash and survival, proving that he was too old to rock and roll, but too young to die. The most pop-oriented song Tull had ever recorded, "Too Old" features an observation about the greasers who "sold out" to become "respectable" (ironically something John Evans would do three years later):

Married with three kids up by the ring road,
sold their souls straight down the line.
And some of them owned little sports cars
and meet at the tennis club do's
For drinks on a Sunday, work on Monday.
They've thrown away their blue suede shoes.

"Pied Piper," a bizarre variation on the 1960s acoustic folk style, depicts Lomas' recovery and comeback as his style of pop music again becomes the vogue. And his fantasies are fulfilled as he seduces a young girl:

So follow me, hold on tight.
My school girl fancy's flowing in free flight.
I've a tenner in my skin tight jeans.
You can touch it if your hands are clean.

Of course the title "Pied Piper" refers to Ray-as-seducer, but it also pertains to the fluted-one himself.

The closing song, "The Chequered Flag (Dead or Alive)," the musical highlight of the album, is one of the most beautiful and moving pieces ever composed by Anderson. Backed by elegant, tasteful, clean electric work by Barre and a gorgeous Palmer string arrangement, Anderson wrings genuine passion from his voice, which is in fine form throughout the album.

The song is about the end of life, yet it offers an optimistic view that, although myriad difficulties are inevitable, the race is worth it after all. The final stunning verse, which segues into a powerful crescendo and the last chorus, makes reference to Anderson's musical hero, Ludwig van Beethoven:

> The still-born child can't feel the rain
> as the chequered flag falls once again.
> The deaf composer completes his final score.
> He'll never hear his sweet encore.
> The chequered flag, the bull's red rag,
> the lemming-hearted hordes running
> ever-faster to the shore singing,
> "Isn't it grand to be playing to the stand, dead or alive?"

The anthem-like melody is very reminiscent of English classical music, particularly that of Elgar. (In fact, the band has played arrangements of Elgar's music during encores at their concerts.) "The Chequered Flag" is a breathtaking coda to a somewhat bizarre but extremely interesting concept album. A single version of the title track also was issued, but, taken out of the conceptual context, led to the critics' misinterpretation of it as autobiographical.

The *Too Old to Rock 'n' Roll* Tour

To support the album's May 1976 release, the band set off on a three-week European tour, hitting Belgium, France, the Netherlands, Sweden, Germany and Spain, before taking a two-month hiatus. After catching one of these gigs, which featured large-screen monitors Anderson dubbed "Tullevision," journalist Tony Proops commented:

> Sound is superb and the band extraordinarily ambitious, at one point working through the complexity of Beethoven's Ninth. There's precision, professionalism, excitement and an emphasis more on the show's content than any distracting visual extravaganza.[151]

On July 15, they opened a North American tour in Providence, Rhode Island, which ended in Calgary, Alberta, on August 25. While at the airport in Jackson, Mississippi, Barre noticed a beautiful young woman, Julie Weems, whom he offered a ticket and backstage pass for the show that night. An unusual move for the reserved and gentlemanly Martin, it led to their marriage the following year.

Songs from the Wood

11 February 1977 (U.K.) / 21 February 1977 (U.S.)
Highest chart position: 13 (U.K.) / 8 (U.S.)
[Rating: 5]
Producer: Ian Anderson / Chrysalis 1132
All songs written by Ian Anderson
(Additional material by David Palmer and Martin Barre /
arrangements by Jethro Tull)

Ian Anderson: vocals, flute, acoustic and electric guitars, mandolin, tin whistles, percussion
Martin Barre: electric guitar, lute
John Evans: piano, Hammond organ, synthesizers
John Glascock: bass guitar
David Palmer: piano, synthesizers, portative organ
Barrie Barlow: drums, glockenspiel, bells, nakers, tabor

Recorded at Morgan Studio, London, and with the Maison Rouge Mobile Studio, autumn 1976
Recording engineers: Robin Black, Thing Moss and Trevor White
Front cover painting by Jay L. Lee
Back cover by Shirt Sleeve Studio
Wood-cutter: Keith Howard

Tracks: Songs from the Wood
　　　　　Jack in the Green
　　　　　Cup of Wonder
　　　　　Hunting Girl
　　　　　Ring Out, Solstice Bells
　　　　　Velvet Green
　　　　　The Whistler
　　　　　Pibroch (Cap in Hand)
　　　　　Fire at Midnight

　　As an artist, Ian Anderson always has responded to his environment, and this fact never has been more apparent than on *Songs from the Wood*, the first album he wrote and recorded with the band after taking a lengthy

Ian Anderson, in classic flute pose, and Martin Barre, on stage during the *Songs from the Wood* tour, 1977. (Photograph by Richard E. Aaron; courtesy of Ian Anderson.)

hiatus from touring and buying a farm west of London. Looking back on that period of transition, he said:

> After only ever living in hotels, or in the middle of London, or in other cities or town environments, I was, I think, the last member of the group to move out of town and go to live in the country. And when I went living in the country, I really went living in the country, not just in a leafy suburb or a village, but actually on a working farm. So suddenly what had been part of my childhood, spending a lot of time outdoors and being in more remote and rural places, was now a reality of day to day life.... That gave me some definite place to put down some roots, and I think that gave the music a suitable anchoring point. But for me the important thing about the album is that it did bring together the guys in the band musically in terms of their involvement. Probably that was one of the albums ... in which the guys contributed with ideas and arrangements.[152]

Praising *Wood* for being an "album ... where the band did really click together again," Anderson further explained:

Martin Barre frets a mighty power chord on his Gibson Les Paul, on stage, 1977. (Photograph by Richard E. Aaron; courtesy of Ian Anderson.)

> I deliberately would leave the studio and let them come up with some arrangements and ideas … that shouldn't be how it is—unfortunately it became the way of working, because it took my overbearing musical influence away and allowed them to contribute.[153]

Prior to *Songs from the Wood*, Tull had incorporated elements of music from various parts of the world, including Britain, the United States, Europe and India—and there always had been a vaguely historical, particularly medieval, component—but now the band produced an album that was thoroughly British. Describing the title track as "fiendishly difficult," Anderson called the project a tribute to their "country of origin":

> I think we had spent so many years away on tour and recording in different countries, it was a kind of natural reaction against all that internationalism that brought us back into, not only recording in the U.K., but making an album of songs that had their roots in terms of musical style and lyrics back more in our home place.[154]

Both Anderson and Barre have voiced their dislike of folk music, in part because the term "folk" conjures up the 1960s American coffeehouse style of bad singing and even worse musicianship. While *Songs from the*

Martin Barre appears to confer with an off-camera Barrie Barlow as he plays his Les Paul, in concert, 1977. (Photograph by Richard E. Aaron; courtesy of Ian Anderson.)

Wood includes elements of folk—here developed from a solid British tradition passed down by Anderson's fellow Scots Robert Burns and Sir Walter Scott—it draws from a wider spectrum of British culture and not just the "folk." Ancient themes and characters (both in the music and lyrical content), tales of decadent aristocrats (not "folk" by any means), courtly music from the Elizabethan Renaissance, and mournful Scottish sounds are blended into a rock style that often incorporates a 19th-century classical structure. Far from being merely a folk-rock album, *Songs from the Wood* is actually rock that distills several centuries of British Isles history into a brilliant 42-minute presentation. Not even Ian Anderson realized how much of a masterpiece he had created; in 1993, when asked about the historical component in his songs, he claimed that such a connection was never a conscious decision on his part.[155] With *Songs from the Wood*, he was able to transcend even his own ambitions.

The Tracks of *Songs from the Wood*

Though Anderson often had included sexual references and imagery on past albums, here he had a concrete reason to incorporate such material:

The ever-flamboyant John Evans, on stage, 1977. (Photograph by Richard E. Aaron; courtesy of Ian Anderson.)

the fact that traditional English songs are rampant with erotic content, especially those celebrating pagan festivals like May Day, or "Beltane" in Celtic parlance. On the final evening of April, in pre–Christian times and after, young maidens would give themselves to the most virile men in their communities, even out in the open fields, to inaugurate spring and ensure a hearty crop. Recalling historical songs (such as those by Robert Burns), Anderson depicts such outdoor *amour* in "Hunting Girl" and "Velvet Green." "Jack in the Green" also suggests the fertility rite of Beltane, which involved this sprightly creature also known as "the Green Man," a character associated with St. George in Christian versions of the legend. Judson Caswell noted:

> Anderson applies this powerful healing spirit to a very modern question. Considering the environmental terrorisms of industrialization as a kind of winter, he asks "Jack do you never sleep? Does the green still run deep in your heart? Or will these changing times, motorways, powerlines keep us apart? Well I don't think so, I saw some grass growing through the pavements today."[156]

The title song musically and lyrically invites the listener into the

John Glascock demonstrates the enthusiasm that made him a fine bassist, on stage, 1977. (Photograph by Richard E. Aaron; courtesy of Ian Anderson.)

experience of *Songs from the Wood*. As Anderson's multi-tracked a capella vocals open the piece, the words also attract anyone within earshot:

> Let me bring you songs from the wood:
> to make you feel much better than you could know.
> Dust you down from tip to toe.
> Show you how the garden grows.
> Hold steady as you go.
> Join the chorus if you can:
> it'll make of you an honest man.

Here, Anderson welcomes the listener to his celebratory realm, actually challenging him to join in if he is capable—an act that will make him "honest." This song, both in narrative content and musicality, is indicative of the high level of sophistication permeating the album, which is very orchestral in its lush layers of instrumentation as well as its structure.

"Jack in the Green," the most thoroughly Celtic Tull song to date, is a multi-tracked solo piece performed entirely by Anderson, while "Cup of Wonder" features the band back in fine form, presenting a pleasant and bright paean to the ancient druidic community, the lyrics incorporating references to Beltane, Celtic standing stones and pagan rituals. Featuring lush synthesizer "orchestrations" by David Palmer, "Cup" is one of several such songs, on the first Tull album to dispense with actual string arrangements.

The innuendo-laden "Hunting Girl" is a steamy and driving Renaissance rocker featuring beautiful drumming by Barrie Barlow, who approximates the sound of galloping horses' hooves with his double-bass drum set-up as he punctuates the breaks between verses with precision cymbal and tom-tom work. As elsewhere on the album, dynamic choral and "symphonic" flourishes end the song in pleasingly dramatic style.

The very upbeat "Ring Out, Solstice Bells," which ends side A on the original LP, celebrates the druidic winter Solstice (December 21 or 22) that became the inspiration for the Christmas holiday. "Solstice Bells" actually had been released as a Yuletide single in the U.K. the previous autumn, on a four-song 45 that also included "March the Mad Scientist," 1968's "A Christmas Song," and "Pan Dance," the lovely piece written and recorded three years earlier. Incredibly, in the raging age of punk, "Solstice" reached number 28 in the charts. (Fans in the U.S. finally were able to acquire "March" and "Pan" on the 1988 box set.)

The ancient ambiance of "Solstice" is echoed in "Velvet Green," the piece that begins the album's second half. The most intricate Tull song up to that time (and most difficult to play, as Anderson attested during the *Wood* concert tour), its traditional Elizabethan basis is elegantly conveyed through a brilliant arrangement of a harpsichord synthesizer voice, an actual lute deftly fretted by Barre, Anderson's acoustic guitar and flute, John Glascock's expert Renaissance-style bass line and Barrie Barlow's astounding period percussion (including the nakers and tabor, which date from the Middle Ages). This tale of verdant seduction includes a flawlessly played, sophisticated instrumental, during which Anderson's mandolin, Palmer's keyboards and Barlow's percussion rise to the fore.

Barre's electric guitar and Anderson's tin whistle create an incredible atmosphere in "The Whistler," wherein the lyrics and musical arrangement hark back to days of ancient troubadours. The driving jig heard after each chorus adds a particular pleasantry to the album, providing stark counterpoint to the thoroughly Scottish melancholia that follows.

Certainly one of the most accomplished pieces ever written by Anderson, "Pibroch (Cap in Hand)" is a musical and lyrical masterpiece blending Scottish music with classical flourishes and a blues tempo. Inspired by the traditional Gaelic *pibroch* (Anderson likes to pronounce it "pee-break"), a set of variations played on the Highland bagpipes (a sound recalled by Martin Barre's powerful and innovative guitar work), it features

Barrie Barlow, captured behind his drum kit, on stage, 1977. (Photograph by Richard E. Aaron; courtesy of Ian Anderson.)

one of Anderson's finest melodies and an impeccably performed folk instrumental in its mid-section.

A true Tull tour de force, the song opens with Barre's mournful multi-tracked guitar wails, one of the most unusual introductions in rock history. Creating more atmosphere than any rock song deserves to have, his playing, in part, is remarkable because of its grounding in an earlier, time-less musical form, providing the perfect aural backdrop for Anderson's tale of romantic longing, disappointment and loss. The folk-based instrumental section is thoroughly Scots Celtic, as opposed to the more aristocratic English passage in "Velvet Green," its communal component of a "crowd" clapping along giving it a rougher, more "common" quality than the sophisticated and studied sound of the earlier song. A retard incorporating a choral passage leads back into an impassioned vocal by Anderson, the song's musical dichotomy prefacing the personal rejection a lover feels when he sees "strange slippers by the fire, strange boots in the hallway."

The perfect foil for "Pibroch," "Fire at Midnight" is a Scottish-based romantic ballad celebrating hearth and home. As warm as an actual blaze, the song reflects Anderson's enjoyment of being with his new wife in their recently acquired country abode after spending so many endless months on the road. Another superb instrumental break, combining Anderson's mandolin with Barre's evocative lead guitar, lends an anthem-like coda to an utterly flawless album that opens with a choral anthem.

The *Songs from the Wood* Tour

In early 1977, Tull took a brief, seven-date tour of the U.S. On January 16, they played an unusual benefit concert at the Dorothy Chandler Pavilion in Los Angeles. To help raise money for the L.A. Music Center, they accepted Terry Ellis' invitation to entertain 471 black-tie guests in the Founders' Circle. The first rock band ever to become associated with the venue, the band again played David Palmer's arrangement of excerpts from Beethoven's Ninth Symphony.

Following this "mini tour," Tull played their first British dates in more than two years, opening with two shows in Scotland and closing at Bristol's Colston Hall on February 14. English fans were treated to a quieter, gentler version of the Anderson madman, shorn of some hair and attired in a classier version of the minstrel's garb, strumming "Wond'ring Aloud" as he innocuously strolled onto the stage to begin the shows. The February 10 gig at the Golders Green Hippodrome was filmed and recorded for broadcast on BBC television and radio's one-hour *Sight and Sound in Concert* programs one week later.

On March 1, 1977, they began a 34-gig North American tour that closed in Miami five weeks later, in time for the band to fly to Nuremburg for a two-week German excursion. After a month-long holiday, they played Sweden, Denmark, Germany, France, the Netherlands, Belgium, Switzerland and Austria. Another holiday allowed them to set off on a two-week tour of Australia before heading back for another 31 U.S. gigs.

Before fans had a chance to buy the new LP, Anderson shamelessly promoted it, referring to "this great new album of ours," during the shows. To provide suitable support for "Jack in the Green," "Songs from the Wood," "Velvet Green" and "Hunting Girl," the band interspersed earlier folk-based songs such as "Skating Away," but also cut loose on "To Cry You a Song," "Minstrel in the Gallery," "Cross-Eyed Mary" and "Back-Door Angels," as well as including the Beethoven suite.

Songs from the Wood re-established Tull as a major band in both the United States and Britain, and was popular with both the public and critics. "Cup of Wonder" and "The Whistler" (backed with the non-album track "Strip Cartoon") were released as singles on both sides of the Atlantic. During the lengthy 1977 tours, Anderson spoke of how he felt about blending the older Tull songs into the new, more rustic repertoire:

What works on stage is the here and now. You can bend emotion-
ally to fit the song, hopefully without getting into nostalgia. You should
sing the song because of what the song is about rather than because it
reminds you of something. It's an emotional interaction and I can still
feel the passion in those songs. And although one's emotions have
become a little more complicated and there are more complex interac-
tions of different feelings, those songs, I think, those songs are still
strong enough to cut through it all. Particularly on stage.[157]

In October, Anderson furthered his retreat to ruralism by purchasing the 15,300-acre Strathaird Estate on the Isle of Skye, where the locals
initially flinched at the prospect of a "rock star" taking over such a sizable
piece of land, which, on its northern border, includes a large portion of
the breathtaking Black Cuillins mountain range. But his intentions were
more than honorable from the beginning, when he first read an article about
salmon farming in a "dreadful" airline magazine and then developed a
plan to revitalize the economy in the depressed Skye region. While the
estate farm consists of only 350 acres, the rest of the land includes about
50 crofts, grazing areas for sheep, Highland cattle and deer, and 6,000
acres that, according to Anderson, "are probably pretty vertical." Addressing the negative reactions, he said:

I was warned by the late Willie McCrea of the Scottish Nationalist
Party that it was a big mistake coming up here to buy Strathaird. It was
a big mistake to be involved in any way with the … complexities of the
social scene up here. That I would not be respected. That I would not be
liked … I argued with Willie McCrea about it, and said, "I just don't
believe that people are that simple-minded."[158]

Heavy Horses

21 April 1978 (U.K.) / 10 April 1978 (U.S.)
Highest chart position: top 20 (U.K.) / 19 (U.S.)
[Rating: 5]
Producer: Ian Anderson / Chrysalis 1175
All songs written by Ian Anderson

Ian Anderson: vocals, flute, acoustic and electric guitars, mandolin
Martin Barre: electric and acoustic guitars
John Glascock: bass guitar

John Evans: piano, Hammond organ
David Palmer: portative organ, keyboards, string arrangements
Barrie Barlow: drums, percussion
Darryl Way: violin

Recorded at Maison Rouge Studios, Fulham, London, January 1978
Recording engineer: Robin Black
Front cover photograph: James Cotier
Back cover photograph: Shona Anderson
"Barley" and "Sir Jim" courtesy of the Courage Shire Horse Centre

Tracks: ...And the Mouse Police Never Sleeps
Acres Wild
No Lullaby
Moths
Journeyman
Rover
One Brown Mouse
Heavy Horses
Weathercock

After moving into the country, Anderson also bought some property to build his own recording studio, Maison Rouge, in South London. Shortly after returning from the *Songs from the Wood* tour, the band guested on *Woman in the Wings*, an excellent solo album by Steeleye Span vocalist Maddy Prior, in January 1978. Barre, Barlow, Glascock and Palmer all played on various tracks, and Anderson, who also played flute, co-produced with veteran Tull engineer Robin Black. The track "Gutter Geese," featuring Prior's haunting lilt throughout, suddenly becomes a Tull piece during the bridge, featuring a bouncy Renaissance style similar to the mid-section of "Velvet Green."

Playing at peak performance, the band then began working on *Heavy Horses*. Three months later, the album was ready for release. As a promotion, Anderson was interviewed by Dougie Gordon of the Finnish magazine *Soundi*, whose feature "Flashes from the Archives" provided an insightful retrospective of the band's first decade: "[T]his band has not achieved its innumerable gold discs by churning out the same stuff all the time: the scale varies from smooth ballads to exploding rock and emotive blues which all have Ian's flute as a constant trademark."[159]

At the height of his rustic phase, Anderson demonstrated that his iconoclasm also had reached a peak. Claiming, "I don't have much in common with most people," he admitted:

I don't listen to music ... my whole record collection consists of twenty
or thirty albums. My single access to music is my tape recorder which I
carry with me to listen to Beethoven, who is my only idol. I listen to
Beethoven when I feel I need sound. I live in a world of sounds and
noise, but when I'm not playing myself or thinking about music I'd
rather be in silence.[160]

(Anderson's comments help explain why his own compositions are so
unique.)

At the time of its release, Anderson described *Heavy Horses* as "*Songs
from the Wood*, Part II, plus a little more Jethro Tull," apparently meaning
that some of the band's own peculiar sound would be more prominently
fused with its recent gravitation toward traditional British music. Whereas
Songs from the Wood can be situated primarily within an English Elizabethan influence, *Heavy Horses* borrows more from 18th-century Scottish
music.

Craig Thomas perceptively wrote that "Heavy Horses,"

so reminiscent of Edwin Muir's poem on the same subject of shire
horses, is perhaps my personal favorite amongst the band's repertoire.
The strings are necessary, as is every other element of the arrangement,
and the lyrics have a poetic subtlety and diamondlike brilliance. No
other band, no other songwriter, would have produced anything remotely
akin to this; the celebration of life and the evocation of a vanished rural
world with a nostalgia that is never sweet, together with the insistent
difference of the modern world are all elementally captured in the
imagery of the heavy horses.[161]

Judson Caswell noted that, like the previous album's "Jack in the
Green," "Heavy Horses" demonstrates Anderson's "faith in old symbols of
power and rejuvenation to overcome [the] industrial winter"[162]:

And one day when the oil barons have all dripped dry
and the nights are seen to draw colder,
They'll beg for your strength, your gentle power,
your noble grace and your bearing,
And you'll strain once again to the sound of the gulls,
in the wake of the deep plough, sharing.

Like the title track, each song on the album is a fully realized, highly
polished piece of music; similar to the previous album, it is not necessarily rock music, but poetic, folk-oriented material played by musicians
using a combination of rock and more traditional, acoustic instruments.

It is the ultimate Tull exercise in musical fusion, one that future members of the band (Dave Pegg and Andy Giddings) preferred. At the time of its release, Anderson said:

> It is a rather more menacing album than *Songs from the Wood*, in a positive way. And I think the guys in the group are playing better, probably due to the different ways we used to record the songs.... We probably recorded about 20 songs, many of which were discarded or not finished. And the songs were written in different environments. I wrote some as usual in hotels on tour, another one on the train, which I tend to do a lot. And some were written at home surrounded by animals. Writing songs at home, rather than on tour or on holiday, tends to give you a more objective look at your life, so obviously the subject matter is going to be more personal and possibly relevant to most of the people who listen to the songs.[163]

As the years passed, however, Anderson came to view the album's "menace" in a negative way:

> *Songs from the Wood* had the fun, the humor ... *Heavy Horses* is missing that warmth.
> I didn't really realize at that time how important the humor or the fun element was in Jethro Tull, which is why some of these albums lack maybe a little bit of levity—a lightness, a kind of "Let's not try to make every song a masterpiece, let's play some songs that have no reason to be here other than they are amusing. They may not be startlingly original, they may not be terribly intricate or difficult to play, they're just fun to do." Maybe it's because the mood in the band was responsible for that.[164]

Truth to tell, all the songs on *Heavy Horses* are little masterpieces, very original, most of them fairly intricate and difficult to play, certainly by rock standards. When Anderson made this assessment, 14 years after the album was released, he again was focusing on much simpler, blues-oriented songs, in part because popular tastes were running in that direction.

But just after completing *Horses*, Anderson thought very highly of a very menacing song such as "...And the Mouse Police Never Sleeps":

> [W]hen I'm home, cats are an important part of my life, but when I'm away, I tend to think, "What is a cat, anyway? Why do I like my cats?" Taming cats and their nature of the beast, for our good rather than the good of the cat, causes me some concern. So the record reflects the state of my normal life, the interesting bits, the loves and hates and so on.[165]

In 1978, Anderson felt very satisfied with the state of his musical output, reflecting the fact that much of the material on the album is very warm and comforting:

> Ten years ago I didn't just have musical problems but also the questions of daily bread and the frustrations that shortage brought. I'd much rather be in where I am today because in my opinion I make better music—at least I'm satisfied—compared to the music that came out of misery ten years ago. I'm rather sure that if I were to start living in hotels again or become a tax exile again it would be reflected in my music; it would be more depressed and aggressive. Today I'm cynical, angry and depressed only when I tour in America, but that is one of the bad sides to my job.[166]

The Tracks of *Heavy Horses*

Many of the songs on *Heavy Horses* are about animals: cats, moths, mice, horses and even a symbolic one, the weathercock. "Mouse Police" truly has a sinister sound, opening with acoustic guitar riffs that suggest the stealthy pitter pat of cat paws and ominous flute punctuations that announce its prowling breath. Anderson said:

> What I really like about [cats] is that they appear to be such passive, lovable creatures who just lie there doing nothing, when in reality they are nasty, vicious animals that do terrible things to other furry little animals. People always have this idea that nature is lovely and fluffy and cute, but the truth is nature is actually too tough for almost all of us. That's why we live in towns, in nice warm houses. The natural, animal world is a horrific place....[167]

The lyric, "Look out little furry folk!" and the song's title are the album's first hints of the influence of Robert Burns, which becomes obvious in "One Brown Mouse" several tracks later.

"Acres Wild" is a Tull masterwork in a jaunty march tempo, one of the band's most thoroughly Scottish songs, both musically and thematically—"under black mountains in open spaces," "through far marches where the blue hare races"—and particularly in the chorus (set on the Isle of Skye):

> Come with me to the Winged Isle—
> northern father's western child.
> Where the dance of ages is playing still
> through far marches of acres wild.

The song's lyrical dichotomy of country ("Winged Isle") and city ("Come with me to the weary town") is musically matched by the juxtaposition of Barre's electric guitar and the first use of authentic bagpipes since *War Child*'s "The Third Hoorah" blended superbly with Anderson's flute.

Barre opens the epic "No Lullaby" in "Pibroch" fashion, his mournful guitar soon being joined by the powerful rhythms of Glascock and Barlow, who once again single-handedly sounds like an entire orchestral percussion section. Like "Pibroch," the song's verses unfold in a slow 6/8 blues tempo, but the 4/4 choruses shift "No Lullaby" into high gear, with Barre's unique multi-tracked "symphonic" guitar work flawlessly underpinned by the driving rhythm section. While the verses warn the listener not to let down his guard—"there's dragons and beasties out there in the night to snatch you if you fall"—the choruses call him to action: "So come out fighting with your rattle in hand. Thrust and parry. Light…."

The primarily acoustic "Moths" features some of Anderson's most accomplished and memorable poetry, its vivid imagery countering the "suicidal" wedding of insects at the candle with the romance of the narrator and his lover. The song begins in classic Anderson style, his acoustic guitar and voice first joined by Barlow, then Glascock, his own flute and David Palmer's beautiful string arrangement, which Barre brilliantly accompanies with electric guitar.

Though its title suggests a much earlier period in history, "Journeyman" describes the plight of the modern commuting worker who has no free time due to his exhausting everyday schedule. The subject matter is musically supported with the first few notes of Glascock's bass, which, accented by Barlow's bass drum, introduces this ominous, strangely R&B-tinged song. Demonstrating Anderson's understanding of effective vocal technique, his phrasing draws out the unpleasantness of the lyrics:

> Sliding through Victorian tunnels
> Where green moss oozes from the pores.
> Dull echoes from the wet embankments—
> Battlefield allotments. Fresh open sores.

Adding powerful dynamics to the piece, Barre unleashes a series of angry, vicious leads, reminding the listener that Anderson's words paint the working man "like a faithful dog with master sleeping in the draught beside the carriage door."

Side B of the original LP begins with "Rover," in which the spirit of adventure is embodied in the song's gypsy-like protagonist:

The long road is a rainbow and the pot of gold lies there.
So slip the chain and I'm off again—
You'll find me everywhere. I'm a Rover.

Providing a perfect contrast to "Journeyman," this song is bright and pleasant, its "colorful and carefree" character offering an optimistic viewpoint
on an album Anderson subsequently has noted for its dark thematics. The
upbeat nature of "Rover" is particularly enhanced by Barlow's xylophone
part, which he plays in unison with Barre's muted electric leads and Evans'
keyboards.

Inspired by Robert Burns' "To a Mouse...," "One Brown Mouse"
offers a safer look at the "little furry folk" that first rear their tiny heads
in "...And the Mouse Police Never Sleeps." Anderson introduces the song
with lush acoustic guitars, soon to be joined by Palmer's medieval portative organ, and the drone-based melody is punctuated potently by the
rhythm section during the heavier, driving choruses. An anthem-like
instrumental section resembling a Scottish march adds just the right Burn-
sian musical touch to Anderson's charming descriptive lyrics, which give
the mouse a considerable depth of character:

Smile your little smile—take some tea with me awhile.
Brush away that black cloud from your shoulder.
Twitch your whiskers. Feel that you're really real.
Another tea time—another day older.
Puff warm breath on your tiny hands.
You wish you were a man
who every day can turn another page.
Behind your glass you sit and look
at my ever-open book—
One brown mouse sitting in a cage.

The album's feline menace, insect self-destruction and rodent charm
is followed by powerful equine dignity on the title track, which Anderson referred to in a humorous vein:

I suppose it's almost an equestrian *Aqualung* in a way. Once powerful and majestic creatures find themselves on the scrap heap, forgotten by
society and replaced by machines. I'm not particularly obsessed by the
animals, and it's not intended as a heartfelt campaign to bring them back
into service, but I do have a soft spot for horses.[168]

At Anderson's request, Barre wrote the music for the pseudo-symphonic
midsection of "Heavy Horses," which features some of the most breath-

taking playing of his career (a feat he was able to duplicate during countless concerts).

Perhaps the greatest of the Tull "epics," it unfolds in a series of movements—much like lengthy pieces on *Aqualung, Minstrel in the Gallery* and
Songs from the Wood (and, of course, *Thick as a Brick* and *A Passion Play*)—
but with a seamless grace that often eludes earlier songs. The introduction features Barre playing an emotive, somewhat mournful melody that
seems to call out to the horses in the field, but melancholia eventually
segues into a more merry ambiance as the rest of the band joins in. The
verses, featuring vocals, Evans' lightsome piano and a striking Palmer violin arrangement, are among Anderson's most beautiful, both musically
and lyrically:

> Iron-clad feather-feet pounding the dust
> An October's day, toward evening
> Sweat embossed veins standing proud to the plough
> Salt on a deep chest seasoning
> Last of the line at an honest day's toil
> Turning the deep sod under
> Flint at the fetlock, chasing the bone
> Flies at the nostrils plunder.
>
> The Suffolk, the Clydesdale, the Percheron vie
> with the Shire on his feathers floating
> Hauling soft timber into the dusk
> to bed on a warm straw coating.

After the listener is lulled by the pastoral nature of the verse, the chorus raises the song to a trot, first offering optimism and then bringing it
down to cold reality:

> Heavy horses, move the land under me
> Behind the plow gliding—slipping and sliding free
> Now you're down to the few
> and there's no work to do
> The tractor's on its way.

The driving bridge section cowritten by Barre brings the heavy horses back
to the fore as Barlow offers an even more impressive variation on his "galloping" bass drum technique first used on *Songs from the Wood*'s "Hunting Girl." Here, and again during a reprise near the end, Anderson includes
one of his most impressive stanzas, loaded with visual imagery:

Bring me a wheel of oaken wood
A rein of polished leather
A heavy horse and a tumbling sky
Brewing heavy weather.

Anderson included the following dedication on the album's back cover, mentioning not only the plow horses, but also his cats, wife and infant son:

> This album is dedicated to: The Highland, Welsh Mountain, Shetland, Fell, Dales, Cleveland and the other indigenous working ponies of Great Britain who, however tiny or great in stature, can truly count themselves as being amongst our HEAVY HORSES; also, Lupus, Fur, Tigger and Mistletoe—and of course, Shona and young Master James.

Harking back to *Songs from the Wood*, *Heavy Horses* closes with a comforting, Scottish-influenced ballad, "Weathercock," in which an actual personality is bestowed upon the iron icon that proves beneficial to the rural inhabitant. Opening in Celtic folk mode with acoustic guitar, portative organ and Anderson's vocal melody doubled by mandolin, this lovely song, which brackets another Scottish march with two heavier sections featuring Barre on lead guitar, lends an upbeat end to the album:

Good morning weathercock: make this day bright.
Put us in touch with your fair winds.
Sing to us softly, hum evening's song.
Point the way to better days we can share with you.

The album helped bring Tull back into the good graces of *Rolling Stone*. In his September 21, 1978, review, Michael Bloom amazingly proved that it was the folk element that accomplished the feat:

> Tull restrains its tonality to basic chord changes and folk-song melodies. But the rhythms are lavish—particularly the instrumental arrangements, where no two players are allowed the same part.... *Heavy Horses* is merely the follow-up to last year's *Songs from the Wood*, which may well have been the group's best record ever. Anderson warns that this is the end of the folk-tinged Tull, that the band will return to boogie forthwith. That's a pity because this genre has suited Jethro Tull wonderfully.[169]

"Moths" was released as a single in Britain, but failed to make a dent in the charts. Originally scheduled to be backed with a track called

"Beltane," which was cut from the album, it ultimately was released with the seven-years-older "Life Is a Long Song" on the B-side. ("Beltane" remained on the shelf until the release of the *20 Years* box set 10 years later.)

"Beltane" would have fit nicely onto the album, along with the Isle of Skye–inspired "Broadford Bazaar" and the sprightly folk song "Living in These Hard Times," which also were deleted (the latter was included on the *20 Years* box, but the former was held out for *Nightcap*, a two-CD collection released in the U.K. in 1993). Another example of Anderson's joyous music-critical lyrics counterpoint, "Hard Times" deals with the special-interest nature of modern politicians who are unwilling to help the unemployed man who resorts to begging when his family is starving. At the time of the album's release, he recently had purchased his salmon farm:

> I have invested my capital so that it creates jobs for people.... I am only involved in a particular corner of the world, and that is Scotland. I am a Scot, born in Dunfermline and lived 'til I was twelve in Edinburgh. My interests lie north of the border. I have experimental contacts with the Scottish Nationalist Party ... today I am responsible for three cities [townships], two churches, a post office, and many people living in the limits of poverty. I want to create a local growing community that is not dependent merely on tourism.... I just hope that I can create enough wealth so that people don't have to leave the island. I would rather leave behind such an achievement than all the records I have made. I would rather be remembered for my accomplishments in employing people than as the Ian Anderson of Jethro Tull.[170]

Of the punk movement's reaction against progressive rock music, he said:

> If you have useable brains and a pair of ears, you refine both in relation to what you want to listen to and what you compose. It is unavoidable. People tending towards punk and new wave may say that the minute you begin to refine you lose your touch for the heart of music, raw enthusiasm and sincerity, but that it not always the case. I'd still rather listen to music that is sincere and inspired, be it that it would be played more badly than a bad Italian symphony, but I demand that it is also individual and original, not just an imitation of the Rolling Stones or the Who. Good singing and meaningful lyrics are also needed, in my opinion, rather than repeating old phrases and dull slang words borrowed from the States.
>
> However naive music may be, there is always some degree of refinement, and the Sex Pistols, Generation X, the Clash, et cetera, are of

the lowest degree, some sort of primitive reaction by man with a guitar in his hand. People have confused ideas of this music being some kind of ground form. That it is not: it is a pile of old tricks and clichés badly played.[171]

On another occasion, he added:

> [I]t's a shame that the punk rock thing is so laden with the fact that it's very derivative musically of things that you and I are familiar with—the rock, the riffs, the beat. We've all heard and experienced it probably twice already. Punk rock is just another time for the same old tried and tested elementary rock riff, same old electric guitar, same old drum kit set up the same old way. And it's so class-ridden, "the music of the working class." The great thing when I came in was that it was classless. It was great back then. People did cross the borders of style and class. But the punk thing is a working class thing and so you only get someone hyphen something following punk out of a terrible mixed-up rebellious thing.[172]

When queried about changing his persona from the *Aqualung*-ish tramp to that of the English country squire, he responded:

> I had a number one record and I still lived in a three pound a week bedsit and it was obviously not right anymore. I wasn't kidding anyone and it would be silly for me to do that now. I like my dogs and cats and horses and my house and the things that I have, that I've worked really hard for. These are the things I enjoy. They're not things I own—I don't believe in ownership of these things—they're things that I've somehow paid in hard cash for the right to enjoy. And I do enjoy them. They mean an awful lot to me.... I try to write songs that aren't too different from the way I live and so my songs have necessarily had to change, as I've grown away from having a working group sort of life. As the logic of success prevailed we made a commitment to going first class in the world and then it suddenly dawned that it's not on to sing as if we're sitting down there. We're not anymore. We're sitting up here. And we can't really sing about sitting up here because that's irrelevant to most people and sounds a bit cocky, so it became a little more abstract. Lyrically things became more abstract and started taking on weird and weighty connotations, which were amusing for a bit, amused me, but after a while you want to get back to the direct meaningful songs that are about something and actually deal in fairly accessible English. You're forced to think what is there to write about, what moves me, and that's what I write about now, whatever it is that's left.[173]

The *Heavy Horses* Tour

"Rover" received a fair amount of airplay on U.S. radio stations, and a promotional video of "Heavy Horses" was included on the popular late-night show *The Midnight Special*, which featured both live and taped performances. From May 1 to June 6, the band played 28 shows in Britain and Europe, several of which were recorded for an intended live album, the first ever produced by Tull.

While on the road, John Glascock began to feel ill. "We used to share the same dressing room," Barrie Barlow recalled, "and he sat down one night with his hand on his chest, complaining of heartburn."[174] However, when the problem persisted throughout the remainder of the tour and after they returned to Britain, Glascock's girlfriend, Jackie, had him rushed to the hospital, where he underwent open-heart surgery. An untreated tooth infection had spread into his bloodstream, damaging a weak heart valve, a condition he had inherited from his father, Walter, who died when John and his brother, Brian, were teenagers.

Live: Bursting Out

22 September 1978 (U.K.) / 29 September 1978 (U.S.)
Highest chart position: 17 (U.K.) / 21 (U.S.)
[Rating: 4.5]
Producer: Ian Anderson / Chrysalis CTJ4
All songs written by Ian Anderson (except where indicated)

Ian Anderson: vocals, flute, acoustic guitar
Martin Barre: electric guitar, mandolin, marimba
John Glascock: bass guitar, electric guitar, vocals
John Evans: piano, Hammond organ, accordion, synthesizers
David Palmer: portative organ, synthesizers
Barrie Barlow: drums, glockenspiel

Recorded "somewhere in Europe" with the Maison Rouge Mobile Studio, summer 1978
Recording engineers: Robin Black, Christopher Amson and Pavel Kubes
Photography by Brian Cooke and Ruan O'Lochlainn
Sleeve design by Ramey Communications

Tracks: No Lullaby
Sweet Dream

Skating Away
Jack in the Green
One Brown Mouse
A New Day Yesterday
Flute Solo Improvisation/God Rest Ye Merry Gentlemen (trad.)/
    Bourée (J. S. Bach)
Songs from the Wood
Thick as a Brick
Hunting Girl
Too Old to Rock 'n' Roll: Too Young to Die
Conundrum (Barre)
Minstrel in the Gallery
Cross-Eyed Mary
Quatrain (Barre)
Aqualung
Locomotive Breath
The Dambuster's March (Eric Coates)

Compiled from three European shows during the *Heavy Horses* tour, *Bursting Out*, a commemoration of Tull's 10-year anniversary, was the first full-length live album the band released. Having given the band such a positive review for *Heavy Horses*, *Rolling Stone*'s Michael Bloom became decidedly mixed about the new offering:

> Jethro Tull's double live album is almost too perfect. *Bursting Out* can't be faulted on any of the usual live-record stumbling blocks: the performances exemplify Tull's technical mastery and omnipresent energy, the track selection runs the stylistic gamut and provides a quick academic history of everything the group's ever been about.... Of Jethro Tull's fourteen previous records ... only three aren't represented here. There are five title tracks. These guys even reach back nine years to *Stand Up* for a hoary old blues, "A New Day Yesterday." Other characteristic Tull sounds include folksy strumming ("Jack in the Green"), precise orchestration ("Thick as a Brick"), crunching guitar fireworks (Martin Barre's interlude in "Minstrel in the Gallery") and such ancient beer-blast standbys as "Aqualung" and "Locomotive Breath." One could quibble about the choice of material ... but it's a program notable for its balance.... So what's wrong with it? In a word, familiarity. The Jethro Tull concept of progressive professionalism precludes a lot of spontaneity.[175]

Since when is a nine-year-old song "hoary" and a seven-year-old one "ancient?" Bloom's remarks indicate his (and perhaps *Rolling Stone*'s) bias that all rock music has to be youthful (therefore quickly disposable). (When

Ian Anderson, sporting natty tartan vest and leather boots, in concert, 1978. (Photograph courtesy of Ian Anderson.)

Bursting Out was released in October 1978, the oldest member of Tull, Martin Barre, was just reaching the hoary, ancient age of 32.)

The Tracks of *Bursting Out*

After the band is introduced, Barre and Anderson launch into a driving introduction; joined by Glascock and Barlow, they soon segue into a meticulously performed "No Lullaby." As on the entire album, Barre's playing is a thing of wonder, as he recreates all his rhythm, riff and melodic lead parts simultaneously. After his final bluesy strain fades, he then lashes into a version of "Sweet Dream" considerably heavier than the *Living in the Past* original. David Palmer's portative-organ dominated instrumental break is particularly effective.

"Skating Away," featuring Barre on marimba and Glascock on electric guitar, is a folksy treat, as is "Jack in the Green," featuring Palmer on organ and Barre switching from mandolin to electric guitar. Announced as "the last of the acoustic songs for the time being" (with Anderson acknowledging his debt to Robert Burns), "One Brown Mouse" rocks a bit more than its *Heavy Horses* ancestor. When the crowd fails to display much enthusiasm during his introduction, he quips, "Well, that's good enough. Don't strain yourselves."

Referring to it as "a very old song," Anderson describes "A New Day Yesterday" as the only number they do "in a blues tempo ... not surprising." Vastly rearranged from its original *Stand Up* simplicity, it features an extended instrumental section allowing Barre to flex his fretwork before Anderson leaps in with his bizarre "Flute Solo Improvisation" incorporating "God Rest Ye Merry Gentlemen" and "Bourée." An abbreviated "Songs from the Wood" is then followed by a 12-minute *Thick as a Brick* suite. "Now then, let's see if we can spot the over twenty-fives in the audience. See if you remember this one," Anderson announces prior to strumming the first famous chords of the song, which includes the "Poet and the Painter" passage, after which Barre pours forth a blazing solo. Played with mind-boggling expertise, it is the finest live recording of material from *Brick*.

The second LP of the original vinyl set opens with "Hunting Girl." During the introduction, when Anderson speaks of "laying to rest any rumors that John Glascock is a kinky bastard who likes to be thrashed severely across the bum," an electronic "beep" censors the "offending" word. "Too Old to Rock 'n' Roll" also receives an annoying censor's beep, when Anderson mentions the music critics "back in old Blighty" who assumed the song referred to his own musical decrepitude. "Conundrum," an instrumental workout written by Barre and giving Barlow his obligatory drum solo, is followed by Palmer's portative organ introduction to "Minstrel in the Gallery," which is somewhat shorn of its original Barre-dominated opening.

Bursting Out closes with three classic songs from *Aqualung*, broken only by the inclusion of the Barre instrumental "Quatrain." Anderson absurdly opens "Cross-Eyed Mary" by playing "Pop Goes the Weasel" on his flute. "Quatrain" then leads to the familiar encore of "Aqualung" and "Locomotive Breath," on which John Evans' piano introduction is quite jazzy and laid-back until Barre joins in with his stinging blues soloing, culminating with a classical-rock arrangement of Eric Coates' patriotic piece "The Dambuster's March," allowing Barre to demonstrate his prowess for playing melodic anthems. (While the U.S. CD release of *Bursting Out* was limited to one disc, which lopped off "Sweet Dream," "Conundrum," "Quatrain" and most of Anderson's stage banter, the entire double LP set was issued as a two-CD package in the U.K.)

The live version of "Sweet Dream" became the B-side of a single, a new studio track called "A Stitch in Time," on which Anderson also played bass.

The *Bursting Out* Tour

To support the live album, Tull booked an October 1–November 17 East to West Coast trek across the U.S., with two Canadian dates worked in. But before the band could play the dates, including three Madison Square Garden shows, one of which would become the world's first transatlantic concert broadcast via satellite, a new bass player had to be recruited. Barlow rushed off to Blackpool to collect his "geezer" Tony Williams "and taught him all the bass parts—because I knew them all."[176] Williams elaborated:

> Barrie ... said, "I've been waiting five years to give you this call. Do you want the Tull gig?" I said, "No, I can't handle it! Not playing bass. There's no way I can do that." He just said, "Yes, of course you can," and that was it. He had a cottage near Blackpool and we spent every available moment going through, literally, the show. He'd worked out what we'd be doing on stage, and Martin remixed some of the tracks and brought the bass track right up, in fact over the top, so that all you could hear was the bass track, with no association with the tunes at all. So I literally learned everything parrot fashion ... with Tull, there's no element of improvisation through any of the set.[177]

For two months, they rehearsed on a soundstage at Pinewood Studios outside London, where Anderson demonstrated one aspect of his attraction to fish. Williams recalled:

> Ian called a halt and said, "Let's get some grub in." And Barrie started nudging me and whispering, "Watch, watch—seafood!" And sure enough, Ian asks for some mussels and cockles and so on. Barrie just said, "Wait!" The thing is, Ian loves the stuff, but he goes green. And when he'd eaten it he had to go and lie down on some packing cases! But he can't stop eating the stuff. We went to a Japanese restaurant in San Francisco, and I was sliding my sushi across to him, and he was really digging into it—but he's actually allergic to it. That's why I thought it was so ironic that he went out and bought a salmon farm![178]

Following the Madison Square Garden shows, *Rolling Stone*'s John Swenson wrote:

> With a meticulously paced set that completely did away with the excessive self-indulgence and pretense that has cost the group so much (especially critical support) over the past few years, Jethro Tull made a strong comeback during its three-night stand at Madison Square

Garden.... Anderson's singing, histrionic stage antics and flute playing have become neatly stylized: in an apparent effort to pace himself, he strikes much less of the abandoned-wildman posture of his earlier years. "One Brown Mouse" and "Heavy Horses" ... came across well, the latter mainly because of Martin Barre's guitar playing.[179]

In 1978, Anderson also was commissioned by the Royal Scottish Ballet to compose music for a future production. Encouraged by his brother, Robin Anderson, who was administrator of the ballet, he asked David Palmer and Martin Barre for assistance, and the former set to work in earnest, recognizing it as a great opportunity to exercise his compositional talent. Although Anderson wrote a major theme and several key pieces, Palmer became the mastermind, working closely with choreographer Robert North to create the ballet sequences. Eventually completing a one-hour score titled "The Water's Edge," Palmer ultimately was frustrated by the whole affair. He recalled:

> [W]e had a press conference in London to launch the ballet. I walked into the room, which was full of the leading London ballet critics and so on, and I picked up one of the handbills on the table. It announced, "*The Water's Edge*—a ballet written by Ian Anderson." I walked out. Maybe it was petulant, but I think it was merited.... I was distressed, having worked so hard on it. Ian apologized for the error, but it should never have happened.[180]

Though the ballet was performed only a few times (at Glasgow's Theatre Royal on March 7–24, 1979; at Edinburgh's Kings Theatre on April 3–14; and for a handful of dates in Aberdeen, Inverness, Liverpool and London), Anderson was very displeased:

> [I]t was awful, hideous! The Scottish Ballet Orchestra, as with all ballet orchestras, were not very good.... They did struggle very badly with it and it was embarrassing. There were bits in it, time signatures and things, and they just could not cope with it at all.... *Swan Lake* for the thousandth time is fine, but to run through something completely new just once or twice before you have to play it live to an audience is likely to result in a mess. And it was a mess....[181]

Titled *Underground Rumours*, this three-part work consisting of "Unsprung" written by Jon Anderson of the progressive rock band Yes, "The Water's Edge" and Duke Ellington's "Such Sweet Thunder" was intended to depict traditional Scottish lore and legends. Two pieces from "The Water's Edge"—"Kelpie" and "Elegy"—eventually were rearranged and recorded by Tull.

Stormwatch

14 September 1979 (U.K. and U.S.)
Highest chart position: 27 (U.K.) / 22 (U.S.)
[Rating: 4.5]
Producer: Ian Anderson / Chrysalis CDL 1238
All songs written by Ian Anderson (except where indicated)

Ian Anderson: vocals, flute, acoustic guitar, bass guitar
Martin Barre: electric and classical guitars, mandolin
John Evans: piano, Hammond organ, synthesizers
David Palmer: sythesizers, portative organ, string arrangements
Barrie Barlow: drums and percussion
John Glascock: bass guitar
Francis Wilson: narration on "Dun Ringill"

Recorded at Maison Rouge Studios, Fulham, London, and with the Maison
    Rouge Mobile Studio, Isle of Skye, Scotland, spring-summer 1979
Recording engineers: Robin Black and Leigh Mantle
Cover concept by Ian Anderson
Art direction by Peter Wagg
Cover painting by David Jackson

Tracks: North Sea Oil
        Orion
        Home
        Dark Ages
        Warm Sporran
        Something's on the Move
        Old Ghosts
        Dun Ringill
        Flying Dutchman
        Elegy (Palmer)

Following the operation to replace his weak heart valve, John Glascock's health had improved enough for him to return for a brief North
American tour in April 1979, before the band prepared to record the next
studio album. The tour ended in San Antonio on May 1, the third anniversary of Glascock's first Tull gig.

The BBC filmed portions of two concerts—Seattle on April 10 and
Portland on April 12—for inclusion in a major one-hour television program on Tull to be aired on BBC2's *Arena* the following January. Over
the ensuing months, the band members were interviewed and Anderson

also was filmed at work on both his Buckinghamshire and Strathaird estates. Songs featured in the show were "My God," "Thick as a Brick," "Heavy Horses," "The Water's Edge," "Sweet Dream" and an ever-developing "Dark Ages," which can be heard during a studio rehearsal and on stage, including a verse that was dropped before the final version was recorded.

Back in Britain, Anderson prepared to write the new material:

> Being at home again I was probably reading more newspapers, reading more magazines, watching current affairs and became more interested in things around me—even the weather, because of my involvements with farming and fish farming. So I think some of the ideas for songs came from these sources. There is a foreboding about the album, there is a kind of slightly threatening feel to it, but it's not a bleak, cold record. Even things like "North Sea Oil" have got a bit of a bounce about them. They're not meant to be taken as serious political statements, they're just wry or cynical, but not negative or complaining, I hope![182]

When the recording sessions began during the late spring, Glascock made the trip to Maison Rouge, but poor blood circulation left him fatigued and unable to play as he once had. He only performed on three of the album's tracks, "Orion," "Flying Dutchman" and "Elegy," so Anderson chose to play bass on those remaining:

> I'm not particularly proud of my bass playing—if I'd been auditioned for the part I wouldn't have got it. On the other hand, I don't think it would have been any better if we'd got in a session player and said to him, "This is the music, these are the chords." It would have been weird crediting some faceless person that would never play with us again. I actually enjoyed the experience very much, playing on an intimate basis with Barrie Barlow and Martin Barre. The drummer, bass player and guitarist have a close musical relationship. Normally I'm way out front, my flute lines are twittery things way above everything else, and acoustic guitar is so quiet. It was like meeting two people you know very well on a completely different footing. It certainly adds a new dimension to the group—it produced a rhythm section which had its life line—a risky rhythm section, but I think it worked. It's tight and punchy.[183]

Anderson recorded some of the album's prettier bits, including acoustic guitar and flute work, at a small studio he had set up at his home in Scotland.

The Tracks of *Stormwatch*

"North Sea Oil" is Anderson's statement about the precariousness of intensive offshore petroleum drilling; but late in the song he sings, "Before we all are nuclear—the better way! Oh, let us pray, we'll want to stay in North Sea Oil," lyrically reinforcing the image on the album's back cover, which depicts an enormous polar bear stomping an atomic reactor into the tundra. As he has said, the song does have a "bouncy" feel, jigging along, though its message is a distinctly pragmatic one.

Like "Aqualung," "Orion" inverts the familiar Tull structure, beginning in a heavy rock mode and then settling down into a quieter, acoustic verse during which Anderson asks for guidance from the familiar constellation featuring the hunter and his faithful dog. Martin Barre's threatening electric guitar work is offset by a superb David Palmer string arrangement (one of several he would contribute to this, his final Tull album).

One of Anderson's favorite songs, "Home," like "Fire at Midnight" on *Songs from the Wood*, is like a warm blaze at the hearth, featuring a beautiful melody, arrangement and perhaps Barre's finest "symphonic" harmony guitar work. Yet another of Anderson's pieces obviously influenced by Beethoven, "Dark Ages" is one of the most classically oriented Tull performances, perhaps even more cohesive than "Heavy Horses." Paralleling modern society with medieval feudalism, the song, though it too prominently stresses Anderson's bass playing in the mix, features sterling performances from all the band members, particularly Barre and Barrie Barlow, who executes some of the most astounding snare drum rolls in the history of rock.

The march "Warm Sporran" finishes the album's first half, an instrumental tune that segues from a traditional Scottish style to John Evans' synthesizer and Anderson's fluttering flute and back again. The second half of *Stormwatch* (side B of the original LP) ranks among the very best of Tull, opening with the hard driving, Martin Barre–led "Something's on the Move"—which features one of the guitarist's most inspired solos—and moving on to the atmospheric "Old Ghosts," an ominous acoustic-based song dealing with mysterious Celtic standing stones.

A favorite of Tull fans, the acoustic, traditional-style "Dun Ringill" is a tribute to a remote locale on the coast of Skye once inhabited by Clan MacKinnon. Near Loch Slapin, the 900-year-old ruin of Castle Ringill was then part of Anderson's estate, evoking in him an ancient tale of a romantic rendezvous. The second verse, referring to the album's title, is a lyrical masterpiece that evokes the work of the great Scottish poets:

We'll wait in stone circles
'til the force comes through—
lines join in faint discord
and the stormwatch brews
a concert of kings
as the white sea snaps
at the heels of a soft prayer
whispered.

Inspired in part by the plight of the Vietnamese boat people, the operatic "Flying Dutchman," in which the band expertly blends nearly every genre in their musical repertoire (folk, blues, classical and rock), brilliantly uses the tale of the ship forced to sail against the wind until Judgment Day as a metaphor for our own haphazard existences. Of this song, Craig Thomas has written, "This is the dance band on the *Titanic*, playing louder and more insistently to quieten the future."[184] The stark nature of Anderson's lyrics—"Death grinning like a scarecrow—Flying Dutchman"—is musically matched by his passionate, bluesy flute playing.

The album ends with the beautiful David Palmer tune "Elegy," a tribute to his deceased father, which features portative organ, flute, mandolin and further brilliantly expressive electric soloing by Barre. Three additional tracks, "Kelpie," a sprightly rock jig weaving the tale of a legendary Scottish loch monster, "Crossword" and an untitled blues instrumental, were recorded but not included on the album. (Although none of the songs were released until their inclusion in the *20 Years* set, Anderson would use the "Kelpie" melody in live instrumentals.)

The *Stormwatch* Tour

The maritime motif of the album also was used for the tour, which included a rigged stage replete with ratlines, sailors' rain slickers and Anderson prancing about the stage with a pirate's cutlass. Having replaced the critically ill Glascock, Dave Pegg, having learned an incredibly complex set list in only two weeks, was attired in a less flamboyant deerstalker cap, paying close attention to his bassist duties. (Anderson's first choice to fill Glascock's role was old mate Jeffrey Hammond, who, after running through some old songs with the band, decided he wanted to remain a solitary painter.) Barrie Barlow, who recently had seen Fairport Convention's "Farewell Concert" on television, claimed that enlisting "Peggy" was his idea:

Ian wanted to get this guy who had been at Harvard Music Academy or something in Boston; a sort of pseudo-funk player. He was a very good player but he wasn't the right guy for Tull, and I was quite surprised that Ian wanted him. So I said, "Look, Richard Thompson is playing at the Hexagon. I'm gonna go and check Dave Pegg out." So I went there and I thought Peggy would be absolutely ideal, so I got Peggy down here [to London] and he got the gig. And he was great ... learned it all quickly and so on ... a very nice man, a great player.[185]

After hiring Pegg, Anderson said:

[H]e fits in so well, same sort of personality and sense of humor as the rest of the group, same sort of background and age—old! He's also not much taller than the shortest member of the group—so we shouldn't intimidate him too much. He also has a musical tradition which is not too dissimilar from our own—he's played everything from commercial jingles to ethnic folk. He has a broad background of Britishness in his music which suits Jethro Tull.[186]

Having inherited musical talent and interest from his banjo-playing grandfather and his vocalizing father, Albert Pegg, Dave was exposed to traditional English sounds at a young age, and his later interest in local R&B and rock 'n' roll bands such as the Spencer Davis Group (fronted by one of Pegg's favorite singers, fellow Birminghamian Steve Winwood) aided him in developing the style that eventually would gain him notoriety as folk-rock's greatest bassist. (Another of his vocal heros is American folk-pop legend James Taylor.) Prior to joining Tull, he played with the Uglies (supporting future Led Zeppelin stars Robert Plant and John Bonham) and the Ian Campbell Folk Group, wherein he learned scores of traditional tunes. After mastering the acoustic double bass and the mandolin, he joined Fairport Convention in 1969, after group founder Ashley Hutchings left to form another pioneering rock band, Steeleye Span. Over the next ten years, Pegg and his various bandmates (including Richard Thompson, Simon Nicol, Sandy Denny, Dave Swarbrick, David Mattacks and many others) experienced uneven success, and when the band folded in 1979 (due in part to Swarbrick's hearing loss), he was available for the Tull gig.

Ironically, Pegg first was puzzled by an offer from Ian Anderson:

My wife, Chris, had had several calls from Ian Anderson, and we didn't put two and two together. We thought it was a different Ian Anderson, the guy who writes *Folk Roots* magazine in England. We didn't think it was Ian Anderson from Jethro Tull, so I hadn't answered the phone on the occasions or hadn't called back ... because I had just thought it was for some sessions through Ian *A.* Anderson. So I was very pleased when I got the call. And, apparently, Barrie Barlow ... had seen Fairport on television, in those heady days when Fairport used to get on the TV. And Barrie had ... thought I played OK—and the combination of that and the fact that Jo Lustig and Bernard Docherty, who did some PR for Jethro Tull, also knew of Fairport and knew of myself, because Jo used to manage Fairport some years previously ... so they put in a good word for me as well, I think.

And I was asked to go along to Maison Rouge Studio in Fulham Road to meet the guys in the band. I was very excited and a bit nervous about it, actually. But off I went to Fulham Road. It was a fabulous studio and I was very impressed. And Ian and Martin and Barriemore Barlow were there. Not the other guys in the band ... David Palmer and John Evans weren't there.... And they seemed like very nice chaps, and they just asked me a few questions ... and the next thing that happened was I had to go up to Pophleys, a house and farm in Buckinghamshire, which Ian used to own ... in between London and where I lived in Cropredy, in Oxfordshire.

So it was quite convenient. It was only about forty-three miles away from Cropredy.... So I had to do this audition. Ian was in and out of the audition.... He'd come in and write a few chord sequences down. It was all ... new stuff. It wasn't any established Tull stuff.... And we'd all play them and that was it. And we did that for two or three hours, and then we went to the pub for lunch.... Ian didn't come to the pub for lunch, but Martin and Barrie ... were very sociable people.

And the next thing I knew was that I'd got the job and could I do an American tour which started in about two weeks' time ... which meant that I had to frantically cram all this Jethro Tull music. There wasn't a set list ... at the time....[187]

At that point, Anderson asked Pegg again to join him at his country home, where they convened in the dining room. According to Pegg, he said, "You may not see much of me. It's ... a seven-week tour, and I'm very busy. I have to do interviews ... and we're a bit of a strange band. It won't be like Fairport ... because we tend not to socialize too much with each other. We're definitely not a party band. Can you cope with all this? You may not see too much of me, but good luck with it."[188]

Pegg recalled:

So I said, "Fine, OK," and he gave me the gig and arranged for me to receive some money for the tour ... which to me was an awful lot of dosh at the time, which wasn't really in terms of Jethro Tull, I found out at a later date! But that's not to say that I wasn't looked after eventually, by Ian and Martin, because they always looked after me financially. It was just for this first tour, I was paid a wage and per diem. It was quite a long tour, but I really enjoyed it and I was very pleased to be offered the gig....[189]

Anderson also told him about relationships with the other band members and how he should react to their behavior:

He went through the other guys ... he said, "Don't pay any attention to what they think. You have to form your own opinions"—which I would have done, anyway. But it was strange, because he gave me these pocket analyses of ... the other people's opinion of *him*—and they were all incredibly accurate, I later found out ... what he thought they thought of him was actually very true.[190]

To prepare for the *Stormwatch* tour, Pegg had to practice relentlessly:

I went on holiday to my good friend Ralph McTell's cottage in Cornwall for a couple of weeks, and swatted and swatted all this stuff. Some of it was very strange music to me. And there were things like odd time signatures which were quite *baffling*—and when we started rehearsing, Martin Barre was very, very helpful to me. And I went and stayed at Martin's house. He lived near Henley-on-Thames at the time, and Martin was really good, and he ... simplified these things for me. And Martin was from Birmingham, so I instantly got on well with him. I didn't feel out of place with Martin![191]

In Jacksonville, Florida, on October 2, 1979, the U.S. leg of the *Stormwatch* tour opened with a host of material from the new album: "Dark Ages," "Home," "Orion," "Dun Ringill," "Something's on the Move" and "Elegy." At Omaha, Nebraska's Civic Auditorium on November 9, Anderson, wearing a pair of dark sunglasses to protect an eye that recently had been pricked by a red rose tossed at him by an over-enthusiastic fan at Madison Square Garden, was at his peak, flawlessly playing a silver concert flute and tossing another, cheaper one into the air and catching it behind his back.

"Songs from the Wood" and "Heavy Horses" were revelatory performed live, and a true instrumental highlight was "Pastime with Good Company," an Elizabethan tune attributed to the pen of a certain Tudor king. "If Henry VIII had had a rock 'n' roll band, it would have sounded like this," announced David Palmer as the band rollicked into one of the most incredible performances ever heard by a rock audience. (The band, including Pegg on bass, also recorded the number, arranged by Palmer as

"King Henry's Madrigal," for release on a U.K.-only EP, which also included "Home" and "Warm Sporran" from *Stormwatch*, and "Ring Out, Solstice Bells." [U.S. fans would not have the chance to hear the track until the release of the *20 Years* box.])

Another instrumental, showcasing Pegg's instrumental prowess, was "Jams O'Donnell's Jigs," a mandolin piece he had written for Fairport Convention. He later revealed,

> I had never played at those huge stadium venues before, and it was a very invigorating experience for me. It also gave me a big kick up the arse musically, because with Fairport, we'd been doing our own thing all the time. We were a very undisciplined band, really. And this was going from a bunch of mates who liked getting together and having a few drinks and playing music, to a band where everything was worked out in advance and was run like an army operation. And you had to be very conscientious and you had to be on the ball all the time. Otherwise, you felt you were letting the side down.[192]

Pegg also remembered the attire the band was required to wear during the tour:

> We'd been measured up for these ... cozzies that we were going to wear ... which was all very professional, I thought. Nobody knew what they really were going to get—we'd just seen some kind of designs. Anyway, it was about 2:30 on the afternoon of the first show, they'd turned up in these boxes, like six boxes that had arrived. It was like a scene from *Help!* the Beatles movie. I remember ... it was a big hotel, a big posh hotel. We all had adjacent rooms, and word had it that the clothes had arrived, and these boxes were all delivered ... there was a knock on the door, and I stuck my head out the door—there was a cardboard box—and I looked down the corridor, and there were five other people grabbing their cardboard boxes and rapidly opening them up and putting their outfits on. I must confess that I put mine on, and I looked in the mirror and I nearly cried, because it was *dreadful*, a towel kind of outfit. It was like toweling, yellow toweling. It was painted with ... green dabs all over ... I looked absolutely ridiculous in it. And I thought, "This is some kind of joke. They've wound me up to be laughed at".... But when I stuck my head 'round the door, *everybody's* outfit was really, really ridiculous. We all looked, well, stupid, to put it mildly. And we all pissed ourselves laughing. The only person that did look really good was Barrie Barlow ... who'd got ... blue shorts and ... this see-through ... pale blue top with a zip down the front. And he looked really good, because he used to wear shorts to play the drums....

And I said, "Barrie, you look great ... you look fine. You're the only one that's come out of it okay."

And he went, "Well, it's fine when I stand up, but when I sit down...." and the whole top ... stuck out, and he looked like he'd got a sixty-five-inch stomach! You know, he looked *ridiculous*.

Anyway ... we had to wear them the first night, and I got through the gig okay. I think I was absolutely terrified. We met up in the hotel bar afterwards, and Ian presented me with a pipe, which I still have to this day. It was a very nice thought, and I was made to feel very welcome. I didn't see very much of Ian. I got to know the other chaps quite well during the tour.

It was quite strange, because ... there would be a fight to avoid getting in the car with Ian. And it wasn't just because of what was ... non-stop pipe smoking at the time. There was a general avoidance. There were always two limousines. Often he and David Palmer, who also smoked a pipe, would get in the first one. The rest of us would get in the second one.

And nobody ever went to the bar at the end of the night, unlike the Fairports. At the end of gigs we would socialize quite heavily. But I did try and persuade Jethro Tull to become more friendly towards each other, and we did finish up in the bar as the tour progressed, on several occasions—although I must confess, it was often me that was buying the drinks!... They didn't tend to put their hands in their pockets very often, to put it mildly. But it was a great tour....[193]

When the U.S. leg of the *Stormwatch* tour ended in California in mid–November, Barrie Barlow phoned John Glascock, proposing that they start their own band:

[H]e was absolutely elated. So I called David Allen [from Carmen] and he was up for it. I met him, we had lunch. He had booked his flight that very day. And the next day John died! And ... we had one more gig to do, and I didn't want to do it, but the management bludgeoned me into doing it ... and I cried all the way through the gig.[194]

By this time, Glascock's heart had rejected the new valve and he passed away very suddenly on November 17. No one had been prepared for it.

During March and April 1980, Barlow agreed to play one last set of dates, to support *Stormwatch* in Europe, before forming his own band, which he hoped would be picked up by Chrysalis. Following the final Hammersmith Odeon gig on April 14, they played completely acoustic renditions of "Heavy Horses," "Dun Ringill" and "Peggy's Pub" on a Capital radio show hosted by Barlow's friend Richard Digance, who had supported them on their 1978 U.K. tour. Television weatherman Francis Wilson also was on hand to reprise his spoken introduction to "Dun Ringill."

Having reached an amicable agreement with Anderson, Barrie Barlow thought all was fine until the next issue of *Melody Maker* was published. In an article on the band, the magazine reported that Anderson was presenting Barlow, Evans and Palmer with their walking papers, ending the most elaborate and musically accomplished lineup in Tull's nearly 12-year history. Palmer found out about the "firing" from his young daughter, who had been teased by her classmates on the playground, while Barlow, who "went fucking mental," recalled:

> John Evans was really shattered.... He just didn't know what to do. When you are on the road with a major band, everything is done for you, and suddenly to take that away from him ... he didn't know where to start. He came to live here [Henley on Thames] for about six months. Took his piano with him and he used to practice all day long—nearly drove us crazy![195]

Evans recounted:

> I got the news in a letter.... After the last tour it was agreed we'd have a decent break rather than the usual few weeks, to give us a chance to go off and do our own thing for a while.... Then in July I got a letter—it was a carbon copy from a typewriter. It said, "Dear Barrie, David and John. I'm sorry this is so rushed, but basically *Melody Maker* is coming out tomorrow and the story in it—which I couldn't prevent, I didn't want it in but Terry Ellis put it in without my knowledge—is that the group has split up. Really, I'm going to do something on my own, maybe called Jethro Tull, maybe not. But I am using different people and I thought I ought to let you know." I can't remember if Ian had signed it or if that was a bloody carbon copy as well.[196]

Of his own musical contributions to the band, Barrie Barlow admitted:

> I think I played far too much with Tull. I was too busy, got in the way of things. But having said that, for the majority of songs we didn't know what the top line was going to be.... I cringe when I hear some of the things I used to play.... But that aside, Ian has often had a go at me. He always did.... But really that is something I don't want to talk about, because I have got immense respect for Ian as a musician, but I disagreed with a lot of personal things that he did. It's much too personal for me to talk about.[197]

Pegg claimed that he sometimes found Barlow "difficult," "hard to get along with" and "a pain in the ass,"[198] while Glenn Cornick recalled:

> He seemed to be very precise, but he's not the kind of drummer I particularly enjoy playing with. Clive is. Clive is a great drummer, dead solid. Not nearly as technical as Barrie, who will tell you how great he is.[199]

But Tony Williams pointed out an undeniable fact about Barlow's contribution to Jethro Tull:

> [O]ne of the amazing things about Tull at the time I was there was the tightness of the band. It was unbelievably tight. And that was down to one guy who was driving the engine, and that was Barrie with his sense of timing and the way he held things together, and the way he worked with everyone in the band. He didn't just work himself, he worked everyone in the band. All the cues came from him.[200]

A great deal of discord in the band was created by Anderson's seemingly insensitive treatment of the unfortunate Glascock. The superb bass player's name had appeared only in tiny type, beneath the others', on the back cover of *Stormwatch*; and Anderson, writing the songs and producing, as well as playing bass on most of the tracks, listed his own name in large type in each instance. Having become dear friends with Glascock, Barlow revealed:

> He couldn't do anything other than play the bass and guitar.... And he was like a shot in the arm for Tull, a marvellous player.... Jeffrey really wasn't a bass player, but he was a friend of Ian's ... Jeffrey's input was very ... "off the wall" artistically, and was very exciting, but his execution of the bass parts took a very long time.... I love Jeffrey, but with all deference to him, having a *proper* bass player ... was fantastic.... And the band improved; without a doubt, the band improved. But although he was a great bass player, Ian didn't really like him, and I think he got a really bad deal all round. And I used to get really angry on John's behalf, to see the way he was treated.[201]

In December 1997, Anderson, who respectfully had attended Glascock's funeral in solitary silence, finally responded to the inquiries about his treatment of the late musician:

> There were no bad feelings at any time between me and John Glascock. Indeed we always got along very well although it is true to say that

I did my best to discourage him from smoking, drinking and late nights following his first heart surgery, and during which time we hoped he could fulfill his ongoing activities with Jethro Tull.... He was an amiable and invariably cheerful character who never had a bad word to say about anybody and, although he liked to "party," he could always be relied upon to fulfill his professional duties as required.... But like many people in similar situations, he found it impossible to modify his lifestyle to accommodate the realities of precarious health. I rather wish that everyone around him had echoed my occasionally stiff and warning tones instead of actively encouraging him in his return to late night party life with the usual attendant health risking social activities.[202]

David Palmer viewed his own departure from Tull as a mixed blessing, but one that advanced his career as a serious composer, arranger and conductor:

[W]hen I left, it was necessary ... if I was ever going to develop any further.... It was really like cutting off an arm because it took a long time to stop writing original material that sounded like Jethro Tull.... When you are writing television under-scores and they keep turning up sounding like Jethro Tull, people are gonna get fed up! So it was a timely departure even though it was a wrench.[203]

Of the era during which he was an official member, Palmer said, "I would say that the best Jethro Tull was the band that existed in the mid- to late-'70s. That band produced live performances together with recordings that were pretty damn good! I'm certainly very proud to have been a part of that."[204]

─────────────── *A* ───────────────

29 August 1980 (U.K.) / 1 September 1980 (U.S.)
Highest chart position: 25 (U.K.) / 30 (U.S.)
[Rating: 4]
Producer: Ian Anderson / Chrysalis CDL 1301
All songs written by Ian Anderson
(Additional musical material: Eddie Jobson)

Ian Anderson: vocals, flute, acoustic guitar, mandolin
Martin Barre: electric guitar

Dave Pegg: bass guitar
Eddie Jobson: keyboards, electric violin
Mark Craney: drums and percussion

Recorded at Maison Rouge Studios, London, and with the Maison Rouge
    Mobile, summer 1980
Recording engineers: Robin Black and Leigh Mantle
Cover concept by Ian Anderson
Art direction by Peter Wagg
Photography by John Shaw

Tracks: Crossfire
        Fylingdale Flyer
        Working John, Working Joe
        Black Sunday
        Protect and Survive
        Batteries Not Included
        Uniform
        4.W.D. (Low Ratio)
        The Pine Marten's Jig
        And Further On

What had happened to induce Anderson to "sack" such long-term, excellent musicians? In truth, executives at Chrysalis, originally planning to release his new project as the first Ian Anderson solo album, developed different marketing ideas. And the *Melody Maker* article? Well, it is well known that British musicians and members of the fourth estate often share a pint or two at the local pub. Such an imbroglio would not have to be invented by the magazine.[205]

Placing the Tull band members on hiatus, Anderson had recruited new talent for the intended "solo" project. After hearing Eddie Jobson play with opening band U.K. every night on the previous tour, he hired him to play piano, keyboards and electric violin. Following stints with Curved Air, Roxy Music and Frank Zappa, Jobson had formed U.K. with bassist John Wetton (who later gained fame as a member of Asia) and drummer Bill Bruford (who had been succeeded by Terry Bozzio prior to the *Stormwatch* tour).

Anderson then shopped about for a percussionist. Minnesota-born Mark Craney, who had played with Jean Luc-Ponty and Tommy Bolin, became the first American ever to infiltrate the solidly British ranks of Tull. Craney explained how he got the job:

> A friend told me Eddie Jobson had an ad in *The Village Voice* for a
> drummer, so I sent him a demo. He liked it so he flew me out there, low

budget. I took the subway, carrying my cymbals and suitcase and groaning all the way…. And we did a demo and then I grumbled my way back to L.A. And I was out mowing my lawn one day, and Kenny Wylie, Tull's main man, called and the next day I was on my way over to England. It was going to be an Ian Anderson solo album, and the record company liked it, so they wanted us to be Jethro Tull. So Ian called and said, "Do you fancy joining the band … can you tour?" And that was it. Off I went.[206]

Craney greatly enjoyed the experience:

[T]hat was a really creative period for me, coming up with that stuff and just being involved in the record and being really into it. It was such a difference from … in the States. When I got there, we were doing it at Ian's estate, and then we'd hop on these motocross bikes for a break, and me and Dave Pegg would go down to the rifle range and shoot some clay pigeons. I couldn't believe it!… you know how it is here [Los Angeles], the clock is running and everybody is stressing.[207]

Anderson not only used Pegg on the album, but Martin Barre as well. Although much of the material did not sound like "traditional" Jethro Tull, Chrysalis decided it would sell better under the band name. In the end, songs like "Black Sunday," "The Pine Marten's Jig" and "And Further On" added familiar classical and folk elements that evoked the Tull ambiance. Anderson revealed:

Originally *A* was to stand for "Anderson," not "Anarchy" as it was sometimes misunderstood, but indeed the album was far from rousing feelings of anarchic defiance. It was actually more often about the warning against such things. Lots of songs arose from things to do with current real-life scenarios, not so much about relationships, but more about things, about realities, about world-scale phenomena.[208]

Anderson created many of the songs very quickly:

[S]ongs that I literally … wrote in the morning, and would be based on whatever was on the news programs the night before. And the whole album was done in the … spirit of … great rush … that wonderful feeling with the first cup of coffee, when you actually get a song going and you know you're going to rehearse it that morning, you're going to arrange it in the afternoon, and record it in the evening.[209]

Dave Pegg said:

That was a really great album, I thought. I really enjoyed playing on that ... and it was done very, very quickly, by Tull album standards. We'd rehearse some of the stuff—Ian, Martin and myself—and when Mark and Eddie came over, I think it was only about ten days ... of recording and mixing. It was a very, very enjoyable period.[210]

The Tracks of *A*

Eddie Jobson's brief keyboard introduction to "Crossfire" immediately casts *A* in a non-"traditional" direction for the band. Dealing with law and disorder in modern London, particularly an attack on Britain's Iranian Embassy, the song immediately suggests 1980, rather than the centuries-earlier atmosphere of the three previous albums, though Anderson and Barre's unison flute and electric guitar riffs keep it musically grounded within a familiar Tull sound.

"Fylingdale Flyer," which concerns the fear of a potential nuclear attack, has a very "futuristic" sound: here the thematic content (which harks back to *Stormwatch*), rather than the music, is familiar. This may be the album's most "non–Tull" song, sounding the most like a "solo" Ian Anderson piece.

A blend of folksy acoustic strumming and straightforward 4/4 rock 'n' roll, "Working John, Working Joe," reflecting the nature of England's "socialist" welfare state in 1980, musically resembles material on *Too Old to Rock 'n' Roll*; while "Black Sunday," another "futuristic" piece, with its classical structure and virtuoso performances by the band, is pure "epic" Tull. The excellent rhythmic interplay between Dave Pegg and Mark Craney really shines on this track, as does the fine acoustic piano soloing of Jobson. The overwhelming sense of urgency and foreboding created by the music strongly reinforces Anderson's lyrical content involving the incessantly hurried nature of modern life.

Jobson's electric violin was saved to open side B of the original LP, on "Protect and Survive," which begins with a frenetic driving tempo that recurs during instrumental breaks following each verse. In his criticism of a government pamphlet advising citizens how to live through a nuclear bombardment, Anderson takes one of his classic swipes at politicians, referring to them as "self-appointed guardians of the race, with egg upon their face." The rhythm section shines again in "Batteries Not Included," a song heavily influenced by Jobson's techno-pop keyboards, which fortunately are joined by Barre's familiar "power slides," reminding the listener that this is still Jethro Tull. Anderson's son James, then a toddler, made his recording debut in the song's opening narration.

The slightly funky "Uniform," a song about yuppie "suits," sounds like an avant-garde jazz version of Fairport Convention, due in part to Jobson's violin work. Opening with a fade-in on Craney's drums, "4.W.D. (Low Ratio)" is another funky, bluesy number blending acoustic piano, flute, fretless bass and electric guitar, with Barre contributing a vicious solo. The album ends in a much more traditional mode: after "The Pine Marten's Jig," combining flute, mandolin, bass and some expert folk-rock drumming with innovative electric fiddle, suggests a hybrid of Tull and early 1980s jazz-rock fusion, "And Further On" takes the listener back to the symphonic style of the epic tracks on *Songs from the Wood*, *Heavy Horses* and *Stormwatch*. Opening with acoustic piano and fretless bass, this closing track is a very comforting counterpoint to the furious energy of the previous Celtic jazz instrumental. After Anderson introduces the melodic leitmotif on flute and sings the first verse, Barre, Pegg and Craney powerfully punctuate the second with dynamic chords, after which Barre plays an Elgar-like electric guitar solo, one of the finest anthems of his career. For the third verse, the rhythm section raises the dynamic to *triple forte*, bracketing Anderson's vocals with Herculean power chords. The song then concludes with Anderson's voice and flute, backgrounded by a sensitive fade-out on Jobson's piano—the perfect counter to the electric keyboard sequence that opens the album. This song is one of Tull's all-time masterpieces.

The *A* Tour

A received a number of highly positive reviews from critics who, having grown tired of Anderson's grandiose eclecticism, were pleased to hear rock 'n' roll–oriented songs utilizing current sounds. "Working John, Working Joe" was released as a single in early October, eventually reaching number 30 on the U.S. charts. From October 4 to November 12, the new Tull toured the U.S., startling audiences with an equally fresh look, attired in stark white jumpsuits with a red electric "A" hovering over them. Anderson also had electrified his flute with a remote pickup, which adversely affected his tone but allowed him freely to roam about the stage. They played a varied selection of material on the tour, trying to merge older, more organic songs with the new, high-tech material.

On October 26, they played St. Louis' Checkerdome, a show from which excerpts were later taken for a *King Biscuit Flour Hour* radio broadcast. Not surprisingly, songs such as "Crossfire," "Batteries Not Included" and "Protect and Survive" all were given top-notch performances, but slightly older material, especially the grand "Songs from the Wood," suffered from Jobson's limited keyboard technique. "Heavy Horses," however, was beautifully driven by Pegg and Barre, who magnificently re-created the melodies he had recorded in the studio nearly three years earlier, at times joining Anderson's flute and Jobson's electric violin for unison parts. And while the original version fades out at the conclusion, here it was given a powerful, classical-style ending. And the straightforward rocker "Bungle in the Jungle" sounded much better than on the *War Child* album, primarily due to Barre's heavier approach, masterfully playing both the rhythm and lead guitar parts while Pegg (who also sang harmony vocals) and Craney thumped away.

A November 12 gig at the Los Angeles Sports Arena was filmed for a future video release. Ending the trek in L.A., the band then flew back to London for two shows at the Royal Albert Hall on November 20–21. Barrie Barlow attended one of them:

> I thought it was dreadful. I walked out, I really did.... Okay, there were some really ropey nights when I was part of the band, but I tried my hardest all the time. I think we all did. But it seemed like Eddie Jobson was "doing them a favor" by being in the band....[211]

Being new to Tull, Mark Craney found the live dates just as enjoyable as the recording of the album:

> [P]robably my favorite story in a song is "Heavy Horses." For some reason I can almost see the horses, veins bulging and sweating, working away. It is a great song. And I can really appreciate what a special person Ian is.... And I always liked "Hunting Girl" ... and ... "Skating Away" because I got to come out and play bass guitar.[212]

Pegg was able to indulge his love of folk music by playing mando-cello on "Skating Away," another successful revamping of an older song. "The *A* tour," he recalled, "was great fun for me ... fantastic bunch of musicians. It was really inspirational stuff to play with everybody. I was very, very proud and very happy."[213]

Of course, "Aqualung" and "Locomotive Breath" also were played each night. Following the November 21 gig, the "A" team took a respite until February 1981, when they toured Europe, hitting Belgium, Germany, Sweden, the Netherlands and France, after which Jobson and Craney retired from the lineup.

The Broadsword and the Beast

10 April 1982 (U.K.) / 19 April 1982 (U.S.)
Highest chart position: 27 (U.K.) / 19 (U.S.)
[Rating: 5]
Producer: Paul Samwell-Smith / Chrysalis CDL 1380
All songs written by Ian Anderson
(Additional musical material by Peter-John Vettese)

Ian Anderson: vocals, flute, acoustic guitar
Martin Barre: electric and acoustic guitars
Dave Pegg: bass guitar, mandolin, vocals
Peter-John Vettese: piano, synthesizers, vocals
Gerry Conway: drums, percussion

Recorded at Maison Rouge Studios, Fulham, London, winter 1981-82
Recording engineers: Robin Black and Leigh Mantle
Illustrations by Ian McCaig
Calligraphy by Jim Gibson

Tracks: Beastie
Clasp
Fallen on Hard Times
Flying Colours
Slow Marching Band
Broadsword
Pussy Willow
Watching Me, Watching You
Seal Driver
Cheerio

Anderson spent the majority of 1981 tending to his farming endeavors as well as writing a large number of songs for the next Tull album. The band members rehearsed and recorded a great deal of material that eventually was dropped from *The Broadsword and the Beast* in April 1982.

Having become more familiar with production techniques while working in his own home recording studio in Devon, Martin Barre approached the *Broadsword* sessions in a relaxed manner, commenting that it was the first Tull album "he truly enjoyed recording."[214] Dave Pegg, however, remembered the experience differently:

> *Broadsword* ... took a long time to record. It was quite a frustrating period. It was over a year in the making. And ... we had some famous

American producer ... who came over and recorded us for a day. Keith Olson, I think it was. It all went terribly wrong.... It wasn't working out. We wasted quite a bit of time, only a couple of days in the studio, but that didn't work out and he went back. And then we started recording it all ourselves, with Ian producing. Ian's a very good producer. And we recorded an awful lot of stuff back at Maison Rouge which didn't see the light of day on the eventual album which came out....

The *Broadsword* album is still my favorite Tull album that I've been involved with—although I love *Songs from the Wood* and *Heavy Horses*. If I had to pick two of my favorite albums, it would be those two. Definitely that period.... The songs Ian was writing....[215]

To join Pegg in powering the new material, Anderson recruited veteran folk-rock drummer Gerry Conway, who had played with Fotheringay (which included past and future Fairports Sandy Denny, Trevor Lucas and Jerry Donohue) and Cat Stevens a decade earlier:

Gerry was a great drummer.... Very musical drummer whenever he played. Even though he had a fairly simple style, it was all very musical, very well thought out with structured kind of parts that he would play. But unlike a lot of guys who think about it too much, and then lose the feel, Gerry was just great on feel. I mean a really good guy to play with when he was confident with the parts that he had. So we did quite a bit of rehearsals....[216]

Though the sessions proved quite a challenge for Pegg, he simplified matters by moving into an office at Maison Rouge:

It was too far to commute every day.... We'd be there about eleven o'clock in the morning and then we'd work to eleven or twelve at night. And you do that for ... three or four months ... you're just really exhausted. But it was a very exciting record to make. It was nice having Gerry Conway on drums....[217]

Anderson also brought aboard an innovative 25-year-old keyboard player, the half–Scottish, half–Italian Peter-John Vettese, who not only added a bold new synthesizer sound to the band, but also played fine acoustic piano on several tracks. Having a diverse musical background incorporating classical, jazz and pop, Vettese had been playing in pubs and small clubs in Scotland with the band R.A.F. ("Rich and Famous") when he saw an ad Anderson had placed in *Melody Maker*. Pegg said:

Peter Vettese ... is an absolutely incredible musician and probably my favorite keyboard player in the whole world. And also one of the

The *Broadsword and the Beast* band: Gerry Conway, Peter-John Vettese, Ian Anderson, Dave Pegg and Martin Barre, 1982.

> nicest and funniest people you could ever wish to be on tour with. Peter's just a remarkably talented guy, and such a bundle of laughs—a very inspirational musician.[218]

But Anderson's most drastic decision was his hiring of an outside producer—former Yardbird Paul Samwell-Smith—something he never had done. Even during Tull's earliest days, Terry Ellis had acted only as executive producer, and not as a creative influence, and Anderson's 1970 meeting with George Martin had convinced him to retain his production role. Anderson said:

> [A]bout four years ago, when I thought it'd be nice to work with somebody else just to get ... a little fresh input, another objective opinion; and

we started looking and, finally, after another two or three albums, we found somebody in the form of Paul Samwell-Smith, but not until we'd had a couple of false starts last year that cost us about six months in time and led to the usual last-minute rush in making a record....[219]

Slipstream Interlude

The one-hour video *Slipstream*, which had been in production for nearly a year, finally was released in Britain in August 1981. (Nearly two more years would pass before it hit shops in the U.S.) Ten tracks from the past decade were included, six recorded live in Los Angeles on the previous tour and four adapted for the increasingly popular music video market. Though all four videos suffer from then-current electronic editing and overused special effects, "Dun Ringill" is the most effective due to its visual atmosphere, having been shot at a remote beach location; the others— "Fylingdale Flyer," "Sweet Dream" and "Too Old to Rock 'n' Roll"—all feature varying degrees of absurdity. "Black Sunday," "Songs from the Wood," "Heavy Horses," "Aqualung" and "Locomotive Breath" are the live numbers, with "Horses" proving worth the price of the tape (or laserdisc, if a fan was lucky enough to land this superior 1984 U.S. release), if only to *see* Martin Barre recreate his unparalleled fret work. Also worth the price of admission are Eddie Jobson's violin contributions on "Heavy Horses" and "Aqualung," and Anderson's brief keyboard work as the violinist bows away on the instrumental epilogue to "Locomotive Breath."

The Tracks of *The Broadsword and the Beast*

"Beastie" opens *The Broadsword and the Beast* with a dark, foreboding atmosphere. Peter Vettese's keyboards immediately dominate the sound, and Pegg's superb bass work and Gerry Conway's solid, economical drumming provide the perfect backdrop for Barre's power chords as Anderson weaves his tale of modern psychological angst dressed up in ancient Scottish folklore.

"Clasp" also opens with swirling, moody keyboards, then adds flute and Pegg on mandolins as Conway serves up some fine "ethnic" percussion. This song, dealing with the inability of leaders (or humans in general) to reach amiable accords, is both medieval and futuristic—a timeless musical quality that reinforces this age-old problem.

The state of England's Thatcher-ized economy returns in "Fallen on

Hard Times," a bluesy folk-rock number brilliantly combining flute, mandolins and excellent Anderson harmony vocals with Barre's tasty slide guitar work (both acoustic and electric). The hard-hitting nature of this number immediately is offset by Vettese's sensitive acoustic piano and Anderson's passionate vocal during the introduction to "Flying Colours," a song about crumbling personal relationships. A startling snare drum rim shot by Conway leads to the classic Tull motif of the band entering with a vengeance, and an excellent instrumental section, culminating with a tremendous Barre power slide, makes this track a standout.

Side A of the original LP ends with "Slow Marching Band," a soothing folk-rock ballad about a man who is bidding adieu to his lover. An outstanding blend of flute, mandolin and acoustic piano is augmented by Conway and Pegg on the chorus, one of the finest ever written by Anderson. Highlights of the song are Barre's multi-tracked electric guitar harmonies, which provide a symphonic backdrop for the beautiful chorus melodies and lyrics:

> Walk on slowly
> Don't look behind you
> Don't say goodbye love
> I won't remind you.

Following the final Barre flourish, a Conway drum roll dynamically ends the song on a lightly plucked acoustic guitar harmonic.

The second half of the album is ushered in with more atmospheric keyboard work, which segues into Conway's Native American–sounding tom-tom beating—a style that makes a musical connection between the similarities of harsh treatment suffered by these people and the Scottish Highlanders. "Broadsword" is an Ian Anderson and Jethro Tull masterpiece, opening with near-operatic vocals and continuing with bone-crunching Barre power chords. On this song, Gerry Conway is as symphonic as Barrie Barlow, while eschewing adornment for a more basic rock-solid style. The instrumental section includes some playful solo trade-offs between Barre and Vettese.

"Pussy Willow," which tells the tale of a slender working woman, opens with mandolin, clean electric guitar and portative organ-style keyboards. (Acoustic piano and synthesizers subsequently join the mix.) And Pegg again is given a chance to demonstrate his prowess on the fretless bass. (This song would prove a favorite of Anderson's, as he went on to perform it over the span of many years in various arrangements.)

"Watching Me, Watching You" is a move into synthesized techno-pop,

Broadsword's only stylistic connection to the *A* album. Including Tull's first use of a keyboard sequencer, it is an interesting song enlivened by Conway's tom-tom fills and Barre's ever-present power chords. Bringing the listener back into more familiar territory, "Seal Driver" is one of the album's finest tracks. The musical contrast between the atmospheric introduction featuring keyboards and bass and the subsequent entrance of drums and electric guitar is paralleled lyrically by the pairing of romantic maritime images with modern references such as "two-hundred diesel horses thundering loud." As sonically dynamic as "Flying Colours," this song segues from pensiveness to intensity (a driving instrumental section capped by a fiery Barre solo) and back again (a funereal passage interrupted by Beethoven-like power chords but returning to the atmosphere of the introduction). Resembling a traditional bagpipe tune, "Cheerio," including only flute, keyboards and voice, lends a very soothing conclusion to a highly dynamic album.

The additional songs recorded during the *Broadsword* sessions remained unreleased until the *20 Years* set appeared six years later. (Others would remain under wraps until the 1993 release of *Nightcap*.) Several ("Overhang," "Too Many Too," "Down at the End of Your Road," "I'm Your Gun," "Motoreyes" and "Rhythm in Gold") would not have jibed comfortably with the material included on the album, but three, "Jack Frost and the Hooded Crow," "Mayhem, Maybe" and "Jack-a-Lynn," would have fit into the overall Celtic-medieval style. The first, a solstice-oriented number recalling "A Christmas Song" in its call for sharing one's Yuletide cheer with the unfortunate, is a slow-paced yet lively jig featuring Dave Pegg's virtuoso mandolin work and some impeccable harmony vocals by Anderson. (Pegg also included a version of the song on his bizarre experimental solo album *The Cocktail Cowboy Goes It Alone*, released on his own Woodworm Records in 1983.) The second, "Mayhem," is as good as any folk song Anderson ever wrote, here completely acoustic, telling the rousing tale of a band of roving brigands. And "Jack-a-Lynn," a beautiful love song that eventually explodes into Tull truly at high tide, has become a favorite of fans across the globe. (In writing this piece, Anderson was inspired by his wife, Shona, whose middle name is Jacqueline.)

Anderson recalled the fertile recording sessions and the public response:

> A very popular album in Germany, possibly because of its symbolism. It is a good combination of heavy rock and folk elements plus some quite electronic stuff. I was playing keyboards on it. I wasn't a keyboard player, so my doing that job kept things from getting too crazy, kept things nice

and fairly simple. Peter Vettese came in towards the latter part of that recording and did some of the tracks, but mostly the songs had come out of rehearsals where things were kept from getting too complicated.... A lot of the stuff was recorded in the studio pretty live with vocals which may or may not have been done again, but it was done very much as a group.[220]

When the album was released in April 1982, Anderson went on an extensive promotional tour of the U.S., including an appearance on *Late Night with David Letterman*. In the early days of his show, Letterman often spent more time insulting guests than actually interviewing them, but the comedian displayed real respect for Anderson, asking him about legends and lore, salmon, and if he was "buying up most of Scotland," to which he replied:

> A little bit at a time.... It's rather unpopular in our country to be a landowner these days. It's supposed to be a sort of vaguely ... socialist climate we live in. So you have to be quite careful when you're buying land. I must say, quite truthfully, I'm not a land*owner*. I'm merely some-one who's bought the right to be custodian of it for a while. So that's how I look at it.... Where things were, a lot of bracken and heather—we plant new grass and plant new trees, the sort of thing Robert Redford would do on a Sunday afternoon.
>
> But ... I'm a bit selfish about it as well, because, being a Scotsman, it is my native heath, after all, and ... I ... brave the occasional vitriolic ... slap on the wrist from some of the local newspapers. But I think, overall, people are kind of on my side, and it's *public* land. Don't take me up on this when I'm sort of *there*, but ... people can wander on the hills, do what they like, and it's a little bit better now, I think people would say.[221]

Asked about how the culture of his homeland had affected his music, he said:

> Well, indeed ... it's obviously difficult to live in that kind of envi-ronment, where you're surrounded by the tangible evidence of three-and-a-half thousand years worth of civilization ... without taking on some of the sheer *terror* ... when you're standing by some deep loch at night and the old hairs on the back of the neck start to prickle, and you start to believe. Even I believe it sometimes. There's a little bit of truth in it, I think.... I pass Loch Ness on my way from the airport to where I live, and I always have one eye sort of going this way and one eye on the road, but, so far, no luck.[222]

In a later interview, Anderson described a specific example of that "terror," which occurred on his Strathaird estate:

> I can remember fishing up the river, just by the Beaker's Peoples' mounds … one night, probably about ten o'clock, as it was getting dark. And I was with my big, black dog, who was at my side—and suddenly every hair on the animal's back shot up, and he slunk back across the bridge, and … whatever I did, he would not come back to me and just made a bee-line for the house. And the hairs on my neck went up as well, like there were a thousand eyes on the back of my neck.[223]

The *Broadsword* publicity tour also included an appearance on the *Mike Douglas Show* and a visit to live satellite radio program *Rockline*, whose host, Bob Cockburn, attempted to analyze the juxtaposition of "Beastie" and "Broadsword," and passed on (mostly inane) questions from callers. Queried about his "favorite" Tull album, Anderson replied that *Broadsword* "is a good, balanced, solid Jethro Tull album. If you pressed me, I would go for *Songs from the Wood*, and maybe *Stormwatch*, as being good, honest Jethro Tull albums."[224] Unfortunately, even after his personal promotion, *Broadsword* did not sell overly well in North America:

> I thought it was a good all 'round Jethro Tull album. I think really its lack of popularity in the U.S. had more to do with the mood of the times because it was that sort of period when people were still flirting with punk and the New Wave thing, and bands like us were definitely right out of fashion. I think we really suffered by not having a terribly convincing amount of radio play or promotion at that time. It was a shame, because it was a really good album. Certainly one of my favorites, and one in which I know [Martin] played unbelievably well.…[225]

Though penned by a different journalist, Parke Puterbaugh, *Rolling Stone* contributed its typical Tull review, criticizing Anderson's didactic thematics but praising much of the musical content:

> Leave it to Ian Anderson and Jethro Tull to anoint the Eighties with a concept album about the erosion of old values in today's rapidly devolving world.… Though it's hard to believe this is happening in 1982, there is something comfortingly antiquarian about *The Broadsword and the Beast*. Anderson often embellishes his morality plays with entrancingly lyrical, flawlessly executed ensemble passages, and "Clasp" and "Flying Colours," in particular, have a restless, brooding grace about them. At the same time, there's something disarming going on. The alienation and foreboding of Peter-John Vettese's synthesizer, combined

with the heavy-handedness of many of Anderson's lyrics, seems at odds with Jethro Tull's more lissome English folk leanings.... There's nothing wrong with living in the past, perhaps. Indeed, Ian Anderson can make the wisdom of the ages seem preferable to the rootless philandering of the present day. But on *The Broadsword and the Beast*, the real beast may be Anderson's penchant for ponderous sermonizing.[226]

Anderson said:

I'm ... singing songs which are all still relevant to today. They're not in any way historical, in the sense that I'm singing about times gone by. They're all basically about something today; but I try and put them in a musical context where they have that little ... timeless romanticism. Maybe they feel like they're set in...a distant past, maybe they feel like they're in a science-fiction future, but whatever it is, they're songs about today that suitably disguise themselves so they hopefully won't sound dated in five or ten years' time.... But how people ... if they listen to the lyrics, think that I'm actually only singing about something ... in the days of pirates ... and swords and sorcery and dragons.... I would have thought the songs presented themselves as being really present-day songs. And I think they've always been like that. I've never been into the Elizabethan age or anything as precisely historical as that. I just try and go for ... this timeless quality; so I sometimes elude to early folk sounds, and also to quite futuristic electronic sounds from time to time....[227]

The *Broadsword* Tour

While the band set off on a European tour, opening in Oslo on April 1, "Beastie" received radio play, as did the entire album, in some areas of the U.S. Peter Vettese became the official keyboard player, and the mood, like the new album, returned to the more traditional Tull experience: once again, audiences delighted in seeing Anderson in a medieval-style jacket (leather this time) and knee boots. To illustrate the album's two sides, he was menaced by a beastie on his back during one portion, but brandished a huge broadsword during another. One German concert, taped at Hamburg's Congress Centrum Halle on April 8, also was broadcast on American airwaves.

Just as Barre had played "unbelievably well" on the album, he may have reached his all-time peak during the tour, performing with profound expressiveness and sheer passion on "Broadsword," "Seal Driver" and a breathtaking instrumental arrangement of "Pibroch (Cap in Hand)," which included a bit of "Black Satin Dancer" for good measure. As he had on the album, Pegg added just the right amount of traditional folk impetus, and "The Clasp" and "Fallen on Hard Times," as well as *Heavy Horses'* "One Brown Mouse" and "Weathercock" (combined with "Fire at Midnight" from *Songs from the Wood*) were played superbly. "The Swirling Pit," one of Peggy's own compositions that he recorded with Fairport Convention, was also a highlight, inducing Anderson briefly to switch to tin whistle. Pegg recalled, "The *Broadsword* tour ... was fantastic for us. I thought we played incredibly well every night.... It was a great period in my life. I really enjoyed the ... tour. We were very, very good."[228]

Even though he enjoyed his own solo spot, Peter Vettese contributed a powerful keyboard complement, filling out the overall sound of the band, rather than grandstanding as Eddie Jobson often had done two years earlier. (On "Seal Driver," for example, he played the harmony part that Barre plays on the album.) And Gerry Conway unobtrusively held the entire performance together.

In May, "Broadsword," backed by "Fallen on Hard Times," was released as a single. During a four-date stint in Italy during the first week of May, some shenanigans occurred with Peter Vettese's luggage, some atrocious 1950s pink American Tourister relics that the band could no longer tolerate being within eyeshot. After purchasing some new bags, Vettese tossed the offending rejects onto some train tracks but later was shocked on stage when they began to dance in midair about his head during a keyboard solo.[229]

Following a few British dates in late May, Tull played two gigs in Dortmund, Germany, before taking a 10-week holiday that was interrupted only by a guest appearance for the Prince's Trust at London's Dominion Theatre on July 21. Sharing the stage with Pete Townshend, Robert Plant, Kate Bush, Joan Armatrading, Gary Brooker and others, they filled in for an absent David Bowie. After Gerry Conway "and Ian had a bit of a falling out,"[230] the drummer's seat was taken up by Phil Collins, who played with all the acts during the show. On "Jack in the Green," Collins perfunctorily backed up Anderson, Barre, Pegg and Vettese, but proved more inspired on "Pussy Willow." Only Anderson was billed, and he chose two songs that come very close to being solo pieces. Sometime after the show, Prince Charles described Anderson as "one of the most interesting and intelligent men in the music business."[231]

On September 1, these four were joined for the second leg of the tour by drummer Paul Burgess. Pegg added, "Gerry Conway played magnificently on the whole tour. It wasn't a problem for me. I don't know what happened ... it was a political thing. And Gerry was replaced by Paul Burgess, who ... is another fine drummer."[232] Headlining the Theakston

Brewery's open air festival at Nostel Priory in Wakefield, North Yorkshire, on August 28, they moved on to Barcelona, Spain, for a September 1 show and then worked in two more German gigs before flying to the States for 40 North American shows. (The relationship with Theakston was established through Pegg's longtime friendship with Neil Cutts, erstwhile owner of the White Bear in Masham, North Yorkshire, where the excellent microbrewery and inn is located.)

After the *Broadsword* album and tour, Anderson sold Maison Rouge:

> I sold my studio around 1982 because I saw it coming that all the original equipment that had gone in would be unfashionable within two or three years…. The … digitals were coming in. It became very threatening to realise that we might have to invest something in the region of £500,000 to re-equip both studios with new gear. And there was no way that I was going to make that kind of profit in a couple of years.[233]

Discovering that professional-grade home recording equipment could be purchased for a quarter of the cost, Anderson decided to set up a new studio at his country estate and re-invest the Maison Rouge capital in his fish farming operation on Skye. In an interview given after the tour, he described a parallel between his two professions:

> We use mandolins alongside sequencers and synthesizers and the technology of today, so I would like to think that Jethro Tull does musically what I think should be the approach towards … agriculture today: that you utilize the best of traditional methods along with the best of today's technology, and try and make them work side by side.[234]

Walk into Light

18 November 1983 (U.K.) / 5 December 1983 (U.S.)
Highest chart position: 78 (U.K.)
[Rating: 3.5]
Producer: Ian Anderson / Chrysalis CDL 1443
All songs written by Ian Anderson (except where indicated)

Ian Anderson: vocals, flute, acoustic, electric and bass guitars, drum programming
Peter-John Vettese: piano, synthesizers, backing vocals

Recorded at Farmyard Studios, spring-summer 1983
Recording engineer: Ian Anderson

Cover concept by Ian Anderson
Art direction by John Pasche
Photography by Martyn Goddard

Tracks: Fly by Night (Anderson-Vettese)
Made in England (Anderson-Vettese)
Walk into Light
Trains (Anderson-Vettese)
End Game
Black and White Television
Toad in the Hole
Looking for Eden
User-Friendly (Anderson-Vettese)
Different Germany (Anderson-Vettese)

Jethro Tull went on hiatus during 1983, when Anderson split his time between fish farming enterprises and the writing and recording of a solo album. Later he admitted:

> I took the dangerous step of working with our new keyboard player, Peter Vettese, to do some recording on my own as, this time, the real solo album. I can't for the life of me remember … why I was doing it, other than I think I wanted to get away from doing guitar type things and acoustic things which I was known for, and go for more of an electronic sound…. I think they suffered really from being just so keyboard dominated, and also the fact that it was a drum machine. Given real drums and a bit of real guitar type playing, I think it would have been a much more popular effort.[235]

Truth to tell, this "solo" album actually was the most collaborative musical work Anderson had made. Vettese, who co-wrote the music for five songs, also had an enormous influence on the overall style and sound. Anderson said:

> It wasn't a case of having a lot of songs already written that didn't fit in with Jethro Tull, there was nothing written at all. It was all worked out in the studio, and the whole album was recorded in one intensive series of sessions rather than over a period of months. We went into the studio and worked solidly every day all the time with new sounds and new ways of making our music.[236]

A year after the album's release, Anderson claimed, "I haven't played my solo album since we made it. I've sort of forgotten it. I can't really remember what it's about."[237] But, by 1997, he had re-evaluated the record:

> I really do have a soft spot for a lot of the songs. I just wouldn't want to record them that way again. But the … album was a good experiment, and one that I enjoy in retrospect because of the songs more than the actual sound of the end result.[238]

Rather than "make the obvious album with acoustic guitar, flute and mandolin," Anderson took the most innovative move in his career since devising *Thick as a Brick*. With that album, he had expanded the scope of rock music; here he tried "to experiment with what was then new technology: sequencers, samplers and the beginnings of the techno age."[239]

Continuing his interest in his former "leader's" work, Barrie Barlow said:

> I thought his solo album was really good … apart from the production. He really should have got somebody in to produce it, because there are some really good songs there but it is flat all the way through. No dynamics at all.[240]

To the contrary, there is a surprising use of dynamics in several songs, even though Anderson used a Linn Drum Computer (which played samples of Ludwig drums) throughout.

The Tracks of *Walk into Light*

A pleasant, musically ambitious opening track, "Fly by Night" sounds a bit like a synthesized pops orchestra, with Anderson having done a remarkable job of utilizing the Linn computer to approximate the sound of live percussion. An Anderson-Vettese collaboration, it is followed by another, "Made in England," which is introduced by some fine melodic lead guitar work. One of the best songs on the album, if arranged differently, it could have fit onto *Songs from the Wood* or *Heavy Horses*:

> Somewhere in a town in England.
> Could be Newcastle, Leeds or Birmingham.
> And were you made in
> England's green and pleasant land?

"Walk into Light," another track driven by well-programmed percussion, actually establishes a groove (a quality rarely achieved by synthesized music). Good use of dynamics, electric guitar and vocals (including Anderson's only *scat* performance sans flute) add up to an excellent song about taking an optimistic approach to one's lot in life. "Trains," with music cowritten by Anderson and Vettese, may be the album's least interesting track, though the incessant clickety-clack drum pattern is redeemed by some fine keyboard work reminiscent of the playing of Genesis' Tony Banks. The next three songs—"End Game," "Black and White Television" and "Toad in the Hole"—all combine atmospheric introductions, eccentric Tull-style riffs, excellent melodies and a variety of keyboard sounds. "Toad," with its blend of acoustic piano, organ and various synthesizer settings, is a highlight of the album.

The occasionally symphonic "Looking for Eden" includes a brief visit by Anderson's Martin acoustic guitar, but the final two tracks—"User-Friendly" and "Different Germany"—are the most computer oriented of all. However, "Germany" is a true high point, featuring a powerful introduction and an excellent instrumental section during which Vettese gets to stretch out a bit.

In November, "Fly by Night," backed by "End Game," was released as a single but, like the album, failed to generate much public interest. The only live performances Anderson gave during the year were promotional appearances on European television. On November 15, after performing three songs for a show in Munich, he attempted to have a drink with one of his heroes, Jack Bruce, who also had played on the show, but suddenly was asked to return to the stage. Fumbling around for his flute, he still was trying to put it back together as he and Bruce rushed out to jam with the late African musician Fela Kuti. Anderson said:

> [T]here was this bunch of very untrained guys, all very rough and ready, and Fela Kuti, who was a total con man. He couldn't play at all, just musical bullshit which he passed off as avant garde playing. As far as I was concerned he just traded off being a black African militant, and all the critics were taken in by him. He didn't like me at all; to him I was "Capitalist Whitey," but he was happy to get me up there promoting his career. Me and Jack Bruce and everybody else, we all got dragged up there, and it was chaos. It was just a rambling mess that went on and on until it ran out of steam.[241]

In December 1983, journalist Chris Welch wrote:

> Along with Frank Zappa, Paul McCartney and very few rockers, Ian Anderson has that quality of exuding intelligence, while putting people at ease. He's funny, just a trifle tetchy, takes a delight in gossip, and has an active mind that wants to probe and rapidly share with others his interests and discoveries.[242]

Under Wraps

7 September 1984 (U.K.) / 8 October 1984 (U.S.)
Highest chart position: 18 (U.K.) / 76 (U.S.)
[Rating: 2.5]
Producer: Ian Anderson / Chrysalis CDL 1461
Songs written by Ian Anderson (except where indicated)

Ian Anderson: vocals, flute, acoustic guitar, drum programming
Martin Barre: electric and acoustic guitars
Dave Pegg: bass guitar, mandolin, vocals
Peter-John Vettese: piano, synthesizers, vocals

Recorded at Farmyard Studios, spring 1984
Recording engineers: Ian Anderson, Martin Barre, Dave Pegg, Peter-John Vettese
Cover concept by Ian Anderson
Sleeve design by John Pasche
Group photograph by Sheila Rock
Cover photograph by Trevor Key

Tracks: Lap of Luxury
Under Wraps #1
European Legacy
Later, That Same Evening (Anderson-Vettese)
Saboteur (Anderson-Vettese)
Radio Free Moscow (Anderson-Vettese)
Astronomy (Anderson-Vettese) [CD and cassette only]
Tundra (Anderson-Vettese) [CD and cassette only]
Nobody's Car (Anderson-Barre-Vettese)
Heat (Anderson-Vettese)
Under Wraps #2
Paparazzi (Anderson-Barre-Vettese)
Apogee (Anderson-Vettese)
Automotive Engineering (Anderson-Vettese) [CD and cassette only]
General Crossing (Anderson-Vettese) [CD and cassette only]

Under Wraps is the most controversial album Jethro Tull have released. In 1989, Anderson admitted that, like *Walk into Light*, it primarily was an experiment with his new home studio and the emerging technology of the time:

> *Under Wraps* ... was mainly drum machines and synths and sequencers.... That technology had been established for home recordists and to ignore it would have been a mistake. Examining these possibilities and what

they would mean to us was something we felt we should do, but I don't think we got an album out of it that was important for us. I think we all look back on it and feel that it was quite good in terms of the songs and the way we did them, but the general feel of it was clearly not something we would want to pursue again.[243]

While Anderson wanted to experiment with current technology, including drum programming (again, no live percussion was used in the recording), the content of the album was a result of his interest in spy novels. The band enjoyed recording the material, being able to convene comfortably at Anderson's own studio to play, engineer and mix the songs. Anderson said, "There was nobody else here, it was just us, the guys, the musicians in one room and we operated the equipment. We didn't have an audience so we could be a little braver in trying things out."[244]

Able to contribute many of his own ideas (including the cowriting of two songs), Barre really appreciated the experience:

> It was a lot of fun to record.... It's one of my personal favorite Tull albums, even though now I can see that maybe it wasn't the right thing for us to do. When you are locked away in a studio for a year with only yourself to please, it is difficult to judge the results in an impartial way. We were making music to please ourselves, which is maybe a bit selfish. Music should be for everybody, not just for an elite bunch of people. Having said that though, nowadays it is one of the few Tull albums that I play to enjoy rather than for reference. Funnily enough, *A* is the other one that I think sounds really good. But *Under Wraps* is a great album.[245]

Eternal folk-rocker Dave Pegg did not share Barre's opinion, believing that the "out-takes from *Broadsword* would have made a better album."[246] But the most violently negative reaction came from Terry Ellis, when he and the band convened at Pophleys to have a few drams and listen to the final mix. When first hearing the techno-rock strains emanating from the hi-fi, he exclaimed, "If you think I'm going to release this fucking pile of crap on my label, you can think again! This isn't Jethro Tull. It's shit!"[247] Ellis parted company with Chrysalis, and his partner, Chris Wright, now in charge, was persuaded to release the album in September 1984. After all, Tull literally had created the Chrysalis label during the late 1960s.

The Tracks of *Under Wraps*

Even for fans who had become familiar with Anderson's solo album, the first moments of "Lap of Luxury," with the drum machine featured up front in the mix, proved a shock. Producing an album under his own name was one thing—but this was Jethro Tull! Though the arrangement and style are highly atypical, this song about materialism is quite excellent and includes fine guitar work by Barre. While the springy title cut "Under Wraps #1" features a few wisps of acoustic guitar, "European Legacy" actually sounds like Jethro Tull. Acoustic guitar–based, bolstered by interesting Scottish lyrics, and including a good instrumental section, "Legacy," if arranged in a more "traditional" fashion, would not have sounded out of place on the *Broadsword* album. Another highlight, "Later, That Same Evening," with music by Anderson and Vettese, benefits from lyrical imagery; but "Saboteur," though featuring odd time signatures and an excellent solo by Barre, treads too close to disco dance music.

Spiced with a bit of Russian flavor, "Radio Free Moscow" is a pleasant folk-pop song blending a Cold War topic with some traditional Tull sounds, particularly during a section featuring mandolin and voice. Two Anderson-Vettese songs issued on CD and cassette only, "Astronomy" and "Tundra," are very pedestrian, computer-oriented affairs (and the listener easily can hear that Anderson strained his voice while recording this material).

The second half of the album opens with "Nobody's Car," a driving number with effective guitar work by Barre, who collaborated on the music with Anderson and Vettese. While this song includes a reggae-tinged introduction, the next track, "Heat," with music by Anderson and Vettese, begins with a pleasant blend of flute and keyboards before it shifts into high gear. Though plagued by the ubiquitous drum machine, "Heat" allows Barre to contribute some trademark riffs, a welcome melodic passage during the instrumental break, and a blistering solo at the end.

The album's one true "consolation" to Tull fans, "Under Wraps #2" is an acoustic rearrangement of the title track. Though Pegg is often lost in the mix on other songs, here his double bass is allowed to shine. This version of the song demonstrates that, if arranged in a more traditional Tull style devoid of the electronic trappings, the music of *Under Wraps* is actually quite impressive. However, the computerized nature of the album soon returns on "Paparazzi," a song about celebrity-hounding photographers, with music by Anderson, Barre and Vettese, and "Apogee," another Anderson-Vettese collaboration, which uses maritime lyrics to tell a space-age tale. Here Anderson again intertwines the past ("standing stones") and the future ("stainless veins of steel"). The CD and cassette editions of *Under Wraps* end with two additional Anderson-Vettese tracks, "Automotive Engineering" and "General Crossing," the former sounding like Thomas Dolby and the latter mere filler.

Of his performances on the album, Anderson, who played very little flute, said:

> The best I've ever sung was on that record. Sadly it was the singing of that material on tour in '84 that actually caused the difficulties with my larynx. Whether it was the nature of the songs or just the intensity of it I don't know, but it was a shame. I can understand why a lot of Jethro Tull fans would be less satisfied with the sound of the album....[248]

(Interestingly, the drum programming on this album is far more synthetic and stiff than it is on the superior *Walk into Light*.)

The *Under Wraps* Tour

Doane Perry, a longtime Tull fan who had met Clive Bunker backstage after a concert in 1971, answered Anderson's advertisement in *The Village Voice* and landed the drummer's seat for the *Under Wraps* tour. Born in Mt. Kisco, New York, in 1954, he had played with a vast array of musicians and now became the second Yank to "infiltrate the ranks of Tull." Interestingly, he and *A* drummer Mark Craney had been good friends for years. Perry remarked:

> [M]y tastes in pop music initially were formed by all the British bands, starting with the Beatles and going to all the progressive stuff that was coming out of England, which to me was far more interesting than the American stuff.... Maybe it's just because ... familiarity sort of breeds contempt.... And the whole sense of humor that they had was so foreign and bizarre and intriguing....[249]

Perry described the unique challenges of playing Tull music:

> I think one of the biggest challenges was to try and keep a clear sense of the feel in the original part, not necessarily everything note for note. I had to try to create parts that remained identifiable and true, but also something that would fall comfortably and naturally under my own hands. The music differed in terms of the form, the structure of it—quite a bit more than some of the American music I'd played. The song forms didn't really traditionally adhere to what is known as "AABA" song form. It was more linear, and you had parts that didn't really repeat at predictable places; and, when they did repeat, they often repeated with a great deal of change. So it was more like classical music in that way. I found that the easiest way to learn the parts was to think of them in a

very linear fashion, rather than if you thought of them in a sort of block-
like form. It wasn't just eight bars of this, and eight bars of this, and sixteen bars of that. Tull music doesn't always have a verse-verse-chorus
feel; and that was really challenging and different about the music.

Some of the earlier music was simpler in terms of the form, but as
the music evolved and became more complex over the years, it probably
borrowed from some of those [classical] forms. There would be certain
familiar motifs that would appear here and there. The idea was to try
and create an evolving series of parts that didn't necessarily have to be
repeated the way you would predictably hear music performed in a more
pop format.

I think I was fortunate to have a background in a lot of different
kinds of music, beginning with pop music and rock, and then jazz and
orchestral music, ethnic music, folk music, R and B, fusion—all these
different styles have really helped me within the context of Jethro Tull,
though Jethro Tull is probably none and all of the above at the same
time, because it has elements of all of those kinds of music. I think I was
better prepared for dealing with the music than had I come strictly from
a pop or rock background. And I think that might be said about everybody in the band. Everybody brings different influences. Their primary
influences might be somewhat different from each other, but all together,
it seems to make a cohesive whole. And we all like different kinds of
music and have influences that are pretty diverse. And yet, somehow,
when we come together and play, hopefully there's a real unity of purpose.[250]

Having been a longtime Tull fan, Perry noted his favorite songs:

Some of them involve quite an active drum part, and actually some
of them don't have any drums or minimal drums. In no particular order,
"Black Sunday," "Songs from the Wood," "Heavy Horses"—I love playing
those. I love the story in "Heavy Horses." Going back to "With You
There to Help Me," I remember as an early song, when I first heard that,
loving that.

"My Sunday Feeling" is a really sentimental favorite, because I
wrote Clive Bunker a fan letter when I was about fifteen and I actually
got to meet him. I didn't know how to play "My Sunday Feeling"—and
he showed me how to play it in the dressing room of the Fillmore East.

"Life Is a Long Song" is another one. I just love that as a piece of
music. "Nothing to Say" from *Benefit*—love that.

Thick as a Brick: There are a lot of parts that we don't play, whole
sections of that that are just wonderful. "Minstrel in the Gallery." "Third
Hurrah" from *War Child*. "Dharma for One"—I used to love listening to
Clive Bunker's solo on that. On *Aqualung*, "Cheap Day Return,"

"Wond'ring Aloud"—great little short pieces of music. "Clasp." From the *Under Wraps* album, which I think is an incredibly underrated album, "European Legacy," "Heat," "Under Wraps Two," that little acoustic piece. And there's a song on Ian's first solo album, *Walk into Light*, called "Trains"—I just love that song.[251]

Opening a nine-day British tour in Dundee, Scotland, on August 30, 1984, the band then played gigs in Spain, France, Sweden, Denmark, the Netherlands, Belgium, Germany and Switzerland before undertaking 31 North American dates. A September 9 show at London's Hammersmith Odeon was taped by the BBC for broadcast on Radio One. An uneven concert, it was condensed down to include classics such as "Locomotive Breath" and (a slightly re-arranged) "Living in the Past," and two tracks from *Under Wraps*, the title song and "Later That Same Evening," which were only slightly livelier than their studio counterparts. (The concert was released on compact disc six years later.)

When the tour reached New York in October, Doane Perry talked the band into seeing Rob Reiner's brilliant rock "mockumentary" *This Is Spinal Tap*:

It wasn't out in Europe, so by the time we got to America several months later, fortunately it was still playing, so we all went to see it. They loved it. It was such an inside thing. Anybody who has seen it who is a musician totally got it. But, even though they loved it, the next day this wave of depression swept through the band, and everybody started saying, "Oh, my God. I can remember when that happened. Oh, no." And everybody realized they had relived some part of their life on the road in that movie. That was the funny part of it, the tragic part of it, because we all had lived that in some way on the road, and nobody wants to believe they've lived some part of Spinal Tap's existence within their own band. It was made more clear when, some months later, when Christopher Guest, who played Nigel Tuffnel in the movie, came out in a *Rolling Stone* interview and said they had drawn on all kinds of influences, a lot of heavy metal bands and a lot of non-heavy metal bands like Jethro Tull. We were actually cited.

We had our Spinal Tap moment, in fact, on stage in Oxford a few years later. It was the last night of the tour, and we had this little Irish guy who worked with us—tiny little guy—and actually in the middle of this piece of Celtic music that Martin Allcock, Dave Pegg and myself were doing as a little trio out at the front of the stage, unbeknownst to us, they were lowering down a little, eleven-inch Stonehenge behind us.

We thought, "This is really going down great tonight. We must really be playing well." The audience started going completely crazy. We were quite pleased with ourselves, and little did we realize that, not only was it this eleven-inch Stonehenge lowered down directly behind us, but this little Irish gnome in a Santa Claus stocking hat doing this little "Stonehenge dance" around this ridiculous little statue. Some people realized what it was, but I'm sure a lot of people thought, "Why in the world are they having this little, eleven-inch rock coming down behind them with this little guy dancing around?" He actually, in fact, knocked it over because it was so little. We thought it was very funny afterwards.[252]

A show at Philadelphia's Spectrum on October 19 was videotaped for inclusion in a special on progressive rock broadcast by MTV. Featuring some material from *Under Wraps*, the program also included "Aqualung," "Locomotive Breath" and an excerpt from *Thick as a Brick*. Prior to breaking for the Yuletide holidays, they played five gigs in Australia.

Not long after the tour began, Anderson experienced a muscle spasm in his throat that continued to worsen with every gig. Although he found it difficult to sing after only a few numbers each night, he continued to push himself, particularly on the difficult *Under Wraps* material. (His voice sounded particularly rough during the MTV special.) Tull fan Rob Curtis, who attended the October 13 concert at the Continental Arena in the New Jersey Meadowlands, recalled:

> Throughout the late '70s ... my friends would come back from a Tull concert explaining that they were the greatest live band they'd ever seen. In 1984, my girlfriend (and now, wife) and I went to the *Under Wraps* tour at Continental Arena.... Suffice it to say, it was a concert best left forgotten. She spent the next 15 years thinking, "Tull sucks live." It wasn't until 1999 that we had the opportunity to see Tull live again.... This time, we were blown away by the musicianship and sheer volume of terrific and unique tunes. My wife, who is not a big fan, just said, "They're incredible."[253]

During his first series of dates on the Tull drum stool, Doane Perry had to remain focused on a specific musical challenge:

> The hardest part about the gig initially was just trying to remember the complexity of the arrangements. I realized the key to remembering all the parts was simply to be able to sing the entire piece of music from beginning to end. If I had a pretty good idea from singing it—whether I was singing a vocal melody or a flute melody, or a guitar part or a keyboard part—I could always keep my place. And it also helped me not to have to be counting odd bar lengths and unusual forms.[254]

Perry also commented on the necessity of injecting musical feeling into some of the more complex songs:

> The thing that is uppermost in my mind when I am creating a part or re-creating a part that one of the other drummers came up with is trying to make the music groove and feel good, even though there are a lot of odd bars and odd time signatures that we play in. And there are certainly a lot of points in the music where there is a deliberate increase or decrease in tempo, just the way there would be in orchestral music. Drummers, these days, get so used to starting in one tempo and keeping it all the way through. There are some songs that are like that, but there are other songs where we deliberately move it a little ahead, a little behind, depending on the section of music, in order to create a certain feel or tension.
>
> Within all the complexity of the arrangements, if I can make the music *groove*; and, to a certain extent, if the technical part of what I'm doing, and what we're doing as a band, becomes invisible to the audience, I feel like I'm doing my job right. If I look out into the audience— even if we're playing something that might be in an unusual time signature—if I see them moving to it, then I think, "Okay, we're doing our job." I think it's good if the audience is largely unaware of whatever technically it's taking to play the music. That it feels right to them, I think, is much more important.[255]

After ending the *Under Wraps* tour on December 18, 1984, Anderson wisely chose to give his voice a much-needed rest, putting the band on another extended hiatus in order to convalesce while tending to his farming business. Back in New York, fresh from his first tour, Doane Perry trotted out photos while playing host to his parents. He recalled:

> I remember that Peter Vettese had this habit: Every time there was a camera out, whether it was mine or somebody else's, Peter liked to expose himself. One time after that tour, my folks came over to my house, and I was showing some pictures of the tour. I realized all these pictures were in there, and my mother kept saying, "Why is that little guy with the glasses always taking his trousers off?" And I really didn't have an answer for that—and I still don't really have an answer for that. Pete had a penchant for exposing himself. He was a very dirty young man, and especially pictures that I was in, I would often get them home, and see that Peter was standing behind me, and perhaps he was resting "himself" gently on my shoulder, unbeknownst to me, or somewhere close by, giving himself a little "airing out."[256]

Anderson brought the lads out of temporary retirement (Pegg had resurrected Fairport Convention with Simon Nicol and Dave Mattacks, adding Ric Sanders on violin; while Barre was getting physically fit and writing songs) when representatives in Germany asked that Tull be involved in a concert celebrating the 300th birthday of J. S. Bach to be held at Berlin's International Congress Centrum on March 16, 1985.

Eddie Jobson "rejoined" the band for this one-off gig featuring a diverse selection of material. Anderson's vocal problems were obvious on "Black Sunday," but were not noticeable on most of the other songs, including "Hunting Girl," "Living in the Past," "Too Old to Rock 'n' Roll," "Wond'ring Aloud," "Aqualung" and "Locomotive Breath." Being a tribute to Bach, the set list was graced with several beautifully played instrumentals: "Elegy," "Serenade to a Cuckoo" (including an extended bridge blending several musical styles and featuring Jobson on violin), "Bourée" and Bach's "Double Violin Concerto" (a 1717 piece actually titled "Concerto for Two Violins in D Minor"). The band segued into "Happy Birthday" at the close of this last number, as Anderson strutted onto the stage with a huge cake adorned with three candles, blowing them out with a New Year's Eve "noisemaker." It was the last gig they would play for 15 months.

A Classic Case: ## *The London Symphony Orchestra* — *Plays the Music of Jethro Tull* —

31 December 1985 (U.S.) / 14 June 1993 (U.K.)
Highest chart position: 93 (U.S.)
[Rating: 2.5]
Producer: David Palmer / RCA Red Seal XRL1-7067
All songs written by Ian Anderson (except where indicated)
The London Symphony Orchestra conducted by David Palmer

Ian Anderson: flute
Martin Barre: electric guitar
Dave Pegg: bass guitar
Peter-John Vettese: keyboards
Paul Burgess: drums

Recorded at CBS Studios, London, summer 1984
Art direction and cover photograph by Manfred Vormstein
Cover design by Ariola-Eurodisc/Studios J. Schlogl

Tracks: Locomotive Breath
Thick as a Brick
Elegy (Palmer)
Bourée (J. S. Bach)
Fly by Night (Anderson-Vettese)
Aqualung
Too Old to Rock 'n' Roll: Too Young to Die
Teacher/Bungle in the Jungle/Rainbow Blues/Locomotive Breath
Living in the Past
War Child

Arranged and orchestrated by David Palmer, *A Classic Case* is not a proper Jethro Tull album, but a collection of pseudo-symphonic instrumental versions of familiar songs by the band. However, the presence of Anderson, Barre, Pegg and drummer Paul Burgess gives it considerable Tull presence.

What could have been a remarkable album is instead a somewhat disappointing foray into symphonic rock. Palmer's retention of the original rock tempi and arrangements (using a brass or string section simply to play one of Barre's riffs or progressions, for example), rather than completely rearranging the songs in an orchestral style, defeated its possibilities. Anderson remarked:

> The original idea as I understood it was that he was going to orchestrate those songs in a creative and totally different context, but all it turned out to be was really the same things. The same tempo with the wretched rock drumming and the orchestra just honking the tune. I thought it was very uninspired, and I felt that David was under a lot of pressure from the record company to do something that really was not adventurous. I had made a personal commitment to David to do it, so I felt obliged to do it.[257]

The selection of songs certainly was unadventurous, merely being a "greatest hits" package. Aside from "Bourée" and "Elegy," which are classically oriented pieces, the rest of the material is standard Tull radio fare. How Palmer could spend time scoring songs like "Too Old to Rock 'n' Roll" and "Bungle in the Jungle" nearly boggles the mind.

The Tracks of *A Classic Case*

The introduction to "Locomotive Breath" is purely orchestral, but as soon as the band joins in, the London Symphony sounds like the Boston Pops. Curiously, the interplay between the brass and the percussion section lends the track a somewhat Native American style. Due to its classical elements, *Thick as a Brick* was a good choice to orchestrate; "Elegy" features a beautiful solo by Barre; and "Bourée" segues from baroque to the *Stand Up* arrangement, to Anderson's smoking jazz soloing and back to baroque before the original Tull sound again emerges.

On "Fly by Night," Palmer regrettably chose to layer his orchestration on top of Anderson's original drum machine program, and "Aqualung" repeats the stodgy style, tempo and Native American overtones of "Locomotive Breath," though Barre contributes another fine solo. "Too Old to Rock 'n' Roll," the "Teacher/Bungle in the Jungle/Rainbow Blues/Locomotive Breath" medley and "Living in the Past" merely take up space, but "War Child," aside from intrusive sound effects, concludes the album with a lovely orchestration devoid of rock elements.

Anderson, Barre and Pegg, accompanied by Gerry Conway on drums, rejoined Palmer to record the title song for the BBC television series *The Blood of the British*. Written by Palmer and released as a single in the U.K. on June 20, 1986, "Coronach" is one of the most beautiful and powerful pieces ever played by the band. A lyrical balled praising the virgin land that once was England (Albion), it was based on a traditional Celtic musical form, the *coronach* (core-a-nuck), a funeral dirge usually sung or played on the bagpipes. Reflecting the classic Tull fusion of ethnic folk and hard rock, the song blends Anderson's melodic voice and a mournful oboe with the raw power of Martin Barre's guitar. (The track was not released in the U.S. until it became part of the *20 Years* box set.)

During the summer of 1986, Tull were persuaded to play a few European dates after being resuscitated by the band Marillion, who were headlining a show at the Milton Keynes Bowl on June 28. Asked to appear as special guests, they decided to utilize all their hard practice by visiting Israel, Hungary, Denmark and Germany for one-off gigs, returning to England in early July. Dubbed the "Jethro Tull Summer Raid," the minitour was shorn of any stage props, and video footage shot at the Milton Keynes show (at which Anderson's voice did not hold up well) later was included in *Sheep and Fish and Rock 'n' Roll*, a British television documentary about the fluted one's farming activities.

Crest of a Knave

11 September 1987 (U.K.) / 16 September 1987 (U.S.)
Highest chart position: 19 (U.K.) / 32 (U.S.)

[Rating: 4]
Producer: Ian Anderson / Chrysalis CDL 1590
All songs written by Ian Anderson

Ian Anderson: vocals, flute, acoustic guitar, keyboards, synthesizer and drum programming, percussion
Martin Barre: electric and acoustic guitars
Dave Pegg: bass guitar, acoustic bass
Doane Perry: drums, percussion
Gerry Conway: drums, percussion
Ric Sanders: violin

Recorded at Woodworm Studios, Farmyard Studios and Black Barn Studio, spring 1987
Recording engineers: Ian Anderson, Martin Barre, David Pegg, Robin Black, Tim Matyear
Remix engineer ("Steel Monkey"): Stephen Taylor
Calligraphy and heraldry by Andrew Jamieson
Art direction by John Pasche

Tracks: Steel Monkey
Farm on the Freeway
Jump Start
Said She Was a Dancer
Dogs in the Midwinter [CD and cassette only]
Budapest
Mountain Men
Raising Steam
The Waking Edge [CD and cassette only]

In late 1986, Anderson, Barre, and Perry joined Dave Pegg at his Woodworm Studios in Oxfordshire to begin working on the first new Tull album in nearly three years. Having recovered sufficiently from his throat ailment, Anderson chose to write songs in lower keys than usual, keeping the melodies simpler than on previous efforts. Perry, who had been touring Europe with an Australian band, recorded the drum tracks, but had to return to New York when his mother became ill and subsequently passed away. During his absence, Anderson brought in Gerry Conway to play on some new recordings at Robin Black's Black Barn Studio (drum programming was also used on a few songs). With the backing tracks completed, the remainder of the recording was done at Anderson's home studio.

Reflecting on his creative approach, Anderson admitted:

I was very, very selfish about making this one. I really just didn't want anybody else to have any creative input at all, other than playing the final parts in the studio. The last few albums involved the other guys quite a lot, in the arranging and in writing bits of music, and I felt this time that I wanted to get away from having input from other people— not because I thought I could do it better, but just because I wanted to be very selfish about it and take total charge.[258]

During the process of deciding which tracks to include on the album, Anderson, via radio station KBCO in Boulder, Colorado, arranged a pre-release listening party for 300 Tull fans at a Marriott Hotel in Denver. Taking all comments and suggestions into account, he then tailored the final product to the potential record-buying public, a commercial move that critics viewed as an artistic sell-out. But Chrysalis, not wanting to repeat the dismal sales of *Walk into Light* and *Under Wraps*, needed to know what the fans expected from Jethro Tull. Confident that the new material was a return to form for his band, Anderson said:

We had stopped, taken stock, and made a really good album.... We didn't want to make another album that was dominated by keyboards, and certainly not something that sounded like we were trying to update ourselves. That's why Peter Vettese is not on the album. He was never going to be a full time member of the band.... Jethro Tull was always going to be something that he could come in and out of as required. And it had got to the stage where, unless he had a great deal of involvement in the writing, or at least a lot of input into the music, he felt very frustrated. The rest of us felt we didn't want to follow the direction of the previous album, and we wanted to get back to a more guitar driven sound.[259]

Of the album's musical style, Anderson said:

Although ... some ... were keyboard oriented, they ended up with a good healthy dose of fairly bluesy rock kind of guitar. So when we finished that album, as yet untitled, having done songs like "Steel Monkey" and "Budapest" and "Farm on the Freeway," it had that definite feeling of being an album that whilst, on the one hand, revisiting some earlier Jethro Tull territory, still had a contemporary feeling. Although a few pundits did point out, fairly in some ways, and unfairly in others, that there was a little bit of Dire Straits, or even a ZZ Top feel to some of it.[260]

Former member Barrie Barlow agreed with many fans and reviewers in thinking that the combination of Anderson and Barre "was Mark

Knopfler from Dire Straits."[261] When asked about this similarity, Anderson responded:

> I had to tell that hoary old story about Paul Hamer from the Hamer Guitar Company, who used to make [Barre's] guitars. When he told me that he got a call from Mark Knopfler saying, "Could you make me a guitar, please, Paul?" And Paul said, "Sure, well what kind of guitar are you looking for? What sort of sound do you want?" And he said, "Well, I want to try and get that sound that Martin Barre from Jethro Tull gets." And soon people were saying, Oh, Jethro Tull sound like Dire Straits. It's the Dire Straits guitar sound." So there you go.[262]

Realistically, the similarities between the Tull and Dire Straits sounds on *Crest of a Knave* can be attributed to at least three factors: that Anderson now was writing in lower keys allowing him almost to whisper his vocals, that Barre was playing with a clean guitar tone more often, and that both Anderson and Mark Knopfler hailed from the Edinburgh area. Barre added:

> It's just a style of music ... there are a lot of people who play with the percussive Strat sound that Mark Knopfler has made famous, but it's not necessarily his sound. I hadn't suddenly started playing it; I think I started playing a Strat around 1982, or maybe before that. It's the best sound you can get on a Strat, and I did it to get some different sounds on the album.[263]

(Actually, Barre used the clean Stratocaster sound as early as 1976, on the *Too Old to Rock 'n' Roll* album.)

While post-production touches were being put on *Crest of a Knave*, Anderson and Barre joined Pegg for Fairport Convention's annual festival at Cropredy, a two-day event that draws more than 10,000 people, on August 15. During the 40-minute set of Tull classics, they were accompanied by Fairports Simon Nicol, Dave Mattacks, Ric Sanders and Martin Allcock, a combination that proved so impressive that Anderson asked the band to open the upcoming North American shows.

Doane Perry was disappointed with the album's liner notes, which included the credit, "Jethro Tull are: Ian Anderson, Martin Barre and Dave Pegg." His trip to visit his ailing mother had prevented him from getting full membership in the band, although he had been touring with them for three years. Perry said:

> Having done the record initially, it went through a couple of changes with Gerry on drums. But I definitely felt very much a part of the band,

not just a sideman. I'd contributed a lot to the live show, and it was a little distressing to be seen as a session player on the album.[264]

In all fairness to Anderson, *Crest* was the first Tull studio recording on which Perry played. Although he had contributed to the *Under Wraps* tour, the record had featured a drum machine; and *Crest* equally included Conway, who played on the epic "Budapest," which had been shortened and rearranged since the recording of Perry's original track.

The renewed interest in the band created by the album led to Anderson appearing as a "guest VJ" on MTV, introducing "some of his favorite videos" (including the live "Aqualung" performance from *Slipstream*) and fiddling about in New York's Central Park. No one there knew him (an elderly couple listened to him play a section of "Bourée" but still didn't realize who he was), except a lovely young waitress–aspiring actress who accepted his invitation to row across the lake.

The Tracks of *Crest of a Knave*

"Steel Monkey," with its straightforward, ZZ Top–inspired rock style, provides an effective bridge from *Under Wraps*. Though driven by a drum machine and a keyboard sequencer, these elements are well mixed into a blend of Barre's guitar, Pegg's bass and Anderson's vocals. Unlike the tracks on the previous studio album, this song actually rocks.

"Farm on the Freeway" is one of two masterpieces on the album, musically combining tasteful flute, bluesy electric guitar, virtuoso instrumental passages and lyrics pitting traditional ruralism against the encroachment of inevitable technological progress. Making his most substantial contribution to the album, Perry powers this exciting song with dynamic yet unobtrusive drumming.

In the tradition of "Working John, Working Joe" and "Fallen on Hard Times," "Jump Start" laments the plight of the British worker. And, at this point, Anderson knew this situation well, having hired scores of formerly unemployed people at Strathaird. For the second time, he mentions Prime Minister Thatcher: "Hey, Mrs. Maggie, won't you come on over. Hook me up to the power lines of your love." Two verses later, he sings, "And if you're fighting for your shipyards, you might as well just blame the sea." During a driving instrumental section, Barre plays a very Scottish-sounding melodic solo, musically reinforcing the lyrics.

Barre (on clean electric guitar) and Pegg (on acoustic bass) contribute a soothing introduction to "Said She Was a Dancer," the album's first "Dire

Straits–like" number. While this comparison may have fit the period in which the song was recorded, this style is very much in keeping with the folk genre that developed in the Scottish Lowlands, as well as throughout much of England, in the late 1960s and 1970s. Even cursory exposure to such singer-songwriters as Archie Fisher, Richard Thompson and Martin Carthy proves this. Lyrically this song, with its Cold War subtext, could have been included on *Under Wraps*, but here it possesses too much subtlety and passion to have been so consigned.

On CD and cassette only, "Dogs in the Midwinter," another drum-machine and sequencer driven track, is a generalized portrait of ineffective politicians, yet the final verse admits, "We're all running on a tightrope, wearing slippers in the snow ... we're all dogs in the midwinter." The listener must remember that, when this track was recorded, the Soviet Union existed and Thatcher and Reagan were still in power: "And it's hard to find true equilibrium when you're looking at each other down the muzzle of a gun."

Doane Perry recalled the experiences the band had while playing behind the "Iron Curtain":

> We were probably one of the first bands that went into the Eastern bloc before the Berlin Wall came down. It was very interesting to me playing in those places, really seeing it the way it probably had been for many, many years, before a lot of Westerners got to see it in its "newly revitalized" life after the wall came down. The first time we went to Budapest in 1986 and started playing in Eastern Germany—some of the places were very depressing and very gray—and it was very sad to see the poverty and what I saw, as a Westerner, probably a general unhappiness with life and work there. For a lot of them there wasn't the prospect of anything approaching what people had in Western Europe and America—the standard of living that most of us had—and yet I'm sure there are many of the people, probably the older generation, who feel that they might like it to go back to the old way.[265]

The second half of *Crest of a Knave* begins with "Budapest," a chauvinistic tribute to a Soviet sprinter the band had viewed while setting up for their July 2, 1986, concert in the Hungarian capital. Anderson recalled:

> I remember writing [it] in a hotel there, the morning after a show, about the vision of some slender and tall athletic creature who was serving sandwiches backstage. It was an easy lyric to write, ten minutes to scribble down half the lyrics for that one. I was having a cup of coffee, overlooking the not-so-blue Danube.[266]

Originally recorded as a 22-minute piece to cover an entire LP side, this rearranged 11-minute epic opens with atmospheric keyboards and Barre's acoustic soloing, building consistently toward a pleasant instrumental blending flute and classical guitar before Anderson and Fairport fiddler Ric Sanders join the mix. Barre then pumps up the volume with some familiar—and welcome—power chords. Doane Perry, whose drumming was supplanted by that of Gerry Conway, recalled: "Ian, I'm sure, has a tape of the original twenty-two minute version, which had a lot of other sections. I don't know if he had words for all of that, but eventually he cut it down to a nice, short eleven minutes. I like playing 'Budapest' live, but I'd love to hear the original some time."[267]

A classic Barre chord progression opens "Mountain Men," the guitarist's heavy multi-tracked harmony parts musically supporting Anderson's straightforward lyrics about a poacher and daughter filching fish from the laird's land. This tribute to the Scottish Highlanders is followed by "The Waking Edge," a Knopfleresque ballad (available on CD and cassette only) featuring the "Dire Straits–style" yet including a Celtic-type melody that is buoyed out of its complacency by Pegg's sensitive fretless bass playing. Ending the album as it begins, "Raising Steam" combines ZZ Top tones with a drum program and keyboard sequencer.

"Steel Monkey" was released as a single, backed with "Down at the End of Your Road" from the *Broadsword* sessions.

The *Crest of a Knave* Tour

The *Crest* tour officially began in Edinburgh on October 4, 1987, then moved to other parts of Britain and mainland Europe before returning to England for a show at London's Hammersmith Odeon on the 29th. The North American dates began in Providence, Rhode Island, on November 7, closing in Los Angeles on December 16 after a three-night stand at the Universal Amphitheater. Pegg got an enormous workout at every U.S. and Canadian gig, playing double duty with Fairport and Tull. Ric Sanders played his violin part on "Budapest" each night, and the entire Fairport ensemble joined in for a tremendous version of "Skating Away."

Having recently recorded their excellent "live" album *In Real Time*, Fairport took the opportunity to promote it heavily. Although it was produced live in the studio without overdubs, the album (which includes a dubbed-in crowd) is a bit misleading: Pegg later lamented that "it wasn't recorded at Cropredy."[268]

After Peter Vettese proved unavailable, Don Airey, a keyboardist with hard rock-heavy metal experience (Black Sabbath, Rainbow, Gary Moore) was hired for the tour. Although Anderson had sent him a tape, Airey, assuming he would be ready, failed to listen to it until the night before his audition. Shocked to hear the complexity of the songs, particularly "Songs from the Wood," which he recognized as "a work of genius," he stayed up until the next morning, learning the material. He admitted, "I had heard a lot of Tull's music before, but it was through hotel walls when I was with Rainbow, because Ritchie Blackmore is such a big Tull fan!"[269] Unfortunately, Airey, often resorting to sequencing and sampling techniques, did not fit easily into the Tull sound.

Doane Perry recalled a humorous incident that occurred when the tour reached North America in early November:

> We were rehearsing in upstate New York, and on the night before the first concert, there was no place open to eat. I was hungry and wanted a bite after a long technical rehearsal, so we stopped at a Dunkin' Donuts. And when I went in there, for some reason, the owner seemed to know who I was—I don't quite know how—but he insisted upon giving me a box of a dozen donuts.
>
> I said, "Look, I'm never going to eat a dozen donuts. Thank you very much. I'll give them to some of the band members tomorrow." So off I went with this box of donuts back to my room. The next day, when I was going off to the sound check—when I got to the arena—I realized I'd forgotten the donuts in the room, and they were going to go bad. Well, I figured I could give them to the crew and the band and anybody who wanted one.
>
> I gave our tour manager my room key and I said, "Would you go to my room and get the box of donuts and bring it down to the gig?"
>
> He came back later on and said, "Well, the cleaning ladies were in there and the box was gone, so I think they threw it out."
>
> I thought, "Great. Well, never mind." I didn't think too much more about it.
>
> That was opening night, and we got to the section of the show where we did this keyboard and drum solo thing; and I got to my drum solo and the audience started going completely crazy. I was thinking, "Oh, yeah. Well, I'm really showing them here!" It had gone down well in Europe, but they were really digging it here in America. I was puffed up like a peacock—and then, as I'm playing, I noticed that people had gathered at the side of the stage, looking at me.
>
> I thought at one point I'd cut my hand—and I've done that, hit my finger between the stick and the rim of a drum, and I see blood all over the drum. There's times when it's the Texas Chainsaw Massacre: blood all over my drums and cymbals and everything. But this was like a big

red splodge on my floor tom. I thought I'd cut myself—and sometimes you don't really feel it.

Anyway, I finished, and the crowd was going completely bananas. So, when I came off stage, Dave Pegg showed me a Polaroid, and what they had done was taken the box of donuts, and they had lowered them down on little pieces of string, so during my solo, eleven or twelve donuts slowly started to get lowered down over me—and they were hovering over me like little UFOs circling around my head. I didn't see this at all, but the jelly one had sprung a leak, and so this big splodge that I mistook for some blood in the heat of battle was only raspberry filling on my floor tom.

I still have the picture somewhere. I'm certainly glad they took it, because I'm not sure I would have believed it—and it must have looked absolutely fantastic from the front. And I'm sure nobody had the slightest idea why all these donuts were being lowered down over my head in the middle of my drum solo. Needless to say, none of my subsequent drum solos had quite the impact on the audience. So all I can say is "Thank you very much, Dunkin' Donuts."[270]

On November 17, the band appeared on *The Howard Stern Show*, during which the "shock jock" actually sang on "Aqualung." Later that day, Tull made a rare appearance on MTV, performing two songs live in the studio. On the 21st, they flew from Montreal back to New York to play a three-song benefit for "Hungerthon 1987" at the United Nations. Following a performance of "Skating Away," "Budapest" and "Serenade to a Cuckoo," they caught a plane to Worcester, Massachusetts, for a gig at the Centrum. Referring to the next evening's show at the Meadowlands Arena in East Rutherford, New Jersey, journalist Don Kaye wrote:

> Class. That sums it up in a word. Everything about Jethro Tull brims with class, from their musicianship to their songs to their sense of humor to their stage show. And it's because Jethro Tull are such a class act that they keep bringing in the crowds, old fans mingling with new generations of Tull devotees who could be the children of the men they had come to see.[271]

20 Years of Jethro Tull

5 LP / 3 compact disc collection
27 June 1988 (U.K.) / 26 July 1988 (U.S.)

Highest chart position: 78 (U.K.) / 97 (U.S.)
[Rating: 4.5]

Ian Anderson: vocals, flute, acoustic guitar, mandolin, tin whistle, harmonica
Mick Abrahams: electric guitar
Martin Barre: electric and acoustic guitars
Glenn Cornick: bass guitar
Jeffrey Hammond: bass guitar
John Glascock: bass guitar
Dave Pegg: bass guitar, acoustic bass, mandolin, mandola, octavius
John Evans: piano, Hammond organ, synthesizers
David Palmer: portative organ, synthesizers
Peter-John Vettese: keyboards
Martin Allcock: bouzouki, electric guitar
Clive Bunker: drums and percussion
Barrie Barlow: drums and percussion
Gerry Conway: drums and percussion
Doane Perry: drums and percussion

Tracks: THE RADIO ARCHIVES AND RARE TRACKS
    A Song for Jeffrey
    Love Story
    Fat Man
    Bourée (J. S. Bach)
    Stormy Monday Blues (Ecstine/Crowder/Hines)
    A New Day Yesterday
    Cold Wind to Valhalla
    Minstrel in the Gallery
    Velvet Green
    Grace
    Jack Frost and the Hooded Crow
    I'm Your Gun
    Down at the End of Your Road
    Coronach (Palmer)
    Summerday Sands
    Too Many Too
    March the Mad Scientist
    Pan Dance
    Strip Cartoon
    King Henry's Madrigal (traditional, arr. Palmer)
    A Stitch in Time
    17
    One for John Gee (Abrahams)
    Aeroplane (Anderson-Cornick)
    Sunshine Day (Abrahams)

FLAWED GEMS AND THE OTHER SIDES OF TULL
Lick Your Fingers Clean
The Chateau D'Isaster Tapes
a. Scenario
b. Audition
c. No Rehearsal
Beltane
Crossword
Saturation
Jack-a-Lynn
Motoreyes
Blues Instrumental
Rhythm in Gold
Part of the Machine
Mayhem, Maybe
Overhang
Kelpie
Living in These Hard Times
Under Wraps 2
Only Solitaire
Salamander
Moths
Nursie

THE ESSENTIAL TULL
Witch's Promise
Bungle in the Jungle
Farm on the Freeway
Thick as a Brick
Sweet Dream
Clasp
Pibroch/Black Satin Dancer
Fallen on Hard Times
Cheap Day Return
Wond'ring Aloud
Dun Ringill
Life Is a Long Song
One White Duck/0^{10}=Nothing at All
Songs from the Wood
Living in the Past
Teacher
Aqualung
Locomotive Breath

Dave Pegg's multi-instrumentalist Fairport cohort Martin Allcock, who had studied at the Huddersfield School of Music before becoming involved in the Celtic music scene, recalled:

> In the backroom of this pub on New Year's Day '88, Peggy said, "Ian wants you in the band playing keyboards." And I said, "Well, you know, Peggy, that I haven't got any keyboards and I can't play them!" Apart from that it was no problem! But I rang him and he said he only wanted somebody to play the simple parts and could play the guitar as well, so the advantage of the lack of technique, I suppose, got me in![272]

Having briefly worked as a chef in the Shetland Islands, Allcock, four days before his 31st birthday, was pleased to accept Anderson's offer—which meant that Don Airey had been dropped from the Tull roster. Allcock claimed, "I think I got the job because Ian didn't want a 'busy' keyboards player, and I am not physically able to do that," revealing that Airey "thought [Tull] was some kind of folk gig ... wasn't really into it."[273] Of his status in Jethro Tull, Allcock claimed that only three full-fledged members existed: "I'm just an operator—a hired hand ... I am in the same boat as Doane."[274] On January 14, Tull—comprising only Anderson, Barre and Pegg—were inducted into Hollywood's "Rock Walk," placing their hand prints in cement during an official celebration. (However, Doane Perry did graduate from "hired hand" to full-fledged member status during this period.)

Though Anderson initially resisted a 20-year gala, Chrysalis decided to give the band the royal treatment, including a three–compact disc (and five-LP) box set, a retrospective video collection, a double album featuring material culled from the box, and a radio series on the history of the band. All but the last project were completed, and the box set proved the jewel in the crown, a 65-track collection of radio and live recordings, studio out-takes, rare singles and remixes. (Only 11 of the tracks previously had been issued in the same form.) And Anderson himself, assisted by Tull aficionados Martin Webb and David Rees of the Tull fanzine *A New Day*, pored through the archives to select the material. When it was released in July 1988, *20 Years of Jethro Tull* was one of the first such box sets on the market.

The Tracks of *20 Years of Jethro Tull*

The three-CD set rightfully opens with six live BBC radio tracks recorded in 1969—"A Song for Jeffrey," "Love Story," "Fat Man," "Bourée," the old chestnut "Stormy Monday Blues" and "A New Day Yesterday"—

giving the listener a good taste of what the band sounded like when making the transition from *This Was* to *Stand Up*. Continuing with live material, this first disc, titled "The Radio Archives and Rare Tracks," jumps ahead to the "Elizabethan-Celtic" period with the acoustic portions of "Cold Wind to Valhalla" and "Minstrel in the Gallery," a superbly performed "Velvet Green" and "Grace."

Three excellent songs from the *Broadsword* studio sessions follow. "Jack Frost and the Hooded Crow," another of Anderson's songs concerning the true meaning of the holiday season, "I'm Your Gun," a common-sense and factual portrait of firearms, and "Down at the End of Your Road," a delightful tale of suburbia in which a "respectable" real estate agent leads a nasty double life, are highlights of the collection—whereas "Coronach," the *Blood of the British* theme written by David Palmer in 1986, is a Tull masterpiece combining a superb Anderson vocal, an impassioned oboe and absolutely savage Barre power chords. "Summerday Sands," a bluesy folk number featuring Barre on slide guitar, was recorded at the time of *Minstrel in the Gallery*, "Too Many Too" is another track from the *Broadsword* sessions (and, like "Watching Me, Watching You," anticipates *Under Wraps*), the brief acoustic piece "March the Mad Scientist" and the classically oriented "Pan Dance" were recorded in 1974 (and released on the 1976 "Winter Solstice" EP), "Strip Cartoon" was an out-take from the *Songs from the Wood* sessions, "King Henry's Madrigal" (featuring Pegg's Tull debut) is the 1979 studio version of David Palmer's rock arrangement of "Pastime with Good Company," and "A Stitch in Time" (with Anderson on bass) was a *Stormwatch* out-take.

The first disc concludes with the rarest of the rare, Anderson's "17," which sounds like an early Eric Clapton track, Mick Abrahams' "One for John Gee," Anderson and Glenn Cornick's "Jethro Toe" classic "Aeroplane," and Abrahams' "Sunshine Day," the most pop-oriented pre–"Too Old to Rock 'n' Roll" number the band recorded.

The second disc, "Flawed Gems and the Other Sides of Tull," begins with "Lick Your Fingers Clean," the original version of *War Child*'s "Two Fingers," recorded during the 1970 *Aqualung* sessions. Following are three excerpts from the "Chateau D'Isaster Tapes," which provide an interesting reference into the creative process that resulted in *A Passion Play*. "Beltane" is hardly a flawed gem, though perhaps a bit repetitious, an out-take from *Heavy Horses* celebrating the ancient Celtic feast of May Day. While "Crossword," including some fine guitar work by Barre, is a funky number recorded at the time of *Stormwatch*, "Saturation" is a somewhat tedious *War Child* out-take.

Another masterpiece, the love song "Jack-a-Lynn" weaves a beautiful melody and fine acoustic instrumentation with an eventual eruption of pulse-pounding hard rock—perhaps Anderson's finest such 180-degree shift. Here, the musical segue directly supports the lyrical content: After his nostalgic longing is accompanied by a lovely acoustic backdrop, the narrator cries out for his partner—"Magpies that shriek. Cold boots that leak!"—and the band explodes—"Call me to Jack-a-Lynn!"

Sandwiched between "Motoreyes" and "Rhythm in Gold" (two more *Broadsword* out-takes that could have fit onto *Under Wraps*, albeit superior with live drums) is "Blues Instrumental," an interesting 1979 fusion piece featuring John Glascock on bass and Anderson on wind synthesizer. "Part of the Machine," written specifically for the set, returned the band to its Celtic-oriented material of several years before. Having composed the introduction on flute, Anderson decided to play it on tin whistle and add Martin Allcock's bouzouki to the mix. Later in the song, during an extended instrumental passage, Allcock also plays electric guitar in his tell-tale fluid style (but unfortunately mixed well below that of Barre). The Scottish flavor of this number is given full reign in "Mayhem, Maybe," a medieval-style acoustic piece recorded for *Broadsword* but left incomplete until this set was issued. Also a *Broadsword* out-take, "Overhang" is followed by the superb "Kelpie," another "beastie" song (recorded at the time of *Storm-watch*), here involving legendary Scottish loch monsters, and "Living in These Hard Times," a *Heavy Horses* out-take using a rustic feel to communicate the then-current state of British poverty. Disc two ends with five previously released but remixed tracks: "Under Wraps 2," "Only Solitaire," "Salamander," "Moths" and "Nursie."

The third and final disc, "The Essential Tull," includes previously released tracks ("The Witch's Promise, " Bungle in the Jungle," "Sweet Dream," "Cheap Day Return," "Wond'ring Aloud," "Life Is a Long Song" [with Barrie Barlow's drums brought prominently into the mix], "One White Duck/0^{10}=Nothing at All," "Living in the Past" and "Teacher") and live arrangements of classics recorded during the early– to mid–1980s ("Farm on the Freeway," "Thick as a Brick," "Clasp," "Pibroch/Black Satin Dancer," "Fallen on Hard Times," "Dun Ringill" [a superb version, with Pegg on mandola], "Songs from the Wood," "Aqualung" and "Locomotive Breath").

The box set was chosen as one of the recommended albums of 1988 by Britain's *Q* magazine and received many positive reviews on the opposite side of the Atlantic. Writing for the Berkshire (New York) *Eagle*, Seth Rogovoy observed: "Listening to *20 Years of Jethro Tull* ... leaves a listener awestruck by the band's richness, diversity and compelling musicality."[275] Devoting three pages to a lengthy review, the esteemed *Record*

Collector magazine noted, "This collection sets the standard that future boxed sets must try to follow."[276] The 80-minute companion videotape blends live archival footage, music videos, an interview with Anderson, and the comments of Tull fans partying in a pub.

The *20 Years of Jethro Tull* Tour

From June 1 through 27, 1988, the *20 Years* tour roamed the U.S., from the West Coast through the South and into the East, bidding farewell at the Pier in New York City. "Part of the Machine" was played at most of the shows but eventually had to be dropped from the set list. Anderson explained:

> I play that to myself quite often, sitting in the dressing room, because I really like that song, but I don't know why it just doesn't work onstage … it never really settled down and felt comfortable. I thought about doing an acoustic version of it on my own, but I didn't in the end....[277]

Playing up the "advanced" age of the band members, the concerts concluded with Anderson, Barre and Pegg collapsing, only to be carted off via wheelchair, stretcher and crutches.

Beginning on July 3, the second leg of the tour hit Italy, Austria, Germany, Switzerland, Hungary, Greece, Germany and London's Wembley Arena for one show before the band played its first ever South American concerts during a tour of Brazil. The initial show at Belo Horizonte's Mineirinho Arena on July 26 was followed by Dave Pegg's joyous discovery of the Caipirinha, the local version of the Mexican margarita, in Rio de Janeiro four days later. In an effort to offset Anderson's previous comment that he cared little for Brazilian music, the band included a few unmistakable notes from Antonio Carlos Jobim's "The Girl from Ipanema" as an introduction to "Aqualung," delighting the 13,000 fans. At Porto Alegre in Southern Brazil on August 2, Anderson became very angry during "Fat Man" when an overzealous fan (one among a 15,000-strong sell-out crowd) tossed a bottle onto the stage, where it smashed a few feet away from Barre. Tull "correspondent" Jerome Ryan reported:

Opposite: The 1988 Fairport Convention lineup who supported Tull on the *20 Years* tour: Dave Pegg, Ric Sanders, Simon Nicol, Dave Mattacks and (kneeling) Martin Allcock. All but Nicol became members of or recorded with Tull between 1979 and 1995. (Pegg's inscription refers to the bass he is holding, a custom five-string model built by Scottish instrument maker Mike Vanden and used on Fairport's *Red and Gold* [1988] and Tull's *Rock Island* [1989].) (Author's collection.)

> It was strange to see Martin standing at the lip of the stage shaking his fist at the audience and motioning for the offending person to come up to the stage so that he could punch him out! But all was soon forgiven and the rest of the show went off without incident.[278]

Suitably recovered from the Porto Alegre incident, Tull journeyed on to the large city of Sao Paulo for three additional shows on August 6–8, the last being a televised affair at Ibirapuera Arena.

Even more shocking than Tull making a musical "comeback" after the bizarre *Under Wraps* release was their winning the first hard rock-heavy metal Grammy Award for *Crest of a Knave* in February 1989. The band, absent from the ceremony, were booed by fans of speed-metalists Metallica and were written up in the press as a "dinosaur" group. (The other two nominees were Alice Cooper and AC/DC.) In the February 28, 1989, Los Angeles *Herald Examiner*, Anderson said, "I really felt that we should be at the Grammys, but we were advised by our record company that we had no chance of winning."[279] Even when Doane Perry, who was at his Los Angeles home at the time, offered to represent the band at the ceremony, Chrysalis replied that they could not give him tickets.

Perhaps David Rees, in *A New Day*, put it best: "This [was] a new category and therefore possibly the first time Tull have suited *any* category no matter how tenuously.... Tull are not a 'hard rock band,' but they *are* a band that plays hard rock. *Crest* is many things, but if it must be condensed into a single narrow category then it is a 'rock' LP."[280] After receiving his statuette, Pegg inconspicuously displayed it, along with his gold records, in his Oxfordshire home, while he claimed that "Martin Barre keeps his in the back window of his car."[281] Barre added:

> We don't apply adjectives to our music. It doesn't matter who buys it or what it's called. It's good or bad.... It [the Grammy] meant a lot when I heard about it, but it fell flat for me personally.... We're hard to pigeonhole. We've always been unusual, out on a limb. I don't see us having a place in rock history. We're not a pure rock band like Led Zeppelin or the Who, doing the same thing for so many years.[282]

Having been out of the band for nearly a decade, David Palmer observed:

> That [heavy metal tag] is beyond the bounds of any comprehension. I don't think it is some kind of inverted compliment or some nasty person at the Grammy committee saying, "Well, let's just do this and sink Jethro Tull once and for all." I feel that this award, however misnamed it

might be, was directed to all the "old boys" that were in Jethro Tull and all the guys who are in it right now. We earned it. We earned public approbation, recognition. We were unique....[283]

In August 1988, Anderson and Barre again joined Pegg at the Cropredy festival. The weekend lineup was impressive, with Richard Thompson and Steeleye Span among the additional acts on the bill. On the evening of Saturday, August 19, during Fairport's four-and-one-half hour set, Barre joined in on "Set Me Up," a track from the band's excellent 1988 album *Red and Gold*, before launching into an instrumental medley culled from *Minstrel in the Gallery*'s "Requiem" and "Black Satin Dancer." (Earlier in the week, he had sat in with Fairport during the band's annual Cropredy "warm up gigs" at the Half Moon pub in Putney.) Toward the end of the set, Anderson added flute to "John Barleycorn" and the thunderous, eternally crowd-pleasing "Matty Groves," during which he created some engaging musical interplay with his "Budapest" collaborator, violinist Ric Sanders.

Rock Island

21 August 1989 (U.K.) / 12 September 1989 (U.S.)
Highest chart position: 18 (U.K.) / 56 (U.S.)
[Rating: 3.5]
Producer: Ian Anderson / Chrysalis CHR 1708
All songs written by Ian Anderson

Ian Anderson: vocals, flute, acoustic guitar, mandolin, keyboards, drums
Martin Barre: electric guitar
Dave Pegg: bass guitar, mandolin
Doane Perry: drums and percussion
Martin Allcock: keyboards
Peter-John Vettese: keyboards

Recorded at Farmyard Studios and Woodworm Studios, spring 1989
Engineer: Ian Anderson
Mixed by Ian Anderson and Tim Matyear, assisted by Martin Barre and Mark Tucker
Illustrations by Anton Morris and Jim Gibson
Art direction by John Pasche

Tracks: Kissing Willie
The Rattlesnake Trail

Ears of Tin (Mainland Blues)
Undressed to Kill
Rock Island
Heavy Water
Another Christmas Song
The Whaler's Dues
Big Riff and Mando
Strange Avenues

In November 1988, Anderson, Barre and Perry rejoined Dave Pegg at Woodworm Studios to begin working on musical ideas for a new Tull album. In just 10 days, eight songs began to take shape.

Pegg recently had designed two custom five-string basses with Scottish instrument maker Mike Vanden. During these sessions he played an active (or preamplified) model of rosewood, ebony, brass and mother of pearl that he subsequently took with him on the *Rock Island* tour. The previous year, he had played it on Fairport's *Red and Gold*, which he recalled as a far easier group of sessions: "I recorded all the bass parts for that in eleven hours, but that Tull album was a pain in the ass!"[284] One individual who disagreed with Pegg was Matthew Davis, a neighboring schoolboy, who was allowed to get a week's work experience as assistant engineer during the recording of the instrumental backing tracks at Woodworm. Having observed the working methods of the band, Davis wrote, "I can see why their music has stayed alive.... They are all real perfectionists, especially Ian Anderson.... All of them were instantly friendly and welcoming, inviting me to have dinner with them everyday at the local [the George pub]."[285]

Reading Anderson's own description of the meticulous recording process appears to bear out Pegg's point of view:

> Martin, Dave and I get together and rough out a few songs and put them on cassettes for some reference. Then we go to rehearse in Dave Pegg's room with a drummer. He's got a bigger studio room. Once we're satisfied with the format and arrangement of the song, we record the drum tracks in a room where we can all see each other while we're playing, so there is human contact. We play the finished song all together in the studio in one go.... But all we're going to keep is the drums, not because of everybody else's playing not being right, but because you want to be able to sit back and say, "What is the real guitar sound we need here and what quality of keyboard do we need there?"[286]

During an interview shot for the *20 Years* video release, Anderson said:

[Recording] is a lot more fun these days than it used to be, in commercial ... studios, when you are ... working with an engineer, a tape operator, and various people who are buzzing around. Doing it at home is much more private.... It's very private to come in here at eight o'clock in the morning or eight o'clock at night. You feel that you can do your best work....[287]

In the United States, *Stereo Review* gave Anderson high marks for a sterling recording, mentioned the swirling mandolins and Barre's "Teutonic" guitar work, but singled out Pegg's bass playing as the album's finest component.[288] Having played on scores of albums (including several by his old Fairport mate, the incomparable Richard Thompson), "Peggy," like Martin Barre, was now the recipient of free guitars from major companies. When asked why he had parted with the basses of his own design, he replied, "I don't have room to keep them in the house—they're just collecting dust—and Ibanez started giving me guitars."[289] At the age of 21, Jethro Tull were far from being a has-been band.

After a five-year stint with the band, Doane Perry finally was able to play on an entire album (aside from a few percussive contributions by Anderson). Of the Tull arranging process, he revealed:

There was certainly the latitude within the band to try different things ... in terms of form, and parts, collectively and individually. The parts evolved quite quickly out of the music that Ian had written. The parts are very directly suggested from everything that I hear when I am presented with some music. I try not to impose any sense of something that I *can* play. Often I'll hear something and I'll have to sit down and work out what the music has suggested to me, because it might be something that I don't know how to play or don't know how to play very well. And I'll have to work at it, but sometimes it comes quite quickly. I try to really stay away from imposing something or bringing a preconceived idea about what I might like to play into a piece of music. When I can let the music dictate what I'm going to play, I think it feels and sounds better. After the initial burst of inspiration, there's usually a lot of hard work in refining the part, to try to work out all the details and the nuances.

There are times that I had wished we had recorded an album after we had played it on tour first, because you would have developed a lot of things that might have sounded really good on the original record. But it's impossible to do that, you really practically can't do that, because audiences wouldn't be familiar with a whole body of music. We always put in something new that they haven't heard, but rarely have we had the luxury of being able to play it for a month or two and then go into the studio and record it. So with the process in the studio and then going out and trying to perform it live—you have to record these things with a view toward how you could perform it live. Very often, things that work in the studio don't come across live quite as well. Sometimes they just remain a studio track and they're better off that way.[290]

The Tracks of *Rock Island*

A steamy blues lick from Barre introduces Anderson's none-too-subtle tribute to fellatio, "Kissing Willie," a song that provides quite a contrast to cleverly ribald past compositions such as "Hunting Girl" and "Velvet Green." Upon hearing the final verse, the listener may wonder just where *Rock Island* is headed:

> Willie stands and Willie falls.
> Willie hangs his head behind grey factory walls.
> She's a—nice girl, but her bad girl's better.
> Me and Willie just can't help come when she calls.
> Now she's kissing Willie. (My best friend, Willie.)

Curiosities on an album that is lyrically excellent (arguably the best since *Broadsword*), these lyrics would seem more at home in the mouth of Mick Jagger. But aside from the content, musically "Kissing Willie" is a very pleasant rocker offering a taste of the subtle way Anderson uses mandolins throughout *Rock Island*.

"The Rattlesnake Trail," with its ZZ Top riffs and Mark Knopfler-like vocals, features the band still in the mode established on *Crest of a Knave*, while "Ears of Tin (Mainland Blues)," with Peter Vettese returning on keyboards, is thoroughly Scottish, both musically and lyrically:

> Now the sun breaks through rain as I climb Glen Shiel
> on the trail of those old cattlemen who drove their bargain south again.
> And in the eyes of those Five Sisters of Kintail
> There's a wink of seduction from the mainland.

Similar in arrangement and production to "Part of the Machine," this song is a fine blend of flute, mandolins and a pleasant folk melody with driving hard rock. Anderson's love for the Isle of Skye is apparent here:

> There's a coast road that winds to heaven's door
> where a fat ferry floats on muted diesel roar.

And there's a light on the hillside—and there's a flame in her eyes
but how cold the lights burn on the mainland.

After "Undressed to Kill" shifts the tone back to the steamy worka-
day world of "Kissing Willie," the title track, like "Farm on the Freeway"
and "Budapest" on the previous studio album, provides a more familiar
Tull style: the epic rock song with prominent elements of folk and classical music. "Rock Island," again featuring Vettese, is an impressive piece
primarily pairing electric guitar with flute but also blending in bits of
acoustic guitar and giving Pegg a rare solo spot. Tempo changes are reminiscent of "Dark Ages" on *Stormwatch*, and, with Pegg, Perry holds it
together with rock-solid precision. The contrast created by these shifting
tempi reinforces the lyrics, which refute the old adage that "no man is an
island": "Doesn't everyone have their own Rock Island? Their own little
patch of sand?" and "all roads out of here seem to lead right back to the
Rock Island."

"Heavy Water" is a simple, straightforward rocker crediting Vettese
on additional keyboards (though much of this is a sequencer) and juxta-
posing two of Anderson's favorite topics—sex and environmental destruction:

> I watched the little black specks running down her leg.
> Didn't seem to mind that dirty rain coming down—
> shirt hanging open. She was wet and brown.

One of the best songs on the album, "Another Christmas Song" is
another of Anderson's Yuletide tributes blending Celtic-style melodies and
instrumentation with classical and rock elements. Opening with a lightsome keyboard part that brings to mind glass-globe curios with their winter scenes and shook-up "snow," this piece, unlike earlier Tull holiday
fare—"A Christmas Song" and "Jack Frost and the Hooded Crow"—is
lyrically more optimistic, a quality reinforced by the pleasant combination of flute, bright electric guitar countermelody and bouncy percussion
(played by Anderson). Pegg's tasteful acoustic bass work and Barre's multi-
tracked harmony guitar parts hark back to *Broadsword*'s "Slow Marching
Band" as Anderson's vocal (still imbued with moments of Mark Knopfler
influence) weaves his warm Scottish verse:

> Sharp ears are tuned into the drones and chanters warming.
> Mist blowing 'round some headland, somewhere in your memory.
> Everyone is from somewhere—
> even if you've never been there.

So take a minute to remember the part of you
that might be the old man calling me.

The warmth of this Christmas fire is soon quenched by the icy chill
of "The Whaler's Dues," arguably *Rock Island*'s best track, which truly
leads Tull back into their late 1970s epic mode. Musically the track is a
combination of hard rock, blues, English folk and Beethoven; lyrically,
another of Anderson's excellent tales about man's disregard for nature, in
this case the continued hunting of Earth's true leviathans. As the song
begins, Anderson's shimmering keyboards and sparse flute suggest the
mysterious, seemingly infinite span of the ocean. Barre enters playing one
of the most mournful lead parts of his career, then joins Anderson in an
ominous unison passage that segues to flute and keyboards, creating the
image of a whaling ship slowly creeping out of fog-bound waters.

The verses are accompanied by dual mandolins, which lend a further
sea-song ambiance to the piece. But this is no pleasant shanty:

Been accused of deep murder on a North Atlantic swell
but I have three hungry children and a young wife as well.
And behind stand generations of hard hunting men
Who raised a glass to the living, and went killing again.

At the end of the verse, Anderson asks, "Are you with me?" and the band
shouts in reply, "*No!*" Here, the doom-laden maritime atmosphere of
"Flying Dutchman" returned for the first time in a decade. A driving
instrumental section, blending bluesy hard rock with Beethoven-like progressions, is beautifully rendered by Barre is all his multi-tracked glory.
After the guitarist approximates whale song with some subtle, weeping
blues licks, Anderson plays a brief flute solo, returning to the mandolins
and a final verse:

Now I'm old and I sit land-locked in a back-country jail
to reflect on all of my sins and the death of the whale.
Send me back down the ages. Put me to sea once again
when the oceans were full—yes, and men would be men.
Can you forgive me?
No!

"Big Riff and Mando" personifies the two ends of the Tull spectrum,
both musically and lyrically. "Marty," a mandolinist, has his instrument
stolen by "Big Riff," a would-be rock 'n' roll singer. As the story plays out,
the mandolin-based folk verses alternate with the hard rocking choruses,

and the song breaks in the middle for melodic, jig-like interplay between the electric guitar and flute (which brings to mind "Part of the Machine"). Anderson gets very self-reflective when he has Big Riff admit that he's "got a proposition for those English boys," offering to give back the mandolin for a chance to sing. The concluding song, "Strange Avenues," also includes a lyrical reference to the band:

> Strange avenues where you lose all sense of direction
> And everywhere is Main Street in the winter sun.
> The wino sleeps—cold coat lined with the money section.
> Looking like a record cover from 1971.

Martin Allcock makes his second of two keyboard contributions, joining Anderson and Barre in a variation on the introduction to "The Whaler's Dues" before the song kicks into high gear and then settles down for the Knopfleresque verses. Drawing the content of the album full circle, "Strange Avenues" concludes by tying in the title track:

> Heading up and out now, from your rock island.
> Really good to have had you here with me.
> And somewhere in the crowd I hear a young girl whisper,
> "Are you ever lonely, just like me?"

In his Fort Lauderdale *Sun Sentinel* column, book editor Chauncey Mabe singled out particular *Rock Island* tracks and summed up the band's current status:

> "Ears of Tin" begins with the folky Elizabethan grandeur that is one of Tull's trademarks, but features a fast break in the middle that is distinguished by searing guitar work by Barre. It's the kind of satisfyingly complex melody that the band's enduring popularity is based on; after two or three hearings it sticks in the mind like flypaper.... When the Who toured earlier this year without a new album ... Pete Townsend admitted his group was "creatively spent." *Rock Island* is the work of an outfit in full possession of its creative intensity.... The group puts on a theatrical show that sacrifices none of its musicality, and indeed, often sounds better live than on record.[291]

British journalists also offered positive reviews, with *Q*'s Rob Beattie giving it four stars:

> There's less acoustic guitar than before, and less solo grandstanding, so the feel is much more of an ensemble performance, though Martin

Barre's electric guitar and Ian Anderson's hustle-bustle flute are well to
the fore ... honest Dave Pegg plucks both bass and mandolin beautifully....[292]

John Blennin, in a column called "It's Hip," wrote:

When so many groups pride themselves on their facelessness, thereby
being able to fit in with all the other vague slop current rock is swim-
ming in, Jethro Tull remains as common to other groups as the Grand
Canyon is to a sewer canal.... Ian Anderson's distinct vocals and flute
work and Martin Barre's guitar phrasings have never been duplicated and
it's to their credit that on this album that they're still finding new ground
to break.[293]

"Kissing Willie" was released as a single, receiving enough airplay in
the U.S. to earn a high ranking among the "most played" songs on album-
oriented radio stations.

The *Rock Island* Tour

The *Rock Island* tour began September 18, 1989, at the Eden Court
Theatre in Inverness, Scotland, home office of Strathaird. Two days later,
they played an energized date at Newcastle's City Hall, where *Evening
Chronicle* reporter Peter Feasby wrote:

Twenty years since Ian Anderson first stood on one leg, rolled his
eyes and leered at the audience, Jethro Tull can still produce a show of
classic and eccentric genius ... they showed a wealth of subtlety, humor
and power that was sometimes breathtaking.... Guitarist Martin Barre
and the rest of the band are individually and collectively more than
accomplished—they lend a quality and range that is rarely surpassed.[294]

The *Sunderland Echo*'s Graeme Anderson also was on hand to form a similar opinion:

[T]he place was packed with those wanting to pay homage to one of the
most individual bands ever to get on vinyl ... it's no mean feat for a 42-
year-old to sing, play guitar and flute *and* leap about the stage like a
madman for that long without so much as a single loss of breath control.
Anderson managed it though as he led from the back as well as the
front of the stage, like some demented musical farmer, dressed in trilby,
waistcoat and tails.... During the entire two-hour set I never once found
myself losing interest.[295]

Following a night in Edinburgh, the band played two dates at the Apollo in Manchester, where the *Evening News'* Paul Taylor wrote:

> To my certain knowledge, Ian Anderson is rock music's only flute-playing fish farmer.... Anderson is not the band's only virtuoso. Martin Barre is one of those rare guitarists who dazzle with their passion and precision rather than their rate of notes across the fretboard. And Martin Allcock is one of those multi-instrumentalists who could get a tune out of a kitchen sink, given the chance.[296]

Four more dates in Britain were followed by shows in Germany and Switzerland. The October 13 Zurich concert was followed by a brief, primarily acoustic jam in the dressing room. The original "A Christmas Song," "Cheap Day Return," "Mother Goose" and "Locomotive Breath" were recorded to DAT for inclusion on a second CD single, "Another Christmas Song," which only was played in Europe, a disappointing fact for Anderson, who acknowledged that current disc jockeys saw Tull as "some quaint, hippy sort of thing.... They probably know we exist, but would not be aware that we do actually go out and play the same places as lots of other people that they hear about every day."[297]

Following a pair of gigs in Italy, the band flew to the U.S. to begin a two-month stretch, opening in Troy, New York, and ending in San Francisco. Preceding the October 23 concert at Troy's R.P.I. Fieldhouse, the *Berkshire Eagle's* Seth Rogovoy pointed out some salient facts about the band:

> Of the many dinosaur Rock 'n' Roll bands who belied their presumed extinction and returned to the concert circuit this year in an unprecedented display of musical nostalgia, perhaps only Jethro Tull can boast that, since 1968, it has continued to tour and record without a break.... Yet curiously, one of rock's oldest and most durable acts is all but forgotten and overlooked by the mainstream rock press.
>
> In fact, from its beginnings ... Tull ... has been woefully misunderstood and underestimated by the rock establishment.[298]

Concerts on the U.S. tour featured much of the new album, opening with the atmospheric "Strange Avenues" and ranging from the phallic excess of "Kissing Willie" to the ominous power of "The Whaler's Dues." "Do you like whales?" Anderson asked the audience in St. Paul, Minnesota, just before a slide show depicting harpoons and scenes of whaling "harvests" filled the huge screen behind the band. Barre, playing exceptionally well on his 43rd birthday, emitted eerie "whalesong" that filled

"Peggy" shows off his 1989 Grammy Award, Woodworm's Hilton, Oxfordshire, September 18, 1990. (Author's collection.)

the auditorium as Anderson "harpooned" himself with his flute toward the end of the performance. The entire concert featured moments of raw power, with the band performing as well as it ever had.

Martin Allcock playing rhythm guitar, allowing Barre to stretch out with his lead work, was a great asset of this tour. Of this experience, All-cock said:

> [Y]ou have to follow the flute.... In Fairport it is a bit easier because there is a lot of room to do what you want in all the arrangements. Even though the arrangements are fairly set, you can still play more or less what you want, whereas with Tull it is much more like playing in a symphony orchestra, because you are playing almost, but not actually, written parts.[299]

Flawless renditions of "Farm on the Freeway," "Budapest" and "Jack-a-Lynn" were matched musically by tight, note-perfect and invigorating instrumentals. Just before the band moved to form a cozier enclave at stage left, Anderson announced, "Now we're going to play some folk music," and launched into a medley of "The Pine Marten's Jig" and the traditional Irish tune "Drowsy Maggie." Perry played some ethnic percussion on this piece, but stayed on his drum stool for a roof-shaking instrumental version of "Sea Lion" (with nods to "The Third Hoorah" and Beethoven's Ninth Symphony) and a *Minstrel in the Gallery* medley of "Requiem," "Black Satin Dancer" and "Cold Wind to Valhalla" featuring some of the most sublimely beautiful soloing ever fretted by Barre. Many Tull fans greatly enjoyed the extended reworking of *Stand Up*'s "Nothing Is Easy" and "Bourée," as well as five songs from *Aqualung*, including "Cheap Day Return," "Mother Goose" and "My God," which was enhanced by slides of stained-glass windows projected behind the band. Unexpectedly, and much to his momentary chagrin, Barre's guitar cable became unplugged just before "Aqualung," forcing the band to begin again.

A week later, Tull reached the warmer climes of Florida, where the band members thawed out, but a new source of unpleasantness returned. At Orlando's Civic Centre, the drunken portion of the crowd screamed through the entire show, prompting Anderson to yell and swear at them on several occasions. The show's two epic highlights, "Budapest" and "The Whaler's Dues," actually were dropped, and, during "My God," Ian angrily kicked his stool across the stage. He later said:

> In reference to the "noisy crowds" ... it's a very subjective thing because what may impose itself on me, in the context of someone sitting three rows in front of me, screaming, "Whoah-Yeah!" when I'm playing or singing some quiet piece, and I'm trying to listen to what I'm doing and what everybody else is doing, as well as trying to actually enjoy what I'm doing. Some clown is there just inanely screaming; the quieter the music, the louder he, she, or they will be. And it's not the whole audience, it may be just a few people, but it really ruins the mood. And when it happens night after night, as it does to some extent—usually in America—it gets you down a bit.[300]

At the close of 1989, *Kerrang* magazine writer Mark Putterford observed:

> Tull, satirical sires in out-sized suits, remain encased within the stratosphere of their own eccentricity. They live in a world populated only by them and their die-hard disciples, and wear their quaint, quirky uniqueness—embodied in that perennial flute/mandolin sound—like a birthmark.[301]

This unique style received some equally unusual exposure in December 1989, when President George Bush ordered U.S. Marines to invade

Panama and capture dictator Manuel Antonio Noriega. Implementing a CIA plan to flush the drug-trafficking general out of his stronghold, the troops blasted loud rock music night and day. One of the songs used to drive him to distraction was "Too Old to Rock 'n' Roll," one of the most famous radio-friendly Tull songs. Required to play it live incessantly, Doane Perry said:

> I actually used to sing live background vocals on stage. Now, I love to sing—and I'm not too bad if I don't have to play and hyperventilated and huff and puff. This little incident sort of signaled the end of my singing career in Jethro Tull, at least in terms of any kind of strenuous vocal parts. We were in the middle of "Too Old to Rock 'n' Roll," and I heard these wheezing and heavily strained sounds coming from all over the stage, only to discover that they had cranked up my vocals in all of the monitors—I hope not in the front-of-house mix—unbelievably loudly. So every kind of wheeze and huff and puff in between every line going horribly out of tune was in full stereophonic glory for every band member and crew member alike to enjoy. I looked around, and every-body was laughing—and I didn't actually realize that I was the source of all the laughter until I realized that it was my voice! Whereupon I instantly stopped singing and was horrified, because at that moment I realized that's what I actually sounded like when I was trying to play and sing at the same time. And I think after that, even though I had a mike on stage, I believe that it was probably plugged into an old pizza box under the stage. I don't think it got switched on after that. But that hasn't discouraged me from singing, nonetheless, though I'm sure they wish that it had.[302]

On December 16, CNN Headline News, reporting that Tull "still tour," featured a brief interview with Anderson, "who still plays the role of a crazed, eccentric Englishman," and a clip from "Kissing Willie." He admitted:

> Maybe coming to see Jethro Tull is like ... buying a very used Austin-Martin ... something that has about a hundred and twenty thousand miles on the clock, but it'll probably go for a few more years yet, and you're gonna have a bit of fun in it.... By and large, it's more fun doing it now than it was twenty years ago.... I'll give it maybe another five years before the slowing down and the inevitable tolls of age begin to catch up on us. But, who knows, we might even manage our farewell concert in the year Two Thousand.[303]

During May 1990, Tull made another tour of Britain, playing smaller halls in 19 cities, opening at Aberdeen's Capitol Theatre on the 4th and closing at the Oxford Apollo on the 28th. To please their fans in England and Scotland, they appeared at venues missed in the past. Anderson said:

> We are taking the music to the people, rather than having them drive through the night to see us. And we will only advertize locally, so people in Birmingham will be able to go to the show in their town without Londoners snapping up all the tickets first![304]

The music was performed in two sets, the first opening with Anderson reprising his "Wond'ring Aloud" solo bit before the rest of the band crashed into "Steel Monkey" from *Crest of a Knave*. A brief *Thick as a Brick* medley and "Living in the Past" were followed by "Rock Island," Barre's instrumental titled "Nellie (The Revenge)" and Anderson's solo medley of "Cheap Day Return," "Nursie," "Mother Goose" and "Jack-a-Lynn," which was concluded, as usual, with awesome power by the entire band. The set ended with "Farm on the Freeway," "Serenade to a Cuckoo," "A Christmas Song" and "Budapest."

Set two began like the *Rock Island* shows, with "Strange Avenues" giving way to "Kissing Willie," but then Anderson gave the spotlight to folkies Pegg and Allcock, who were joined by Perry for the "The Pine Marten's Jig"/"Drowsy Maggie" medley. The Celtic material continued with "Dun Ringill" and "Jack-in-the-Green" before "Said She Was a Dancer" led into the thunderous grandeur of "My God" (this time with "Bourée" serving as the bridge), an instrumental medley of "Pussy Willow" and the majestic "Pibroch," the soothing "Another Christmas Song" and a surprising rendition of *Living in the Past*'s "Love Story," which they only had played live in 1969 for the BBC. The shows culminated with the familiar "Too Old to Rock 'n' Roll," "Aqualung," and "Locomotive Breath," with "Cheerio" thrown in as a final encore.

At Caird Hall in Dundee, Scotland, on May 5, reviewer Alan McCrorie particularly appreciated the folk elements:

> With two members of Fairport Convention lurking in the ranks, the folk instruments figured greatly. Bassist Dave Pegg and keyboards/guitarist Martin Allcock brought to life the creaking "Love Story," "Christmas Song" and even "Bourée" with mandolin and bouzouki....
> Anderson's flute freak-outs recall[ed] the halluceogenic [sic] '70s on *Bursting Out*, with much snorting and whistling to be heard for full effect.... Aaah, they simply don't make 'em like this anymore! Still, bearing in mind the 'orrible checked trousers Pegg was wearing, we have to be thankful for even the smallest and most wretched of mercies, don't we?[305]

During the fourth concert, at the Livingstone Forum on May 8, Pegg became noticeably angry and smashed his bass against a wall behind the stage. He later admitted, "I just had a little too much to drink. I repaired the bass and it's fine."[306]

Journalist Philip Widdows attended the May 13 show at Preston's Guild Hall:

> Jethro Tull are a steel hand in a velvet glove. They stroke the listener into [a] contented, relaxed mood and then blast them with full force rock, with a tight bass-drum combo hooked to a wailing lead guitar and rumbling keyboards while over the top is Anderson's savage flute spitting notes.... Playing as well as ever, Jethro Tull proved that they can succeed where many bands fail....[307]

The following evening, the band was in Hanley, where no Tull lineup had performed in 18 years. In his article "Gems from Tull's ageless minstrels," John Fradley enthusiastically reported:

> Originality is an increasingly rare commodity in the music business—particularly in this, the age of computerized mediocrity, dominated by pre-programmed trivia and candyfloss throwaway lyrics.
>
> The Victoria Hall, Hanley, last night excelled with an act that cuts across the age gap because of its sheer timeless brilliance. Last seen here in 1972, Jethro Tull have retained all their magic.
>
> The original [sic] members of the band are "Mr. Tull" himself, Squire Ian Anderson, of Skye, and Martin Lancelot Barre, a guitarist of rare lyricism.... It was good of Ian to bring his ageless minstrels to Hanley after all these years.[308]

Liverpool *Daily Post* critic Tony Kenwright, however, addressed a problem created by performers who remain on the road for so many years. Following the May 22 concert at Liverpool's Empire—where the band may have been uninspired at that point in the tour—he wrote:

> Fronting a rock band with acoustic guitar is not unique but the sound Jethro Tull make is. Influenced almost exclusively by the English folk tradition it manages to encompass both hard driving rock and gentle eloquent moments.
>
> The band are splendid musicians and Anderson is still a marvelous showman but what this show lacked was an edge. There was no risk-taking here.... Jethro Tull may not be too old to rock 'n' roll but they shouldn't be such old dogs that they can't learn a few new tricks either.[309]

After a summer break, the band regrouped for a four-city tour of Germany in late August, interrupted by a sidetrack back to London to play Wembley Stadium with Fleetwood Mac on September 1. Appearing third, after sets by River City People and Daryl Hall and John Oates (a strange segue, to be sure), they offered an abridged, 75-minute version of the current tour, impressing the Fleetwood fans with (not surprisingly) "Too Old to Rock 'n' Roll" and "Aqualung." Anderson said:

> I think we all hated that, because it was a very uncomfortable thing. We felt very strange about it because the atmosphere was not good. As far as Fleetwood Mac were concerned it was their gig, and they all arrived in separate—not even separate limos—but separate buses with their entourage. I wasn't allowed to use certain parts of the stage; they cordoned them off so I couldn't use them! I couldn't believe how petty it was!... We were asked to help out because it was selling so badly to begin with. I'm not saying that we made that much of a difference but we were certainly responsible for some of the ticket sales anyway.[310]

During the second week of September, they then flew back to Brazil for a second "South American tour," although this one would consist of only five dates. Upon returning, Dave Pegg described the poverty and crime he had witnessed in Rio de Janeiro, particularly an unpleasant incident involving him and Martin Barre, whose leather jacket had been stolen by a passerby. After chasing the thief and his accomplice to a toilet farther down the beach, they decided to "bugger off" when a knife was brandished.[311] Pegg later elaborated on Barre's obsession with leather garments:

> Once, we were in Mexico City. It was about eighty-five degrees. My wife, Chris, was with me at the time. And there was a knock at the door, and Martin was standing there, and he was wearing this full-length, Gestapo-type leather coat, which, to be honest, was about three sizes too big for me.
> And he said, "What do you think?" and we both just stood there flabbergasted! It was touching the floor and about four inches too wide at either shoulder.
> We went, "Yeah, it's great, Martin! Who's it for?" And he had to buy it. It was such a bargain....
> Every tour, he would buy a leather coat.... I'm sure he's got a room at his house which smells like a leather shop.... I remember once, being in the market in Istanbul—the famous market—with Martin. And we went out shopping and Martin wanted to buy a leather bag. And he spotted this big, black leather bag.... There were lots of stalls, and we all finished up buying carpets ... but there was this leather bag, and it was

fantastic. You'd pay a hundred-and-fifty, hundred-and-seventy-five pounds for it in England, but it was advertised at fifty quid, and Martin eventually knocked the guy down by bartering. He got him down to about twenty pounds. Even I was embarrassed by Martin. He was very good at it....

And the guy said, "Right, it's a deal," and he took the twenty quid off of Martin. He took all the newspaper stuffing out of the bag.

And Martin proudly picked up the bag and he walked about five yards. And there was another store next to it, and the guy came over to him and he went, "You want to buy a *new* one?" Which I thought was funny at the time.[312]

On Saturday, September 22, 1990, a truly historic moment in the band's career occurred at the Woughton Centre in Milton Keynes, where the annual Jethro Tull Convention attracted some surprise guests. Though the attendance of Mick Abrahams and Clive Bunker (with their band Blodwyn Pig) had been advertised, their being joined by Ian Anderson, Martin Allcock, the elusive John Evans and the reclusive Jeffrey Hammond startled and thrilled the 400 fans who managed to get tickets. Playing together for the first time in 22 years, Anderson and Abrahams got bluesy on "Someday the Sun Won't Shine for You" and "So Much Trouble" before Allcock and Bunker joined in on bass and bongos, respectively, for "Fat Man," which Ian dedicated to Mick, who hadn't played on the original.

Although Allcock handled the bass work, Hammond said afterward:

I enjoyed the convention very much. I was a bit dubious about it at first, to be honest, because obviously I had no idea of what it would be like or what sort of people would be there. But I thought there was a very nice atmosphere there, and I was quite touched in a way that people should actually remember me and recognize me from what was really quite a long time ago. It was a bit of a humbling experience in a way to realize that it was and is important for many people. And I do remember somebody saying as I was leaving, "Thanks for giving up your Saturday to come here." That was nice....[313]

Live at Hammersmith '84—
—— *The Friday Rock Show Sessions* ——

10 December 1990 (U.K.)
[Rating: 2.5]
Producers: Tony Wilson and Dale Griffin / Raw Fruit FRSLD 004
All songs written by Ian Anderson (except where indicated)

Ian Anderson: vocals, flute, acoustic guitar
Martin Barre: electric guitar
Dave Pegg: bass guitar, mandolin
Peter-John Vettese: keyboards
Doane Perry: drums and percussion

Recorded live for the BBC at the Hammersmith Odeon, London, September
9, 1984
Recording engineer: Dave Dade
Digital remastering by Don Walker

Tracks: Locomotive Breath (instrumental)
Hunting Girl
Under Wraps
Later, That Same Evening (Anderson-Vettese)
Pussy Willow
Living in the Past
Locomotive Breath
Too Old to Rock 'n' Roll: Too Young to Die

Initially broadcast by the BBC on December 27, 1984, a truncated
version of the band's Hammersmith Odeon *Under Wraps* show was released
on LP and compact disc by London's Raw Fruit Records in mid–December
1990. Fading in on a drum program and a pre-recorded voice stating,
"Under Wraps," the introduction segues to Barre's guitar and Pegg's bass
before Perry drives the band into an instrumental version of "Locomotive Breath" recalling David Palmer's arrangement on *A Classic Case*. Soon,
"Hunting Girl" rears her head, featuring an atypically inferior tone from
Barre, whose guitar lashes out with metallic shrillness and feedback—a
quality that unfortunately plagues much of the album.
    While the drum machine fits into the studio "Under Wraps," here it
sounds insufficient, and some live acoustic drumming from Perry could
have improved the track. Also featuring programming, "Later, That Same

Evening" is a slight improvement, though the un-dynamic nature of the *Under Wraps* album is made openly apparent.

The sound of Anderson's woodsy mandolin, Vettese's portative organ-like keyboards, Pegg's bass and Perry's cymbals on "Pussy Willow" now reminds the listener that this is a *Jethro Tull* concert. The traditional arrangement of "Living in the Past" is then introduced on claves by Perry, who displays a very deft touch on the jazzy drum part. After the second chorus, the song shifts into jazz-fusion high gear, with Pegg and Perry contributing some of the tightest Tull rhythm section work ever recorded.

Peter Vettese provides fine jazzy improvisation on John Evans' "Locomotive Breath" introduction before Barre burns through a nasty solo and the rest of the band thunders in on this Tull warhorse. Bits of "Black Sunday," "Living in the Past" and "European Legacy" are included in the lengthy ending, which is followed by the inevitable encore, here "Too Old to Rock 'n' Roll." Vettese contributes some good "old time" rock and roll piano on the solo break before the band kicks into another fusion-style instrumental sequence ending with Anderson strumming and singing the introduction to *Thick as a Brick*.

At the close of 1990, Anderson played flute on an album by the New York thrash-metal band The Six and Violence, whose attitude one would expect to oppose that of the Jethro Tull leader. What do progressive rock and punk have in common? The Six's Kurt Stenzel explained:

> [A] lot of our musical mayhem came from the Jethro Tull spirit that music should be fun, and that the music that you play should sound like no one else's.... Jethro Tull is it's own genre, and that is what we're all trying to be.... Very few [bands] play on their own terms, fewer still play well, and so few do it on such a grand underground scale as Jethro Tull. Theirs is a fine instrument, the Six and Violence a blunt one, but both are an attempt at honesty.[314]

During a Yuletide trip to Colorado in December 1990, Barre was involved in a skiing mishap that injured his left hand: the tendon at the base of his thumb was torn after he fell, requiring a cast that temporarily prevented the band from finishing the next studio album. All the backing tracks had been completed before Christmas, but the master guitar work would have to wait a while.

In May 1991, Pete Prown, a contributing editor for the magazine *Guitar for the Practicing Musician*, wrote:

> [B]ehind [Anderson's] broad musical vision over the years has been a revolving cast of players whose main constant has been guitarist Martin

Barre. Barre's crunching electric rhythms and tasteful leadwork have been the perfect foil to Anderson's whimsical acoustic strumming, and have also allowed Tull to generate the kind of exciting acoustic-electric interplay in their stage shows that other top bands have found impossible to pull off, Led Zep included.[315]

Prior to the release of the new studio album, the band played a month-long series of European dates during June and July 1991. Beginning the tour at Denmark's Aalborg Festival on June 22, they impressed a huge crowd, as reported by an astute musical observer in the following day's *Aalborg Stiftstidende*:

> The one and one-half hour set showed that on the whole Jethro Tull has not progressed since the early seventies, but also showed that this does not matter at all. The band has found a niche to which it holds onto proudly and rightly, and that is no bad thing in our shifting age. The niche consists of a broad and complex, rather symphonic style, perfectly balancing with great technical skill 17th-century English music and something like heavy rock. In spite of a most advanced and complicated structure the music still reaches out to the audience....[316]

Another newspaper, *Jyllands-Posten*, agreed, printing an article titled "Jethro Tull—the experience of the year in Aalborg":

> The performance of the band developed into something you could compare with a warm embrace from an old friend.... Ian Anderson['s] ... complex rock music—with a touch of symphony—has not lost a single inch during the years.... The older ones amongst us had to fight against the lump in the throat emotions, while the younger generations enthusiastically applauded Ian Anderson.[317]

Five concerts in Germany were followed by three Austrian gigs, one each in the Czech Republic, France, Luxembourg, Greece and Switzerland, and four in Turkey, where the band is very popular. Doane Perry remembered:

> The first time we played in Turkey, in Istanbul, and later in Ismir, at an amazing ten-thousand-year-old ampitheater called Ephesus: The wonderful luxury we have as a band is that we can go and play in many places in the world, and people do seem to know our music. It's wonderful. We're very fortunate to do that, and part of that is because the band has been going for so many years. But music really is the international language. They don't really even have to understand the lyrics. They might like the sound of things, and they might know what Ian is singing about, but they respond to the music, and that's incredibly gratifying.[318]

Finally, Tull returned to the crumbling Eastern bloc for a festival in Tallinn, Estonia. Perry said:

> We played a huge outdoor concert for about one-hundred and fifty or one-hundred and sixty thousand people. It was quite a surprise to us; and yet the sound of the crowd was probably similar to playing for a couple thousand Westerners. I think the people were so intimidated by the police there. They had this huge crash barrier that was kind of a wire fence that was in front of the stage, and then there were police with billy clubs behind that. The really avid fans were down in front. Some of them periodically would try to climb the fence, and they would get told to get down by the cops. The cops were pretty strident and pretty physical. They'd push them off and, at one point, a kid climbed up and got pretty far up the wire, and a cop pulled out a billy club and whacked him on the head and he fell. At this point, Ian got really pissed off and he stopped the concert. And he said if any more policemen hit any more kids that we were going to stop playing and just leave the stage. And the audience was so intimidated by the police—not just the ones down in front—even the people way in the back. They just didn't know quite how to respond at a Western rock concert. I think it was one of the first big Western rock concerts that ever happened in Estonia, and they did not know how to behave. They were afraid to be too demonstrative, because they were afraid they were going to get whacked over the head with a billy club, as well.[319]

Perry also elaborated on the unique nature of the band's lodging accommodations in Tallinn:

> I can recall some amazing incidents in the hotel that we were in. The second floor, which from the outside looked like a normal part of the hotel, actually didn't officially exist. You couldn't get to it by elevator. And I noticed when I looked at our room numbers, we were all in a vertical line up and down the hotel, like 315, 415, 515, 615 and 715. And the crew were all spread out. And I thought, "Well, that's kind of unusual," because the rooms themselves weren't that great or unique. And if you wanted to make a phone call, it took about eight hours to get through to the West.
> I recall going out shopping with our interpreter, and I just said jokingly, "So, I guess our rooms are bugged," and she said, "Oh, yes, of course they're bugged." And I looked at her, and I thought she was joking, and she said, "No, no, no, your rooms are bugged." And she told me that the second floor was the KGB headquarters in the hotel, where they monitored everything because it was sort of a big, fancy hotel in Tallinn, which in reality wasn't all that fancy.

I actually found the bug in my room, and I felt like James Bond. I took out my very trusty Swiss Army knife after discovering this huge panel in the closet and unscrewed it, and I found this grill. And behind the grill was another panel, and I unscrewed that with my knife, and behind that I found the bug. But then I thought better about removing it or playing some practical joke, pretending there were a lot of people in the room, because I thought, "Well, I don't know if they have a really great sense of humor about these things!"

Remembering a friend of mine who had been over to Moscow on tour and had found a bug in his room—he pulled it off the wall, and within about a minute and a half the KGB were at his door—I thought, "I don't think I'll do that." But I was sort of amused and entertained and *shocked* at the same time. I can't imagine why they thought bugging our rooms would be remotely interesting. So they probably have hours and hours of incredibly tedious tape that hopefully somebody had to listen to.[320]

Catfish Rising

10 September 1991 (U.S.) / 23 September 1991 (U.K.)
Highest chart position: 27 (U.K.) / 88 (U.S.)
[Rating: 2.5]
Producer: Ian Anderson / Chrysalis DCHR 1886
All songs written by Ian Anderson

Ian Anderson: vocals, flute, acoustic and electric guitars, acoustic and electric mandolins, keyboards, drums
Martin Barre: electric guitar
Dave Pegg: bass guitar
Doane Perry: drums and percussion
Andy Giddings: keyboards
John Bundrick: keyboards
Foss Paterson: keyboards
Matthew Pegg: bass guitar
Scott Hunter: drums (uncredited)

Recorded at Farmyard Studios, Woodworm Studios and Presshouse Studios, winter-spring 1991
Engineered by Ian Anderson and Tim Matyear, assisted by Mark Tucker
"This Is Not Love" and "Doctor to My Disease" mixed by John Williams and Geoff Foster at Air Studios

Sleeve design by Phil Rogers and John Pasche
Illustration by Jim Gibson
Logo and monogram by Geoff Halpin

Tracks: This Is Not Love
            Occasional Demons
            Roll Yer Own
            Rocks on the Road
            Sparrow on the Schoolyard Wall
            Thinking Round Corners
            Still Loving You Tonight
            Doctor to My Disease
            Like a Tall Thin Girl
            White Innocence
            Sleeping with the Dog
            Gold-Tipped Boots, Black Jacket and Tie
            When Jesus Came to Play

  Catfish Rising generated an equal amount of positive and negative opinions from Tull fans, some who enjoyed Anderson's return to the band's early roots, and others who criticized it as a commercial move to capitalize on the resurgence of blues popularity. Anderson claimed:

> [I]t was an album born out of having fun making a kind of rock music using more traditional, woody sort of instruments and with an emphasis on blues as being the musical feeling behind most of it, rather than having classical or any folk references. A couple songs in there are rather like "automatic writing" songs.... They don't necessarily tell a big story. They're just like lots of little ideas linked together.... Again for me that's an album that does have the humor, the warmth, a slightly careless feel about it which I like.[321]

Having previously said that Beethoven was his "only hero," now he again embraced the workingman likes of Howlin' Wolf and Muddy Waters during interviews. How could a lover of only Beethoven play the blues? Many who heard the album agreed that, at this point, Tull couldn't.
  Anderson explained how he approached writing the material:

> Most of the songs were written on open tuning mandolins, so therefore they have a kind of bluesy feel about them, although they are not "the blues" as such. I've taken those ideas and feelings and tried to go somewhere else with it, both musically and lyrically. I've made it a bit less Louisiana, and a bit more Surrey![322]

Nonetheless, fans who saw Anderson's return to the blues as a commercial one had some ground to stand on. In 1971, after attaining enough success to forget about how he had sounded on *This Was*, he told an interviewer:

> It's black music and I'm not black and I'm not being racist in saying this so why should I pretend to be black by playing their music? You know, try to become absorbed in what they're singing about because I'm not black, I don't know how it feels to be black and I don't know how it feels to be black and proud or black and down or any of the variations of the feelings that everybody in humanity goes through without being black so why should I try and sing those kinds of songs?[323]

Having written so many of the songs on mandolin, Anderson played all the parts himself, admitting, "We have a great mandolin player in the band; in fact, *two*, in the form of Dave Pegg and Martin Allcock ... but it's sort of my sacred territory. And just as I don't tread on other people's toes too much of the time, nobody treads on mine...."[324] Although using sparse keyboards, Anderson went through three musicians: Who veteran John ("Rabbit") Bundrick; a Scottish player, Foss Paterson; and Andy Giddings, who had come to his attention through drummer Steve Jackson, who had sent an audition tape featuring "The Chase," a pub band with whom the 27-year-old keyboardist had been playing. (Martin Allcock did not play on the album, though he was retained for the subsequent tour.)

The Tracks of *Catfish Rising*

Beginning with a Doane Perry drum fill, "This Is Not Love" is a straightforward, Rolling Stones–type rocker featuring Giddings on keyboards and Pegg's son, Matthew, on bass. (Pegg wrote all the bass parts for the album, during his absence touring with Fairport Convention, Matt very capably sat in for his father.) Lyrically, *Catfish Rising* is another very strong album, as demonstrated by the second verse, which easily could have fit into *Heavy Horses* or *Stormwatch*:

> Empty drugstore postcards freeze
> sunburst images of summers gone.
> Think I see us in these promenade days
> before we learned October's song.
> Out on the headland, one gale-whipped tree;

curious, head-bent to see.
How come you know better than me
that this is not love.

"Occasional Demons," an earthy, steamy blues number, is a more "rural" sounding, acoustic version of *Rock Island*'s "Kissing Willie" and "Undressed to Kill," while "Roll Yer Own," Anderson's lighthearted advice about female masturbation, is a jazzy, mandolin-based folk-blues (featuring Pegg on acoustic bass guitar) stylistically reaching back 22 years to the *Stand Up* album.

"Rocks on the Road" is arguably the album's best song, featuring an atypical acoustic guitar style and a fine, jazzy instrumental break allowing Giddings to stretch out on piano and Matt Pegg deftly to play another of his father's bass parts. Barre adds a sensitive solo just before the piano and flute segue back into an acoustic verse. The lyrics create an indelible image:

> There's a black cat down by the quayside.
> Ship's lights, green eyes glowing in the dark.
> Two young cops handing out a beating:
> know how to hurt and leave no mark.
> Down in the half-lit bar of the hotel
> there's a call for the last round of the day.
> Push back the stool, take that elevator ride.
> Fall in bed and kick my shoes away.
> Rocks on the road.

Of this song, Anderson said:

> It's one of those songs about ... being on the road, but not necessarily in a rock band. I mean, if you're a traveling salesman, and you're traveling in vacuum cleaners ... selling them. Or fish, for that matter ... It's ... hotel life, and I get to talk about my favorite subject, which is plumbing.[325]

"Sparrow on the Schoolyard Wall," another mandolin-based number, is advice directed at teenagers, while "Thinking Round Corners," a Celtic blues containing the most bizarre lyrics ever penned by Anderson and musically reminiscent of *Benefit*'s tartan psychedelia, is another highlight:

> Let's bathe in malt whisky: covet gold finery
> through the eyes of a Jackdaw, dressed to the nines.

Let's go in wet corridors: dive down drains.
Draw strength from machinery, it's all the same.
Thinking round corners. Think round corners, I say.
Thinking round corners.

Unleashing a vicious solo that matches the neurotic nature of Anderson's vocals, Barre contributes perhaps his most intense moment on the album. The oddity of the song actually became magnified for Doane Perry, who, while first listening to Anderson sing and play it on acoustic guitar, developed a drum part that situated the downbeat in the wrong place. He explained:

> I was trying desperately to *unlearn* the way I had learned it. I was upside down. I had to transcribe my part and move everything over by an eighth note, in my head. But, when we got to the chorus, it was still too confusing, so I had to have the engineer group mute the whole band. So when we got to the chorus, all I heard was the click track and the drums. Then, when I finished, I went up to the control room. He put the whole band in, and it was like some other guy playing the drums, because it still sounded totally backwards to me. I thought, "Oh, man, I'm in big trouble if we have to play this live!" Every time I hear that song, I'm inclined to want to hear it in this upside-down way, which sounds quite natural and sort of syncopated with a really interesting groove. But, in fact, it's actually *wrong*![326]

"Still Loving You Tonight," including subtle lead guitar work by Anderson and Barre, Matt Pegg's final contribution and a guest spot from drummer Scott Hunter, is a slow 6/8 blues played with classical precision, but "Doctor to My Disease" is an unimaginative rocker squarely in the ZZ Top mode. Another good acoustic, folk-based song, "Like a Tall Thin Girl," musically and lyrically recalling "Fat Man," may be the most "classically Tull" piece on the album. Like "Budapest," it was inspired by an attractive young woman who impressed the band, specifically Doane Perry, who had spied her while eating in an Indian restaurant. Mentioning his love for this type of ethnic cuisine, Anderson wrote a verse about the percussionist:

> Big boy Doane, he's a drummer. Don't play no tambourine
> but he's Madras hot on the bongo trot, if you know just what I mean.
> Stands six foot three in his underwear;
> going to get him down here and see
> if this good lady's got a little sister 'bout the same size as me.

A non-blues, more "epic"-oriented song, "White Innocence" is a lesser version of "Budapest" including the album's only moments of Mark Knopfler–style vocals. Though the chorus features Barre and Perry creating Native American–sounding riffs that recall "Broadsword," and the instrumental break includes nice interplay between Anderson's flute and Foss Paterson's keyboards, there is not enough musical variety to sustain a song than runs nearly eight minutes. However, Perry recalled, "'White Innocence' was a very memorable song to record and to play live."[327]

A funky bass introduction by Pegg opens "Sleeping with the Dog," another slow 6/8 blues that steams along nicely, occasionally punctuated by effective rhythm section kicks and alternating solos from Anderson's flute and Barre's guitar. Graced by a title worthy of ZZ Top's Billy Gibbons, "Gold-Tipped Boots, Black Jacket and Tie" is an acoustic, mandolin-based boogie; and "When Jesus Came to Play," featuring the same instrumentation, provides a fun, humorous conclusion to the album:

> He sang about three or four numbers, but we'd heard it all before.
> We boys were getting restless: no girls were moving on the floor.
> Those parables, they were merciless and the tables overturned.
> And there were no minor miracles but false prophets, they were burned.
> Well, maybe he was Jesus; but his hair could have used a comb.
> Long before he hit the last notes, we boys had all gone home.
> Oh yeah. When Jesus came to play.

Several additional songs were recorded but not included on the final release. About half of them arguably are superior to what is on the album, and the remaining tracks are some of the strangest Jethro Tull ever, particularly two country-flavored numbers, "I Don't Want to Be Me" and the incomprehensible "Truck Stop Runner." Incredibly, during the spring, Anderson, while performing as a guest disc jockey on Greater London Radio, had plugged "Runner" in between interviewing a Scottish National Party MP and Francis Wilson, the television weatherman who narrated the introduction to "Dun Ringill." Anderson later admitted:

> I was mixing songs at the time and I took along the two that I'd finished, but afterwards I decided that it was a bit wet, so I chucked it out. Gone!… It was okay, but it didn't quite click. It was actually quite fun when it was just me singing and playing guitar, but we had real problems trying to make it into a credible band piece. Martin and I did a demo of it which was all right and sounded quite promising, but when it came to it, it didn't quite gel as a Jethro Tull song. So that one went by the board. You'll never hear that again.[328]

The "country-western" influence on Anderson actually came from a song that American guitarist Steve Cropper had sent to him via Chrysalis. Though the demo did not particularly impress him, Cropper's finger-picking style of acoustic guitar playing did:

> I think actually the original "Christmas Song" was played with my fingers.... But it was one of those things where, in learning somebody else's song I had to learn to play that way, and it sparked off other things on the album. If I hadn't had that song from Steve Cropper I wouldn't have played "Rocks on the Road" in the same way....[329]

Country hardly seems appropriate for Jethro Tull, who have successfully worked nearly every other kind of music into their eclectic mix. The other out-takes, "Rosa on the Factory Floor" and "Silver River Turning," are quite good (and would be made available two years later on the two-CD set *Nightcap*). Another ZZ Top–style song, "Night in the Wilderness," was included on the U.K. "This Is Not Love" CD single, along with a live version of "Jump Start" recorded in Philadelphia during the 1987 tour. These two tracks also were released on the U.S. "Rocks on the Road" CD single, which also includes live versions of "Rocks" and "Bourée," and Anderson's 1981 home demo of "Jack-a-Lynn."

At the time *Catfish* was completed, Martin Barre spoke about his playing style:

> I'm sure it's changed over the years, though I don't think of myself as having a style or anything. I'm not a technician, who really works out a way of playing, like the way Steve Vai or Larry Carlton would do it. I look at myself as a jack-of-all-trades on guitar, because I can play Bach, blues, rock 'n' roll, and something that sounds like jazz, but probably isn't. I don't get influenced as much by guitar players as I do by a good melody, like in Edward Elgar's *Symphony Number One*. I just love the harmony, the melody, and the emotion of that piece....[330]

Immediately after the album was released, Anderson, Barre and Pegg made the rounds of American East Coast radio and television stations. On August 20, 1991, Anderson and Barre appeared on *Late Night with David Letterman*, where they played a medley of "Aqualung," "Locomotive Breath" and "Black Sunday" with band regulars Paul Shaffer, Will Lee and Anton Fig. Letterman introduced only Anderson, who stopped to mention "Mr. Martin 'Da Da Da Da Dah Dah' Barre" before allowing his axeman to unleash the famous opening riff. Pegg, who was not invited, later said, "It didn't matter to me. I don't like David Letterman, anyway."[331]

After the *Late Night* taping, Anderson, Barre and Pegg packed off for Jimi Hendrix's famous Electric Ladyland Studios in Greenwich Village, where they played a live semi-acoustic set for broadcast over WNEW radio: "Rocks on the Road," "Tall Thin Girl," "Mother Goose/Jack-a-Lynn," "Bourée" and the "Aqualung"/"Locomotive Breath"/"Black Sunday" medley. Following the intimate concert, all three were supposed to enjoy a meal courtesy of Chrysalis at a New York restaurant. However, only Anderson was provided for, and Barre and Pegg were ignored entirely, leaving them stranded until they could find their way back to the hotel. The next morning, while doing another live broadcast, this time on Philadelphia's WMMR, Anderson attributed the band's survival to "Julie Barre's credit cards." Pegg then proposed "a tour of old people's homes when Tull are in their 70s."[332]

Over the remainder of the week, they did similar spots in Boston, Chicago and Los Angeles, where the publicity tour culminated on *Rockline* with Bob Cockburn. Callers again asked typical questions, but this time Barre and Pegg were able to field a few, in between joining Anderson for semi-acoustic renditions of "When Jesus Came to Play," "Rocks on the Road," an extended "Fat Man" and the "Aqualung"/"Locomotive Breath"/"Black Sunday" medley. "Fat Man" was the highlight, featuring Barre on flute as Anderson played mandolin (and tambourine with his left leg), and then a bass solo by Pegg while his cohorts switched to electric guitar and flute, respectively. Following his flute solo, Anderson returned to mandolin as Barre again twittered the 22-year-old flute licks.

Reviews of the album were mixed, with critics noting its uneven quality but praising the folk and blues oriented songs. Although critics such as Patrick Kampert blamed Anderson's attempt to make Tull more palatable to current fashions—"In recent years, the members of Tull seem to have their eye more on pleasing and appeasing the tastes of the marketplace rather than playing to their strengths.... *Catfish Rising* seemingly tries to please everyone, and thus its accomplishments are limited"[333]—others mentioned that his hard rock songs often have been plodding affairs. American audio publications particularly admired the eclectic material. *Goldmine*'s Michael P. Dawson wrote:

> The surprising jazz flourishes in the moody, rambling "Rocks on the Road," the return to "Fat Man" territory in "Like a Tall Thin Girl" and the indescribable Beefheart-gone-Celtic weirdness of "Thinking Round Corners" help make those songs stand out over relatively mundane rock fare....[334]

Stereo Review agreed, calling the performance "strong" and the recording "excellent":

> "Roll Yer Own" is a particular delight, harking back to the walking gait and blues/jazz sound of *This Was*.... "Gold Tipped Boots, Black Jacket and Tie" is a bouncy near-rockabilly number with mandolins and flute thrown in, giving it, too, the woodsy flavor of vintage Tull. Then there's "Thinking Round Corners," an audacious creation that could have sprung only from a mind as original as Anderson's. What, exactly, is it? Well, if you were as charmed and fascinated by albums like *Stand Up* and *Benefit* as I was many years ago, you'll understand that labels simply can't be hung on music as delightfully deranged and eclectic as this.[335]

At about the time *Catfish* was released, the introductory bars of "Locomotive Breath" were being used as the soundtrack for a Michelob Beer commercial on U.S. television. During the *Rockline* interview, Anderson said:

> [N]ormally speaking, we wouldn't do that stuff ... if it was in Britain or anywhere else, especially if it was alcohol or cigarettes ... but here, people don't mind you being associated with it. I mean, Paul Newman has his salad dressing, and the money goes to charity. And I'm just the Colonel Sanders of smoked salmon in a mysterious and horrific way, so being involved with a particular brand of beer is okay....[336]

Finishing his comment, Anderson mentioned that it was not really his playing that was featured in the commercial, but that of Barre, who added, "My in-laws phoned me to tell me about it.... They were very excited.... They all drink Southern Comfort down there [in Mississippi]. They have a lot of spirit."[337]

The *Catfish Rising* Tour

Just before the *Catfish* tour began, Anderson revealed how he and his bandmates devised ideas for their stage shows:

> [A]ll those things that you would consider "production values" ... things like stage setting and whatever bits and pieces go with it—we really only decide that in the final couple of weeks of rehearsal, because if you plan these things way ahead of time, they become so contrived and so theatrical, so *showbizzy*, that it's not really our style. So ... we try and do those things at the very last minute....[338]

In early October 1991, the band played six dates in England—two at
the Manchester Apollo, one in Birmingham, and three at the Hammersmith Odeon—before heading back to mainland Europe for three gigs in
Italy, one in Switzerland and 13 in Germany, where they hit every major
city. Completing that leg of the tour in Hagen on November 1, they had
only a few nights off before opening the U.S. tour five days later in Providence, Rhode Island, where Anderson received the key to the city from
Mayor Buddy Cianci.

Supporting the album's back-to-blues style, the U.S. tour, featuring
Allcock on keyboards but leaving all the electric guitar work in the hands
of Barre, included impressive versions of songs reaching all the way back
to *This Was*, particularly a superb, eerily recreated version of "Serenade to
a Cuckoo," with Anderson's improvisatory talent on the flute being light
years beyond what he could do 23 years earlier. Obviously spending more
time with his instrument and less on writing complex songs, he later said:
"I *do* quite often practice the flute these days and I have the feeling that
I might actually be getting better at it."[339] The band also unleashed a
thunderously rearranged version of *Stand Up*'s "A New Day Yesterday,"
with Anderson back on "mouth organ" for the first time since *Too Old To
Rock 'n' Roll*, and an equally savage performance of "Cross-Eyed Mary."
The concerts' true highlight of musical intensity and sheer power arrived
when Barre, Pegg and Perry were left as a trio to perform a wicked instrumental rendition of *Songs from the Wood*'s "The Whistler." Perry described
the tour's stage design:

> We had a set that looked like an Italian bistro that had a rise in the
> middle, and I was set up on stage right, and Martin Allcock's keyboards
> looked like an English pub, and he had beer pulleys; and we had a dart-
> board. During this one song when Ian was playing a little acoustic song
> by himself, I got up from the drums and went over to the pub part of the
> set. I started playing darts.
>
> Now, I never ever drink alcohol on stage. I just really can't play if
> I've had the slightest bit of alcohol. I always have Gatorade—and we had
> this particular flavor of Gatorade, and it was kind of like the color of
> whiskey. So they got these shot glasses and they poured the Gatorade out
> of a whiskey bottle—and I took seven or eight shots, very, very quickly.
> So the audience thought I had seven or eight shots of whiskey—and
> Martin Allcock and the crew members swear up and down they never
> did this, but somebody spiked me, and I think it was vodka because I
> couldn't taste it.
>
> It wasn't whiskey—I would have tasted that. It tasted like Gatorade,
> but by the time I'd finished my eighth shot, I noticed that the darts—

first I was hitting Martin's speaker grill, and they were going off to the monitor desk at stage left, everywhere except the dart board—I realized I was having some sort of trouble controlling the aim of the darts.

After a couple minutes of this, I was a little bit *over refreshed*, and I thought, "Oh, no! I've got about another hour and twenty-five minutes to go, and I was like a Gumby man, just rubber limbed, legless; and I staggered back to the drum seat, and somehow I finished the rest of the show, just being completely like rubber bands. My limbs and everything felt totally elastic.

And I actually kind of had fun—I didn't feel guilty, because I hadn't really done it to myself, but I realized that I had in fact been spiked—and I thought, "Oh, this is how Dave Pegg feels every night when he goes out to play!"

I don't think I would ever elect to do that, because it affects the motor control that's necessary to play the drums. As a sheer novelty, it was kind of fun for an evening. And I think the crew got a big kick out of it, but nobody's ever admitted to it. I don't believe that it was psycho-somatic.[340]

The future of the tour seemed in jeopardy after the second U.S. show when, in Portland, Maine, on November 8, Anderson was stricken with laryngitis. Writing for the Portland *Press Herald*, freelance reporter Jim Sanville had a field day criticizing Anderson but displayed his ignorance of the subject by referring to Pegg as the "*former* Fairport Convention bassist."[341] But Anderson was not averse to being self-deprecating, opening the concerts by entreating, "I'll take your pity. You're looking at a bunch of really *old bastards!*"

The tour also included some of *Catfish*'s weaker songs, including "White Innocence" and "Doctor to My Disease," which Dave Pegg complained about after the sold-out Chicago show on November 24: "Ian's a good songwriter, but … I hate playing *that* damn song!"[342] That same show was cut short due to Anderson's illness with the flu, which he attributed in part to "bad American hotel air-conditioning"; in fact, several of the concerts on the tour suffered from his recurring throat problems. Nothing from *Rock Island*, which had dominated the much more elaborate previous U.S. tour, was played, but "Farm on the Freeway" impressed the true Tull fans in the audience.

Following the Chicago concert, Pegg discussed his feelings about the current status of the band, remarking that he much preferred playing dates with Fairport Convention: "Ian won't play any of the folk-oriented material in the States, because no one understands it. We do in Europe, though, particularly Germany. 'Heavy Horses' is a big favorite there."[343]

The sheer volume of the Tull concerts was problematic at this stage of the band's career, with the sound level remaining uniform, whether for a large stadium or a small theater. Noting that Doane Perry wore earplugs while playing, Pegg referred to being on stage as "fucking cacophony."[344] However, a highlight of the tour was the souvenir program, which increasingly had become more elaborate, in the tradition of great album packages like *Thick as a Brick* and *Living in the Past*. This time the booklet, one of the best they ever devised, featured each band member's "favorite recipe," reflecting the catfish in the album's title. While Anderson offered his own "Cheating Catfish Jambalaya," Martin shared "Barre's Veggie Lasagne," Dave revealed "Peggy's Mussles," the younger "Maart" described "Allcock's Eggs Benedict Souffles," and Perry listed "Doane and Xam's Beanless Cajun Turkey Vindaloo." Both Anderson and Perry demonstrated their love of hot chili peppers, an ingredient "Peggy" also included in his seafood dish, which he often cooks at his summer home on the coast of Brittany. Referring to the programs, Pegg said:

> Fantastic. A lot of work goes into them. Once, everybody had to write about somebody else. It's not that easy, because you don't want to upset anybody. So I had to write about Martin [Barre].That was all right. I mean, I could never write about Ian ... but Martin had to write about Ian. I mean, it was quite funny, quite accurate. Ian's a very intelligent guy.... I still have a lot of respect for him....[345]

However, Pegg also remarked that Anderson generally avoided having a drink with the rest of the blokes, instead isolating himself, always with Gerd Burkhardt at his side. Cindy Redmond, an employee of Chrysalis' press and promotions department in New York, explained:

> Of course, every band has schedules, but none operate on Ian Standard Time. I mean, a new employee asked me recently what it's like working with Ian—and I wasn't entirely joking when I said, "Invest in a stopwatch." See, Ian Anderson is a guy who likes things to run with military precision. He hates inefficiency and he hates surprises. In short, "Shit happens" is not a philosophy that has much appeal for him. That puts him in the minority in the world of rock 'n' roll.[346]

During March and April 1992, Tull set off on another series of *Catfish* dates, again playing smaller venues in Britain, including shows in both Edinburgh and Glasgow, before heading for mainland Europe, hitting capitals and other cities in Denmark, Sweden, Norway, Germany, Holland, Belgium, France and Spain. Allowing the talented Andy Giddings to fill the keyboard post, Anderson gave Martin Allcock the axe. "Maart" revealed:

> Ian didn't tell me face to face that I was out of the band. I just got a letter, from his secretary I think, telling me that Ian wanted to experiment with different players, so my services were no longer required. He congratulated me on the improvement in my keyboard playing while I'd been in the band, and offered me a reference should I need it to find further work! I was really hurt. I didn't mind that he wanted to use somebody else—it's his band, and I respect that, obviously. But it would have been nicer to hear it from him personally.[347]

But the Fairport contingent in the band numerically remained the same: unavailable for more dates, Doane Perry left the drummer's stool to reliable Dave Mattacks, who became the third member of the folk-rock legends to join the Tull ranks.

A versatile musician, Giddings had toured with various performers but now was faced with a unique challenge, as he explained:

> I spent a solid week, every day from nine in the morning 'til one the next morning, with all the stuff set up at home, and went through all the tapes and made myself learn it. There is nothing predictable about any of the material, so it's not the sort of thing you can just jump in and busk. There is a lot of homework to be done before you can even attempt to play it.... It's probably the most taxing stuff I've ever had to play, both mentally and physically.[348]

Giddings not only wanted to learn the material properly, but he became the first Tull keyboard player to recreate the original parts played by John Evans and David Palmer. He gathered various samples: "A tune on a piano is one thing, but you have the piano down here, bells and flute over there, string parts, et cetera, up there, and so on."[349] He also was the first keyboardist in a decade to set aside the computerized sequencers in favor of playing everything live. Of his first concert experience, he recalled:

> Ian is a real stickler for punctuality. I mean, nobody likes to be kept waiting. On the way to the venue, Ian was enlightening me as to the importance of prompt hotel departures and the like, and of course I was agreeing emphatically, eager to appear responsible. The next morning I overslept. I couldn't blame it on my alarm clock, as I didn't have one. Ian was less than impressed, although he did offer to buy me an alarm clock at the railway station.[350]

The Tull lineup of 1991–1995: Martin Barre, Ian Anderson, Doane Perry (standing center), Andy Giddings and Dave Pegg. (Photograph by Marek Smejkai; courtesy of Ian Anderson.)

A Little Light Music

14 September 1992 (U.K.) / 22 September 1992 (U.S.)
Highest chart position: 34 (U.K.) / 150 (U.S.)
[Rating: 3.5]
Producer: Ian Anderson / Chrysalis CHR 1954
All songs written by Ian Anderson (except where indicated)

Ian Anderson: vocals, flute, acoustic guitar, mandolin
Martin Barre: electric and acoustic guitars
Dave Pegg: acoustic bass guitar, mandolin
Dave Mattacks: drums and percussion, keyboards

Recorded live on 8-track DAT in Germany, Switzerland, Austria, Czechoslovakia, Greece, Turkey and Israel, spring 1992
Engineered by Leon Phillips
Mixed by Ian Anderson

Sleeve design and illustrations by Bogdan Zarkowski
Photographs by Martyn Goddard

Tracks: Someday the Sun Won't Shine for You
Living in the Past
Life Is a Long Song
Under Wraps
Rocks on the Road
Nursie
Too Old to Rock 'n' Roll: Too Young to Die
One White Duck
A New Day Yesterday
John Barleycorn (traditional)
Look Into the Sun
A Christmas Song
From a Dead Beat to an Old Greaser
This Is Not Love
Bourée (J. S. Bach)
Pussy Willow
Locomotive Breath

Back in England in mid–April 1992, the band rehearsed for yet another tour, this time a semi-acoustic set to encompass Europe and parts of the Middle East, to be recorded for a live album titled *A Little* Light *Music*. Was Anderson pandering to the marketplace by mimicking the currently fashionable "unplugged" shows and albums? He said:

> We've been going to radio stations with just an acoustic guitar for a long time now, and we went and played that way on MTV in its early days. Right from the beginning, my role has always been as the acoustic musician in a rock band, and I am almost alone in the history of rock music in that regard.
> The instruments I play have always been very acoustic instruments.... I've been giving you the health-food version of rock 'n' roll: The more organic Ian Anderson will not harm your health.[351]

Putting Andy Giddings on hiatus (and turning over a modicum of keyboard work to Dave Mattacks), Anderson resurrected folkie gems such as "Life Is a Long Song," "Nursie," "One White Duck" and "Under Wraps II" to be played by Barre on acoustic and electric guitars, Pegg on acoustic bass guitar and mandolin, and Mattacks on a stripped-down drum kit, as well as his own flutes, mandolin and acoustic guitar. After opening with two English dates on May 1–2, they were off to Germany, Switzerland, Austria, Czechoslovakia, Greece, Turkey and Israel, including two dates in Tel Aviv. Toting along an 8-track DAT deck on loan from Yamaha, they captured enough alternate takes of the songs to ensure a releasable 80-minute album. Anderson nearly included as much heavy material as usual, offering somewhat watered down renditions of full-tilt rockers such as "This Is Not Love" and "Locomotive Breath," which he believed could not be left out of Tull concerts, for the simple reason that fans might be disappointed.

Of the small theaters, Anderson remarked:

> I think the most scary thing wasn't actually the change to the music, because it really wasn't an acoustic tour. It was just a little bit more emphasis on quieter songs that we had recorded, most of which were more acoustic anyway. It still had its loud and up tempo moments as well, but it was actually the size of the venues I found really very terrifying. I remember one theatre we played in—I don't know whether it was Berlin or Munich—it was about 1,100 people or something, and it was just scary. You could almost reach out and touch the back row. I found that absolutely, really, really frightening to feel everybody in the room could really see everything and hear everything that you did. It was a strange, strange thing to get used to. But after the first couple of songs it was really enjoyable. You felt the sort of intimacy that you really were contacting all the audience, and once you got used to the idea, it was great, but it was very frightening walking on stage.[352]

The Tracks of *A Little* Light *Music*

Anderson's return to the blues is apparent in a reworking of the *This Was* track "Someday the Sun Won't Shine for You" recorded in Athens. After he opens with harmonica, Barre enters playing Mick Abrahams' riffs from 1968, then the rhythm section joins in, ending the song with a brief blues jam that segues into a driving instrumental rearrangement of "Living in the Past" from a concert in London.

The long-dormant "Life Is a Long Song," from a show in Frankfurt, Germany, follows. Barre's electric guitar is joined by Pegg's bass and Mattacks' glockenspiel, which introduce Anderson's acoustic strumming. Recorded in Zurich, Switzerland, "Under Wraps" is presented as a primarily acoustic instrumental. While introducing the song, Anderson humorously refers to his former experimentation with computerized music: "Back in eighty-four ... we toyed with the world of synthesizers and technology, and then decided it was easier just to keep Dave." Due to the absence of Andy Giddings' piano, "Rocks on the Road," recorded in Caesarea, Israel, sounds a bit thin during the jazzy instrumental section, but is nicely rounded out by Pegg's bass work.

Another acoustic classic from *Living in the Past*, "Nursie," taped in Mannheim, Germany, is given an extended rearrangement: after the familiar lone verse featuring Anderson's voice and guitar (with minimal keyboard backing by Mattacks), the rest of the band joins in, with Barre adding some powerful, melodic solos. Also radically reworked, "Too Old to Rock 'n' Roll" (referred to by Anderson as the "reggae version") is a Latin-tinged piece from a show in Ankara, Turkey, allowing Barre to lend some fine acoustic work to a lengthy introduction. A welcome return to material from *Minstrel in the Gallery*, "One White Duck," recorded in Prague, Czechoslovakia, adds some more of Mattacks' tasteful keyboard work to Anderson's strumming.

In Graz, Austria, Pegg opens "A New Day Yesterday" as Anderson returns to harmonica, then flute on the instrumental section lifted from "Kelpie." A second track taped in Athens, "John Barleycorn" takes Anderson into territory trodden by many British folk groups and one of his early progressive rock influences, Traffic. (One version of this traditional song was collected and published by Robert Burns.) Though Greek singer George Delares also sang on this track, his voice was mixed out and Anderson recorded additional vocals for all CD releases outside of Greece. Compared to Anderson's previous fusions of traditional material and rock—whether his own compositions or a David Palmer–arranged piece such as "Pastime with Good Company"—this performance is stark in its simplicity, due in part to a lack of keyboards.

Two more songs recorded in Caesarea follow: The first is a blues instrumental arrangement of *Stand Up*'s "Look into the Sun," during which Barre and Pegg trade off expert acoustic guitar and bass solo parts before launching into a laid back yet inspired boogie spiced up by Anderson's harmonica. (If the song's title was not listed, even diehard Tull fans would have trouble identifying it.) Mattacks again mallets the glockenspiel, on the album's third track from *Living in the Past*, "A Christmas Song," and Anderson cannot help adding some irreverence to the set-up:

> [R]eally, we should remember, this is a time for spiritual uplift. A time for oneness with the universe—and Donovan. It is *not* a time for heavy drinking, overeating and casual sex with farm animals. That's out of the question! So be warned, David Pegg!

Peggy often was the brunt of Anderson's sexual innuendoes, usually a joke about the aging Englishman's bum. When asked what he thought of such

Ian Anderson, decked out in his *A Little Light Music* garb, 1992. (Photograph by Fabio Nosotti; courtesy of Ian Anderson.)

on-stage hijinks, Pegg replied, "It depends on whose wife is in the audience that night."[353]

Too Old to Rock 'n' Roll's "From a Dead Beat to an Old Greaser" may have been an odd choice for the tour and album, but the audience in Munich applauded this downbeat number, which is electrified by the punchy drumming of Mattacks and an explosive, passionate solo by Barre. Mattacks repeats his percussive pick-ups to shift the band into high gear on "This is Not Love," a fourth track from the Caesarea concert. Perhaps the highlight of *A Little* Light *Music,* an extended arrangement of "Bourée" is a superb J. S. Bach medley befittingly recorded in Berlin. Mattacks, again on glockenspiel, sensitively accompanies Pegg's bass solo before Barre and the bassist perform a masterful classical-jazz duet. Anderson then joins in, driving the band into alternating swing and funk rhythms. The entire recording, concluding with a reprise of the classic "Bourée" melody, may be one of the greatest performances ever achieved by a rock 'n' roll band.

An instrumental "Pussy Willow," taped in Dortmund, Germany, opens with great interplay between the two Fairports, Pegg and Mattacks (on keyboards), who soon are joined by Barre and Anderson, who forgoes vocals for flute (as he previously had done to spare his voice). As Tull tradition would have it, "Locomotive Breath," from a Jerusalem show, is the album's coda, here made newly interesting by Anderson (flute), Barre (acoustic guitar) and Pegg (bass) recreating the original piano-electric guitar introduction. Switching to electric, Barre cranks out his classic, savage "Loco" licks, creating the usual frenetic, exciting culmination to a Tull show.

While *Q*'s Robert Renton praised the "exhilarating instrumental work," *Vox*'s Chas de Whalley found much more to appreciate:

> Does the world need another Jethro Tull album? Well, when it's a live one like this, featuring a selection of well-chosen oldies from the band's 25-year career, played by a semi-acoustic lineup featuring Fairport Convention stalwarts Dave Pegg and Dave Mattacks on bass and drums, the answer is "Yes."
>
> Admittedly, Ian Anderson's somewhat inane schoolboy asides between songs are an unnecessary irritant, but those who number *Stand Up* and *Aqualung*

Ian Anderson tips his new straw hat, 1992. (Photograph by Fabio Nosotti; courtesy of Ian Anderson.)

among the finest example of very late-'60s British progressive rock will be happy to ignore them and enjoy this album for the sheer quality of its musicianship and the clarity of its recording alone. It perfectly captures the romantic, softwood textures of Tull's semi-medieval style songs.

And not only have most survived the passing of time wrinkle-free, some (like the instrumental "Bouree") may even have improved with time.[354]

The "Light and Dark" Tour

On Saturday, July 18, Anderson made an unexpected appearance at the 1992 Jethro Tull Convention in Milton Keynes, delighting the crowd by introducing Martin Barre's "Summer Band," who were headlining the show, and mingling before leaving to mix the new album. At the end of the month, the band reconvened for three major festivals in Switzerland and Italy before *A Little Light Music* was released on September 14. On September 22–23, two English dates were followed by an additional festival, at Akranes, Iceland, on the 25th, before the "Light and Dark Tour" of North America began in Boston on October 2. Comprising 30 concerts, the tour took them throughout the U.S., south to Mexico, and then across Canada and back, with two Detroit gigs squeezed in for good measure.

Split into two separate sets, the first primarily folk and blues oriented and the second classic Tull, this concept worked far better than the previous "acoustic" tour, which had been misrepresented. A great deal of *This Was* material was resurrected, including "My Sunday Feeling," "A Song for Jeffrey" and "Beggar's Farm," as well as *Benefit*'s "With You There to Help Me," which included some effective "mandolin" playing by Giddings on a remarkably musical-sounding sampling keyboard. A quarter of *Thick as a Brick* (similar to the 1978 *Bursting Out* arrangement) was played with a welcome freshness, as well as the Bach-medley version of "Bourée" from the new live album, the lovely yet hard-hitting "Jack-a-Lynn," a jiggy Celtic rearrangement of an excerpt from *A Passion Play*, the hard-rock instrumental version of "The Whistler," and an astounding version of "My God" replacing *Aqualung*'s chant and neurotic flute solo with a medieval-style rendition of "God Rest Ye Merry Gentlemen"(included in earlier live treatments of "A New Day Yesterday," also heard on *Bursting Out*) that eventually segued into a swinging jazz version.

Again, Anderson was experiencing obvious problems with his voice, which sometimes was painful to hear amplified over the wall of sound unleashed by Barre. After the October 11 concert at Chicago's Riviera, Andy Giddings explained that this strain on Anderson's throat was caused, in part, by his flute playing, which stretches the muscles in the direction opposite to that which is required for singing.[355] After 24 years of such constant strain, his insistence on still treading the boards so often seemed rather masochistic, but at least he was beginning to relieve some of the constant abuse by rearranging some songs as instrumentals, a stylistic choice that forced him to begin practicing the flute. Anderson later explained:

> The flute has very much become the trademark of Jethro Tull. I felt it wasn't something I should leave behind, even when I felt I'd exhausted the possibilities of the instrument. I persevered a bit more with it, and I'm really glad I did. One of the reasons I worked on [refining technique] was that when I tried an expensive flute, it made no difference. It

sounded just the same. And I thought, "There's something wrong. If I sound the same on a $300 flute as I do on a $10,000 flute, there's something wrong with me, because I know the instrument's got to be better." So that caused me to really work on technique a bit more.

These days, I use almost all of the flute's three-octave, proper range. For a long time I was only playing the instrument in the middle octave-and-a-half, because I only really had the volume in the middle of the range. The difference is I never, ever practiced. I would pick the flute up five minutes before I walked out on stage and simply make sure it was mechanically functioning. Then I'd go out and play a show. Now I keep a flute with me wherever I am.[356]

Six days after the Chicago gigs, the sold-out show at San Diego's Spreckels Theatre had to be canceled. Anderson truly regretted the decision, but as he indicated in the local press, he had no choice:

Having to cancel the first [Tull] concert in eight years, and one of less than ten cancellations in 24 years of touring, was not an easy decision. It had to be taken, sadly, only at the last minute after exhaustive attempts to revive my sagging vocal chords [sic] which were suffering from a bronchial infection contracted a few days ago.... I must now write to offer my humble excuses for ruining your evening, as well as my own.... If I had enough flowers to send you all, I just hope you would find yourselves able to accept them. Thanks and sorry.... Too old to rock 'n' roll? Well, some might think so, but never too old to apologize.[357]

As usual, reviewers focused on the musicians' ages—something Anderson kept playing up by referring to the band as "the Exceedingly Old Jethros"—but most concluded that it mattered little. Helen Metella, reporting on the October 26 show at the Jubilee in Edmonton, Alberta, observed, "Anderson and his colleagues proved that old is not synonymous with decrepit—especially when ideas are original and craftmanship stellar."[358]

During the 1960s, a jazz giant such as Duke Ellington was not referred to as a "dinosaur," nor were the tunes he had written and performed during the 1920s and '30s called "ancient" works. But rock musicians have been looked upon differently, regardless of the fact that jazzmen like Ellington, Count Basie and particularly the great innovator Louis Armstrong were also youngsters when they first began to play. Jazz was just as shocking and rebellious in its first days as was rock three and four decades later, but perhaps the fact that rock 'n' rollers burned out faster created the impression that the later genre was appropriate for youths only. The day after the September 22 show at the Regent's Theatre in

Ipswich, England, Mark Hindle opened his review with the sentence "Balding dinosaurs they may be, but the aging rockers of Jethro Tull held a packed crowd spellbound for more than two hours ... last night."[359]

Some rock musicians undoubtedly became dinosaurs very quickly, but few have argued that Tull are among them. Even critics who have mentioned the term (even Anderson used it as early as 1978, and the entire band recorded a song with that title at one point) also have noted that the band's consistent inventiveness and abilities have more than compensated. Anderson said:

> I haven't done what Genesis or Eric Clapton have done, which is to adopt a more middle-of-the-road rock style in order to have greater lasting success in a rather smooth and middle-aged way. Rock musicians are not put on this planet to age gracefully; they are put on this planet to be like Keith Richards and age disgracefully.[360]

In his article "Dinosaur, Sr.," published in *Guitar World* in July 1993, Doug Caldwell wrote:

> Back in the mid-Eighties a magazine editor impatiently dismissed my idea for an article on Jethro Tull, calling the band a rock "dinosaur." Now, almost ten years later, he and his Clash albums are fossilized relics.... Far from being dinosaur-ish, Tull concerts reveal a polished, confident and ambitious musical team, hardly content to rest on their laurels. Rather, they rework and rearrange what is already complex music into consistently awe-inspiring performances.[361]

A majority of those who reviewed the "Light and Dark Tour" agreed that the revamped "My God" was the highlight—as did Rick Overall in the Ottawa *Sunday Sun*: "They took this biting thesis on organized religion and turned it into a musical tour-de-force—sliding effortlessly into chamber orchestra and jazz versions of 'God Rest Ye Merry Gentleman' as a bridge."[362] Another Ottawa paper, the *Citizen*, also carried a review of the November 7 show, pointing out Anderson's demands that the crowd behave itself:

> A gracious but temperamental host, the veteran British musician treated his guests to a fine evening of music, but he expected some basic politeness in return. No smoking in the hall. No drinking during the concert. No wandering in front of the stage. No loud, loud noises while he was playing a quiet part....
>
> Rolling his eyes at the audience and spitting, groaning and belching

into his flute, the 46-year-old [sic] Anderson transformed the instrument from a thing of delicacy to a formidable weapon of rock 'n' roll....

Anderson is not as flamboyant as in his early days, but he is in better shape than most 30 year olds. He may have been pacing himself during the two-hour-show ... but he showed plenty of energy, stalking the stage, kicking up one foot and making bad jokes.[363]

The final show of the tour, at Montreal's St. Denis Theatre on November 9, resulted in the loss of an expensive Hohner harmonica custom made for Anderson, who believed the instrument had been stolen prior to an encore. According to Brian Rabe, a freelance reporter who spoke to Anderson after the show, a reward was being offered to anyone who could drop off the harmonica at the offices of the Montreal *Gazette*.[364]

—— *Jethro Tull: 25th Anniversary* ——

4-compact disc collection
26 April 1993 (U.K.) / 20 April 1993 (U.S.)
[Rating: 3.5]
Chrysalis CD CHR 60044
All songs written by Ian Anderson (except where indicated)

Ian Anderson: vocals, flute, acoustic guitar, keyboards, percussion
Mick Abrahams: electric guitar
Martin Barre: electric, acoustic and classical guitars
Glenn Cornick: bass guitar
Jeffrey Hammond: bass guitar
John Glascock: bass guitar
Dave Pegg: bass guitar, mandolin, acoustic and electric guitars, keyboards, drum programming
John Evans: piano, Hammond organ, synthesizers
David Palmer: synthesizers, portative organ
Eddie Jobson: keyboards
Peter-John Vettese: keyboards
Martin Allcock: keyboards, electric guitar
Andy Giddings: keyboards
Clive Bunker: drums, percussion
Barrie Barlow: drums, percussion
Mark Craney: drums, percussion
Gerry Conway: drums, percussion
Doane Perry: drums, percussion

"The Beacons Bottom Tapes" recorded November–December 1992
Recording engineer: Leon Phillips
Package and sleeve design by Bogdan Zarkowski

Tracks: REMIXED
My Sunday Feeling
A Song for Jeffrey
Living in the Past
Teacher
Sweet Dream
Cross-Eyed Mary
The Witch's Promise
Life Is a Long Song
Bungle in the Jungle
Minstrel in the Gallery
Cold Wind to Valhalla
Too Old to Rock 'n' Roll: Too Young to Die
Songs from the Wood
Heavy Horses
Black Sunday
Broadsword

LIVE AT CARNEGIE HALL, 1970
Nothing is Easy
My God
With You There to Help Me
A Song for Jeffrey
To Cry You a Song
Sossity: You're a Woman
Reasons for Waiting
We Used to Know
Guitar Solo (Barre)
For a Thousand Mothers

THE BEACON BOTTOM TAPES
So Much Trouble (McGee)
My Sunday Feeling
Some Day the Sun Won't Shine for You
Living in the Past
Bourée (J. S. Bach)
With You There to Help Me
Thick as a Brick
Cheerio
A New Day Yesterday
Protect and Survive
Jack-a-Lynn

The Whistler
My God
Aqualung

POTPOURRI: LIVE ACROSS THE WORLD AND THROUGH THE YEARS
To Be Sad is a Mad Way to Be
Back to the Family
A Passion Play Extract
Wind Up/Locomotive Breath/ Land of Hope and Glory
Seal Driver
Nobody's Car (Anderson-Barre)
Pussy Willow
Budapest
Nothing Is Easy
Kissing Willie
Still Loving You Tonight
Beggar's Farm (Abrahams-Anderson)
Passion Jig
A Song for Jeffrey
Living in the Past

In February 1993, all current and past members of Jethro Tull were obliged to congregate at the Westmorland Arms pub in London to celebrate the 25th anniversary of the band. Most attended: along with the then-active group of Anderson, Barre, Pegg, Giddings and Perry were Mick Abrahams, Clive Bunker, Glenn Cornick, Barrie Barlow, John Evans, Jeffrey Hammond, Tony Williams, Mark Craney and Martin Allcock. Although he only played on one track in the band's quarter-century catalog, Ric Sanders also was invited (as well as Fairport's Simon Nicol). Absent were David Palmer, Eddie Jobson, Peter-John Vettese, Don Airey, Paul Burgess, Gerry Conway and Dave Mattacks. The festivities were taped for a one-hour television special.

A year after the reunion at the Westmorland Arms, Tony Iommi, the man who could have been Tull's second guitarist, looking nearly as youthful as he had back in 1968, observed the photos snapped at the pub and responded:

> Bloody hell! Is that Glenn Cornick? I wouldn't have recognized him. Woah, look at Mick! And is that Clive? Bloody hell! I wouldn't have recognized him, either.... Ian looks well there. Ha, ha—Dave Pegg. He's always got a drink in his hand, has Dave. I know Dave from old. The music scene in Birmingham was so small that everyone knew everyone else. I used to go and see him many years ago when he was playing

Andy Giddings, Ian Anderson, Martin Barre, Doane Perry and Dave Pegg pose to promote *Jethro Tull: 25th Anniversary*, 1993. (Photograph by Martyn Goddard; courtesy of Ian Anderson.)

with people like Plant and Bonham. He seemed to be in a different group every week.[365]

The following month, Anderson traveled to Bombay for a two-day promotional visit. During a press conference, he announced that plans were being made for Tull to tour India in early 1994. While there, he could not resist mentioning the age angle: "Unlike Elton John who has taken to wearing a dead cat on top of his head, some of us older guys are losing our hair and proud of it."[366] After his Indian visit, he then moved on to South America to organize some concerts in Brazil, Venezuela and Chile, where he held a press conference on April 18. When a reporter remarked that his use of the flute in rock music was "very original," he replied:

> And stupid as well! The role of the flute is the role of a very small voice desperately trying to find some space to be heard, with a power-crazy drummer behind me, a deaf guitarist who has his amplifier turned all the way up, and a bass player too drunk to know whether this is Chile or Iceland. So God help the poor flute player, to say nothing of the problems faced by the mandolinist, the acoustic guitar player and the harmonica player![367]

At the 25-year juncture, "power-crazy" Doane Perry had been with Tull off-and-on for nine years. Of the band's other drummers, he remarked:

> I really appreciated when Mark Craney first joined the band. How he interpreted the Tull music was very different from what Barrie did and what Clive did. I just loved what he played and what he came up with naturally. I would have to say the same for Barrie Barlow, Clive Bunker and Gerry Conway. They all came up with great, really imaginative, musical drum parts that were very creative. Their own personalities were very much in evidence to me—they all played very differently and brought a different strength to the band. I can appreciate all of that, and I think that's one of the harder parts of my job—to try to keep all those parts that came naturally to them and to try to make it natural to me to play. There are certain things that they all played that wouldn't be comfortable for me to play, just because they had an ability to do things that somebody else just doesn't come by naturally.
>
> Clive Bunker was such an early influence on me. I really dissected his style very closely and analyzed some of the techniques that he used. And the same with Barrie, though Barrie and I play very differently; but I could really understand why he was doing certain things and they made so much sense in the context of the music he was presented with. He came up with these incredibly creative, imaginative parts. Some of them are really hard for me to play naturally, so I had to alter some of them to fit my style. But there are certain elements of his style that are similar to my own. He had a certain degree of ornamentation and decoration which I always liked and I think is evident in my playing. It's kind of an orchestral approach, and that was kind of natural for me to do that, too. He did a lot of great cymbal work and some incredibly intricate drumming, some of which I still haven't figured out![368]

The Tracks of *25th Anniversary*

"Remixed: Classic Songs" includes 16 tracks, 10 of which were engineered by longtime Tull collaborator Robin Black. The remaining six were given a more current studio sound by Ian Taylor, who had done production work for Irish rocker Gary Moore. Black remixed the first two selections, "My Sunday Feeling" and "A Song for Jeffrey" from *This Was*, adding a noticeable amount of reverb to the instruments and Anderson's voice. Though these songs still retain their late 1960s sound, they are given a somewhat more modern ambiance. "Jeffrey" in particular features a punchier rhythm section, with Cornick's bass and Bunker's drums providing a heavier foundation for Abrahams' blues riffs and Anderson's voice and harmonica.

"Living in the Past," sonically light years ahead of the previous two tracks, is given a brighter mix by Taylor. Bunker's percussion (including his sticks knocking together) stands out noticeably, as does Lou Toby's excellent string arrangement. Taylor's remix of "Teacher," however—like his work on other tracks—adds an unnecessarily thick and muddy equalization to the drums that destroys the original crispness of Bunker's playing. "Sweet Dream," engineered by Black, rescues another *Living in the Past* song from its original murky mix; though adding additional reverb, he does not unduly electronically enhance the sound of Bunker's jazzy snare drum.

Black also handles the next three tracks. On his remix of "Cross-Eyed Mary," the band sounds less tight than on *Aqualung*, due to an overabundance of added arena-style reverb. Returning to *Living in the Past* material (25 percent of this disc), the engineer wisely kept the processing to a minimum on "The Witch's Promise" and "Life is a Long Song," both of which are brighter and better defined, yet the latter features a heavier rhythm section (Hammond's bass finally can be heard) that sometimes distracts from the song's folk basis. (Anderson's spoken "Take five" is included in the mix.)

Taylor returns for "Bungle in the Jungle," equalizing Barrie Barlow's drums so they sound more like Doane Perry's. Black is back on "Minstrel in the Gallery," adding similar thick processing to Barlow's percussion—an effect that somewhat alters the musical precision the drummer brought to his playing. "Cold Wind to Valhalla" gets the Taylor treatment, though here the enhancement of the bass and drums fits, lending additional drive to Barre's Teutonic riffs and solo slide work. Taylor also remixed "Too Old to Rock 'n' Roll," giving the song a livelier, fuller sound.

Black's remix of "Songs from the Wood" reveals a wealth of material edited from the original release. However, additional guitar, percussion and keyboards detract from the 1977 masterpiece, as they do from "Heavy Horses." Though these versions are of interest to the diehard Tull enthusiast, they are inferior to the originals. (For example, the processing of the percussion on "Horses" destroys the brilliantly precise bass- and snare-drum fill that Barlow plays after the line "And you'll strain once again to the sound of the gulls in the wake of a deep plow sharing.") On "Black Sunday," Black sticks fairly close to his original *A* mix, here adding a bit of thickness to the bass and drums but sharpening the other instruments effectively. Disc one ends with Taylor's remix of "Broadsword," a song that needed no enhancement to make it more magnificent. Inexplicably, some of Barre's solo spots were "eliminated" (though bleed-throughs can be heard).

Disc two includes the majority of the November 4, 1970, Carnegie Hall concert. Except for "By Kind Permission Of" and "Dharma for One"—the two tracks released on *Living in the Past*—the show is represented in its entirety, consisting of one track from *This Was*, four from *Stand Up*, three from *Benefit*, the then-unreleased "My God" and Barre's interminable "Guitar Solo."

The third disc was titled "The Beacons Bottom Tapes" after the location at which 8 rearranged Tull classics were recorded in November 1992. Six additional multi-tracked solo numbers, four by Anderson recorded at his home studio, Pegg's Fairport-influenced "Cheerio" produced at Woodworms Studio in Oxfordshire, and Barre's classically tinged rendition of "Protect and Survive" cut at his Presshouse Studio in Devonshire, were completed the following month.

Anderson's solo acoustic version of Brownie McGee's "So Much Trouble," on which he plays guitars, harmonica and percussion, carries on the back-to-basics blues style prevalent on *Catfish Rising* and parts of *A Little Light Music*. Following this laid-back introduction, the entire band explodes on a rousing "My Sunday Feeling" featuring a near–Big Band sound created through the fusion of Pegg's jazzy bass, Barre's power chords, Giddings' wall-of-sound keyboards, Perry's punchy drumming and Anderson's heady flute licks. Having learned the "Sunday" drum part from Clive Bunker, Perry particularly enjoyed the sessions: "Re-recording lots of the classic Tull songs was great fun for me, to be playing those songs that I grew up listening to, and getting to do a rearrangement."[369]

"Someday the Sun Won't Shine for You" is Anderson's solo take on the *This Was* blues song originally revived for the *A Little Light Music* tour, and is followed by his unusual acoustic folk-blues reworking of "Living in the Past," the first version to include harmonica. The fluted one's solo excursions end with an excellent version of "Bourée," given yet another classical-meets-jazz interpretation and displaying his talent as a tasteful arranger and multi-instrumentalist. (Giddings also adds some keyboards during the swinging bridge.)

As played on the "Light and Dark Tour," "With You There to Help Me" is beautifully resurrected after 22 years, combining Barre's heavy blues riffs with Giddings' excellent keyboard parts, including the mandolin-like sound he created by sampling a Japanese koto.[370] Giddings' brilliant recreations of John Evans' original Hammond organ parts are a highlight of the nine-minute "Thick as a Brick" medley, a superb "live in the studio" performance that also provides a good example of Barre's ability to play rhythm and lead guitar simultaneously. And Anderson's occasional improvisations on the flute add a new texture to portions of a very familiar song.

Pegg characteristically lends his bright and cheery disposition to "Cheerio," expanding Anderson's brief *Broadsword* epilogue into a folk-rock instrumental on which he plays mandolin, acoustic guitars, electric lead guitar, organ, bass and drums. He then leads off the savage rearrangement of "A New Day Yesterday" with a funky harmonic bass line. Giddings again contributes some fine Hammond work, particularly during a solo spot prefacing the "Kelpie" section.

Barre begins "Protect and Survive" in pseudo–Spanish style on classical guitar, segues into a multi-tracked acoustic instrumental interpretation of the verse, then adds his trademark lush electric harmonies and an anthem-like melody before returning to Spanish form at the end. The pleasant folk strains of "Jack-a-Lynn" follow, with this version considerably toned down from the alternately bucolic and ferocious original recorded during the *Broadsword* sessions. Though the song is well done, the powerful dynamics never arrive, due primarily to Barre's use of a clean guitar tone except in a few measures toward the end. To the contrary, the next number—Barre's hard rock instrumental arrangement of "The Whistler"—literally blows the lid off the elaborate cigar box that stores the four CDs. A 180-degree turn from the original folk-rock masterpiece on *Songs from the Wood*, this version proves that a truly great song can be equally successful when adapted into another form. Perfectly supported by Pegg, Giddings and Perry, the combined musicality and sheer power of Martin Barre—who perhaps plays a minor chord with more "bite" than any other rock guitarist—is captured at its most spine-chilling.

The high point of "Beacons Bottom," "My God" provides an almost shocking contrast to the rough 1970 live version on disc two. Though the classic *Aqualung* version is a masterpiece, here it becomes a highly polished tour de force incorporating the delightful medieval-cum-jazz "God Rest Ye Merry Gentleman" instrumental bridge. The dynamic shifts from acoustic folk-blues to bone-crunching hard rock are made even more effective by the "live in the studio" nature of the recording. When Anderson sings "and don't call on Him to save" and "you-know-who with his plastic crucifix," the band literally strikes like the very wrath of Jehovah. Arguably anticlimactic on the heels of this 10-minute opus, "Aqualung" attained the closing spot for obvious reasons. Though Anderson's voice sounds strained, the excellent recording featuring Pegg, Giddings and Perry is a welcome addition to the Tull catalog, and Barre once again improvises enough to keep his solo interesting.

"Potpourri: Live Across the World and Through the Years," a compilation spanning 1969 through 1992, makes up the final disc in the set. The first two tracks, "To Be Sad Is a Mad Way to Be" and "Back to the Family," recorded at Stockholm's Concert Hall on January 19, 1969, feature the Anderson-Cornick-Bunker lineup with wet behind the ears Martin Barre, whose playing aptly defies the fact that he had been with the band a mere three weeks. Here, the *Stand Up* sound has not yet taken root—the basic heavy blues sound, driven by Anderson's harmonica, stays well within the *This Was* format. However, "Family," performed prior to the studio recording, incorporates the dynamics, folk elements and flute improvisation that soon would give *Stand Up* its unique ambiance.

Skipping ahead six years, the disc lands the listener in Paris for an extract from *A Passion Play*, providing quite a jarring stylistic transition. Running a little over three minutes, the segment ends just before "The Hare Who Lost His Spectacles" would have made its bizarre appearance. Two years hence in London, a medley of "Wind Up," "Locomotive Breath" and Edward Elgar's "Land of Hope and Glory" is performed by the *Songs from the Wood* lineup. Sparked by the kind of guitar solo mid–1970s audiences craved, the piece includes an Anderson lyrical ad lib during the first verse: "I didn't mind if they groomed me for success, or if they said that I was just a fool—or even worse, a *punk!*" The Elgar passage is particularly effective, superbly arranged by Palmer and brilliantly driven by John Glascock's bass and the precision percussion of Barrie Barlow.

Three tracks from the 1980s follow. Though sonically, "Seal Driver," recorded in Hamburg in 1982, is a disappointment, the performance is superb, reinforcing Pegg's assessment of the band's prowess during the *Broadsword* tour: Peter Vettese's atmospheric keyboards are exemplary, and Barre's dead-on recreation of his blistering solo sets the hair on end. Taken from a 1984 show in London, "Nobody's Car" is superior to its lifeless studio prototype, though the prerecorded elements detract from the "live" performance, and "Pussy Willow" is faithful to its *Broadsword* progenitor.

The remaining eight songs were culled from 1991–92 shows, the first two—the band favorite "Budapest" and the classic "Nothing Is Easy"—edited from a show in Leysin, Switzerland. The former faithfully follows the *Crest of a Knave* original, with Martin Allcock's keyboards filling in for Ric Sanders' absent fiddle, while the latter, due to a mixing problem, briefly drops Barre's guitar out of the potent jazz-blues, heavy rock blend. Recorded in—of all places—Tallin, Estonia, "Kissing Willie" chugs along yet lacks the drive of the original. (Another selection from the 1989 *Rock Island* tour may have enhanced this disc.)

"Still Loving You Tonight," from a London date, a close copy of the *Catfish* song, is followed by four "Light and Dark" tracks. Recorded in Pullman, Washington, and the only Abrahams-Anderson compositional collaboration on *This Was*, "Beggar's Farm" features an excellent bridge allowing Giddings to demonstrate more of his jazzy piano style. "Passion Jig" and "A Song for Jeffrey" were taken from the October 11, 1992, show at Chicago's Riviera Theatre, and provide a fine live example of the Tull fusion of folk-rock, blues and hard rock. Finally, edited from a Montreal show, the rearranged instrumental "Living in the Past" concludes the set.

The *25th Anniversary* Tour

As if the band hadn't been touring enough over the past few years, Anderson organized a mammoth seven-month schedule covering Britain, Europe, the Middle East, North America and then back to Britain before playing gigs in Ireland and South America. This group of musicians, all save one pushing 50, would play a total of 88 highly physical concerts all over the world, with a four-week break during July and August, and two 10-day breaks, at the end of September and October, respectively. By the end of it all, they would play to a half million fans in 20 countries.

In order to reflect the eclectic nature of the band over a quarter-century, Anderson selected even more early material than he had for the past two U.S. tours, including "For a Thousand Mothers" and an instrumental arrangement of "Reasons for Waiting" from *Stand Up*, *Benefit*'s beautiful "Sossity: You're a Woman" and excerpts from "Songs from the Wood" and "Heavy Horses" (though regrettably included in a somewhat cumbersome medley with "Too Old to Rock 'n' Roll"). A highlight was a powerful instrumental rendition of "Seal Driver" from *Broadsword*, an album that hadn't been represented in concert for many years (save for the sporadic

The *25th Anniversary* lineup: Martin Barre, Andy Giddings, Dave Pegg, Ian Anderson (foreground) and Doane Perry, 1993. (Photograph by Martyn Goddard; courtesy of Ian Anderson.)

resurrection of "Pussy Willow"). The shows concluded with Doane Perry practically bringing down the house with a tremendous drum solo on an extended "Dharma for One." A little more than a year earlier, when recalling Barre's misunderstanding of "Sossity," Anderson had said, "It sounded like it was a strange and very feminine, childlike girl's name, and it was amusing at the time, but it's not a lyric that I feel comfortable with now. I couldn't sing you that song."[371]

Perry commented on the experience of touring with opening band Procul Harum (including Matt Pegg on bass guitar):

The official *25th Anniversary* tour program, signed by Ian Anderson, Martin Barre, Dave Pegg, Andy Giddings and Doane Perry, September 1993. (Author's collection.)

We had some great nights with them on the road. On the very last night in San Diego on the American tour, we went out during their set and slowly started picking their equipment up piece by piece and moving it until they were all down to—Ian Wallace, who was drumming at the time, was playing a snare drum and a hi-hat, and we couldn't do much about Matthew Fisher's Hammond organ or Gary Brooker's big piano; but we did remove the bass amp and guitars and microphones.

There was some retaliation planned. During our set, they came on. We had this set which looked like a tacky Fifties living room, and they came on all dressed as women, which wouldn't have been too bad, except it was kind of frightening because a couple of them, particularly Matthew Pegg—he had really long hair and was dressed up in a nurse's uniform—some of them actually looked a little better as women. And Ian Wallace came up behind me dressed in a French maid's outfit, and, as I was playing—we were in the middle of some difficult piece of music—and he came up and planted a big kiss on my lips, and I was trying to play, and I was just laughing and losing my place.

Each one of the Procul guys had gotten one of us, doing something to distract each one of us—so, unfortunately, whatever we were playing, the whole thing completely unraveled and fell apart, to the complete delight of the audience. I don't know if they recognized it was actually Procul Harum. They just thought, "There's these five ugly, or maybe not so ugly, women up there on stage molesting the band"—and the band are letting them do it. I don't know how we really recovered, or if we just bludgeoned our way through that piece of music and stopped—but we had a good time with them.[372]

After returning to Eastern Europe, where the band played gigs in the formerly Soviet-controlled Hungary and Czech Republic, Perry observed:

> My heart breaks a little bit when I go to some of these places that were so unique and beautiful, and so relatively untouched by the West; and to go there and see McDonald's signs. I have to say I find that a little depressing. Though I don't think Andy does, because he loves McDonald's.[373]

In the U.S., critics eager to deride Tull as another nostalgia act were surprised and impressed. *Dallas Morning News* staff writer Tom Maurstad lauded them for giving away free tickets to anyone who arrived at the August 21 show with recyclable materials, resulting in a turn-out of 18,000 fans and 50 tons of aluminum cans, newspaper and plastic containers. After the September 3 show in Darien Lake, New York, Robbie Ann McPherson wrote:

> A remarkably lean, energetic Ian Anderson and the rest of Jethro Tull hit the stage and proceeded to thrash the geezer notions out of my head with one of the finest musical performances I've ever seen.
>
> Anderson's signature flute solos, which featured him kicking and hopping around the stage like a rock 'n' roll "Pan" incarnation could have silenced any skeptics. But woven in with his megawatt showmanship and the stunning complexity of Jethro Tull's music, Anderson and company created an undeniably awe-inspiring musical tapestry.[374]

However, no matter how musically adept Tull remained at the 25-year mark, the fact that Anderson's voice was faltering—due not only to age, but also to overuse—continued adversely to affect the band, as noted by journalist Brett Miller, who attended the August 28th show at Great Woods in Mansfield, Massachusetts:

> [T]he ornate band sound and Ian Anderson's showmanship (which has gotten a lot friendlier over the years) are intact, and the buoyant mix of Anderson's flute with Martin Barre's guitar remains a pleasure. But they have a serious problem: Anderson's losing his voice, and it makes you realize how important his vocals were to the sound all along.[375]

In Burbank, California, with Matt Pegg substituting for his father, who was playing a few dates with Fairport, they appeared on *The Tonight Show with Jay Leno*. After delivering a slick rendition of the rearranged "Living in the Past," Anderson was interviewed by Leno, who asked him to autograph a copy of the new box set for Vice President Albert Gore, Jr. For a few seconds, the fluted one exchanged courtesies with the V.P. on the telephone. Matt Pegg recalled, "We were supposed to play *Thick as a Brick* [actually "Locomotive Breath"] on the show as well, but one of the guests, a football coach who is like bigger than God over there [the U.S.], just wouldn't stop talking and we ran out of time."[376] (This guest actually was New York Yankees manager George Steinbrenner.) The younger Pegg also played a small show at New York's Lonestar Roadhouse, which he described as a "proper old fashioned pub gig, but with Jethro Tull!... There were a few mistakes, but everybody had a good time."[377]

Back on their home turf, the band played two dates at the Hammersmith Apollo (formerly Odeon) in mid–October. As another element of the anniversary celebration, Anderson had phoned the former members, asking if they would like to appear on stage at some point during the shows. Only Mick Abrahams, Clive Bunker and Gerry Conway accepted the invitation. Anderson said:

> Barrie, John and Jeffrey ... I suggested to them if they didn't want to play then just come up on the stage and say, "Hi." There would be some people who would really appreciate just seeing you. Or if you want to come and play something, whatever you would like to do, just for a bit of fun.... Barrie Barlow said, "I've given it some thought and I think I'd rather bow out of this one." He didn't really give any reason why, but it was obviously a decision he had made, so, fair enough. John Evans asked for money, very pointedly, a sum of money with several zeros on the end, and I said, "The thing is, John, this is really not about that, this is just

fun or it isn't." He said, "Well, in that case, it wouldn't be." End of conversation. I don't know how you take that one. Martin, as I was, was deeply pissed off by that ... I think John Evans is conveniently forgetting the fact that twice every year he gets paid a royalty check, and that if nothing else he might just stop to think that maybe he just owes it to a few people who still buy records that he played on, just maybe that it might be a nice and polite and respectful thing to do to say, "Hey, thanks for paying my holiday" or something ... Jeffrey gave it some thought ... but ... he said he would be too terrified to get up on stage....[378]

On October 20, the band finally thrilled their Irish fans by playing a gig at Dublin's National Stadium, where *Hot Press*' Siobhan Long observed:

> [T]he 40-somethings nodded knowingly to their teenage offspring, whispering, "There, lad, *that's* how it should be done."
> An homage to a bygone era, a reminder of just how good they were (and are), Jethro Tull thrashed and tore their way through the night and left a rake of raucous fans baying for more. 'Twas a good night, to be sure.[379]

Other reviews from the tour included the headlines "Jethro's Just Magic" (Tarlair Festival, MacDuff, Scotland), "timeless magic" (Birmingham, England), and "stunning, classic rock" (Asbury Park, New Jersey).

Nightcap: The Unreleased Masters, 1973–1991

22 November 1993 (U.K.) / 11 January 2000 (U.S.)
[Rating: 2.5]
Producer: Ian Anderson / Chrysalis CD CHR 6057
All songs written by Ian Anderson

Ian Anderson: vocals, flute, acoustic guitar, mandolin, tin whistle
Martin Barre: electric and acoustic guitars
Jeffrey Hammond: bass guitar
Dave Pegg: bass guitar, mandolin
Matthew Pegg: bass guitar

John Evans: piano, Hammond organ, synthesizers
Peter-John Vettese: keyboards
John Bundrick: keyboards
Barrie Barlow: drums, percussion
Gerry Conway: drums, percussion
Doane Perry: drums, percussion

"The Chateau D'Isaster Tapes" recorded at the Chateau d'Herouville, France,
    August 1972
Sleeve design by Bogdan Zarkowski

Tracks: MY ROUND: THE CHATEAU D'ISASTER TAPES
    First Post
    Animelee
    Tiger Toon
    Look at the Animals
    Law of the Bungle
    Law of the Bungle, Part II
    Left Right
    Solitaire
    Critique Oblique
    Post Last
    Scenario
    Audition
    No Rehearsal

    YOUR ROUND: UNRELEASED AND RARE TRACKS
    Paradise Steakhouse
    Sea Lion II
    Piece of Cake
    Quartet
    Silver River Turning
    Crew Nights
    The Curse
    Rosa on the Factory Floor
    A Small Cigar
    Man of Principle
    Commons Brawl
    No Step
    Drive on the Young Side of Life
    I Don't Want to Be Me
    Broadford Bazaar
    Lights Out
    Truck Stop Runner
    Hardliner

"Jethro Tull's Other Boxed Set," a three-disc collection, had been advertised on the back cover of the *25th Anniversary* booklet, but by the time this second package was released (in the U.K. only), the set had been shorn to two CDs (the third was to have consisted of live material). While listening to the remaining unreleased material in the Chrysalis archives, Anderson discovered the abandoned Chateau d'Herouville recordings and, to please Tull fans who clamored for their release, decided to include most of the tracks on the first disc in the retitled *Nightcap* set. Naming it "My Round," he remastered the tapes to digital and then added flute parts to unfinished sections. Missing vocals, however, were not completed, as he explained:

> It's OK to add flute to something 20 years after the rest of it was recorded, because it would have sounded the same had I done it 20 years ago. Vocals are a different matter, though: I was a young man then, with a much better voice and a different way of singing things, and it would sound decidedly odd should I try to sing those songs now.[380]

The Tracks of *Nightcap*

"Chateau D'Isaster" is of particular interest to fans of *A Passion Play* and the 1973 Tull lineup. In the liner notes, Anderson writes:

> The infamous ... recording sessions at the Chateau d'Herouville ...
> Not a cup of tea for everyone, but a slightly dizzy night cap for
> old friends in need of that last dram before laying down their
> heads to dream of what might have been.[381]

"First Post" opens the CD with a flute and saxophone "duet" by Anderson, then segues into solo acoustic guitar before the rest of the band joins in on "Animelee," a baroque-style march featuring Evans on harpsichord. "Tiger Toon," a number reworked for *A Passion Play*, keeps the material at a march tempo, here purely instrumental and impressively performed but fading out perhaps a bit too soon; whereas "Look at the Animals," though running only five minutes, seems to drone on far longer, due primarily to its absurd lyrics about the toilet habits of various fauna (a far cry from the serious life-and-death content of *A Passion Play*).

"Law of the Bungle" also includes instrumental material that would be rearranged for *A Passion Play*. In a rare spoken-word contribution, Martin Barre provides a narrative bridge between this song and the next track:

Hello. This is "Law of the Bungle, Part Two." By the way, I'm Martin Barre, but sometimes I'm an owl, and my feathers are really smooth, and when I feel romantic, I like to dress up in men's clothing.

Barrie Barlow adds a brief drum solo during Barre's ramblings and then drives the band into the five-minute instrumental, another lumbering piece indicative of the unfinished nature of the material. "Left Right" begins with a collage of multi-tracked sounds and some heavier riffs from Barre before Anderson adds voice, flute and saxophone. Joined by the rest of the band, they rock a bit here before Anderson returns to acoustic guitar on the original rendition of "Solitaire," which later was remixed as "Only Solitaire" for *War Child*.

"Critic of the black and white, it's your first night" introduces "Critique Oblique." Featuring a primarily acoustic introduction, it sounds like a demo for *A Passion Play*, which in fact it was, though some of the lyrics had yet to be written. Another instrumental, "Post Last," reprises the musical leitmotif and includes more melodic material recycled for *Play*, which would be recorded after Anderson completed the lyrics.

The final three tracks, which previously had been released on the *20 Years* box set, "Scenario," "Audition" and "No Rehearsal," are the highlight of the disc. The only pieces that were not reworked to some extent for *Play*, these three stand alone as good Tull songs. "Scenario," even considering its over-processed vocal, features some excellent acoustic work by Anderson, with Barlow adding effective percussion parts on xylophone and glockenspiel. "Audition," Anderson's perceptive view of one's helplessness at the hands of society, is smoothly succeeded by "No Rehearsal," ending this uneven 13-track suite in a march tempo, with the band alternating between a full-throttle jam and a traditional-style Celtic melody enhanced by tin whistle. Its content concluding with considerable anarchy, the song descends into narrative and musical chaos.

"Your Round: Unreleased and Rare Tracks" opens with five songs from the *War Child* and *Catfish Rising* sessions, the first being the inexplicable "Paradise Steakhouse," a title that would seem more at home on an American "Southern Rock" album released in 1974. Bearing the *War Child* sound, lyrically it is filled with none-too-subtle sexual innuendoes, and "Sea Lion II" is an alternate "instrumental" with strange voice overdubs by Jeffrey Hammond and a bridge sounding as if it was recorded in a London pub.

The first *Catfish* cut, "Piece of Cake" is a middling blues-rock number similar to other 1990 out-takes, including "Night In the Wilderness" and "Truck Stop Runner," which appears later on the disc. "Quartet" is an elaborate, classically influenced, synthesizer-heavy instrumental tune (Anderson worked the melody into his "Flute Solo Improvisation," which was released on *Live: Bursting Out*), while "Silver River Turning" is an excellent, environmentally conscious song unfortunately left off *Catfish*. Opening with flute and a pleasant piano arrangement by John Bundrick, the song kicks in with some steamy riffs from Barre reminiscent of the somewhat "Native American" chord progressions he had played on "Broadsword" a decade earlier (here, as on "White Innocence" from the same 1990 sessions, effectively underpinned by Doane Perry's tom-tom work). Following a reprise of Bundrick's introduction, Perry leads Barre and the rest of the band back in for a bluesy, churning fade out.

"Crew Nights" is the first of six out-takes from the prolific *Broadsword* sessions. Though featuring the excellent lineup of Anderson, Barre, Pegg, Vettese and Conway, the song does not compare favorably (particularly lyrically) with the material on the released album. Clearly an early–1980s, techno-pop number, "The Curse" undoubtedly anticipates *Walk into Light* and *Under Wraps*.

"Rosa on the Factory Floor" is another excellent out-take from *Catfish*, its atmospheric Anderson-Bundrick flute-and-piano duet introducing a folk-rock tale about a female assembly line worker recalling World War II's "Rosie the Riveter." (The reprise of the introduction also includes Anderson on tin whistle, bringing a welcome Celtic element back into the Tull mix.) At the very end, after a sustained flute note, Anderson narrates, "Hey, Santa, pass us that bottle, will ya? Oh, no, we've done that...."

Recorded during the *Too Old to Rock 'n' Roll* sessions, "A Small Cigar" features Anderson accompanied only by David Palmer's piano. What initially seems to be his ultimate tribute to tobacco—"A small cigar can change the world...."—one listen demonstrates that he could be as cynical about smoking as he was about other habits, whether they be social, religious or political. Jumping ahead 13 years, the collection offers the *Crest of a Knave* lineup on "Man of Principle," a mediocre track buoyed by Barre, who blends bluesy lead licks with his trademark melodic riffs. Perhaps the disc's best song, "Commons Brawl," cut from *Broadsword*, combines a classic Anderson lyrical attack on the wrangling of ineffectual politicians with innovative Celtic folk-rock, here a masterful musical counterpoint created by offsetting Pegg's lightsome mandolin picking with Barre's vicious power chords.

Two additional out-takes from *Broadsword* follow: "No Step," another attempt by Anderson (who plays keyboards) to update Tull to an early 1980s style; and "Drive on the Young Side of Life," a return to the full band sound that, sans flute and Barre's unmistakable technique, could have been created by many other groups at the time. "I Don't Want to Be Me" is one of two country-influenced songs recorded for *Catfish* that just cannot be fit comfortably into the Jethro Tull catalog. Ian Anderson sporting "diamond spurs jangling into the sunset?" Perhaps not, but the following track—"Broadford Bazaar," recorded in 1978—lands the disc back into territory where the "Laird of Strathaird" belongs. The most "traditional" of Anderson's Scottish songs, it features him on acoustic guitar, tin whistle, tambourine and voice, and tells the tale of a local market near his fish farm and former estate on the Isle of Skye. (For the Tull fan, it is worth the price of the two-disc set.)

"Lights Out," like "No Step," is an early 1980s experiment from the *Broadsword* sessions featuring Anderson on keyboards—clearly a precursor to the *Walk into Light* material. "Truck Stop Runner," of course, is the most un–Tull song ever written and produced by Ian Anderson, his bizarre attempt to try something radically different—even more so than the electronic experimentation he and Peter Vettese tried nearly a decade earlier. Regardless of the strange instrumental work (Barre's playing begs description), Anderson's lyric, "I want a cup of black coffee and a piece of sweet cake," like the rest of the song, is a play on the most absurd 1970s country-and-western clichés. Tull fan W.S. Gumby wrote, "'Truck Stop Runner' and 'Rosa on the Factory Floor' … should have been on *Catfish Rising* instead of 'Doctor to My Disease' and 'White Innocence'."[382] The closing song, "Hard Liner," lyrically and musically a rather pedantic exercise, was dropped from *Rock Island*.

When *Nightcap* was released, Anderson was asked about any remaining unreleased material. He replied:

> [P]ure and utter crap!… you're never gonna hear that … we're talking real shit, we're talking rubbish, either lyrical or musical crap. There comes a point where my decision really is final on that, there is nothing else left…. So much if it is doodling in the studio that never evolved into anything complete. There are bad notes and dodgy bits in it, and although something like that is sort of amusing, it really is scraping the barrel. There has to be some kind of criteria laid out in this kind of a project, and that is that it's really got to be stuff that could legitimately have found its way onto any Jethro Tull album in the past….[383]

Continued Touring

Anderson's desire to keep the band globetrotting continued into 1994, with a four-concert tour of India, including two in Bombay, followed by jaunts to Hong Kong, New Zealand, Australia (11 gigs), Hawaii and the U.S. West Coast, Canada and the Northern U.S. before they took a three-week hiatus. The first "gig" of the year, however, involved a Jethro Tull convention in Altenkirchen, Germany, on January 8, where Anderson played a "solo" acoustic set during which he was accompanied by a tape of himself on all manner of instruments. Opening with "Someday the Sun Won't Shine for You," he moved on to "Bourée," "Living in the Past," an instrumental (alternately called "Clint Eastwood" [because it had no name] and "Andy Giddings' Parrot"), an excerpt from *Thick as a Brick*, "Heavy Horses," "Wond'ring Aloud" and "Mother Goose." Fairport Convention played the next set, during which Anderson joined in on "Beggars Farm," "Life Is a Long Song" and "Locomotive Breath" (transforming the band into four current or former Jethros, plus Simon Nicol and Ric Sanders). The final act of the evening was Mick Abrahams' Blodwyn Pig, who were just beginning a German tour. Anderson also joined them, including Clive Bunker on drums, making this lineup very close to the original 1968 Tull as they played "My Sunday Feeling," "So Much Trouble" and "I Wonder Who."

From February 16 to February 20, Anderson, Barre, Pegg, Giddings and Perry made their collective debut in India. Perry recalled:

> Wherever we go to play, the greatest reward is that people know the music, or perhaps only know a few songs but come to see us and really enjoy the whole show and perhaps discover music that they never knew existed. We didn't know people would really know us, and we were delighted that so many people did know the music, and though that might not necessarily be reflected in record sales and royalties—because bootlegs and tapes get passed around—and people don't have much money there anyway. Just the fact that they came out and spent what little money they had. We don't make hardly any money, if at all—we're lucky of we break even, particularly playing places like India.
>
> It was probably one of the most memorable tours we've ever done anywhere, apart from the fact that I'm just crazy about Indian food. There's very little in terms of food from other countries that I don't like. I have a pretty wide-ranging palate, particularly when it's hot and spicy stuff, something that Ian and I both have a real affinity for—for hot food. If we can't find an Indian restaurant or a Thai restaurant, we just bring our own spices with us, because we grow our own peppers.
>
> The Indian people were so nice—and it was completely chaotic and disorganized. You had to almost laugh at it, because you couldn't really expect it to be like it would be in the West, but they try so hard to make it right. Half the time we had to be rebuilding the PA. You had to do these ridiculous things to try to technically make everything work. We

had the *one* PA system and the *one* lighting system in all of India. I think Peter Gabriel was wanting to come through, and since we were there and had claimed use of the one sound system, he had to change his tour. It's very hard bringing stuff there. It's very expensive. You're really not going to make any money, even playing for loads of people.[384]

Perry admitted his confusion over "Mr. Nareesh," the band's Indian traveling companion:

> I never quite understood what Mr. Nareesh's function was. I thought he was actually the tour doctor, because he dressed in white all the time. Somebody had said, "Oh, he's the doctor." So, after a concert one night, I asked him, "What do you do?"
>
> He told me he worked with the promoter, but he didn't appear to be doing settlements or anything. And there was a whole army of these Indian touring personnel who came with us. It's hard to know what a lot of them did, but they all had some purpose.
>
> Mr. Nareesh came into his own one night. The band used to do a runner after the gig, back to the hotel. I was always so wet and sweaty that I just wanted to cool down slowly and then go back to the hotel. I was standing outside in the backstage area, because the dressing room was way too hot to go in. In India, even in February, it's still pretty hot. And the concept of security in India is almost nonexistent.
>
> They had these cops there, and there were a lot of kids by the crash barrier, and our dressing rooms were in plain sight of the barrier. I was standing there, not paying a lot of attention to what was going on. They pushed past the crash barrier, and a whole bunch of them started running across the area to the backstage.
>
> Then the cops came after them and tried to stop them. Suddenly it became this big fracas, with cops yelling, and they were waving their billy clubs. They weren't hitting anybody, but they were yelling and trying to push them back, and the kids were yelling. They were just wanting to come over and, I suppose, get an autograph or talk to me since I was the only one in the band left. It was kind of scary, because I didn't really have any place to go.
>
> Suddenly, out of nowhere, Mr. Nareesh appeared like Moses parting the Red Sea, and he walked between the policemen and the kids, and both sides backed off. He said something to the policemen very quietly and something to the kids very quietly. And then the kids respectfully moved away and went off into the night, and the cops disappeared.
>
> I was completely astonished. Mr. Nareesh came over to me, and I said, "What in the world did you say to them?" I can't imagine if this had happened in America or Europe, or most Western countries, those kids wouldn't have paid any attention to some guy walking through there in

what looked like a white doctor's outfit. Apparently this was Mr. Nareesh's job. He was a holy man, and he was there to keep the peace. The policemen and the kids recognized that he was a holy man, and they all deferred to him. Subsequently I witnessed a number of situations where he gently intervened and smoothed things over or stopped a problem from happening.

I thought, "Only in India," because you could never have a guy like that on the road with you in America without it being some big beefy security guard. It was wonderful. I wish that could happen here but, unfortunately, I think people are far too cynical to pay any credence to a guy like that. The Indians are very respectful, and that said a lot about the Indian character.[385]

During the Indian tour, Perry was pleasantly surprised by a percussion-related discovery:

Right before we left for India, the big earthquake in California happened. Unfortunately our home sustained a lot of damage, and one of the things that got damaged—I have a lot of ethnic drums in the living room—things came flying off the walls. And something came off the wall and went through the head of my big tabla drum, which I'd had for years. I hadn't the slightest idea where even to buy a replacement tabla head. I'd never broken one. It's not something you play very hard.

Two weeks later, after this earthquake, we were actually scheduled to go to India, and I thought, "Well, you know, I'm sure I can find a placement tabla head there." And while we were there, I was talking to our promoter—and they were always going to get me down to the music store, but there was just never time. And the very last night, the promoter had us over for dinner at his house, and I asked him about it again.

He said, "Ah, yes, yes, yes. Must take you down to the music store." And he called all the music stores—eight or nine—and they were closed at that point. We were flying out that night to Hong Kong. So I thought, "Well, I'll have to try and find one back in America."

We were taken to the airport about midnight. Everything was closed, and it was a kind of dingy airport. Not much there. And as we were coming up the escalator, there was a guy like a carnival barker standing at the head of the escalator, trying to get people to come into his shop.

He said, "Come in. Come in."

And I said, "Well, I'm sure you don't have what I need."

He said, "What do you need?"

I said, "I actually need a replacement head for a tabla drum."

He said, "Oh, yes. We have those!"

And I thought, "Oh, right. Sure. In a duty-free airport shop, I'm going to buy a drum head! And he took me into this tiny little shop about the size of a single-car garage. It was just stuffed floor to ceiling with all sorts of useless little, touristy junk that you wouldn't want. Plastic replicas of the Taj Mahal and all that kind of nonsense. He climbed up to the top shelf in the back of the store, and came down and produced a tabla head.

He said, "Is this what you want?"

I said, "Why, yes, it is!" And I couldn't believe it. It was exactly the right size and exactly the right head. And I thought, "What are the chances of this?" You know, I probably would have more luck bagging an elephant on the Moon than buying a drum head at a duty-free airport shop! At the last possible place I could have bought anything in India. He probably had a spark plug for a Fifty-seven Chevy, which I could have used. To me, that was just indicative of India and how wonderful and magical and *totally* surprising it was.[386]

On March 14, Anderson again was criticized for substituting more flute for his faltering voice, this time in Perth, Australia. However, reviewer Michael Dwyer also found much to praise:

When anything approaching a higher register was called for, Anderson's voice was conspicuously absent, the shortfall picked up with extended flute shenanigans.... Thankfully, the rest of the band was sonically immaculate. The 25 years in question canonly date from Martin Barre's admission to the ranks, along with Anderson as the only "permanent" member.

Barre's role in establishing the metal guitar tradition shouldn't be underestimated and he still plays like a bald, elderly champion. The whole band shares Anderson's passion for overblown theatrics and the result was never less than spectacular, visually and musically.[387]

On April 29, they then set off on another grueling tour of Europe, which included Norway, Sweden, Finland, Denmark, Holland, Belgium and back to Britain for another 11 shows. During the summer, the band returned to Europe, mainly to play the festival circuit, with appearances in Austria, Norway, Romania, Germany, Switzerland, Denmark and Hungary, as well as one additional date in their homeland, before another English Tull convention was held on October 1 (plans for a 1993 event had fallen through). But the lineup had changed yet again: along with Anderson, Barre and Giddings, Matthew Pegg once more was substituting for his father, and Marc Parnell (who had been playing with Barre, live and on his solo recordings) was temporary warming the drum stool. Scheduled to play the entire summer tour, Parnell was fired after only five shows. Matt Pegg explained:

> [T]hese gigs were kind of thrown together late on, which is why Dad couldn't do it because he [was] working with Fairport.... [Marc] didn't learn the tape properly; it was a bit of a mess ... a nightmare for me. There were lots of songs I'd never played, and I'd learnt the tape with Doane playing, and suddenly you are playing live with someone playing "Locomotive Breath" like a thrash song! It was so fast, all up and down, nothing at the right speed ... it was terrible, and Doane was back in a flash. I mean, they were big gigs, fifteen-, twenty-thousand people, with no sound check and only two days' rehearsal, so it is not easy for a drummer to step into that, but he really should have made a bigger effort to learn the stuff.[388]

Following Doane Perry's return, the band played a July 16 gig at Tutbury Castle, a three-walled medieval ruin in Staffordshire that provided an intimate venue for a twin-bill with Blodwyn Pig. In his review, Tull fan Tim Wilson pointed out the problems with Anderson's choice of material, particularly when playing in such a superb historical setting:

> [G]reat stuff, but too much [was] taken from the first few albums, with only a slight nod towards the classic "middle" period, and nothing at all more recent than 1987. Although the earlier songs[were] reworked in tremendous style ... more recent songs would go down better. Perhaps the older songs suit Ian's vocals better now, which also has some bearing on his recent re-interest in the blues? A mistake in my opinion—the blues has been done to death by others, and it's better that Ian's original talent is allowed to shine.[389]

The 45-minute video *Jethro Tull: 25th Anniversary* finally was released that month. Superior to the *20 Years* program, it was broadcast on the BBC and then combined with full-length music videos for its commercial VHS version. The highlight of the show is interview footage shot at the Westmorland Arms pub gathering (rather than following the style of *20 Years* and restricting the comments to Anderson only). Clips featuring various Tull lineups are interspersed with the then-current perspectives of Anderson, Abrahams, Barre, Cornick, Bunker, Evans, Pegg and Perry, not to mention the surprising appearances of Jeffrey Hammond and Barrie Barlow.

On August 11, "Jethro Tull and Friends" played a benefit concert for the Friends of the Earth organization at Clapham's Grand Theatre. Anderson opened the show with a solo acoustic blues set before he was joined by Giddings and Barre on "Wond'ring Aloud," "Cheap Day Return" and "Life Is a Long Song." The Martin Barre Band followed with material from his solo album *A Trick of Memory* and some blues-rock classics, and when Barre made his exit, Tull, with Mick Abrahams on guitar, took the stage for a set that included the forever-neglected "Move on Alone" from *This Was*. Several more blues numbers segued into more familiar Tull territory when Barre returned. The remainder of the show consisted of a folk set from the eccentric Roy Harper (with Anderson joining in on flute) and an appearance by Procul Harum's Gary Brooker, who performed "Conquistador" and "A Whiter Shade of Pale" with Tull, who then gave in to the fan's demands by playing "My Sunday Feeling" and "Budapest." Incredibly, Brooker's encore choice was Willie Dixon's "Hoochie Coochie Man," featuring Abrahams and Barre playing on stage together for the first time. Tull, not surprisingly, closed with "Locomotive Breath" and "Dharma for One." Doane Perry played on all the Tull material, while Matt Pegg played throughout the entire show.

Eight days later, Tull headlined one day of a week-long rock festival in Budapest, which also boasted nostalgia acts Eric Burdon (with former Tull member Mark Craney on drums), Blood, Sweat and Tears, Jefferson Starship, the Grand Mothers of Invention, the Byrds and current thrash-metal bands from Hungary and Germany. As all such festivals go, nearly a half million people were crammed together in a tiny space, this time to hear Tull play the same basic set they had been using since the beginning of the *25th Anniversary* tour (though this was the only stop in Budapest). On August 20, in a bizarre set indeed, Anderson sat in on flute with Hungarian singer-songwriter-percussionist Leslie Mandoki.

During October 1994, Tull played their first-ever dates in South Africa, including three shows in Cape Town, two in Johannesburg and one each in Pretoria and Durban. The following month, Ian and Shona Anderson moved from Pophleys to another farm, located in Oxfordshire farther away from London. "Unwelcome visitors" had begun to appear at the Buckinghamshire estate. "We thought we were a little too public there," Anderson revealed, "so we decided to move."[390] After settling in, Anderson spent $140,000 converting a horse stable into a modern recording studio where he would rehearse and record with Tull and work on various solo projects.

Jethro Tull in Concert—
At the Hammersmith Odeon
8th October 1991

24 April 1995 (U.K.) / 13 February 1996 (U.S.)
[Rating: 3.5]
Producer: Pete Ritzema / Windsong WINCD 070 / Griffin Music GCD-8615-2
All songs written by Ian Anderson

Ian Anderson: vocals, flute, acoustic guitar, mandolin, harmonica
Martin Barre: electric and acoustic guitars
Dave Pegg: bass guitar
Martin Allcock: keyboards
Doane Perry: drums and percussion

Recorded live for the BBC at the Hammersmith Odeon, London, October 8, 1991
Recording engineer: Mike Engels
Sleeve design by Definition

Tracks: Minstrel in the Gallery/Cross-Eyed Mary
This Is Not Love
Rocks on the Road
Heavy Horses
Like a Tall Thin Girl
Still Loving You Tonight
Thick as a Brick
A New Day Yesterday
Blues Jam
Jump Start

A stunning *Catfish Rising* tour photograph, capturing Ian Anderson holding his flute in the air with one hand while resting the other on the shoulder of a Martin Barre blissfully enraptured by his own playing, his golden locks having grown back from their shorn status of a few years earlier, caught the attention of Tull fans during the spring of 1995. The photo graces the cover of *Jethro Tull In Concert*, the second non–Chrysalis live CD to be released in conjunction with the BBC. Superior in every way to the Hammersmith Odeon show of 1984, this October 1991 gig at the same venue features an excellent blend of songs, a more polished, driving band and a much better recording.

Anderson's voice is a bit rough as he strums a brief introduction from "Minstrel in the Gallery," but switching to flute he leads the band into an absolutely earthshaking "Cross-Eyed Mary" well-powered by Pegg, Perry and Barre, whose live power-chord vengeance is atypically captured in all its intensity by BBC engineer Mike Engels. Perry then leads his comrades into the thumping, Stones-ish "This Is Not Love," during which Pegg's backing vocals come through clearly. Another *Catfish* track, "Rocks on the Road" sounds very similar to the stripped-down version on *A Little Light Music*, due to the sparsity of Martin Allcock's keyboards.

The only officially released live version of "Heavy Horses" is a highlight of the album, particularly for American Tull fans who, unlike their European counterparts, did not get to hear it during the *Catfish* tour. Sans piano accompaniment, Anderson opens the song with acoustic guitar and voice, though Allcock does add his basic keyboards in mid-verse. As he had done in the past, Barre plays the violin part on electric guitar, carrying much of the song through sheer musical prowess (though he accidentally bumps a string at the end of the lengthy instrumental section). Of course this version does not match the live performances of the song by the Tull of 1978–79, but the recording provides an excellent record of how such a complex piece of music was interpreted by the excellent Pegg-Perry rhythm section.

Anderson publicly acknowledges Perry during his introduction to "Like a Tall Thin Girl," mentioning the "*Thick as a Brick*–pajama clad" drummer's 1984 audition and subsequent enamorment with the attractive Indian waitress. Anderson's electric mandolin sounds fuller and more woody here than on other live Tull recordings, and his jaunty Eastern instrumental interplay with Barre is a folky treat. The 6/8 blues "Still Loving You Tonight" works well in a live context, and, though Anderson's voice is strained, he does not push it as far as he does on the original studio recording.

Eight minutes of *Thick as a Brick*—opening with Perry lending some tasteful, dynamic cymbal work to Anderson's acoustic strumming—are followed by three *Stand Up* rearrangements: "A New Day Yesterday" features a lengthy instrumental break including "Kelpie" and "Bourée"; while a section from "Reasons for Waiting," introduced by Allcock's keyboards, becomes the "Look into the Sun"–based "Blues Jam" between Barre's acoustic guitar, Pegg's bass and Anderson's harmonica. Back on acoustic guitar, Anderson introduces "Jump Start," which eventually erupts into its Scottish-style instrumental featuring flute and the electric guitar of Barre, who closes the album with a fearsome solo.

Ian Anderson: Divinities—
——— *Twelve Dances with God* ———

24 April 1995 (U.K.) / 2 May 1995 (U.S.)
[Rating: 4]
Producer: Ian Anderson / Angel-EMI 5 55262 2
All music written by Ian Anderson, with additional material by Andrew Giddings

Ian Anderson: concert and alto flute, bamboo flute, other wooden flutes and
    whistles
Andrew Giddings: keyboards, orchestral tones and colours
with: Doane Perry: percussion
        Douglas Mitchell: clarinet
        Christopher Cowie: oboe
        Jonathon Carrey: violin
        Nina Greslin: cello
        Randy Wigs: harp
        Sid Gander: french horn
        Dan Redding: trumpet

Orchestrations by Ian Anderson and Andrew Giddings
Additional orchestrations and ideas by Gareth Wood and Roger Lewis
Recorded at Ian Anderson's home studio, autumn 1994
Engineered by Ian Anderson, Andrew Giddings and Leon Phillips
Sleeve design by Bogdan Zarkowski

Tracks: In a Stone Circle
        In Sight of the Minaret
        In a Black Box
        In the Grip of Stronger Stuff
        In Maternal Grace
        In the Moneylender's Temple
        In Defense of Faiths
        At Their Father's Knee
        En Afrique
        In the Olive Garden
        In the Pay of Spain
        In the Times of India (Bombay Valentine)

During the past half-decade, Anderson's woodshedding with the flute
really had paid off. Of his diligent attempts finally to learn more about the
instrument, extend his range and practice material outside the existing Tull
canon, he admitted:

If I'd had one day of lessons when I started to play the flute, I would have saved myself 20 years of agony. But by the same token, I might have had one day of flute lessons and given it up. It's only the fact that I couldn't figure out how to play the wretched thing that kept me going. I was determined to beat it.

It took me 27 years before I was really comfortable with it. The first 20 years were hard work, and during the next four or five, I was fairly depressed with it. I wasn't making any progress at all. It's only in the last three years that I've got quite interested in it again.[391]

Roger Lewis, head of EMI's classical division, wanting to offer the public an alternative to the legendary composers and well-known modern orchestral artists, approached Anderson about recording an album of music for flute and orchestra. Accepting the challenge, he chose to collaborate with Andy Giddings, who explained:

I don't know that it is really classical music.... It is classical in the sense that it has orchestral instruments and orchestral sounds. It is a mixture of real instruments and synthesized sounds, almost by accident.... Ian and I recorded it over several months, with him giving me his ideas and melodies that I would develop and play using the sound of an orchestra. The idea was to demo everything that way and then recreate it with an orchestra or quartet depending on what was required....[392]

A third Tull member, Doane Perry, joined the project on percussion, and several members of London's Royal Philharmonic joined Giddings in creating the lush orchestrations backing Anderson's silver concert, wooden and bamboo flutes from various parts of the world. In the end, the music became as much "world" or "New Age" as classical, and record stores had no idea how to promote it or where to stock it. Anderson later said, "This gave us a number one hit in America ... in the *Billboard* Classical Crossover Chart, whatever the fuck that is!"[393]

Anderson's original title was simply "Divinities," but EMI added the "Twelve Dances with God" subtitle, giving the album a heavier religious tone. Was the anti–organized religion Ian Anderson of *Aqualung* no more? Had he been won over by some particular belief? Giddings explained:

It isn't a celebration of Ian's religious beliefs, but it's an acknowledgment of all the religions that are around. It's not aimed at religious people or at any particular religion, it's just a theme for the album. Different religions tend to stem from different countries and continents, and those people all have their own kind of music. It was the musical element that was important to us, in as much as it gives us twelve different styles of music that we could work from, and then develop it in our own way.[394]

The Tracks of *Divinities*

"In a Stone Circle" lends a Celtic druidic tone to the beginning of the album, with the flute beautifully backed by Anderson and Giddings' orchestration seamlessly blending real string instruments with keyboards. Indian-influenced melodies are combined with a European baroque style in "In Sight of the Minaret," in which Giddings contributes fine piano and harpsichord, as well as string parts, and Anderson adds some improvisational soloing on an up-tempo dance section. The light, pastoral "In a Black Box" is reminiscent of incidental film music for a Victorian scene set in the English countryside, perhaps a picnic or leisurely Sunday carriage ride, but when Perry joins in on martial snare drum, the drama increases, briefly adding a hint of suspense. Opening with a tone of definite menace, "In the Grip of Stronger Stuff," another piece with Eastern influences, plays like a series of whirling ethnic dances: a passage featuring Anderson on bamboo flute and accentuated by Perry's percussion is especially effective.

The lullaby-like "In Maternal Grace" transports the listener to the Far East for one of the most beautiful pieces ever written by Anderson, whose bamboo flute is accompanied by more of Giddings' koto keyboard sampling. Different musical characters, represented by wooden flute and keyboards, are dramatically set against one another in "In the Moneylender's Temple," another piece that would work well in a period film; while "In Defense of Faiths," the most English-sounding composition on the album, is a superb Renaissance–early baroque style piece for woodwinds, organ, brass and a stringed instrument resembling a lute. "At Their Father's Knee" may be the most "classical" piece, featuring a fuller, more lush orchestration that includes, yet is not dominated by, a solo flute part. Twice, the rhythms, emphasized by Perry's percussion, recall the "Mars" movement in Gustav Holst's *The Planets;* and, toward the end, Giddings works in a brief countermelody reminiscent of George Gershwin's *Rhapsody in Blue.*

The film scores of Henry Mancini come to mind during "En Afrique," a rhythmic bamboo flute piece that would work well in a modern Disney animated dance sequence or production number. A 180-degree turn, "In the Olive Garden" is a soothing, melancholy piece suggesting Christ's last hours on Earth; while the highly accomplished "In the Pay of Spain," recalling the film music of Miklos Rosza, particularly his masterful score for *El Cid* (1961), the Charlton Heston classic depicting the medieval conflict between Spain's Christians and Islamic Moors, more than proves Anderson's mettle as a composer. The disc concludes with the epic "In the Times of India (Bombay Valentine)," a worthy successor to the previous track and one that, if arranged differently with added vocals, could just as easily work as a monumental Tull track such as "Heavy Horses" or "Flying Dutchman."

While *Q* magazine commented that *Divinities* was "a bit like tuning in to Classic FM by mistake,"[395] *Jazziz* noted that Anderson's "writing recalls Aaron Copland with its dynamic tempo shifts and doubled lines, but there are touches of India, Flamenco, palmas and wooden flute as [he] traverses the world."[396] It is indeed a remarkable achievement for a "rock 'n' roll" musician.

The *Divinities* Tour

The *Divinities* tour consisted of 18 concerts during May and June 1995, with Anderson, Giddings and Perry being joined by bassist Jonathan Noyce, a 24-year-old London Royal Academy of Music graduate who had performed with David Palmer during the latter's "orchestral rock" tours, and local musicians in intimate European and American venues. Opening in Brussels on May 17, they then played three German dates and one each in Switzerland and England before heading to the States for 11 shows ranging from Boston to Los Angeles. Also in the lineup was the superb fiddler Chris Leslie, a well-known folk musician who had been recommended by Dave Pegg. (Leslie subsequently joined Fairport when Martin Allcock left the group in 1997.) The entire *Divinities* album was performed live, as well as orchestrally rearranged Tull songs, even some classics like "Aqualung" and "Locomotive Breath," this time played as mini-suites and bearing none of the rock trappings that had been retained by David Palmer for *A Classic Case*.

Roots to Branches

4 September 1995 (U.K.) / 12 September 1995 (U.S.)
Highest chart position: 20 (U.K.) / 114 (U.S.)
[Rating: 4]
Producer: Ian Anderson / Chrysalis CHR 6109
All songs written by Ian Anderson

Ian Anderson: vocals, flutes, acoustic guitar
Martin Barre: electric guitar

Dave Pegg: bass guitar
Andrew Giddings: keyboards
Doane Perry: drums and percussion
Steve Bailey: bass guitar

Recorded at Ian Anderson's home studio, December 1994–June 1995
Engineered by Ian Anderson
Sleeve design and artwork by Bogdan Zarkowski

Tracks: Roots to Branches
           Rare and Precious Chain
           Out of the Noise
           This Free Will
           Valley
           Dangerous Veils
           Beside Myself
           Wounded, Old and Treacherous
           At Last, Forever
           Stuck (Out) in the August Rain
           Another Harry's Bar

Increasingly committed to Fairport and growing tired of the same set list, his limited input and the enormous on-stage decibel levels, Dave Pegg left Tull during the summer of 1995, after nearly 16 years of faithful service. Prior to beginning the spring tour with Fairport, he had recorded the bass parts for only three tracks on the new *Roots to Branches* album. Anderson, rather than waiting for him to return, hired American session bassist Steve Bailey to play on the remaining tracks before leaving on his *Divinities* tour. Pegg said:

> It got a bit hard for me. The reason I left Jethro Tull was that I was doing all these things with Fairport. We have this festival at Cropredy, which is a big thing in our lives. There were too many clashes, and Ian was very good to me. He let me have lots of time off, and he was even good enough to employ my son, Matt, to dep for me when there were Fairport commitments that I couldn't get out of.
>
> The thing about the Fairports is ... we're only a little band ... It's everybody's livelihood. I had to do it, and I had to have my priorities, which became more and more geared towards Fairport. Without things like the Cropredy festival and our annual winter tour, it would have been very difficult for the guys in the band to survive. And when Tull's itinerary started clashing, I felt it was time for me to go.
>
> Also, I'd had a lot of problems because Ian went through a period where his voice was giving him so much stick, and it was really playing

him up. It kind of hurt to do gigs. I found it really hard to listen to him, because he was suffering, and he was having really great difficulty singing. He always gave it a hundred percent, but it was painful to listen to him. [It was] very unfair that he would have to suffer in order to get through gigs, and I just felt it was time to go, really.[397]

The musical style and lyrical content of *Roots to Branches* was influenced heavily by the band's visit to India the previous year, and the same Eastern sounds prevalent on *Divinities* (particularly Anderson's use of bamboo and wooden flutes) can be heard throughout. In a basic sense, *Roots* is Tull's Indian *Songs from the Wood*. Of the title song, Anderson said:

> Following my return from India, I followed up the title idea by completing the lyrics to the song.... Lyrically the song works on the idea of the darker side of the various world religions' apparent and infinite capability for subdivision, and the (these days) inevitable return to ultra-conservative and fundamentalist beliefs. Oh, beware the scary power of religious fervor, mixed with the dangerous geo-politics and the chip-on-the-shoulder mind-set of separatism, fragmentation, and the wild flag-waving desire to settle old, old scores. And it could be happening in your town. For some of us, it already is.[398]

Obviously, Anderson's basic view of organized religion had not changed since the release of *Aqualung* in 1971, but now his understanding of the connections between religion and sociopolitical realities was more developed, due in large part from the sheer experience of traveling and conducting business the world over.

The Tracks of *Roots to Branches*

An immediate musical extension of the *Divinities* material, "Roots to Branches" proved the strongest song to open a Tull album since "Beastie" on *Broadsword*, 13 years earlier. Introduced by the ominous electric guitar of Barre, it incorporates nearly every musical style in the band's arsenal, including some deftly played jazz passages and Anderson's first-ever use of bamboo flute on a Tull recording.

"Rare and Precious Chain" is a true highlight, another Indian-oriented piece, the development of which was described by Doane Perry:

> It's amazing at times how songs take on their own personality and direction regardless of any resolute conviction on the part of the musician

to steer them somewhere else. ... This song was just such an example ... Ian came to us with this piece about which he said, "I want to record this fairly straight-ahead rock tune—with a sort of loose around the edges, bluesy, rough and ready feel—no frills, raw and stripped down."

With the best of intentions to try to accomplish this task, we set off with the goal in mind of trying to create a "radio ready/friendly" song. Somehow, before we even knew it, we were off in another direction, perhaps initiated by Andy's lewd, suggestive and very funny (at least to me, anyway) keyboard samples which sent me away to some uncharted location roughly between Tangiers, Bombay and a Senegalese village full of drumming tribespeople. And all of this happened while Ian went into the other room to write the bridge melody. While I was out there in the percussive ethers communicating with some Zulu god, Andy remained firmly in an ersatz Bombay recording studio contriving strange string lines for an Eastern pop record.

Meanwhile, Martin retreated into weird '60s wah-wah psychedelia, and Ian kept popping his head in and out to hear how things were going, offering an occasional "Hmm, why not try this?" or more disturbingly, simply raised an eyebrow. Strangely it all seemed to be coming together but it was a completely different song, different than everything three hours before. What in the hell was Ian going to do with this?

At the end of the day, I knew that we really had something very special. I just didn't know what. So it was a very pleasant though not unexpected surprise when I heard how perfect the vocal and lyric fit the music, though I suspect they underwent a great transformation as well.[399]

"Out of the Noise," the album's most hard-driving song, features classic Martin Barre stylings. Barre said:

> This track was built up from the drums and bass [one of the three tracks featuring Dave Pegg]. The guitar part was the result of an hour in the hotel bedroom with a tape machine. Ian left Andy to "produce" my effort in the studio; it was, genuinely, a very exciting day of recording.[400]

Another of the album's excellent "Indian" tracks, "This Free Will," which features Barre at his harmonic best, was literally an afterthought saved from the scrap heap at the last moment. Anderson revealed:

> A failed backing track, contrived on the final day of Doane's recording stint for the album, lay undisturbed for a few weeks during time out for the short *Divinities* tour before being revisited at the eleventh hour with a different set of previously written lyrics and a completely new melody and arrangement.
>
> To save a little time, I popped down the guide electric guitar track,

together with vocals, flute and a couple of other lines, over the original drum track. Andy came into add some keyboard and bass lines, and Martin added some great atmospheric parts to counter the flute and my guitar parts, which I left on the finished track (but did not credit on the album sleeve notes).... Doane finally heard the end result, convinced that we must have used another drummer, since he could not recognize the song or remember recording anything like that.[401]

Perry said:

How Ian wrote stuff around my parts was completely different than how I would have played it if he had presented that piece of music to me without the drums. I would have made completely different musical decisions. But I thought, "That's a very interesting way to write," because he took an already existing performance unto itself, and what he wrote kind of overlapped my part in certain very interesting ways. From a compositional point of view, it gave me some ideas about how you can write certain things and move elements around.[402]

The steamy, mysterious atmosphere of the music is equaled by Anderson's lyrics:

She peeled from a stretch black snake
which slipped up to the hotel door.
Darting looks from piercing eyes—
The stir of memory and then no more.
Well, you know how I have to believe—
She can almost remember my name.

Roots to Branches' "epic," "Valley," another song about social separatism, benefits from Pegg rejoining Perry to create the dynamics necessary to power its dramatic potential—a style that recalls the more ambitious material on *Rock Island*. In contrast to the meticulously multi-tracked "This Free Will," "Dangerous Veils," the album's heaviest song, praised by Barre for embodying "the Tull trademark ... was rehearsed live from its concept"[403]; although a rocker, it allows the guitarist to stretch out with a bluesy solo and Giddings to inject jazzy piano.

"Beside Myself" benefits from the classic Tull alternation of lilting folk and hard-hitting orchestral rock. Andy Giddings described:

We had no idea, when we recorded the backing track, of the lyric or melody, but when Ian suggested "some kind of Indian/Eastern string line in the chorus" I had some idea of direction.

Weeks later I heard the track with vocals and flute and the whole concept was there in my headphones, with references to far away places we had visited and the consequent frustration that accompanies encountering another culture: the desire to "change things for the better," and the realization that intervention of any kind would not only be futile but unwelcome.

The track reflects these mood swings, switching from the intensity of the verse to the relief of the delicate bridge, and then back to the crux of the matter, the chorus: "I'm Beside Myself."[404]

The introduction and initial verse, with acoustic guitar, vocals and electric solo licks, recall "Rocks on the Road," but when the heavy rock kicks in—trading off Barre's power chords with Giddings' "Indian" keyboard part—the listener is treated to high-octane Tull, a far cry from the more laid-back material on *Catfish Rising*.

Though repetitive, "Wounded, Old and Treacherous" blends pop, rock and jazz in a manner unique to Tull, and the narrated vocals suggest the influence of Frank Zappa. Running five seconds longer at 7:55, "At Last, Forever" is a lovely Eastern-influenced folk-rocker dealing with mortality:

> So why are you holding my hand tonight?
> Well, am I feeling so cold to the touch?
> Do my eyes seem to focus
> on some distant point?
> Why do I find it hard to talk too much?
> And who was I to last forever?
> I didn't promise to stay the pace.
> Not in this lifetime, babe
> But we'll cling together:
> Some kind of heaven written in your face.

Sounding like a *Divinities* piece saved for rearrangement by Tull, the song is orchestral rock at its finest (and is worth the price of the CD). Another *Divinities*-like track (with added vocals and percussion), "Stuck (Out) in the August Rain" was the first real Tull "ballad" since *Crest of a Knave*'s "Said She Was a Dancer." Perry said:

> This track contains my favorite section of music on the entire record, which is the eight bars that comprise the bridge. The way the chords move through the changes with the beautiful stately melody on top, the subtle keyboard harmonization underneath, and the bass line is incredibly moving to me. I loved that bridge so much I thought it should

have been the chorus, but … the very reason that it isn't makes me want
to go back and hear it over and over because it never wears out its welcome. The other thing I love about this song is the way it subtly glides
through all these various key signatures without ever really calling attention to the fact that it is doing so.[405]

Dave Pegg makes his Tull curtain call on "Another Harry's Bar," a
jazzy, mostly acoustic "pub" piece that brings to mind the "Dire Straits
influences" of nearly a decade earlier. A good story song, it captures an
element of the everyday lives of many listeners:

> Got the scent of stale beer hanging, hanging round my head.
> Old dog in the corner sleeping like he could be dead.
> A book of matches and a full ashtray.
> Cigarette left smoking its life away.
> Another Harry's bar—or that's the tale they tell.
> But Harry's long gone now, and the customers as well.
> Me and the dog and the ghost of Harry will make this world turn right.
> It'll all turn right.

The album ends with a coda that builds in intensity, with Barre unleashing some blistering solo licks, but then decrescendos, allowing Pegg to
make a final harmonic statement on his acoustic bass.

The *Roots to Branches* Tour

For the *Roots to Branches* tour, Anderson retained Jonathan Noyce, who
had earned a teaching diploma and professional certificate in music, quite
impressive credentials for a youngster joining two aging veterans old
enough to be his father—and who never had taken lessons on their instruments. (On July 15, 1971, Noyce was born in Sutton Coldfield, near Birmingham, while Tull were taking a brief break from the *Aqualung* tour.)

Noyce had been "broken in" on the *Divinities* tour and by working with
Barre on his *The Meeting* solo album. His bass style veered the rhythm
section away from the linear, folkish sound of Pegg toward the earlier Tull
sound, and his re-creation of Glenn Cornick's solo on "Bourée," which again
was played in its original 1969 version, was staggering, both in technique
and tone. Cornick said, "We joke a lot about that. Jon has become a very
close friend of mine. He's a great bloke. I see him when I go to London."[406]

Of his experiences playing with both Pegg and Noyce, Doane Perry
explained:

They're both great bass players in their own right, and they're very different. Dave has a linear style, it's sort of unusual and fits Tull's sound really well. I think because he plays mandolin, that he plays a lot of lines that bass players wouldn't usually play. He always plays with a pick, and so his sound and the way he articulates certain things really fit with the music so well, because he could blend very easily with the lines that either Ian or Martin would be playing. Sometimes Dave would be playing a real direct counterpoint to what I would be playing, and the traditional role of the way a rhythm section operates was a little bit different. I think it's actually the same way with Jonathan in the band, but Jon comes from more of a Motown style of bass playing—a more R&B style. It's very much in evidence in Dave's playing, as well, but Dave also has that folk-rock tradition in his background, and from those years of playing mandolin. I think that makes Dave have a very different style on the bass, and the way that he approached the Tull music was entirely different. In some ways, maybe Jonathan has more of an American style, though Jonathan also had a classical upbringing, so he has a very deep background in music: He's played jazz and pop and classical; he's played in orchestras, and yet he's got a love for the great American R&B bass players.

I don't think I changed the way I play particularly for either one of them; but in terms of the way the rhythm section in Jethro Tull operates, a lot of times you're not playing the way an "American" rhythm section would be, playing a simple part over and over again. It would be the same way whether it was Jon Noyce or Dave Pegg—we would be playing something together, and then we would be playing something that is really a counterpoint to each other. Maybe I'm playing something that is relating more to a vocal melody or a flute line or a guitar part or a keyboard part as much as I am with the bass player. With Dave in the band, we would come together on certain passages, and other times we were playing our parts or perhaps highlighting something somebody else in the band was doing. I sometimes relate quite equally to what everybody is doing, because I'm trying to listen to everybody's parts and interact with them. The whole thing forms a very tightly interwoven fabric, even though the way it's put together, in terms of the foundation, would be very different if you analyzed it from listening to an R&B or jazz rhythm section.

I think everybody is always aware of everybody else's playing, but it's interesting that the roles within Jethro Tull can be very interchangeable in terms of who is doing what functionally: Somebody might be playing the role of a timekeeper—and sometimes we might fall into quite traditional roles of how we would function in a rhythm section, and other times we're playing with and against each other, and in between. But it all has to sound cohesive. The danger is that you can completely fall off the cliff; and if everybody's not responsible for the feel—if you tend to stay in your own little orbit, it doesn't really work very well. At the same time, it's very organic, the way it happens. It's not an intellectualized process at all. I think that if it became an intellectual process, it would probably sound like one, and it probably wouldn't sound or feel very good. If you can keep that part out of it—there are people who deliberately contrive things to be complex—I don't really like music like that. I think if the emotional component and the heart of the music is there, then as long as you don't ruin it by trying to create something that is too clever, I think that is the intangible element that audiences sense right away.

Working with both Dave and Jon has been a wonderful experience, and for completely different reasons. But what the experiences have in common is that they're both wonderful musicians and really easy to work with; and I think that, when they're easy to work with—no matter what they do—it will feel good. To me, that's the most important thing: the feel of it.[407]

The *Roots to Branches* souvenir program was another true highlight of the Tull road experience. This time, Anderson parodied "MTV Unplugged" by creating "J Tull Unpacked," showing the contents of each member's suitcase while on tour. Anderson emphasized his love of hot chili peppers, his need to stay on top of his farming business (the newspaper *International Fish Farming* and his Fish-o-Fax were in there) and the necessity of carrying along a copy of the *Jethro Tull: Complete Lyrics* hardcover book; Barre toted the two-volume *Annotated Sherlock Holmes*, a plastic children's guitar and chilipepper boxer shorts; Perry packed various pepper sauces and Eastern herbs; Giddings carried a feather duster, a roll of toilet paper and a girl's squeaking doll; and Noyce took along pickled onions, a coconut and a monkey suit (no doubt proving that he fit right into the famously eccentric band).

The *Roots* tour opened in Carlisle on September 16, continuing with 10 more British and 20 European dates. After a two-week rest, they returned Stateside for a brief, eight-show tour, beginning at the Boston Orpheum on November 10 and ending at the Los Angeles Universal Amphitheater on the 24th. In another effort to support his native culture, Anderson donated three Celtic-oriented tracks—"Warm Sporran," "Broadsword" and "Cheerio"—to *Heart of the Lion*, a CD intended to raise money for the Scottish Highland Hospice.

Tull took a three-month hiatus prior to another tour of South America, hitting Chile, Argentina, Uruguay, Brazil, Peru, Bolivia and Venezuela during a 12-gig stretch from March 6 to March 23, 1996—dates that proved the most dangerous of the band's career. While performing at one of the Peruvian shows, Anderson was tripped up by an uneven stage, fell and seriously injured one of his knees. Always the indefatigable performer, he finished the concert while sitting in a chair. From March 25 to April 6, they managed to pull off 10 U.S. dates as Anderson performed in a wheelchair, confusing fans who had seen him use this as a "geezer gag" during previous tours.

Having endured illness and food poisoning during the South American sojourn, the band then rested a month before beginning a tour of Australia, where only four shows were played before Anderson was unable to continue. The Tull management were forced to cancel the remainder of the dates in Australia and New Zealand, as well as a series of European concerts, while Anderson, diagnosed with thrombosis, was hospitalized for emergency knee surgery.

By August 28, Anderson was well enough to begin a mammoth U.S. tour, and in six weeks Tull hit 33 venues, many in cities (including parts of the Midwest) where they hadn't set foot before. Anderson explained:

> Those are [the areas] I find quite exciting. It's the nearest I can ever get to the first time I ever played at the Fillmore East or the Boston Tea Party or the Marquee Club in London. I can't go back and recreate those moments; those places don't exist anymore.[408]

Again, the set list closely resembled the greatest-hits approach of the *25th Anniversary* tour, and little material from the new album was heard in the smaller venues. Discussing the tours of younger, higher profile rock bands, Barre observed:

> It must be wonderful to make oodles of money, fly around in your own jet and spend thousands of dollars on better lighting, stage setups and production. There's also a terrible wastage of money in the music business. We're very proud of the economics of our operation. It's very carefully planned, it works well, and there's nothing wasted. And that's the way we survive.[409]

In the Mississippi River town of Moline, Illinois, where Anderson opted to play before "warm-up band" Emerson, Lake and Palmer, Barre opened the show with an ear-piercingly loud "Aqualung." With that inevitable crowd pleaser completed, more greatest hits poured forth. Assuming that fans in the sticks may never have seen the band live, Anderson chose only one song from *Roots*, "Dangerous Veils," dedicating it to all the "exotic Eastern women of Moline," before returning to overly familiar ground. There were some highlights, however, with *Stand Up*'s bluesy

"We Used to Know" adding a soulful note to the evening. But here, as at the 1989 show in St. Paul, Barre's guitar gear failed him: just as he tore into the first note of the legendary solo, nothing emanated from his amplifier; the cable had been pulled out of his wah-wah pedal. This tour's instrumentals were taken from Anderson's *Divinities* and Barre's *The Meeting* solo albums.

At the time *The Meeting* was released, Barre said, "I would never make too little of what Jethro Tull means to me and its fans. I love the companionship within the band, and we have really good, loyal fans. It's something to be respected. I look at my solo work as a bonus, as something to coexist with Tull, not replace it."[410] However, he also pointed out a major challenge to this coexistence and described why he never stopped practicing each day:

> When you're a member of a so-called "classic rock" band, the problem is that no radio stations will play your new music. They'd rather play "Aqualung" for the millionth time…. Every evening on stage [with Tull]is challenging. I know that I can always play better. Eighty percent of what we play live is the same every night. But the rest is open to spontaneity and improvisation. When you try something new, and it clicks, it becomes part of your arsenal. I'm always looking for little oddball, magical things.[411]

In November, the band played its final 11 gigs of 1996 back in the U.K., opening at the Plymouth Pavilions on the 11th and closing at Northhampton's Derngate two weeks later. Following four months off, Anderson again took his crew on a grueling schedule that spanned seven months, with one-month holidays in May and October. From late April to early August, they thrilled crowds in Denmark, Britain, the Netherlands, Belgium, Poland, Czechoslovakia, Slovakia, Hungary, Germany, Austria and Italy. On August 3, they headlined the three-day Guildford Festival in Stoke Park, where 20,000 fans, including a large contingent of bikers, enjoyed their thunderous set. As a compliment to his old "hired hand," Anderson took time to promote Pegg and Fairport's Cropredy Festival, which was held the following weekend. Another North American tour followed during August, September and the first half of November before they finished the year with five more German gigs.

On August 10, 1997, Anderson celebrated his 50th birthday at the Harbor Lights in Boston, where a bagpiper rang in the occasion in Scottish style. In May 1978, he had said:

> I will still write music, make records and play live when I'm 50. I'd rather not be the Bing Crosby of that time—singing hits back from the '60s. I

want to write new music for new people because I can't go on wearing tights and funny clothes forever. It will be a different show, and music that fits a 50 year old without needing to jump up and down on one leg for two hours on stage. That might be a bit too much for me physically![412]

In April 1998, Anderson ended a five-month touring break to play at the German Tull Convention in Bedburg-Hau, where he promoted Martin Barre's upcoming "Summer Band" tour of the Rhineland. Playing songs from his two solo albums, as well as a rearranged version of "To Cry You a Song," Barre's group, fronted by singer Maggie Reeday, was merely the current Tull sans its flute-wielding leader. But soon after, Anderson again was out, manically fronting his band, for 29 July–October concerts in the United States and six November dates in Spain.

Thirty years down the road, the physical limitations began to set in. But was anything else about playing music different for Ian Anderson? He revealed, "Performing live is still the same challenge but easier now that we don't have to open for Led Zeppelin. And the audiences are now a little more drug free."[413]

Meanwhile, Anderson's status as a highly successful businessman received wide exposure on the Cable News Network. On May 5, 1998, CNN correspondent Sissel McCarthy reported that the Strathaird company was the largest independent smoked salmon firm in the U.K.—no small achievement for a rock 'n' roll musician who initially sank some of his hard-earned cash into a fledgling industry. Producing an album of pop music is one thing, running such a huge operation is another. McCarthy described the process involved in "fish agriculture":

> Salmon farming is a complex, time-consuming business. At a hatchery, the salmon eggs are nurtured in freshwater tanks. About 15 months after they hatch, the salmon are transferred to pens immersed in a saltwater loch, or sea inlet. There, the fish are hand-fed for two years. When they are about eight pounds in weight, the salmon are ready for harvest. At a processing facility in Inverness, the fish are gutted, filleted, salted to remove the moisture from the flesh, and smoked for up to 10 hours.... Last year, privately held Strathaird had revenues of $26 million, and turned out 900 tons of smoked salmon.[414]

Over the course of 30 years, Anderson created a lot of unforgettable music, but his contributions to his native heath remained much lesser known, due in large part to his own wish not to use his "rock star" status to promote his other business ventures. When asked about salmon in interviews, he usually replied that no one could possibly be interested in hearing about them. The fact that he transformed a depressed area with little occupational opportunity into a thriving one with jobs for 400 people (while re-investing all his profits to hire more) is remarkable. He admitted, "It's a good feeling that you've been part of the gentle and considerate repopulation of these rural areas, as well as creating the employment opportunities for the local kids to leave school and get a proper job." Of his refusal to use Tull as a promotional tool for salmon, he added, "If I was in America, it would be permissible and, indeed, even expected to do that. But on this side of the Atlantic, it's considered just a teeny-weeny bit tacky."[415]

Understandably, Anderson, almost constantly on the road with Tull, hired excellent managers to run Strathaird:

> Essentially, I'm just the guy who owns the company. It has become a self-contained business with fairly heavyweight management. I don't show up for work every day—more like once or twice a month. And when I do show up, I don't have to wear a suit and tie.
>
> I do, however, have to wear a funny hat and a beard net and white gloves and white boots. Must meet the rigorous government regulations, you know. Even Prince Charles had to dress up when he came here for an opening of one of our fisheries. And, as you can imagine, white gloves, funny white hats and white Wellington boots don't go very well with a kilt.[416]

As to the reputation of the salmon, Anderson said:

> They don't smell. Actually lovely things when they're fresh. All they smell of is the sea. When people say things smell "fishy," that's the most insulting thing you can say, because they think fish smells "fishy" because fish is "off" … past its sell-by date. But fish should just smell of the sea … fresh, exhilarating, and like a mermaid's armpit….[417]

Unfortunately, the original Strathaird salmon factory in Inverness burned down on August 1, 1998.

J-Tull Dot Com

---

23 August 1999 (U.K.) / 24 August 1999 (U.S.)
Highest chart position: 44 (U.K.) / 161 (U.S.)
[Rating: 3.5]

Produced by Ian Anderson/Fuel 2000
All songs written by Ian Anderson (except where indicated)

Ian Anderson: vocals, concert flute, bamboo flute, bouzouki, acoustic guitar
Martin Barre: electric and acoustic guitars
Andrew Giddings: Hammond organ, piano, accordion, chromatic and qwerty
    keyboards
Doane Perry: drums and percussion
Jonathan Noyce: bass guitar
Najma Akhtar: backing vocals on "Dot Com"

Recorded at Ian Anderson's home studio, January–April 1999
Engineered by Ian Anderson, assisted by Martin Barre, Doane Perry, Andy
    Giddings, Jonathan Noyce and Tim Matyear
Production mastering by Declan Burns at Chop 'Em Out
Cover painting by Ian Anderson, based on a sculpture by Michael Cooper
Sleeve design and layout by Bogdan Zarkowski
Photography by Martyn Goddard

Tracks: Spiral
       Dot Com
       AWOL
       Nothing @ All (Giddings)
       Wicked Windows
       Hunt by Numbers
       Hot Mango Flush (Anderson-Barre)
       El Niño
       Black Mamba
       Mango Surprise
       Bends Like a Willow
       Far Alaska
       The Dog Ear Years
       A Gift of Roses
       Bonus track (from forthcoming solo album):
       The Secret Language of Birds

The recording sessions for *J-Tull Dot Com* (a title reflecting the group's
internet website, which first went online in December 1998) were completed in April 1999. Two months later, Anderson added the backing vocals
of Indian vocalist Najma Akhtar to the title track and finished the final
mix, including for promotional purposes the title track from his forthcoming *The Secret Language of Birds* solo album as a bonus. Completing
contract negotiations, Anderson signed with Universal's Fuel 2000 for
distribution in the United States and Canada, while a new Chrysalis Group

label owned by Chris Wright (and unaffiliated with EMI) released the album across the world.

However, Anderson was disappointed that the American edition of the album would not feature in its entirety a painting he created for the front cover of the CD booklet. Based on a statue of the mythological Egyptian Ram–creature Amun that adorns his garden, the image had to

> have the genitals removed, due to the record company's concern that we might give offense to little old ladies, Mothers Superior and former FBI agents, together with the very slight possibility of one or two of our more sensitive fans working up a bit of a lather. Never mind: the full three and a half inches of glory will be there for all to see on T-shirts, the tour programme and [the] website.... All will, I am sure, be amused to learn of the advised necessary amputation, but I was not about to go back and paint CK boxers over the thing at this late stage.[418]

The Tracks of *Dot Com*

Dot Com begins on a solid note as an Anderson flute trill leads into the heavy rock "Spiral," a song dealing with the dream state experienced during the early morning hours just before one awakens. Perry and Noyce keep the rhythm section very simple as Giddings brings forth some welcome Hammond organ recalling the sound of early Tull. Then the title track leads the album in a totally different direction, combining the styles of *Divinities* (Indian-influenced melodies and wooden flute) and *Stand Up* (an ethnic-based number featuring doumbek and bongos). The haunting, gently wailing voice of Najma Akhtar lends the song just the right amount of cultural authenticity. Following a brief flute-and-keyboard introduction, Barre powers up "AWOL," a song about lovers meeting via the internet, a topic reflecting the album's title. The driving instrumental section following the chorus contributes a classic Tull sound, featuring single-note riffing by Barre and lush Hammond work by Giddings.

Giddings is given a quasi-classical solo spot on the brief "Nothing @ All," which leads into "Wicked Windows," one of the album's best tracks. Giddings again shines on Hammond organ here, contributing more "classical" ambiance to a potent rhythm section blend, especially Barre's combination of melodic single-note work (doubling Anderson's vocals) and crunching power chords. Barre, supported by Noyce, then shifts into "Aqualung" mode, opening "Hunt by Numbers" with an ominous, downright predatory riff befitting the song's subject. As explained by Anderson, it "is dedicated to [his favorite felines] and all species of Catus Pussicus everywhere, especially the, arguably, 26 species of small wild cat who don't receive much public attention compared with the big cats."[419] The groove laid down by Barre, Noyce and Perry is perfectly suited to the material, suggesting a stalking feline tracking down its doomed prey.

Absolute off-the-wall weirdness pervades "Hot Mango Flush," a song that elicited reactions of confusion and near-violence from some Tull fans. After Anderson contrived the nonsensical lyrics, which recall the style of "Wounded, Old and Treacherous" on *Roots to Branches*, Barre wrote the bizarre music, which resembles tracks on his solo albums. (On the positive side, the band, driven by Perry's excellent percussion, is incredibly tight on this song.) *Dot Com* regains its appeal on the thunderous "El Niño," featuring Barre at the very height of his power-chord prowess, musically painting the atmosphere of the well-known climatic phenomenon. Anderson's lyric, "Savage retribution makes for a headline feast. Planet-warming, opinion-forming headless beast" is ideally suited to Barre's style of guitar playing.

"Black Mamba" takes the band back to India in a song likening a relationship with a woman to putting one's "hand in the snake pit." (During the instrumental bridge, the melody, particularly Giddings' keyboard voicings, tread uncomfortably close to Led Zeppelin's "Kashmir.") An inexplicably remixed, primarily instrumental reprise of "Hot Mango Flush," retitled "Mango Surprise," mercifully fades out to welcome "Bends Like a Willow," an interesting love song couched in maritime terms that describes a man's ability to learn from the amiably adaptable, level-headed behavior of his mate:

> When I'm caustic and cold, she might dare to be bold—
> Ease me round to her warm way of thinking:
> Fill me up from the cup of love that she's drinking.
> And I find, given time, I can bend like a willow.
> She bends like a willow.

Like other songs on the album, "Far Alaska" begins with flute, which alternates with the heavy rock of the rhythm section, then settles into a funky groove as Anderson's observations about the current time-share real estate craze pour forth. A complex bridge section, featuring trademark Tull stylistic and key changes, is a highlight of the album. Following a driving conclusion, "The Dog Ear Years" begins a two-song treat for the longtime Tull fan. Returning the band to its late–1970s sound, this number includes Anderson's observations about his current status in the music business:

Rusted and ropy.
Dog-eared old copy.
Vintage and classic,
or just plain Jurassic:
All words to describe me.

Lyrics aside, this track could have fit into the *Heavy Horses* experience, or even the folk-dominated section of *Living in the Past*. But it is "A Gift of Roses" that truly offers a return to "Ye Olde Jethro Tull" so beholden to fans of *Songs from the Wood*, *Heavy Horses* and *Stormwatch*. Fading in on Anderson's bouzouki and bamboo flute, the song wonderfully combines Giddings' accordion (a welcome resurrection) and Barre's heavy guitar (reminiscent of his playing on "Mother Goose"). The best Tull fusion of British folk and rock since *Broadsword*, "Roses" lends an optimistic tone to the end of an album that deals with various, often serious, subjects:

Picking up tired feet. Back from a far horizon.
Cleaned up and brushed down. Dressed to look the part.
Fresh from God's garden. I bring a gift of roses.
To stand in sweet spring water and press them to your heart.

Here, the lyrics bring to mind the lovely conclusion of *Songs from the Wood*, "Fire at Midnight."

Just when *Dot Com* seems to be over, the listener is jarred by "Hello, this is Ian Anderson. Congratulations. You have happened upon a bonus track on this edition of the new Tull record. It's a preview of the title track from my solo album *The Secret Language of Birds*. Tweet, tweet. Tweet, tweet. See you in the morning." Though a clever way to pre-publicize an upcoming, long-anticipated release, Anderson's inclusion of this song may be heard by only a handful of *Dot Com* buyers: the song does not play until a full minute of silence has elapsed.

A limited edition single released in the U.K. features slightly edited versions of "Bends Like a Willow" and "Dot Com," as well as an unreleased track, "It All Trickles Down." Fading in on a nasty Barre drone, the bonus track combines lyrics ranging from medieval to modern with a jazz-blues groove—truly a bizarre melange of moods and styles.

The *Dot Com* Tour

Prior to the release of the album, the band took a summer tour through Hungary, the Czech Republic, Poland, Germany and Italy. Much to fans'

Ian Anderson on mandolin, Doane Perry on bongos and Martin Barre on flute play "Fat Man" during the *J-Tull Dot Com* tour, 1999. (Photograph by C. Woodhouse; courtesy of Ian Anderson.)

delight, the set list included "The Witch's Promise" and "To Cry You a Song," which Martin Barre recently had played live with his own group. Andy Giddings recalled an unfortunate incident that occurred during the June 10 show in Rostock:

> [W]e played a large sports hall and it was packed to the gills. As usual, people nearest the stage were jammed up against the barrier, and right in front of me I watched as a young woman was extricated from the heaving mass by the local Red Cross brigade, having just fainted. Her girlfriend was left looking equally worse for wear and so I mimed for Midge [Mathieson], my technician, to give her a glass of water from the stage. She looked mighty pleased to receive it, unlike her suddenly present and over-protective boyfriend, who hadn't been evident up to that point. He spent the rest of the show making sure that any eye contact I had with his girlfriend was minimal. At one point I gestured to him that he was nowhere to be seen when he could have helped. I guess it got lost in the translation![420]

Hard on the heels of the album's August 24 unveiling, Tull opened the U.S. leg of the tour at the Casino Ballroom in Hampton Beach, then moved on to Boston; Albany, New York; Wallingford, Connecticut; Darien, New York; Holmdel, New Jersey; and the Jones Beach Theatre in Wantagh, New York, where 17-year-old Amy Rosenblatt saw her first Tull show: "Ian ... seemed very down to earth, like he was playing for friends."[421] Though Tull failed to sell out the small venue and attracted "mostly middle-aged people," Ms. Rosenblatt believed that the 90-minute show was well worth the "more than $45" her father paid for the tickets.

By contrast, the September 11 show at Chicago's Auditorium Theatre was a sold-out bonanza. Minutes before opening act Viktoria Pratt Keating began her set, eager fans still were inquiring after tickets at the box office, to no avail. Fueled by a full-throttle Doane Perry, Jonathan Noyce's laid-back yet powerful bass lines and Andy Gidding's ever-enthusiastic keyboard prowess, Anderson and Barre sounded as good as ever, playing familiar songs yet adding just the right amount of (often jazzy) improvisation. Particular highlights were Anderson's rearrangement of "Serenade to a Cuckoo" for Indian wooden flute, a "Bourée" complete with a chamber-music introduction, a delightful "Jeffrey Goes to Leicester Square" and four tracks from *J-Tull Dot Com*. Even the stage shtick was refreshing, including a mock phone call in the middle of (it had to be) "Hunting Girl," the band finally returning to a track from the superlative *Songs from the Wood*.

In the audience at the October 7 Greek Theatre concert in Los Angeles, Glenn Cornick found the set list somewhat amusing:

> The *Stand Up* set. They did virtually everything from *Stand Up*. I couldn't believe it! I swear, out of the whole set, there may have been three songs that weren't songs that I was on. I think the only ones I wasn't on were "Locomotive Breath" and two songs from the *Dot Com* album. *Everything else* was something I played on. It was weird. Something we never played on stage: "Jeffrey Goes to Leicester Square." Where did that come from? It was like "The *Stand Up* Tour," and I was thinking, "This is 1999. You have a brand new album out. Why are you promoting a 1969 album? Well, I'm glad that you are, because for every one that's sold, I get some money." But I thought it was a very strange thing, although I can understand why. I listened to the new album, and it's all right, but there isn't anything that just jumps out and grabs you. I haven't really followed the band, so I don't know a lot of the stuff.[422]

The Secret Language of Birds

7 March 2000
[Rating: 5]
Produced by Ian Anderson
All songs and music written by Ian Anderson

Ian Anderson: vocals, flute, acoustic guitar, bouzouki, acoustic bass guitar, mandolin, percussion, piccolo
Andrew Giddings: accordion, piano, organ, marimba, percussion, electric bass, keyboards and orchestral sounds
Gerry Conway: drums
Darren Mooney: drums
James Duncan (Anderson): drums
Martin Barre: electric guitar
Roland Bord-du-Quai: violin

Recorded at Ian Anderson's home studio, 1998
Engineered by Ian Anderson
Production mastering by Nick Webb at EMI Abbey Road Studios
Sleeve design and artwork by Bogdan Zarkowski

Tracks: The Secret Language of Birds
The Little Flower Girl
Montserrat
Postcard Day
The Water Carrier
Set-Aside
A Better Moon
Sanctuary
The Jasmine Corridor
The Habanero Reel
Panama Freighter
The Secret Language of Birds, Part II
Boris Dancing
Circular Breathing
The Stormont Shuffle
Bonus tracks (live with Jethro Tull):
In the Grip of Stronger Stuff
Thick as a Brick

Throughout 1998, Anderson wrote and recorded a new solo album, *The Secret Language of Birds*, a project that had been called "Boris Dancing"

Ian Anderson promotes his long-awaited acoustic solo album, *The Secret Language of Birds*, **2000.**

at one point. Having seen a video-tape of Russian President Boris Yeltsin's attempts at rock 'n' roll terpsichore, he wrote this instrumental piece, but in the end it became just one of the album's tracks, as well as a number in the live Tull set.

Originally scheduled for late 1998, the album's release was moved to February 1999, then summer 1999 and finally late winter 2000, being held back by the record companies' insistence that two "Ian Anderson albums" should not be offered for sale simultaneously. Since the record outlets would not lavish twice as much attention on the releases, it was thought best to separate them by a lengthy span. In April 1999, Anderson wrote, "That's the official 'business' account of the whys and where-fores of it all. Blame the new record company guys. (They said it was all right for me to say this.)"[423]

Sixteen years earlier, Anderson had shocked his fans by producing his first solo album as a techno-pop experiment. Now, after *Divinities* had taken him in yet another direction, he finally returned to what "Tull Heads" had always wanted, a very personal, folk-oriented acoustic album. In December 1999, Anderson revealed how the passage of time had affected his views on recording technology:

> I like to write a piece of music and say, "This music can be enhanced by using this particular technical application" … I don't like music that's driven by technology. I'm more than happy to leave that up to the folks who play around with techno and dance forms, which are basically music composed with a lot of repetition and a lot of very simple motifs; music usually done by people who aren't really trained musicians.[424]

Anderson described the process of writing and recording the long-awaited album:

[T]he first few pieces were worked out as acoustic mandolin, bouzouki or guitar backing tracks with vocal lines and a few lyrics, mostly already with titles. Soon, Andrew Giddings, dropping by on a few occasions, added some subtle additions from accordion, bass, marimba and so on, and the drums or percussion were finalized just before the final mixing down process many months later.... Some of the later songs to be written and recorded tended to be quite personal and emotive and Andy put his additions to the almost completed work at the final stages.[425]

Just prior to the album's release, Anderson, via the Tull website, told fans:

Well, I hope you like the finished work and that the legacy of early Tull lingers on through the songs on this record. It is, at least, a personal document, free from the need to accomodate [sic] the heavier aspirations and tendencies of typical Tull members (including me!) No requirement to Rock-On, Cleveland! More, Strum-On, St. Cleve....[426]

To get his promotional activities off to a good start, Anderson appeared on *The Late Show with David Letterman*, playing with Paul Shaffer and the band throughout the program and receiving a few comments from the comedian. "Is that a flute?" Letterman asked at one point. The music consisted of instrumental versions of Tull material and Led Zeppelin's "Whole Lotta Love," and a Big Band–tinged arrangement of "Aqualung" with Anderson on vocals. On March 8, he was joined by Andy Giddings, Doane Perry and Tim Landers, a bass player friend of Perry's, for a spot on *The Late, Late Show with Craig Kilborn*. Though he was supporting the solo album, Anderson was not allowed to play any of the new material, since the powers-that-be believed that audience recognition would be stronger if some Tull songs were performed instead, even if Martin Barre was not included.

The Tracks of *The Secret Language of Birds*

The Secret Language of Birds is one of the most consistently excellent albums Ian Anderson has released. All 15 tracks blend his ethnic influences—English, Celtic, Indian/Middle Eastern, Spanish, Russian (no African-American blues this time)—with lush acoustic arrangements incorporating folk, jazz and laid-back, primarily non-electric rock. (Two tracks feature subtle electric contributions from Martin Barre.) Reaching back to the days of *Minstrel in the Gallery, Songs from the Wood, Heavy*

Horses and *Stormwatch*, he offers what he does best, at times (beautifully accompanied by Giddings on accordion) suggesting the influence of traditional Scottish folk groups, yet maintaining a style that is totally unique. The only classification that can be placed upon this music is that it falls within the genre of "Ian Anderson."

The title track, concerning the morning after a romantic rendezvous, recalls the acoustic passages on *Minstrel in the Gallery*, with Anderson's acoustic guitars and flute subtly accompanied by Giddings' keyboards and the ever-economical drumming of Gerry Conway. Anderson said:

> It could be a distinct possibility if you invited a girl to "sleep over," as the kids say, then, maybe, to ask her to spend the night and wake up to discover the "secret language of birds" might have a desired effect, being slightly more romantic, perhaps, than the Mick Jagger request to "Let's Spend the Night Together." Or perhaps if Oasis were to record such a piece, in today's rather more blatant and aggressive style, they might just say, "Let's shag!"[427]

Gerry Conway also plays on the following track, "The Little Flower Girl," a tribute to an erotic painting by watercolorist Sir William Russell Flint. Giddings' organ work adds to the *Living in the Past*–era verses, while his "string" arrangement during the choruses is reminiscent of Peter Vettese's keyboard playing on tracks such as "Fly By Night" on *Walk into Light*. "Girl" is a highlight of the album.

"Montserrat" is Anderson's view of the tragic situation on the beautiful West Indies island that practically was turned to ash after the volcano Souffriere began erupting in 1995. A Celtic-style march, featuring flute, accordion and snare drum, opens the song, which alternates between this instrumental passage and verses given a laid back groove by Giddings' squeeze box and Anderson's acoustic bass and percussion.

A song about "holiday guilt," "Postcard Day" (originally titled "Postcard Wednesday") fades in on an atmospheric, Spanish-style combination of bouzouki, flute, Latin percussion and minimal keyboards. Anderson's bass playing on this track is excellent, as is the use of dynamics throughout, a fine achievement in an acoustic piece. "The Water Carrier," on which Martin Barre contributes an electric guitar part, continues Anderson's fascination with Indian music, though this track treads very close to authentic Eastern music, rather than fusing it with heavy rock, as on *Roots to Branches* and *Dot Com*. Giddings' accordion blends effectively with Anderson's mandolin, flute and percussion, as well as Barre's lead part, which sounds like a traditional Indian instrument.

The superb "Set-Aside" is a brief acoustic guitar and flute piece offering the early, minimalist Ian Anderson style, as well as some haunting pastoral lyrics, like "Heavy Horses," lamenting the loss of rural life:

> Hard black crows bobbing where once ran deep furrows.
> Frazzled oak silhouetted in her ivy dress.
> Winter sun catches dog fox through thin hedges:
> throws his long shadow north to the emptiness.
>
> Farmhouse in tatters; shuttered and battered.
> Even lovers don't go there these last few years.
> Spider-web windows on set-aside heroes
> standing lost in a landscape of tears.

Anderson revealed the impetus for the song:

> [T]he agricultural policies that are necessary ... in this day and age: To literally set aside agricultural land in rotation *not* to produce crops. And the biggest irony is, although there are millions of starving people throughout the world, we're actually being paid as farmers in some of the rich Western countries ... not to grow anything. So "Set-Aside" is a rather dubious and mysterious, rather sad reality of modern farming, but ... we seem to have to do it.... I think it's a very depressive state of mind that visits itself upon farmers who, I think, are deeply saddened by the fact that they are being paid *not* to grow crops. It's a sad world. Make the best of it.[428]

"A Better Moon," described by Anderson as a "sultry and subtropical ... fantasy five thousand miles from home,"[429] features south of the equator keyboards and percussion, memorable melodies and a mesmerizing groove. One of the finest songs ever written by Anderson, "Sanctuary" begins with the finger-picking guitar style he used on "Rocks on the Road" and exquisite violin soloing by Breton fiddler Roland Bord-du-Quai (who unfortunately is not listed in the CD booklet credits). A beautiful instrumental bridge is highlighted by solo interplay between the violinist and Anderson on acoustic guitar. The content of the song is equally effective:

> Prince Charles ... was in Nepal, and was very moved to visit a charity-run sanctuary for returning young girl prostitutes ... children who have been abducted or sent away ... to Bombay to work in the brothels.... These girls come back, usually with AIDS, to die back in Nepal.... In the second half of the song, I talk about an almost parallel situation that is the result of unwanted zoo animals, rejects from some of the worst zoos in Europe and elsewhere. The cats, who are disposed of.... A few

> charitable organizations around the world will look after the ex-zoo ani-
> mals.... Some of the cats that I visited in a British sanctuary, although
> they were pretty sad creatures, they had a resigned dignity about them—
> something that called out to me and made me want to put these
> thoughts in a song....[430]

The child prostitute verse recalls the lyric "young bodies whoring" in "Flying Dutchman," while the concluding verse, like "...And the Mouse Police
Never Sleeps" and "Hunt by Numbers," reinforces Anderson's undying
love of wildcat breeds.

A romantic song about a dying man's lifelong love for his wife, "The
Jasmine Corridor" is an eerie acoustic guitar, accordion and organ blend
steeped in the Scottish ballad tradition. (One can imagine one of the great
traditional Scottish singers—Andy M. Stewart, Ian Bruce, Rod Paterson
or the late Davy Steele—"giving tongue to this one.") Endorphin rushing
to the other end of the emotional spectrum, "The Habanero Reel" is Anderson's tribute to the heavy-hitting pepper 100 times hotter than the jalapeno.
Opening with flute, accordion and keyboards, the instrumental reel segues
to Giddings' addition of marimba during the first verse, followed by the
return of the reel (with Anderson on piccolo) during the chorus. The second verse includes a reference to the Caribbean version of the habanero,
chosen for the pepper's resemblance to the Scottish tam o' shanter:

> Troubled skin? Pour oil upon it.
> She's fit to burn in her new Scotch Bonnet.
> Spice up anybody's stew.
> Frogs and goats and chickens too.

The last two lines refer to Anderson's tendency to tour with habanero hot
sauces in an effort to improve various bland cuisines.

How could a Scotsman produce an acoustic solo album without
including a sea song? Shades of "Flying Dutchman" again arise as Anderson delivers "Panama Freighter," another of the album's finest tracks, in
which he sings of a man's genuine love for a native girl he vows not to
"over-rate ... patronize ... educate ... or civilize." Deeply rooted in Scottish style, the song builds to a nice groove during an instrumental bridge
driven by Anderson's bass, Giddings' keyboards and the drumming of
Ian's son, James Duncan Anderson.

Though Anderson wrote separate music for "The Secret Language
of Birds, Part II," the song, a paean to his love for "the thoughtful and
detailed use of language" and "healthy disdain for ... business jargon-
speak,"[431] becomes a narrative continuation of the initial track: but here

the possibility of the woman being "the special person" has left the cliché-aversive protagonist "standing at the station":

> Right time but the wrong idea.
> Well, you're making it all sound just the same.
> Try taking it up a key like that Nightingale
> still over there in Berkeley Square.

Here, Anderson refers to the famous English song by Eric Maschwitz (superlatively recorded by both Frank Sinatra and Nat "King" Cole). The most Tull-like song on the album, "Part II" opens with Giddings' accordion riffs answered by potent kicks from flute, bass and Darren Mooney's drums, which effectively power the driving choruses.

The first of two instrumental tracks, "Boris Dancing" is an excellent, Russian-tinged tribute to the "dear fragile human bear [who has] hand on heart but not any longer, hopefully, on button."[432] Punctuated by hammering percussion, the flute-and-accordion melody occasionally is joined by Barre's electric guitar, making this piece sound as if Tull were playing material from *Divinities*. Anderson described his inspiration for the piece:

> [W]e were relatively safe with ol' Boris. Mr. Putin ... seems to be exhibiting signs of being a fairly war-mongering individual.... Boris was seeking re-election ... and was seen by the world's cameras, specifically in my case, CNN Nightly News, which showed Boris boogying frantically in Red Square in Moscow in front of a young Moscow rock band. I think he was trying to impress the young people, looking for the younger vote.... His dancing was perhaps on a par with his tennis playing, in terms of uncoordination ... rather awkward physical movements—which suddenly suggested itself to me as the basis for a piece of music which would employ some sharp and sudden twists and time signatures....[433]

(Here Anderson had a concrete reason to utilize abrupt shifts in musical time.)

"Circular Breathing" is a somewhat surreal end to the album's lyrical content. In another of several songs inspired by English painters, Anderson here mentions landscape artists John Constable and L. S. Lowry. Introduced by solidly British guitar reminiscent of the playing of Irish folky Gerry O'Beirne (accompanist for Andy M. Stewart), Anderson's quiet voice, singing a fine melody, sounds years younger.

The album concludes with another instrumental, "Stormont Shuffle," in which Anderson fuses traditional Celtic musical styles to suggest his view of the current political situation in Northern Ireland: "Peace, Love, Misunderstanding. Decommissioning the vipers' tongues. Two part tune: north and south, slippery Sams, moaning Minnies. Doublecross, double talk, double trouble."[434] The song opens ominously with hard-strummed staccato chords on acoustic guitar, introducing a flute melody accompanied by an accordion drone—a melancholy sound that alternates with a more sprightly jig featuring bouzouki, flute, accordion, piccolo and bodhran, bringing to mind the early recordings of Scots group Capercaillie, particularly the bouzouki playing of Irish musician Manus Lunny.

This final piece, as well as the entire album, is testament to the fact that Ian Anderson's roots in ethnic music always have given him the potential to create an organic, utterly non-commercial work such as *The Secret Language of Birds*. For admirers of traditional music, particularly Celtic, and fans of Jethro Tull, this project, like *Songs from the Wood* and *Heavy Horses*, reveals Anderson's considerable talent for merging past musical styles with wholly modern ones. On this album, he takes the musical fusion process he honed with Jethro Tull for three decades and moves it to a more refined plane. The songs recall "Skating Away," "Jack in the Green," "Weathercock" and "Warm Sporran," yet, benefiting from many years of musical and wordly experience, converge into one of Ian Anderson's greatest accomplishments as a singer-songwriter-musician-producer. No one said it more succinctly than Doane Perry: "It is an excellent record."[435] And, writing in the respected folk and world music periodical *Dirty Linen* (named after a Fairport Convention traditional medley), Michael Parrish reported:

> The disc includes some of Anderson's best tunes in years, including the airy title tune, the sparkling island pastiche "Postcard [Day]," and the Middle Eastern tonalities of "A Better Moon." "The Habanero Reel," with its dancing accordion and xylophone, likewise explores new stylistic ground for Anderson. All in all, Anderson sounds more energized here, as singer, instrumentalist, and composer, than he has in many a moon.[436]

Classical music aficionado Scott Huntley, a Tacoma, Washington, native descended from an ancient Scottish family, said:

> Although I am a dedicated fan of Jethro Tull, I was lackadaisical about purchasing the new Ian Anderson solo album. Perhaps it's the chequered history of Mr. Anderson's solo efforts…. Now we Tull fans are a dedicated cult … but never had I seen such [u]nanimity of opinion about one of their albums. Even the fans of "early Tull" (the hard rockers) have

never heaped such effusive praise on *Stand Up* as I found [for this album].... That such variation of texture and depth of sound can be produced from such modest means can leave me only to conclude that true genius was at work: Mr. Anderson's is apparent by this time— however, Mr. Giddings must be similarly commended for his remarkable contributions. Has there ever been another member brought to Tull by Mr. Anderson, in all the band's history, who has shown such versatility as we hear in Andrew Giddings?... "Sanctuary" ... is as fine and beautiful a song as [Anderson has] ever written. More poignantly sad than "Flying Dutchman." More ethereal beauty than is found in even "And Further On" ... Simply the brightest star in a vivid constellation.

If "Jasmine Corridor" ... radiates any less beauty than the previous song, it is by a margin too narrow to measure. I can almost guarantee that you will not be able to get "Panama Freighter" out of your head. Andrew Giddings just shines in this wonderfully melodious, offbeat story of Caribbean travel.... There is no logical reason why great musicians should lose their ability with age (a stupid youth culture notion that has gone on way too long). And Tull have produced some of their best works in recent years....[437]

Fan Rob Curtis was very emphatic about where he ranks *Birds* in the arena of contemporary music:

> *The Secret Language of Birds* comes at a time when teen girl strippers perform to drum kit drivel, androgynous and talent-challenged boy bands sing limp dance-pop, rappers spew their special brand of disrespect, wiggers try to do the same thing but even fail at that, hard rock bands have absolutely nothing to say, anything Latin-tinged is good even if it isn't, country is something other than country, adult contemporary is what it's always been—which isn't saying much—and Santana makes his big comeback with *lots* of help from his friends. *The Secret Language of Birds* represents the efforts of one of the most underrated songwriter-musicians in rock history, at once uplifting and thought-provoking. The lyrics and music have depth. *Birds* is crafted, not manufactured.[438]

Two "hidden" bonus tracks are included at the end of the disc. "In the Grip of Stronger Stuff," from *Divinities*, and the opening section of *Thick as a Brick*, with Anderson playing bouzouki rather than acoustic guitar, were recorded live by Tull for a European television show. Of these performances, Perry said, "We had to play so quietly that we could barely hear each other."[439]

Touring in 2000

Anderson rejoined Tull for a series of European dates in late April 2000, opening in Stockholm on the 25th and continuing with dates in Helsinki, Oslo and Copenhagen. During the first two weeks of May, the band played nine concerts in Eastern Europe, including appearances in Poland, the Czech and Slovak Republics, and Turkey. Their considerable popularity in the latter country was attested to by fan Aykut Oral, who has attended shows in Israel as well as the Turkish cities of Istanbul and Ankara. While serving a mandatory eight-month stretch in the Turkish army, "Ayk the Ulu" actually went AWOL to see Tull on May 13. The following day, he admitted:

> My flight to Istanbul was at 8:00 yesterday. I came back to the army location two hours ago. The concert's bill to me is seven days in military prison beginning next week because of running out of the military camp without permission, *but that does not mean anything if there is a Tull night.*[440]

Anderson commented on the effort required to transport the band's gear to Turkey:

> The crew had the nerve-wracking journey through Belgrade to get to Turkey, but the border guards and frequent police-check officers seemed content with a T-shirt or four and English cigarettes. By careful pre-arrangement with the NATO forces, the roads to Turkey had been left intact during the earlier bombings to speed the crew bus on its weary way. I only hope that we are still professionally engaged when it comes time, as one day it must, to visit Serbia in safety and openness to play a concert for the successors to the current regime.[441]

Following a brief break, the band began the North American leg of the tour in Austin, Texas, on June 6. Mark Louis reported:

> Ian ... noted the amazing similarity of "Hotel California" to "We Used to Know" from the *Stand Up* album. The Eagles were the opening band for Tull in 1972 and had "borrowed" the chord sequence. Anderson noted the theft, mentioning that he didn't expect royalties, but would accept a dinner from the Eagles as payback.[442]

During the first three days of July in North Carolina and Virginia, lucky fans were able to see Tull on a double bill with Ireland's greatest traditionalists, the Chieftains. The remaining dates featured the Los Angeles–based Celtic rock band, the Young Dubliners, perhaps the most musically appropriate supporting act since Fairport Convention.

Opening the shows with either *Benefit*'s "With You There to Help Me" or the perennial *Stand Up* favorites "For a Thousand Mothers" and "Nothing Is Easy" (previous tours had featured them later in the set list), the band alternated classic material with more recent pieces from *Roots to Branches* ("Beside Myself"), *Dot Com* ("Hunt by Numbers" and "AWOL") and *The Secret Language of Birds* (the lively ones: "Habanero Reel," "Water Carrier" and "Boris Dancing"). The July 3 concert at the Virginia Beach Amphitheater included Anderson and Perry sitting in with the Chieftains before they took the stage for their own set.

While the current Tull lineup were crisscrossing the United States, some former blokes in the band convened for an Italian Tull convention in July. Glenn Cornick described his appearance with old mates John Evans and Clive Bunker, as well as David Palmer, whom he had known only as a string arranger:

> We tried to get John Evans to play something serious. He claims he doesn't play anymore. We all think he sneaks off to some secret room in his house and practices without anybody knowing. We had him play the introduction to "Locomotive Breath." David Palmer, who is a very close friend of John's, twisted his arm into playing this part. David wrote it all out again for John, so John could pretend that he couldn't remember it. That is how I read it. So John went up and he played that full intro absolutely perfectly. Didn't miss a note. He pretended to read off this music that David had written out. He didn't want to blow his cover that he didn't play anymore.
>
> We had a really good time. I'd never worked with David Palmer on stage. My knowledge of David was the *This Was* and *Stand Up* albums when he did the string arrangements, and that was my only connection with him. We got on quite well. We were together a few days in Italy. It's interesting because he plays keyboards and sings. And we did several Tull songs, but David sings just like Tom Waits, which was very, very cool. Singing like Tom Waits, but doing Tull songs. We considered the possibility of actually getting out and doing some gigs: Clive, David, me and some guitar player or other. I think it would be quite funny.[443]

Managing to persuade Evans to struggle through all of "Locomotive Breath," they also played "We Used to Know," a song that had been recorded prior to the pianist's joining the group in 1970.

Back in America on August 8, an enormous crowd turned out to see Tull at Chicago's Ravinia Festival, located in Highland Park, Illinois. Two huge lawn areas as well as the 3,300-seat amphitheater were packed with patrons whose applause was deafening at times. The double dose from *Stand Up* opened the show, and some of the instrumental highlights included "In the Grip of Stronger Stuff" from *Divinities* and an Andy Giddings–backed Barre guitar solo including the guitarist's famous introduction to "Pibroch (Cap in Hand)." Anderson, however, was a bit annoyed by the behavior of the audience:

> [Y]ou might argue, we are but lucky visitors to a foreign country and must abide by and accept the local culture and customs. Hmm: not too sure, myself. I occasionally go to a show and am well rehearsed with bladder-emptying-with-forethought as well as imbibing whatever is required in the way of liquid or other sustenance suitably in advance of death by thirst or hunger. To get up from a seat in the front few rows and disturb performer and neighbours would fill me with horror and self-loathing. At least wait until the end of a bloody song, you rude buggers. Whoops: there I go. I came out and said it after all. You know, I feel better already.[444]

Completing their Midwest dates, Tull hit two venues in New York state before heading for the West Coast, closing the American tour in Anchorage, Alaska, on September 20. Back in England, Anderson prepared for additional shows in Spain, Portugal and Israel, scheduled for late October through mid–November. At this point, was there—as Anderson once remarked—any chance of the band playing their "farewell concert" in the year 2000? This former prediction soon was tossed to the winds as plans were made for a European tour during the summer of 2001.

The first leg of the 2001 North American summer tour coincided with the release of yet another compilation album, this time called *The Very Best of Jethro Tull* and news of a forthcoming DVD "history of the band." Nearly all 20 songs on *The Very Best* had been included on previous "greatest hits" packages, but, as Anderson states in the liner notes, "I think we have got as close as possible to a broad representation of the big picture."[445] When queried about the reason for such a release, Anderson said, "The record company needed a new replacement for the older compilations."[446] Unfortunately, due to time constraints, three of the songs are "ruthlessly edited": While this does not adversely affect "Minstrel in the Gallery," which had been released as a single, the majestic "Heavy Horses" does not benefit from this practice. One of the highlights of the disc is the inclusion of "Roots to Branches," the only track featuring Andy Giddings and Doane Perry.

Some of the American venues presented the usual problems. The concert at the Chicago Theatre on July 21 was particularly noisy, with "James Bond" author Raymond Benson remarking, "I've never seen so many assholes in a Tull audience."[447] The fluted one was conspicuously less active on stage, Perry was under the weather and Shona Anderson was ill from seafood she ate at the previous evening's Harley Davidson Rally in West Branch, Missouri. The set list was quite eclectic, including "Roots to Branches," "Sweet Dream," "Jack in the Green" and several songs from *The Secret Language of Birds*. An additional highlight was opening act Seven Nations, a Celtic rock band from Nova Scotia.

On August 11, 2001, the day after his 54th birthday, Anderson injured his "dicky" left knee while joining Dave Pegg and Fairport at their annual Cropredy Festival. On the official Tull website, Anderson told fans:

> It might not have been so bad if I had been a guest with a real life manly rock and roll ensemble like Aerosmith, Iron Maiden or Metallica, but to have this happen in the context of a twee and gentle folky moment. Hardly the stuff of VH1's *Behind the Music* series. Oh yeah, that Ian Anderson guy: the one who had the near-death experience at a folk festival...[448]

Three days later, in pain and attempting to get his leg back into shape, Anderson was treading the boards with his bandmates in the American Northeast. Perhaps life was beginning to imitate art too closely: The tour's T-shirts sported the title, "A Leg to Stand On."

CONCLUSION

In a live context, why has Ian Anderson focused on certain songs while ignoring others that were brilliantly performed on recordings? Are they too difficult to play in concert? Did his voice later become too damaged to do justice to them? In May 1992, he revealed:

> All the songs fall into three categories lyrically. There are those that I'm happy to get up and sing, that I have an emotional reaction and feel honest about, and there are those that instantly I know I just cannot sing, in no way. It could be a song from twenty years ago, it could be a song from six months ago, but certain things I just know I'm not gonna be able to get up and do, because I don't feel right about them anymore. Some of those songs are amongst Jethro Tull's most popular songs, but I cannot get up and sing them. I've tried. I can't do it. I don't want to go on and do something which is dishonest....[1]

During that same interview, he said:

> I think people are now a little less volatile and more tuned to the subtleties of old folks like us, who need more of a range of emotion in our performances. The audiences, too, are more receptive to an emotional range of intensity, a broader range of musical style. That's why we're still around and a lot of other people aren't, and why people in our audiences are so different from each other, as opposed to being one social or demographic type.[2]

What has been the guiding force in the innovation and eclecticism that Anderson has brought to his more than three decades of work? He admitted, "With ... music, I'm not interested in objectivity, quite the opposite.

308

I want a solely and totally subjective experience, which is what I'm after when I'm listening to music, whether it's mine or somebody else's."[3]

In his October 29, 1989, review of *Rock Island* in the Fort Lauderdale *Sun Sentinel*, Chauncey Mabe wrote:

> Tull ... is impossible to categorize. Led by ... Ian Anderson and ... the vastly underappreciated Martin Barre, Tull has produced some of the most complex and imaginative music in the rock era. Lyrically, Anderson has tackled thorny themes—from homelessness and child prostitution to religious corruption to the admirable attributes of farm animals—with songs of wit and substance.[4]

Along with the Rolling Stones and a precious few others, Tull are a rare survivor from the 1960s, a rock 'n' roll group who have outlived all forms of cyclic fashion, changing cultural tastes and the shifting values of old and new fans alike to remain essentially true to their own unique musical style. They never have "retired" from recording nor from touring North and South America, Great Britain, Eastern and Western Europe, the Middle East, the Orient, Australasia and Africa. They quickly outlived the "revolutionary" fad of punk rock, which railed against their ilk yet burned out within a few years. While the thrashing guitars and droning screams of the Sex Pistols and the Clash disappeared, the lilting melodies, powerful rhythms and impeccable musicianship of Jethro Tull lived on.

In 1991, Martin Barre said:

> One of the best things about the whole Jethro Tull experience is that we still enjoy playing together after all this time. ...As a musician, I really relate to people by playing live, and it's within that environment that I feel myself really coming into my own. I mean, I'd hate to be in a situation where I couldn't play live. It's the lifeblood of the group, and I've always considered us a touring unit, and I suppose that's one reason why we've been around for twenty-odd years. As far as Ian and I are concerned, we'd like Jethro Tull to be around forever.[5]

Two years later, Anderson offered his own desire for the band:

> [M]y most driving enthusiasm is to continue doing what I can only describe as progressive rock music. Because, for me, it is a progressive area in which to work. It doesn't mean you have to get more complicated—it doesn't have to get more highly structured or academic or cerebral. It actually has more to do with coming up with little ideas and themes and nuances within the music that either I haven't done before—or have done, but am gonna do a little better.[6]

Of his musical trademark, the flute, his conclusions may seem a wee bit ironic:

> Sometimes when I look at it, I think that it would drive me crazy if I was in the audience and had to listen to it in more than two or three songs. At least playing it, I have some physical and intellectual involvement. From an audience point of view, I reckon it must become pretty boring pretty quickly.
>
> It's really a decorative instrument. It's the fairy lights on the Christmas tree, a little condiment that you use to tickle things up a bit. But it's not the meat and potatoes of music. So the degree to which it's used in our music is really quite unnatural, I think, for the instrument. And I can't tell you that it works. I tell you that I use it. I hope that it works.[7]

Reflecting on his considerable contribution to Jethro Tull, Doane Perry explained:

> I feel incredibly lucky to be part of a band that is able to travel all over the world and play music that people really enjoy and ask us to come back and play again. That aspect of what I do never gets by me. I realize I'm incredibly fortunate to be part of a group like that—and you meet amazing people, and I get to see some extraordinary places in the world in the course of my work. I'm pretty lucky. I get to do what I love to do, which is just to play music and to go around the world doing it, eating some incredible food!
>
> I really think of Jethro Tull as my musical home. I have to thank all the people who come to see us every year and go out there and buy our records—that allow us the chance to continue to perform. We owe a lot to the people who have supported us, year in and year out. We also owe a lot to our incredibly loyal and hard-working crew of many years, headed by the always affable and extremely organized Kenny Wylie.
>
> All the years that I was a fan before I was ever in the band, I used to go to see them. And since I've been in the band, I certainly have a great appreciation for how fortunate I am to be playing with a group like this. They're all wonderful people, we're good friends, and that's a really important element in the success of the band, at least internally. We all love going out there and playing the music, and that's really the only reason we're still doing it—because we all *truly* love what we do.[8]

Why has Jethro Tull, after more than three decades of innovative recording and touring, been totally overlooked by the Rock and Roll Hall of Fame? Perry speculated:

I don't know. Maybe we're just too underground or too left field. We're a sort of really popular underground band. If they ever put us in there, that's fine that they recognize us. But if they don't, that's okay. We're still going to continue to go out there and play and hopefully make records. It's a hell of a great job.[9]

In 1979, when asked about his motivation for continuing with Jethro Tull, Anderson, metaphorically reflecting the maritime themes of *Stormwatch*, replied:

If I knew the answer to that, it would be self-defeating. I wouldn't be continuing. On a loftier scale, it's like why Sir Edmund Hilary felt it necessary to climb Everest or why Drake sailed 'round the world. It's the old answer, "Because it's there." There is something about performing, whether it's in the studio or on the stage, that having done it, one has to continue. Rather like the seaman who keeps going off and leaving the wife and kids, that primitive gypsy-like urge to be on the move again. It's more complicated with the stage because there's that tremendous feeling of putting yourself on the line when you perform in front of people—it's a great leveller to go out there and survive on the strength of your wits. It does you a lot of good to do it—even to fail once in a while. It's a further piece of self-examination. It's also wound up with the egotistic motives of peacocks strutting about, showing off and all the rest of it, but that's the side that you can control and rationalize. I'm always trying to inch my way up a ladder to some kind of definitive performance—and, apart from all that, it's good fun.[10]

And during the *25th Anniversary* tour 14 years later, he attempted to account for why the band had been allowed to last so long, while (as always) taking a swipe at current fadism:

As with the Grateful Dead and Status Quo, there's an amazingly strong, loyal following among our fans. Some of them are what we affectionately call the Train Spotters—you know, the ones who are slightly peculiar people who, if they weren't into Jethro Tull, would be just as likely to be jotting down train numbers in a station somewhere. They are unusual folks, God bless them, and very English for the most part. But then you've also got the incredibly die-hard 18- and 19-year-olds. God knows what that's about. They weren't born when we started, and they feel so denied by having missed out on that thing their parents' generation was part of. Right now, the most dangerous thing you're going to get, I suppose, is near-the-knuckle American rap vulgarism, which most of us are pretty uncomfortable with, or Madonna or Michael Jackson grabbing their parts in order to get attention. I find that all of a bit of a fad, really, probably because I'd been doing it as a joke every night onstage during "Locomotive Breath" since 1971—without, I hasten to add, trying to appear sexy in the process.[11]

Six years later, Anderson added:

Same old simple rhythms, melodies, harmonies and verse/chorus/bridge song structures. Nothing changes: nothing is really new. But each generation of young musicians rediscovers the wheel, the Beatles, sunglasses and stretch limousines. As long as they and their fans think it is new, why disappoint them? Give the kids a pot of paint and they will repaint their house. Same old bricks underneath. Techno and Rap? Just nursery rhymes with attitude. Nice idea but going round in very small circles.[12]

Of other musicians who attempt to blend the elements often associated with Tull and contemporaries like Fairport Convention, Glenn Cornick said:

Anybody can play bloody folk-rock or Celtic rock now. You get a fiddle player who knows all the dance tunes. It's so easy because everybody has something to fall back upon. We were, at the time, inventing all the stuff. I don't want to appear "so much greater" because we did this. All the bands in London at the time were all so different. And none of them had anything to refer back to.[13]

The Secret Language of Birds has proved that an artist as talented as Ian Anderson can transcend the commercial dictates of the marketplace, even if a corporation insists that his music be released at a time displeasing to its maker. How many "leaders" of groundbreaking rock 'n' roll bands ever have produced such works, merging the music of everyday folk with that of transcendant forms and what is popular on the radio and in record stores? While some of the Jethro Tull albums released since 1984 have been created in part to attract potential consumers, Anderson's latest work connects with his earliest efforts, assuring admirers of honest music that at least one innovative artist has not "sold out." *Birds*, indeed, may make listeners "get ready for the whistler ... for the tune ends too soon for us all."

AFTERWORD
by David Pegg

I was very proud and very happy most of my time with Jethro Tull. I made many friends in those days as a result of my touring with Tull— people like John Belville, when I first joined the band and we went to America on the *Stormwatch* tour. The first week, we'd be driving into gigs, and I'd always see this guy standing by the stage entrance, and I figured he was one of the crew. And I went out for a walk one night, because nobody knew who I was. It was great being anonymous, whereas if any of the others went out walking by the gig, they'd just be pestered by a lot of autograph hunters and fans. For me, I never had that problem.

So I went out for a walk one night, and I said to this guy, "Oh, excuse me, mate. I've seen you for the last seven nights running. What do you do?"

And he said, "I'm just a fan. I'm from Stoke-on-Trent. I come to every Tull gig. I'm on my holiday."

So I went back and told the others. I said, "There's this guy. He's been here seven consecutive gigs, all over America."

And they all said, "Oh, yeah, well…"

I said, "Well, don't you think that's amazing? Perhaps we should invite him in. We should say, 'Hello.' He'd be really pleased."

So I got him a pass one night. He was a very shy guy, but he did come in and meet us all. And ever since then, John's sort of become another member of the band. He's not at all shy now when he comes to see the band, but he gets really upset if the audiences don't react in a really good manner. He gets really pissed off, like the band do when they have a really bad night! But he's a really nice guy. And I miss seeing my people like that, from not being with Tull.

313

Tull fans—they're all such a good bunch, really. It was a real pleasure being in the band. I did it for 16 years and I had some right good times. I wish everybody in Tull all the best of luck. I'm glad to see they're still going and doing so well, and I hope we remain friends.

And Jethro Tull fans all over the world: It was nice knowing you. I hope, maybe one day, I can come out and play some of that stuff again! Best wishes to you all. Take care.

Dave Pegg
Oxfordshire, England

APPENDIX A:
THE MEMBERS OF JETHRO TULL
(1968–2001)

Michael Timothy Abrahams ("Mick")—Luton, England, 7 April 1943

Don Airey—Sunderland, England, 21 June 1948

Martin Allcock ("Maart")—Manchester, England, 5 January 1957

Ian Scott Anderson—Dunfermline, Scotland, 10 August 1947

Barrie Barlow ("Barriemore")—Birmingham, England, 10 September 1949

Martin Barre—Birmingham, England, 17 November 1946

Clive William Bunker—Luton, England, 30 December 1946

Paul Burgess—England

Gerry Conway—King's Lynn, Norfolk, England, 11 September 1947

Glenn Douglas Cornick (Glenn Barnard)—Barrow-in-Furness, Cumbria, England, 24 April 1947

Mark Craney—Minneapolis, Minnesota, U.S.A., 26 August 1952

John Evans—Blackpool, England, 28 March 1948

Andrew Giddings—Pembury, Kent, England, 10 July 1963

John Glascock—Islington, London, England, 2 May 1951 (died 17 November 1979)

Jeffrey Hammond ("Hammond-Hammond")—Blackpool, England, 30 July 1946

Eddie Jobson—Billingham, England, 28 April 1955

David Mattacks—Edgeware, Middlesex, England, March 1948

Jonathan Noyce—Sutton Coldfield, England, 15 July 1971

David Palmer—England, 2 July 1937

David Pegg ("Peggy")—Birmingham, England, 2 November 1947

Doane Ethredge Perry—Mt. Kisco, New York, U.S.A., 16 June 1954

Peter-John Vettese—Seafield, Midlothian, Scotland, 15 August 1956

Tony Turnbull Williams—Durham, England, 19 August 1947

Appendix B:
Greatest Hits /
"Best of" Releases

M.U.: The Best of Jethro Tull

9 January 1976 (U.K.) / 12 January 1976 (U.S.)
Highest chart position: 44 (U.K.) / 13 (U.S.)
Producers: Ian Anderson and Terry Ellis / Chrysalis CHR 1078
All songs written by Ian Anderson

Ian Anderson: vocals, flute, acoustic guitar, mandolin, soprano saxophone
Martin Barre: electric and acoustic guitars
Glenn Cornick: bass guitar
Jeffrey Hammond: bass guitar
John Evans: piano, Hammond organ, synthesizers
Clive Bunker: drums, percussion
Barrie Barlow: drums, percussion

Recorded at Morgan Studios, London; Vantone Studio, West Orange, N.J.; Island
   Studios, London
Recording engineers: Andy Johns, John Burns and Robin Black
Strings arranged and conducted by David Palmer

Tracks: Teacher; Aqualung; Thick as a Brick edit #1; Bungle in the Jungle; Locomotive Breath; Fat Man; Living in the Past; A Passion Play edit #8; Skating
   Away (On the Thin Ice of the New Day); Rainbow Blues [previously
   unreleased]; Nothing Is Easy

Repeat: The Best of Jethro Tull, Volume II

9 September 1977 (U.K.) / 7 November 1977 (U.S.)
Highest chart position: 94 (U.S.)
Producers: Ian Anderson and Terry Ellis / Chrysalis CHR 1135
All songs written by Ian Anderson

Ian Anderson: vocals, flute, acoustic guitar, mandolin, alto and soprano saxophones
Martin Barre: electric and acoustic guitars
Glenn Cornick: bass guitar
Jeffrey Hammond: bass guitar
John Glascock: bass guitar
John Evans: piano, Hammond organ, synthesizers
Clive Bunker: drums and percussion
Barrie Barlow: drums and percussion
Maddy Prior: backing vocals

Recording engineers: Andy Johns, John Burns and Robin Black
Strings arranged and conducted by David Palmer

Tracks: Minstrel in the Gallery; Cross-Eyed Mary; A New Day Yesterday; Bourée;
    Thick as a Brick edit #4; War Child; A Passion Play edit #9; To Cry You a
    Song; Too Old to Rock 'n' Roll: Too Young to Die; Glory Row [previously
    unreleased]

Original Masters

21 October 1985 (U.K.) / 18 November 1985 (U.S.)
Highest chart position: 63 (U.K.)
Chrysalis JJVT 1

Ian Anderson: vocals, flute, acoustic guitar
Martin Barre: electric and acoustic guitars
Glenn Cornick: bass guitar
Jeffrey Hammond: bass guitar
John Glascock: bass guitar
John Evans: piano, Hammond organ, synthesizers
David Palmer: synthesizers
Clive Bunker: drums and percussion
Barrie Barlow: drums and percussion
Maddy Prior: backing vocals

Tracks: Living in the Past; Aqualung; Too Old to Rock 'n' Roll: Too Young to Die;
    Locomotive Breath; Skating Away (On the Thin Ice of the New Day); Bungle
    in the Jungle; Sweet Dream; Songs from the Wood; Witch's Promise; Thick as a
    Brick; Minstrel in the Gallery; Life Is a Long Song

20 Years of Jethro Tull

Compilation from the box set on double LP and single CD
10 October 1988 (U.K.) / 16 January 1989 (U.S.)
Chrysalis CJT 7

Ian Anderson: vocals, flute, acoustic guitar, mandolin, tin whistle, harmonica
Mick Abrahams: electric guitar
Martin Barre: electric and acoustic guitars
Glenn Cornick: bass guitar
Jeffrey Hammond: bass guitar
John Glascock: bass guitar
Dave Pegg: bass guitar, mandolin
John Evans: piano, Hammond organ, synthesizers
David Palmer: portative organ, synthesizers
Peter-John Vettese: keyboards
Martin Allcock: bouzouki, electric guitar
Clive Bunker: drums and percussion
Barrie Barlow: drums and percussion
Gerry Conway: drums and percussion
Doane Perry: drums and percussion

Tracks: Stormy Monday Blues; Love Story; A New Day Yesterday; Summerday Sands; Coronach [not on CD]; March the Mad Scientist; Pibroch/Black Satin Dancer (instrumental) [not on CD]; Lick Your Fingers Clean; Overhang; Crossword; Saturation [not on CD]; Jack-a-Lynn; Motoreyes [not on CD]; Part of the Machine; Mayhem, Maybe; Kelpie; Under Wraps 2 [not on CD]; Wond'ring Aloud; Dun Ringill; Life Is a Long Song; Nursie; Grace; Witch's Promise; Teacher [not on CD]; Living in the Past; Aqualung; Locomotive Breath

The Best of Jethro Tull: The Anniversary Collection

Two-compact disc collection of remastered songs
24 May 1993 (U.K.) / 6 June 1993 (U.S.)
Reissued 5 October 1999 (U.S.)
Chrysalis CD CHR 6001

Ian Anderson: vocals, flute, acoustic guitar, keyboards, percussion
Mick Abrahams: electric guitar
Martin Barre: electric and acoustic guitars
Glenn Cornick: bass guitar
Jeffrey Hammond: bass guitar
John Glascock: bass guitar
Dave Pegg: bass guitar, mandolin
John Evans: piano, Hammond organ, synthesizers
David Palmer: synthesizers
Eddie Jobson: keyboards

Peter-John Vettese: keyboards
Martin Allcock: keyboards
Andy Giddings: keyboards
Clive Bunker: drums and percussion
Barrie Barlow: drums and percussion
Mark Craney: drums and percussion
Gerry Conway: drums and percussion
Doane Perry: drums and percussion

Tracks: A Song for Jeffrey; Beggar's Farm; A Christmas Song; A New Day Yester-
day; Bourée; Nothing Is Easy; Living in the Past; To Cry You a Song; Teacher;
Sweet Dream; Cross-Eyed Mary; Mother Goose; Aqualung; Locomotive Breath;
Life Is a Long Song; Thick as a Brick Extract; A Passion Play Extract; Skating
Away (On the Thin Ice of the New Day); Bungle in the Jungle; Minstrel in the
Gallery; Too Old to Rock 'n' Roll: Too Young to Die; Songs from the Wood;
Jack in the Green; The Whistler; Heavy Horses; Dun Ringill; Fylingdale Flyer;
Jack-a-Lynn; Pussy Willow; Broadsword; Under Wraps #2; Steel Monkey; Farm
on the Freeway; Jump Start; Kissing Willie; This Is Not Love

Through the Years

23 January 1997 (U.K.)
Produced by Ian Anderson/EMI Gold CDGOLD 1079

Ian Anderson: vocals, flute, acoustic guitar, keyboards, percussion
Mick Abrahams: electric guitar
Martin Barre: electric and acoustic guitars
Glenn Cornick: bass guitar
Jeffrey Hammond: bass guitar
John Glascock: bass guitar
Dave Pegg: bass guitar, mandolin
John Evans: piano, Hammond organ, synthesizers
David Palmer: synthesizers
Peter-John Vettese: keyboards
Andy Giddings: keyboards
Clive Bunker: drums and percussion
Barrie Barlow: drums and percussion
Gerry Conway: drums and percussion
Doane Perry: drums and percussion
Dave Mattacks: drums and percussion

Tracks: Living in the Past [live, from *A Little* Light *Music*]; Wind-Up; War Child;
Dharma for One; Acres Wild; Budapest; The Whistler; We Used to Know;
Beastie; Locomotive Breath [live; from *Live: Bursting Out*]; Rare and Precious
Chain; Quizz Kid; Still Loving You Tonight

The Very Best of Jethro Tull

July 2001
Chrysalis/EMI/Capitol Records, Inc. 72435 32614 29

Ian Anderson: vocals, flute, acoustic guitar, keyboards
Mick Abrahams: electric guitar
Martin Barre: electric guitar
Glenn Cornick: bass guitar
Jeffrey Hammond: bass guitar
John Glascock: bass guitar
Dave Pegg: bass guitar
Steve Bailey: bass guitar
John Evans: piano, Hammond organ, synthesizers
David Palmer: synthesizers, string arrangements
Peter-John Vettese: keyboards
Andy Giddings: keyboards
Clive Bunker: drums, percussion
Barrie Barlow: drums, percussion
Gerry Conway: drums, percussion
Doane Perry: drums, percussion

Tracks: Living in the Past; Aqualung; Sweet Dream; The Whistler; Bungle in the
    Jungle; The Witch's Promise; Locomotive Breath; Steel Monkey; Thick as a
    Brick; Bourée; Too Old to Rock 'n' Roll: Too Young to Die; Life Is a Long
    Song; Songs from the Wood; A New Day Yesterday; Heavy Horses;
    Broadsword; Roots to Branches; A Song for Jeffrey; Minstrel in the Gallery;
    Cheerio

APPENDIX C:
SONG COPYRIGHT INFORMATION

All Words and Music by Ian Anderson

"Aqualung"
"Cross-Eyed Mary"
"Hymn 43"
"Locomotive Breath"
"My God"
"Son"
"Wind Up"
"Wond'ring Aloud"
"Thick as a Brick"

"A Passion Play"
"Critique Oblique"

"Back-Door Angels"
"Bungle in the Jungle"
"Only Solitaire"
"Queen and Country"
"Skating Away (On the Thin Ice of the New Day)"
"The Third Hoorah"
"Two Fingers"

"Baker St. Muse"
"Cold Wind to Valhalla"
"Grace"
"Minstrel in the Gallery"
"Requiem"

"Big Dipper"
"Crazed Institution"
"From a Dead Beat to an Old Greaser"
"Pied Piper"
"Quizz Kid"
"Salamander"
"The Chequered Flag (Dead or Alive)"
"Too Old to Rock 'n' Roll: Too Young to Die"

"Jack in the Green"
"Pibroch (Cap in Hand)"
"Songs from the Wood"

"Acres Wild"
"And the Mouse Police Never Sleeps"
"Heavy Horses"
"Journeyman"
"No Lullaby"
"One Brown Mouse"
"Rover"
"Weathercock"

"Dun Ringill"
"Flying Dutchman"
"North Sea Oil"

"Protect and Survive"

"Seal Driver"
"Slow Marching Band"

"Made in England"

"Dogs in the Midwinter"
"Jump Start"

"Jack-a-Lynn"

"Another Christmas Song"
"Ears of Tin (Mainland Blues)"
"Heavy Water"
"Kissing Willie"

CHAPTER NOTES

Introduction

    1. G. E. Fussell, *Jethro Tull: His Influence on Mechanized Agriculture* (Reading, Berkshire: The Berkshire Printing Co., Ltd., 1973), p. 5.
    2. Fussell, p. 14.
    3. *Rolling Stone* (22 July 1971).
    4. Craig Thomas, *Jethro Tull: 25th Anniversary* booklet, p. 19.
    5. Roy Eldridge, *Jethro Tull: 25th Anniversary* booklet, p. 31.

Becoming Jethro Tull

    1. *Collins Encyclopedia of Scotland*, p. 269.
    2. Collins, p. 723.
    3. *Crawdaddy* (18 July 1971).
    4. Jethro Tull Official Website (1998).
    5. Jethro Tull Official Website (1998).
    6. *Wind Player* (no. 55), p. 18.
    7. *Crawdaddy* (18 July 1971).
    8. *Circus* (no. 124, 9 December 1975).
    9. *Hit Parader* (March 1976).
    10. *Hit Parader* (March 1976).
    11. Jethro Tull Official Website (December 1998).
    12. *Crawdaddy* (18 July 1971).
    13. *Hit Parader* (March 1976).
    14. Glenn Cornick, telephone conversation with Scott Allen Nollen (10 August 2000).
    15. *Rolling Stone* (July 1971).
    16. Glenn Cornick, telephone conversation with Scott Allen Nollen (10 August 2000).
    17. *Hit Parader* (March 1976).
    18. *20 Years of Jethro Tull* video (1988).

19. *Rolling Stone* (22 July 1971).
20. *A New Day* (no. 37, p. 18).
21. *A New Day* (no. 37, p. 18).
22. David Rees, *Minstrels in the Gallery: A History of Jethro Tull* (London: SAF, 1998), p. 22.
23. Glenn Cornick, telephone conversation with Scott Allen Nollen (10 August 2000).
24. *A New Day* (no. 19, p. 20).
25. Rees, p. 24.
26. Jethro Tull Official Website (1999).
27. *Circus* (no. 124, 9 December 1975).
28. *Wind Player* (no. 55), pp. 18–19.
29. *Downbeat* (11 March 1976), p. 14.
30. *Wind Player* (no. 55), p. 19.

The Albums and Tours (1968–2001)

1. Glenn Cornick, telephone conversation with Scott Allen Nollen (10 August 2000).
2. *20 Years of Jethro Tull*, video (1988).
3. Rockline (1982).
4. *Jethro Tull, 25th: Complete Lyrics*, p. 7.
5. *Circus* (no. 124, 9 December 1975).
6. *Jethro Tull: 25th Anniversary*, box set booklet (1993), p. 18.
7. *Hit Parader* (October 1969).
8. Glenn Cornick, telephone conversation with Scott Allen Nollen (10 August 2000).
9. *This Was*, liner notes.
10. *20 Years of Jethro Tull*, video (1988).
11. Glenn Cornick, telephone conversation with Scott Allen Nollen (10 August 2000).
12. Glenn Cornick, telephone conversation with Scott Allen Nollen (10 August 2000).
13. Karl Schramm and Gerard J. Burns, eds., *Jethro Tull, 25th: Complete Lyrics* (Heidelberg, Germany: Palmyra Publishers, 1993), p. 8.
14. *A New Day* (no. 43), p. 17.
15. *A New Day* (no. 37), p. 19.
16. *A New Day* (no. 43), p. 18.
17. *A New Day* (no. 43), pp. 21–22.
18. David Rees, *Minstrels in the Gallery: A History of Jethro Tull*, p. 33.
19. Glenn Cornick, telephone conversation with Scott Allen Nollen (10 August 2000).
20. Glenn Cornick, telephone conversation with Scott Allen Nollen (10 August 2000).
21. Rees, p. 30.
22. Glenn Cornick, telephone conversation with Scott Allen Nollen (10 August 2000).
23. Glenn Cornick, telephone conversation with Scott Allen Nollen (10 August 2000).

24. *A New Day* (no. 37), p. 23.
25. Glenn Cornick, telephone conversation with Scott Allen Nollen (10 August 2000).
26. *A New Day* (no. 38), p. 25.
27. Glenn Cornick, manuscript annotation for Scott Allen Nollen (August 2000).
28. *A New Day* (no. 38), p. 24.
29. *Jethro Tull, 25th: Complete Lyrics*, p. 8.
30. *Home & Studio Recording* (March 1989), p. 44.
31. *Guitar for the Practicing Musician* (May 1991), p. 138.
32. Glenn Cornick, telephone conversation with Scott Allen Nollen (10 August 2000).
33. *A New Day* (no. 23), p. 22.
34. *Jethro Tull, 25th: Complete Lyrics*, p. 8.
35. *A New Day* (no. 37), p. 22.
36. Rees, p. 32.
37. Glenn Cornick, telephone conversation with Scott Allen Nollen (10 August 2000).
38. Jethro Tull Official Website (1999).
39. Glenn Cornick, telephone conversation with Scott Allen Nollen (10 August 2000).
40. Glenn Cornick, telephone conversation with Scott Allen Nollen (10 August 2000).
41. *Jethro Tull: 25th Anniversary*, tour program (1993), p. 6.
42. Glenn Cornick, telephone conversation with Scott Allen Nollen (10 August 2000).
43. Glenn Cornick, telephone conversation with Scott Allen Nollen (10 August 2000).
44. Glenn Cornick, telephone conversation with Scott Allen Nollen (10 August 2000).
45. Greg Russo, *Flying Colours: The Jethro Tull Reference Manual* (Floral Park, New York: Crossfire Publications, 2000), p. 55.
46. Glenn Cornick, telephone conversation with Scott Allen Nollen (10 August 2000).
47. Glenn Cornick, telephone conversation with Scott Allen Nollen (10 August 2000).
48. *Jethro Tull, 25th: Complete Lyrics*, p. 13.
49. Judson C. Caswell, "Minstrel in the Gallery: History in the Music of Jethro Tull," *St. Cleve Chronicle* (vol. 4, issue 92/7 December 1993).
50. *Today's Runner* (May 1990).
51. Glenn Cornick, telephone conversation with Scott Allen Nollen (10 August 2000).
52. Glenn Cornick, telephone conversation with Scott Allen Nollen (10 August 2000).
53. *Jethro Tull, 25th: Complete Lyrics*.
54. *A New Day* (no. 37), p. 23.
55. *A New Day* (no. 37), p. 22.
56. David Rees, p. 37.
57. Glenn Cornick, manuscript annotation for Scott Allen Nollen (August 2000).
58. *New York Times* (23 May 1970).
59. Glenn Cornick, telephone conversation with Scott Allen Nollen (12 August 2000).

60. Glenn Cornick, telephone conversation with Scott Allen Nollen (10 August 2000).

61. Glenn Cornick, telephone conversation with Scott Allen Nollen (10 August 2000).

62. Glenn Cornick, telephone conversation with Scott Allen Nollen (10 August 2000).

63. *Crawdaddy* (8 June 1970).

64. *A New Day* (no. 38), p. 25.

65. Glenn Cornick, telephone conversation with Scott Allen Nollen (10 August 2000).

66. *A New Day* (no. 37), p. 18.

67. *Jethro Tull, 25th: Complete Lyrics*, pp. 8–9.

68. *Circus* (no. 124, 9 December 1975).

69. *A New Day* (no. 28), p. 17.

70. *Jethro Tull, 25th: Complete Lyrics*, p. 9.

71. Glenn Cornick, telephone conversation with Scott Allen Nollen (10 August 2000).

72. *Rolling Stone* (22 July 1971).

73. *Guitar for the Practicing Musician* (May 1991), p. 138.

74. *Jethro Tull, 25th: Complete Lyrics*, p. 13.

75. Ian Anderson, letter to Scott Allen Nollen (1991).

76. *Jethro Tull, 25th: Complete Lyrics*, p. 12.

77. *Rolling Stone* (22 July 1971).

78. *Crawdaddy* (18 July 1971).

79. *Rolling Stone* (22 July 1971).

80. *Rolling Stone* (22 July 1971).

81. *A New Day* (no. 28), pp. 17–18.

82. *A New Day* (no. 19), p. 20.

83. *A New Day* (no. 19), p. 21.

84. *A New Day* (no. 19), p. 21.

85. *Rolling Stone* (22 July 1971).

86. *A New Day* (no. 19), p. 22.

87. *Rolling Stone* (22 July 1971).

88. *Rolling Stone* (22 July 1971).

89. *Rolling Stone* (22 July 1971).

90. *Rolling Stone* (22 July 1971). Ian Anderson, manuscript annotation for Scott Allen Nollen (August 2000).

91. *Audience* (May–June 1972).

92. *Audience* (May–June 1972).

93. *Home and Studio Recording*, p. 44.

94. *Downbeat* (11 March 1976), p. 16.

95. *Jethro Tull, 25th: Complete Lyrics*, p. 15.

96. *Guitar for the Practicing Musician* (May 1991), p. 138.

97. *Guitar World*, p. 55.

98. *Thick as a Brick*, CD interview (1997).

99. Glenn Cornick, telephone conversation with Scott Allen Nollen (10 August 2000).

100. *Jethro Tull: 25th Anniversary*, box set booklet (1993), p. 9.

101. *Jethro Tull: 25th Anniversary*, box set booklet (1993), p. 23.

102. *Jethro Tull: 25th Anniversary*, box set booklet (1993), p. 26.

103. *Rolling Stone* (22 June 1972).

104. *Rolling Stone* (22 June 1972).
105. *Thick as a Brick*, CD interview (1997).
106. *Jethro Tull, 25th: Complete Lyrics*, p. 12.
107. David Rees, p. 49.
108. *Thick as a Brick*, CD interview (1997).
109. Mark Louis, letter to Scott Allen Nollen (21 July 2000).
110. *Jethro Tull, 25th: Complete Lyrics*, p. 15.
111. *A New Day* (no. 41), p. 20.
112. *A New Day* (no. 28), p. 19.
113. *A New Day* (no. 28), pp. 18–19.
114. *A New Day* (no. 28), p. 20.
115. *Rolling Stone* (30 August 1973).
116. *Rolling Stone* (30 August 1973).
117. *Rolling Stone* (30 August 1973).
118. W.S. Gumby's internet review page.
119. *A New Day* (no. 28), p. 20.
120. *Jethro Tull: 25th Anniversary*, tour program (1993), p. 15.
121. Mark Louis.
122. David Rees, p. 63.
123. *Downbeat* (11 March 1976).
124. "Cup of Wonder" website.
125. *Jethro Tull, 25th: Complete Lyrics*, p. 19.
126. *Circus Raves* (vol. 1, no. 9/November 1974).
127. *Soundwave* (no. 1/Fall 1976).
128. *A New Day* (no. 19), p. 22.
129. Judson C. Caswell.
130. Judson C. Caswell.
131. *Circus Raves* (vol. 1, no. 9/November 1974).
132. *A New Day* (no. 28), p. 20.
133. *Rock Island* tour program, 1989, p. 22.
134. *25th Anniversary* tour program, 1993, p. 13.
135. *Circus* (no. 24/9 December 1975).
136. *Downbeat* (11 March 1976), p. 15.
137. *Circus* (no. 24/9 December 1975).
138. *Jethro Tull, 25th: Complete Lyrics*, p. 19.
139. *A New Day* (no. 19), p. 25.
140. "Cup of Wonder" website.
141. *Downbeat* (11 March 1976).
142. *25th Anniversary* tour program, 1993, p. 11.
143. *Circus* (no. 24/9 December 1975).
144. *A New Day* (no. 28), p. 22.
145. *Hit Parader* (March 1976).
146. *Hit Parader* (March 1976).
147. *Circus* (no. 137/10 August 1976).
148. *Jethro Tull, 25th: Complete Lyrics*, p. 20.
149. *Circus* (no. 137/10 August 1976).
150. *Soundwave* (no. 1/Fall 1976).
151. *Circus* (no. 137/10 August 1976).
152. *Jethro Tull, 25th: Complete Lyrics*, p. 21.
153. *Jethro Tull, 25th: Complete Lyrics*, p. 20.
154. *25th Anniversary* tour program, 1993, p. 15.

155. Ian Anderson, conversation with Scott Allen Nollen (12 September 1993).
156. Judson C. Caswell.
157. *25th Anniversary* tour program (1993), p. 14.
158. *Fish and Sheep and Rock 'n' Roll* television program (British Broadcasting Corporation), 1987.
159. *Soundi.*
160. *Soundi.*
161. *25th Anniversary* tour program, p. 34.
162. Judson C. Caswell.
163. David Rees, p. 80.
164. *Jethro Tull, 25th: Complete Lyrics*, p. 21.
165. *Soundi.*
166. *Soundi.*
167. David Rees, p. 81.
168. David Rees, p. 80.
169. *Rolling Stone* (21 September 1978).
170. *Soundi.*
171. *Soundi.*
172. *Cream* (June 1978).
173. *Cream* (June 1978).
174. *A New Day* (no. 19), p. 23.
175. *Rolling Stone* (28 December 1978).
176. *A New Day* (no. 19), p. 23.
177. *A New Day* (no. 31), p. 25.
178. *A New Day* (no. 31), p. 25.
179. *Rolling Stone* (30 November 1978).
180. David Rees, p. 85.
181. David Rees, pp. 85–86.
182. *Jethro Tull, 25th: Complete Lyrics*, p. 21.
183. *Stormwatch* tour program (1979), p. 10.
184. *25th Anniversary* tour program, p. 34.
185. *A New Day* (no. 19), pp. 23–24.
186. *Stormwatch* tour program, p. 11.
187. Dave Pegg, reminiscence for Scott Allen Nollen (24 November 1999).
188. Dave Pegg, reminiscence for Scott Allen Nollen (24 November 1999).
189. Dave Pegg, reminiscence for Scott Allen Nollen (24 November 1999).
190. Dave Pegg, reminiscence for Scott Allen Nollen (24 November 1999).
191. Dave Pegg, reminiscence for Scott Allen Nollen (24 November 1999).
192. Dave Pegg, reminiscence for Scott Allen Nollen (24 November 1999).
193. Dave Pegg, reminiscence for Scott Allen Nollen (24 November 1999).
194. *A New Day* (no. 19), p. 24.
195. *A New Day* (no. 19), p. 24.
196. David Rees, pp. 94–95.
197. *A New Day* (no. 19), p. 22.
198. Dave Pegg, conversation with Scott Allen Nollen (18 September 1990).
199. Glenn Cornick, telephone conversation with Scott Allen Nollen (10 August 2000).
200. *A New Day* (no. 31), p. 29.
201. *A New Day* (no. 19).
202. David Rees, pp. 90–91.
203. *A New Day* (no. 23), p. 21.

204. David Rees, pp. 96–97.
205. Glenn Cornick, telephone conversation with Scott Allen Nollen (10 August 2000).
206. *A New Day* (no. 20), p. 13.
207. *A New Day* (no. 20), p. 14.
208. *Jethro Tull, 25th: Complete Lyrics*, p. 22.
209. *Rockline* radio program, 1982.
210. Dave Pegg, reminiscence for Scott Allen Nollen (24 November 1999).
211. *A New Day* (no. 19), p. 26.
212. *A New Day* (no. 20), p. 15.
213. Dave Pegg, reminiscence for Scott Allen Nollen (24 November 1999).
214. *Rock Island* tour program (1989), p. 22.
215. Dave Pegg, reminiscence for Scott Allen Nollen (24 November 1999).
216. *25th Anniversary* tour program, p. 25.
217. Dave Pegg, reminiscence for Scott Allen Nollen (24 November 1999).
218. Dave Pegg, reminiscence for Scott Allen Nollen (24 November 1999).
219. *Rockline*, 1982.
220. *Jethro Tull, 25th: Complete Lyrics*, p. 22.
221. *Late Night with David Letterman* television program (April 1982).
222. *Late Night with David Letterman* (April 1982).
223. *Fish and Sheep and Rock 'n' Roll* television program (1987).
224. *Rockline* (1982).
225. *25th Anniversary* tour program, p. 25.
226. *Rolling Stone* (10 June 1982).
227. *Rockline* (1982).
228. Dave Pegg, reminiscence for Scott Allen Nollen (24 November 1999).
229. Doane Perry, reminiscence for Scott Allen Nollen (March 2000).
230. Dave Pegg, reminiscence for Scott Allen Nollen (24 November 1999).
231. David Rees, p. 104.
232. Dave Pegg, reminiscence for Scott Allen Nollen (24 November 1999).
233. *Home and Studio Recording* (March 1989), p. 43.
234. *Night Flight* television program (1982).
235. *25th Anniversary* tour program, p. 27.
236. *Walk into Light* CD booklet (1997).
237. *Kerrang* (no. 58/December 1983).
238. *Walk into Light* CD booklet (1997).
239. *Walk into Light* CD booklet (1997).
240. *A New Day* (no. 19), p. 25.
241. David Rees, pp. 108–09.
242. *Kerrang* (no. 58/December 1983).
243. *Home and Studio Recording* (March 1989), p. 43.
244. *25th Anniversary* tour program, p. 27.
245. David Rees, p. 110.
246. David Rees, p. 111.
247. David Rees, p. 111.
248. *Jethro Tull, 25th: Complete Lyrics*, p. 23.
249. *25th Anniversary* video program.
250. Doane Perry, reminiscence for Scott Allen Nollen (March 2000).
251. Doane Perry, reminiscence for Scott Allen Nollen (March 2000).
252. Doane Perry, reminiscence for Scott Allen Nollen (March 2000).
253. Rob Curtis, letter to Scott Allen Nollen (17 July 2000).

254. Doane Perry, reminiscence for Scott Allen Nollen (March 2000).
255. Doane Perry, reminiscence for Scott Allen Nollen (March 2000).
256. Doane Perry, reminiscence for Scott Allen Nollen (March 2000).
257. David Rees, p. 115.
258. Greg Russo, *Flying Colours: The Jethro Tull Reference Manual* (Floral Park, New York: Crossfire Publications, 2000), p. 137.
259. David Rees, p. 120.
260. *25th Anniversary* tour program, p. 28.
261. *A New Day* (no. 19), p. 26.
262. *25th Anniversary* tour program, p. 28.
263. David Rees, p. 122.
264. David Rees, p. 123.
265. Doane Perry, reminiscence for Scott Allen Nollen (March 2000).
266. *Jethro Tull, 25th: Complete Lyrics*, p. 24.
267. Doane Perry, reminiscence for Scott Allen Nollen (March 2000).
268. Dave Pegg, conversation with Scott Allen Nollen (18 September 1990).
269. David Rees, p. 124.
270. Doane Perry, reminiscence for Scott Allen Nollen (March 2000). Doane Perry, conversation with Scott Allen Nollen (8 August 2000).
271. *25th Anniversary* tour program, p. 29.
272. *A New Day* (no. 25), p. 25.
273. *A New Day* (no. 18), p. 25.
274. *A New Day* (no. 18), p. 27.
275. *A New Day* (no. 23), p. 14.
276. David Rees, p. 128.
277. *A New Day* (no. 24), p. 19.
278. *A New Day* (no. 17), p. 21.
279. Los Angeles *Herald Examiner* (28 February 1989).
280. *A New Day* (no. 18), p. 29.
281. Dave Pegg, conversation with Scott Allen Nollen (18 September 1990).
282. *A New Day* (no. 23), p. 14.
283. *A New Day* (no. 23), p. 26.
284. Dave Pegg, discussion with Scott Allen Nollen (24 November 1991).
285. *A New Day* (no. 18), p. 17.
286. *Home and Studio Recording*, p. 44.
287. *20 Years of Jethro Tull* video program.
288. *Stereo Review* (1989).
289. Dave Pegg, discussion with Scott Allen Nollen (18 September 1990).
290. Doane Perry, reminiscence for Scott Allen Nollen (March 2000).
291. Fort Lauderdale *Sun Sentinel*.
292. *A New Day* (no. 20), p. 7.
293. *A New Day* (no. 23), p. 11.
294. *A New Day* (no. 23), p. 12.
295. *Sunderland Echo* (30 September 1990).
296. *A New Day* (no. 23), p. 12.
297. *A New Day* (no. 24), pp. 11–12.
298. *A New Day* (no. 23).
299. *A New Day* (no. 25), pp. 26–27.
300. *A New Day* (no. 24), p. 4.
301. *25th Anniversary tour* program, p. 29.
302. Doane Perry, reminiscence for Scott Allen Nollen (March 2000).

303. *CNN Headline News* (16 December 1989).
304. David Rees, p. 133.
305. *A New Day* (no. 26), p. 22.
306. Dave Pegg, conversation with Scott Allen Nollen (24 November 1991).
307. *A New Day* (no. 25), p. 9.
308. *A New Day* (no. 25), p. 10.
309. Liverpool *Daily Post* (23 May 1990).
310. *A New Day* (no. 29), pp. 21–22.
311. Dave Pegg, conversation with Scott Allen Nollen (18 September 1990).
312. Dave Pegg, reminiscence for Scott Allen Nollen (24 November 1999).
313. *A New Day* (no. 28), p. 7.
314. David Rees, p. 136.
315. *Guitar for the Practicing Musician* (May 1991), p. 137.
316. *Aalborg Stiftstidende* (23 June 1991).
317. Aalborg *Jyllands-Posten* (24 June 1991).
318. Doane Perry, reminiscence for Scott Allen Nollen (March 2000).
319. Doane Perry, reminiscence for Scott Allen Nollen (March 2000).
320. Doane Perry, reminiscence for Scott Allen Nollen (March 2000).
321. *Jethro Tull, 25th: Complete Lyrics*, p. 25.
322. David Rees, p. 139.
323. *Crawdaddy* (18 July 1971).
324. *Rockline* radio program (26 August 1991).
325. *Rockline* (26 August 1991).
326. Doane Perry, reminiscence for Scott Allen Nollen (March 2000).
327. Doane Perry, reminiscence for Scott Allen Nollen (March 2000).
328. *A New Day* (no. 29), p. 11.
329. *A New Day* (no. 29), p. 13.
330. *Guitar for the Practicing Musician* (May 1991), p. 142.
331. Dave Pegg, discussion with Scott Allen Nollen (24 November 1991).
332. *A New Day* (no. 30), p. 20.
333. *A New Day* (no. 32), p. 27.
334. *Goldmine* (4 October 1991).
335. *Stereo Review* (December 1991).
336. *Rockline* (26 August 1991).
337. *Rockline* (26 August 1991).
338. *Rockline* (26 August 1991).
339. *25th Anniversary* CD box set booklet (1993), p. 7.
340. Doane Perry, reminiscence for Scott Allen Nollen (March 2000).
341. Portland *Press Herald* (9 September 1991).
342. Dave Pegg, discussion with Scott Allen Nollen (24 November 1991).
343. Dave Pegg, discussion with Scott Allen Nollen (24 November 1991).
344. Dave Pegg, discussion with Scott Allen Nollen (24 November 1991).
345. Dave Pegg, discussion with Scott Allen Nollen (24 November 1991).
346. *Catfish Rising* tour program (1991), p. 13.
347. David Rees, p. 140.
348. *A New Day* (no. 33), p. 7.
349. *A New Day* (no. 33), p. 7.
350. Jethro Tull official website (March 1999).
351. Chicago *Sun-Times* (8 October 1992).
352. *25th Anniversary* tour program, p. 33.
353. Dave Pegg, conversation with Scott Allen Nollen (18 September 1990).

354. *A New Day* (no. 34), p. 10.
355. Andy Giddings, conversation with Scott Allen Nollen (11 October 1992).
356. *Windplayer* (no. 55/December 1996), p. 20.
357. *A New Day* (no. 35), p. 28.
358. Edmonton *Journal* (28 October 1992).
359. Ipswich *Evening Star* (23 September 1992).
360. Chicago *Sun-Times* (8 October 1992).
361. *Guitar World*, ps. 49, 51.
362. Ottawa *Sunday Sun* (8 November 1992), p. 25.
363. Ottawa *Citizen* (7 November 1992).
364. Montreal *Gazette* (14 November 1992).
365. *A New Day* (no. 43), p. 22.
366. *Mid-day* (16 March 1993), p. 7.
367. *A New Day* (no. 40), p. 12.
368. Doane Perry, reminiscence for Scott Allen Nollen (March 2000).
369. Doane Perry, reminiscence for Scott Allen Nollen (March 2000).
370. Andy Giddings, conversation with Scott Allen Nollen (11 October 1992).
371. *Jethro Tull, 25th: Complete Lyrics*, p. 9.
372. Doane Perry, reminiscence for Scott Allen Nollen (March 2000).
373. Doane Perry, reminiscence for Scott Allen Nollen (March 2000).
374. *A New Day* (no. 40), p. 14.
375. *A New Day* (no. 40), p. 18.
376. *A New Day* (no. 44), p. 17.
377. *A New Day* (no. 44), p. 17.
378. *A New Day* (no. 41), p. 17.
379. *Hot Press* (17 November 1993).
380. David Rees, p. 147.
381. *Nightcap* CD booklet (1993).
382. W.S. Gumby website (17 July 1999).
383. *A New Day* (no. 41), p. 19.
384. Doane Perry, reminiscence for Scott Allen Nollen (March 2000).
385. Doane Perry, reminiscence for Scott Allen Nollen (March 2000).
386. Doane Perry, reminiscence for Scott Allen Nollen (March 2000).
387. *A New Day* (no. 43), p. 26.
388. *A New Day* (no. 44), pp. 22–23.
389. *A New Day* (no. 44), p. 27.
390. *Home Recording* (December 1999), p. 31.
391. *Windplayer*, p. 15.
392. David Rees, p. 153.
393. David Rees, p. 153.
394. David Rees, p. 154.
395. *Q* (June 1995), p. 115.
396. *Jazziz* (September 1995), p. 35.
397. Dave Pegg, reminiscence for Scott Allen Nollen (24 November 1999).
398. *Roots to Branches* tour program (1996), p. 4.
399. *Roots to Branches*, p. 15.
400. *Roots to Branches*, p. 10.
401. *Roots to Branches*, p. 22.
402. Doane Perry, reminiscence for Scott Allen Nollen (March 2000).
403. *Roots to Branches*, p. 9.
404. *Roots to Branches*, p. 19.

405. *Roots to Branches*, p. 13.
406. Glenn Cornick, telephone conversation with Scott Allen Nollen (10 August 2000).
407. Doane Perry, reminiscence for Scott Allen Nollen (March 2000).
408. *Windplayer*, p. 23.
409. *Windplayer*, p. 18.
410. Los Angeles *Times* (19 September 1996).
411. Los Angeles *Times*.
412. *Soundi*.
413. WRPU website.
414. CNN website (8 May 1998).
415. CNN website (8 May 1998).
416. Kansas City *Star* (18 July 1998).
417. *Rockline* (26 August 1991).
418. Jethro Tull official website (August 1999).
419. Jethro Tull official website (June 1999).
420. Jethro Tull official website (June 1999).
421. Amy Rosenblatt, on-line conversation with Scott Allen Nollen (6 September 1999).
422. Glenn Cornick, telephone conversation with Scott Allen Nollen (10 August 2000).
423. Jethro Tull official website (April 1999).
424. *Home Recording*, p. 32.
425. Jethro Tull official website (February 2000).
426. Jethro Tull official website (February 2000).
427. Jethro Tull official website (March 2000).
428. Jethro Tull official website (March 2000).
429. *The Secret Language of Birds* CD booklet (2000).
430. Jethro Tull official website (March 2000).
431. Jethro Tull official website (March 2000).
432. *The Secret Language of Birds* CD booklet (2000).
433. Jethro Tull official website (March 2000).
434. *The Secret Language of Birds* CD booklet (2000).
435. Doane Perry, telephone conversation with Scott Allen Nollen (7 March 2000).
436. *Dirty Linen* (2000).
437. Scott Huntley, letter to Scott Allen Nollen (July 2000).
438. Rob Curtis, letter to Scott Allen Nollen (17 July 2000).
439. Doane Perry, telephone conversation with Scott Allen Nollen (7 March 2000).
440. Aykut Oral, letter to Scott Allen Nollen (14 May 2000).
441. Jethro Tull official website (June 2000).
442. Mark Louis, letter to Scott Allen Nollen (21 July 2000); "Collecting Tull" website (June 2000).
443. Glenn Cornick, telephone conversation with Scott Allen Nollen (10 August 2000).
444. Jethro Tull official website (August 2000).
445. Ian Anderson, *The Very Best of Jethro Tull* CD booklet (Capitol Records, 2001).
446. Ian Anderson, conversation with Scott Allen Nollen (21 July 2001).
447. Raymond Benson, conversation with Scott Allen Nollen (21 July 2001).
448. Jethro Tull official website (28 August 2001).

Conclusion

1. *Jethro Tull, 25th: Complete Lyrics*, p. 9.
2. *Jethro Tull, 25th: Complete Lyrics*, p. 16.
3. *Home and Studio Recording*, p. 45.
4. Fort Lauderdale *Sun Sentinel*.
5. *Guitar for the Practicing Musician* (May 1991), p. 144.
6. *Guitar World* (July 1993), p. 64.
7. *Windplayer* (no. 55/September 1996), p. 21.
8. Doane Perry, reminiscence for Scott Allen Nollen (March 2000).
9. Doane Perry, reminiscence for Scott Allen Nollen (March 2000).
10. *Stormwatch* tour program (1979), p. 11.
11. *Rolling Stone* (28 October 1993).
12. Jethro Tull official website (1999).
13. Glenn Cornick, telephone conversation with Scott Allen Nollen (10 August 2000)

BIBLIOGRAPHY

Primary Sources

Conversations with and Reminiscences of Band Members and Crew Members

Allcock, Martin. Conversation with Scott Allen Nollen, Chicago, Illinois, 24 November 1991.

Anderson, Ian. Conversation with Scott Allen Nollen, Chicago, Illinois, 24 November 1991.

____. Conversation with Scott Allen Nollen, Chicago, Illinois, 12 September 1993.

____. Conversation with Scott Allen Nollen, Chicago, Illinois, 11 September 1999.

____. Conversation with Scott Allen Nollen, Highland Park, Illinois, 8 August 2000.

____. Conversation with Scott Allen Nollen, Chicago, Illinois, 21 July 2001.

Anderson, Shona. Conversation with Scott Allen Nollen, Chicago, Illinois, 11 September 1999.

Barre, Martin. Conversation with Scott Allen Nollen, Chicago, Illinois, 24 November 1991.

____. Conversation with Scott Allen Nollen, Chicago, Illinois, 11 October 1992.

____. Conversation with Scott Allen Nollen, Chicago, Illinois, 12 September 1993.

Cornick, Glenn. Telephone conversation with Scott Allen Nollen, 10 August 2000.

____. Telephone conversation with Scott Allen Nollen, 12 August 2000.

____. Telephone conversation with Scott Allen Nollen and Donald Craig Nance, 19 August 2000.

Giddings, Andy. Conversation with Scott Allen Nollen, Chicago, Illinois, 11 October 1992.

____. Conversation with Scott Allen Nollen, Chicago, Illinois, September 1993.

____. Conversation with Scott Allen Nollen, Highland Park, Illinois, 8 August 2000.

Mathieson, Midge. Conversation with Scott Allen Nollen, Chicago, Illinois, 24 November 1991.

Mattacks, David. Conversation with Scott Allen Nollen, Chicago, Illinois, 10–11 October 1992.

Pegg, David. Conversation with Scott Allen Nollen, Barford St. Michael, Oxford-shire, England, 18 September 1990.
____. Conversation with Scott Allen Nollen, Chicago, Illinois, 24 November 1991.
____. Conversation with Scott Allen Nollen, Chicago, Illinois, 10–11 October 1992.
____. Conversation with Scott Allen Nollen, Chicago, Illinois, 12 September 1993.
____. Conversation with Scott Allen Nollen, Chicago, Illinois, 26 March 1998.
____. Conversation with Scott Allen Nollen, Chicago, Illinois, 3 November 1999.
____. Reminiscence for Scott Allen Nollen, St. Petersburg, Florida, 25 November 1999.
Perry, Doane. Conversation with Scott Allen Nollen, Chicago, Illinois, 24 November 1991.
____. Conversation with Scott Allen Nollen, Chicago, Illinois, 12 September 1993.
____. Conversation with Scott Allen Nollen, Chicago, Illinois, 11 September 1999.
____. Telephone conversation with Scott Allen Nollen, 7 March 2000.
____. Reminiscence for Scott Allen Nollen, Woodland Hills, California, March 2000.
____. Telephone conversation with Scott Allen Nollen, 20 April 2000.
____. Telephone conversation with Scott Allen Nollen, 22 April 2000.
____. Conversation with Scott Allen Nollen, Highland Park, Illinois, 8 August 2000.
Wylie, Kenny. Telephone conversation with Scott Allen Nollen, February 1990.
____. Conversation with Scott Allen Nollen, Chicago, Illinois, 11 September 1999.
____. Conversation with Scott Allen Nollen, Chicago, Illinois, 21 July 2001.

Letters from Band Members

Anderson, Ian. Letter to Scott Allen Nollen, 25 April 1990.
____. Letter to Scott Allen Nollen, 19 June 1990.
____. Letter to Scott Allen Nollen, 8 April 1991.
____. Letter to Scott Allen Nollen, 27 September 1993.
____. Letter to Scott Allen Nollen, 16 September 1997.
____. Letter to Scott Allen Nollen, 6 January 1999.
____. Letter to Scott Allen Nollen, 18 March 1999.
Pegg, David. Letter to Scott Allen Nollen, 24 July 1990.
____. Letter to Scott Allen Nollen, August 1990.
____. Letter to Scott Allen Nollen, 30 July 1992.
____. Letter to Scott Allen Nollen, 17 September 1992.
____. Letter to Scott Allen Nollen, 16 November 1992.
____. Letter to Scott Allen Nollen, 22 March 1993.
____. Letter to Scott Allen Nollen, 17 May 1993.
____. Letter to Scott Allen Nollen, 24 July 1996.
____. Letter to Scott Allen Nollen, 14 August 1996.
____. Letter to Scott Allen Nollen, May 2000.
Perry, Doane. Letter to Scott Allen Nollen, 4 March 2000.
____. Letter to Scott Allen Nollen, 30 May 2000.

Corrections and Additions to the Manuscript

Anderson, Ian. July–August 2000.
Cornick, Glenn. August 2000.
Perry, Doane. March–May 2000.

Interview Segments

CNN Headline News. News report, 16 December 1989.
Fish and Sheep and Rock 'n' Roll. Television program, 1987.
Jethro Tull: The 25th Anniversary Video. Video program, 1993.
Late Night with David Letterman. Television program, April 1982.
Mike Douglas Show. Television program, 1982.
Night Flight. Television program, 1982.
Rockline. Satellite radio program, 1982.
Rockline. Satellite radio program, 26 August 1991.
Thick as a Brick. Digitally Remastered Special Edition. Chrysalis Records, 1997.
20 Years of Jethro Tull. Video program, 1988.
WRDU Radio. Website, 1998.

Books

Schramm, Karl, and Gerard J. Burns, eds. *Jethro Tull, 25th: Complete Lyrics.* Heidelberg, Germany: Palmyra Publishers, 1993.

Tour Booklets, CD Booklets, and LP Liner Notes

Catfish Rising. Tour program, 1991.
Jethro Tull: 25th Anniversary. Box set booklet. Chrysalis Records, 1993.
Jethro Tull: 25th Anniversary. Tour program, 1993.
A Little Light Music. Tour program, 1992.
Rock Island. Tour program, 1989.
Roots to Branches. Tour program, 1996.
Stormwatch. Tour program, 1979.
This Was. Liner Notes, 1968.
20 Years of Jethro Tull. Box set booklet. Chrysalis Records, 1988.

Newspapers, Periodicals, and Websites

Aalborg Stiftstidende (Denmark), 23 June 1991.
Audience, May–June 1972.
Chicago Sun-Times, 8 October 1992
Circus, no. 124, 9 December 1975.
Citizen (Ottawa, Ontario), 7 September 1992.
CNN website, 8 May 1998.
Crawdaddy, 8 June 1970; 18 July 1971.
Cup of Wonder website.
Daily Post (Liverpool, England), 23 May 1990.
Dallas Morning News, 21 August 1993.
Downbeat, 11 March 1976.
Edmonton Journal, 28 October 1992.
Evening Star (Ipswich, England), 23 September 1992.
Gazette (Montreal, Quebec), 14 November 1992.
Goldmine, 10 April 1991.
Guitar for the Practicing Musician, May 1991.
Guitar World, July 1993.

Herald Examiner (Los Angeles), 28 February 1989.
Hit Parader, March 1976.
Home and Studio Recording, March 1989.
Home Recording, December 1999.
Hot Press (Dublin, Ireland), 17 November 1993.
Jazziz, September 1995.
Jyllands-Posten (Aalborg, Denmark), 24 June 1991.
Kansas City Star, 18 July 1998.
Mid-day, 16 March 1993.
A New Day, 17, 18, 19, 20, 23, 24, 25, 26, 28, 29, 30, 31, 32, 33, 34, 35, 37, 38, 40, 41,
    43, 44.
The Official Jethro Tull Website (j-tull.com). December 1998–August 2001.
Press Herald (Portland, Oregon), 9 September 1991.
Q, June 1995.
Rolling Stone, 22 July 1971; 22 June 1972; 30 August 1973; 21 September 1978; 30
    November 1978; 28 December 1978; 10 June 1982, 28 October 1993.
St. Cleve Chronicle, vol. 4/issue 92, 7 December 1993.
Soundi, 1978.
Stereo Review, December 1991.
Sun Sentinel (Fort Lauderdale, Florida), 29 October 1989.
Sunday Sun (Ottawa, Ontario), 8 September 1992.
Sunderland Echo, 30 September 1989.
Today's Runner, May 1990.
Windplayer, no. 55/September 1996.
W.S. Gumby's Website.

Recollections of Fans

Benson, Raymond. Conversation with Scott Allen Nollen, 21 July 2001.
Curtis, Rob. Letter to Scott Allen Nollen, 17 July 2000.
Huntley, Scott. Letter to Scott Allen Nollen, 15 July 2000.
Louis, Mark. Letter to Scott Allen Nollen, 21 July 2000.
Oral, Aykut. Letter to Scott Allen Nollen, 14 May 2000.
Rosenblatt, Amy. Conversation with Scott Allen Nollen, 6 September 2000.

Secondary Sources

Books

Espinoza, Barbara. *Driving in Diverse: A Collective Profile of Jethro Tull*. Kearney,
    Nebraska: Morris Publishing, 1999.
Fussell, G. E. *Jethro Tull: His Influence on Mechanized Agriculture*.
Rees, David. *Minstrels in the Gallery: A History of Jethro Tull*. Wembley, Middlesex:
    SAF Publishing, 1998.
Russo, Greg. *Flying Colours: The Jethro Tull Reference Manual*. Floral Park, New York:
    Crossfire Publications, 2000.

INDEX

*Numbers in **bold** indicate photographs*

A (album) 156–160, 167, 177, 179, 251
Aalborg Festival (Denmark) 221
Aalborg Stiftstidende 221
Abrahams, Mick 28, 29, 30, 32, 33, **35**,
   36, 37, 38, 45, 60, 73, 75, 77, 195, 198,
   218, 238, 245, 247, 250, 254, 258, 265,
   269, 270, 315, 319, 320, 321
AC/DC 202
"Acres Wild" (song) 18, 129, 132–133, 320
"Aeroplane" (song) 29, 195, 198
Aerosmith 307
Air Studios 223
Airey, Don 192–193, 197, 247, 315
Akhtar, Najma 289, 290
Aldrin, Buzz 55
Alexander, Cecil Frances 77
"Alive and Well and Living In" (song)
   53, 76, 78
Allcock, Martin (a.k.a. "Maart") 4, 6, 15,
   181, 189, 195, 196–197, 199, **200**, 209,
   211, 215, 218, 225, 232, 234, 245, 247,
   254, 271, 272, 276, 315, 319, 320; on
   joining Jethro Tull 197; on leaving
   Jethro Tull 234; on playing Jethro Tull
   music 212
Allen, Angela 113, 115
Allen, David 153
Amphitheater (Virginia Beach) 305
Amson, Christopher 139
"And Further On" (song) 157, 158, 160,
   303
"…And the Mouse Police Never Sleeps"
   (song) 18, 129, 131, 132, 134, 300

Anderson, Graeme 210
Anderson, Ian 1, 4, 6, 8, 9, 11, 12–13, 15,
   26, 33, 35, **39**, **46**, **51**, 52, 54, 55, 57,
   59, 76, 78, 84, **90**, 91, 97, 105, **120**, 139,
   141, 145, 150, 151, 153, 154, 161, 162,
   164, 165, 171, 179, 184, 195, 197, 198,
   203, 210, 216, 218, 219, 223, 234, **236**,
   240, **241**, 247, **248**, 250, 251, **255**, **256**,
   271, 283, 284, **293**, 294, **296**, 315, 317,
   318, 319, 320, 321; and blues music 24,
   25, 34–35, 36, 49, 58, 85, 106, 112, 117,
   125, 148, 180, 208, 224–225, 226, 227,
   238, 242, 269, 292, 297; and classical
   music 48, 53, 85, 89, 94, 95, 112, 118,
   125, 142, 147, 148, 158, 180, 186, 198,
   207, 221, 224, 227, 240, 252, 274–276,
   281; and country music 228–229, 264;
   and English/Scottish/Celtic folk music
   17–18, 20, 55, 58, 65, 77, 80, 85, 89, 95,
   98–99, 101, 102, 106, 111–112, 121–127,
   130, 132–133, 134, 136, 147–148, 158,
   160, 167, 170, 178, 180, 181–182, 186,
   192, 198, 199, 206–207, 208, 209, 215,
   221, 224, 226, 230, 242, 262, 263, 264,
   272, 275, 284, 292, 297, 298, 300, 301–
   302, 305; and Indian/Middle Eastern
   music 36, 47, 49, 101, 121, 180, 227, 272,
   275, 276, 278, 279, 280–281, 289, 290,
   291, 297, 298, 302; and jazz music 43,
   47, 85, 89, 94, 95, 106, 160, 180, 186,
   220, 226, 240, 242, 251, 252, 253, 278,
   281, 292, 297; and medieval/Renais-
   sance music 49, 56, 68, 69, 78, 85, 86,

108, 111–112, 121, 122, 125, 129, 167, 198, 199, 221, 241, 242, 253, 292; and 1980 "solo" album 157–158; and politics 159, 301, 302; and problems with voice 178, 179, 182, 183, 184, 187, 233, 242, 243, 258, 268, 272, 277–278; and religion 23, 59, 63, 69–72, 100, 101–102, 103, 274, 278; and Russian music 99, 101, 178, 297, 301; and salmon farming 128, 137, 143, 162, 172, 183, 186, 264, 284, 287–288; and spicy food/hot peppers 12, 13, 265, 284, 300; and the flute 30–31, 60, 160, 232, 242–243, 249, 273–274, 310; as guest VJ on MTV 190; as songwriter/composer 3, 17–20, 48–49, 54, 56, 63, 66–72, 79, 85–88, 98–104, 107–110, 113–118, 119–127, 130–138, 144, 147–148, 158, 165–167, 170, 172, 173–175, 187, 188–192, 255, 275–276, 280, 295–303, 308–309; attitude toward drugs 56; birth 21, 22; childhood 23; education 23, 25, 28; knee injuries 284–285, 307; marriages 61; musical development 23–25; musical tastes 130; nickname of "Elvo" 27, 93; on *A* 158; on aging and rock music 244, 248, 286–287, 308, 311–312; on *Aqualung* 63–64, 68; on *Benefit* 56, 58; on Boris Yeltsin 301; on *The Broadsword and the Beast* 165, 167–168, 169, 170; on *Catfish Rising* 224, 226, 228–229; on cats 131, 132, 290–291, 299–300; on *A Classic Case: The London Symphony Orchestra Plays the Music of Jethro Tull* 185; on commercial endorsements 231, 288; on contemporary pop/rock music 312; on *Crest of a Knave* 187–188, 191; on *Divinities* 274; on Fela Kuti 175; on Fleetwood Mac 217; on *Heavy Horses* 130, 131; on his stage persona 32, 74–75; on J. B. Lenoir 112; on *J-Tull Dot Com* 290–291; on Jethro Tull stage shows 231; on Led Zeppelin 107; on *A Little Light Music* 237, 238; on *Minstrel in the Gallery* 106, 107, 110; on move to Oxfordshire estate 270; on *Nightcap* 261; on 1989 Grammy Award 202; on noisy audiences 213, 244, 306; on other members of Jethro Tull 38, 58, 107, 121, 146, 149, 155–156, 238, 239, 258–259, 272; on *A Passion Play* 92; on punk rock music 137–138; on recording 172, 204–205; on *Rock Island* 204; on rock 'n' roll bands 35–36; on rock radio 211; on *Roots to Branches* 278, 279–280; on *The Secret Language of Birds* 296–297, 298, 299–300, 301, 302; on *Songs from the Wood* 120–121, 131, 169; on *Stand Up* 44, 46; on *Stormwatch* 146, 169; on success 138; on Terry Ellis 34; on the early days of Jethro Tull 31–32; on the "Mark Knopfler" guitar sound 189; on the name "Jethro Tull" 29; on the nature of music 19, 23–24, 28, 115; on *Thick as a Brick* 82–83, 92; on *This Was* 34; on *Too Old to Rock 'n' Roll: Too Young to Die!* 114; on touring 62, 73–74, 89, 96, 111, 128, 215, 233, 238, 304, 311; on *Under Wraps* 176–177; on unreleased Jethro Tull material 264; on *The Very Best of Jethro Tull* 306; on *Walk into Light* 173–174; on *War Child* 98, 100, 102; on *The Water's Edge* 144; Scottish heritage 23, 106, 137, 147–148, 168–169, 191, 192, 206–207, 264, 284, 287–288

Anderson, Ian A. 149–150
Anderson, James 136, 159, 295, 300
Anderson, Jennie 55, 58, 61, 62, 64, 108
Anderson, Jon 144
Anderson, Robin 23, 144
Anderson, Shona 12, 15, 105, 129, 136, 167, 270, 307
Angel-EMI Records 273, 274
"Animelee" (instrumental) 260, 261
The Annotated Sherlock Holmes (book) 284
"Another Christmas Song" (song) 204, 207, 211, 215
"Another Harry's Bar" (song) 277, 282
Anton, Morris 203
"Apogee" (song) 176, 178
Apollo (Hammersmith) 258
Apollo (Manchester) 211, 232
Aqualung (album) 3, 17, 19, 55, 58, 60, 62–72, 77, 79, 81, 82, 85, 89, 100, 103, 107, 134, 135, 138, 142, 180, 198, 213, 241, 242, 252, 274, 278, 282
"Aqualung" (song) 13, 62, 64, 66–67, 72, 83, 89, 142, 147, 161, 165, 182, 184, 185, 186, 190, 194, 196, 199, 201, 213, 215, 217, 229, 230, 247, 253, 276, 285, 286, 290, 297, 317, 318, 319, 320, 321
Arena (TV show) 145–146
Armatrading, Joan 171
Armstrong, Louis 243
Armstrong, Neil 55
Ashton, Sir Frederick 98

Asia (band) 157
"Astronomy" (song) 176, 178
"At Last, Forever" (song) 277, 281
"At Their Father's Knee" (instrumental)
    273, 275
The Atlantics 24, 26"
"Audition" (song) 196, 260, 262
Auditorium Theatre (Chicago) 12–13, 294
"Auld Lang Syne" (Robert Burns song)
    100
"Automotive Engineering" (song) 176, 178
"AWOL" (song) 289, 290, 305

Babbacombe Lee (Fairport Convention
    album) 9
Bach, Johann Sebastian 44, 47, 76, 96,
    140, 184, 185, 195, 229, 237, 240, 242,
    246
"Back to the Family" (song) 44, 48, 247,
    253
"Back-Door Angels" (song) 97, 100, 104,
    127
"Bad-Eyed and Loveless" (song) 113, 117
Bailey, Steve 277, 321
Baker, Ginger 32
"Baker Street Muse" (song) 106, 109
Banks, Tony 175
Barlow, Barrie (a.k.a. "Barriemore") 4,
    25, **26**, 28–29, 76, 80, 82, 86, **90**, 91, 97,
    101, 105, 108, 113, 114, 116, 119, 125, **126**,
    129, 133, 134, 135, 141, 143, 144, 145,
    146, 147, 148–149, 150, 152–153, 166,
    195, 199, 245, 247, 249, 250, 251, 253,
    258, 260, 262, 269, 315, 317, 318, 319,
    320, 321; drumming with Jethro
    Tull 154; on other members of Jethro
    Tull 30, 74, 107, 139, 153, 154, 155, 188–
    189; on the *A* tour 161; on touring 73;
    on *Walk into Light* 174; on *War Child*
    102–103
Barre, Julie 6, 118, 119, 230
Barre, Martin 4, 6–9, 12, 13, 15, 40–42,
    44–45, 46, 47, 48, 49, **51**, 52, 53, **54**,
    55, 56, 58, 60–61, 62, 69, 71, 72, 73, 76,
    77, 78, 79, 80, 81, 82, 85, 86, **90**, 91, 92,
    95, 96, 97, 98, 100, 101, 102, 103, 105,
    108, 110, 113, 114, 115, 116, 118, 119, **120**,
    121, **122**, 125–126, 127, 128, 129, 133,
    134–135, 136, 139, 140, 141, 142, 144,
    145, 146, 147, 148, 150, 151, 156, 158,
    159, 160, 161, **164**, 165, 166, 167, 171,
    176, 178, 184, 185, 186, 187, 190, 192,
    195, 197, 198, 199, 201, 203, 204, 205,
    206, 207, 208, 209, 210, 211, 212, 213,

216, 219, 220–221, 223, 226, 227, 230,
    232, 234, **236**, 237, 238, 239, 240, 241,
    242, 245, 247, **248**, 250, 251, 253, **255**,
    256, 258, 259, 261–262, 263, 264, 265,
    269, 271, 272, 276, 278, 282, 283, 284,
    289, 290, 291, 292, **293**, 294, 295, 297,
    298, 301, 306, 315, 317, 318, 319, 320,
    321; and blues music 229; and classical
    music 229, 252; and jazz music 229;
    attitude toward drugs 56–57; on *Aqua-
    lung* 66–67; on his guitar style 229; on
    Michelob endorsement 231; on 1989
    Grammy Award 202; on playing Jethro
    Tull music 286; on *Roots to Branches*
    279, 280; on *Stand Up* 45; on *The
    Broadsword and the Beast* 162; on the
    "Mark Knopfler" guitar sound 189; on
    Thick as a Brick 83–84; on touring 89,
    285, 309; on *Under Wraps* 177; solo
    recordings 268, 270, 286, 287, 291
Basie, William ("Count") 243
"Batteries Not Included" (song) 157, 159,
    160
"The Beacons Bottom Tapes" 246, 251–
    253
"Beastie" (song) 20, 162, 165, 169, 170,
    278, 320
The Beatles 24, 38, 40, 49, 60, 64, 152, 312
Beattie, Rob 209–210
Beethoven, Ludwig van 60, 66, 70, 85,
    100, 107, 112, 118, 127, 130, 147, 167, 208,
    213, 224
"Beggar's Farm" (song) 33, 36, 37, 242,
    247, 254, 265, 320
"The Beggar's Song" (Fairport Conven-
    tion song) 10
Behind the Music (TV show) 1, 307
"Beltane" (song) 137, 196, 198
Belville, John 313
"Bends Like a Willow" (song) 289, 291,
    292
Benefit (album) 52–59, 64, 65, 68, 71, 78,
    84, 85, 180, 226, 231, 242, 251, 254, 305
Benson, Raymond 307
"Beside Myself" (song) 277, 280–281, 305
*The Best of Jethro Tull: The Anniversary
    Collection* (album) 319–320
"A Better Moon" (song) 295, 299, 302
"Big Dipper" (song) 113, 117
"Big Riff and Mando" (song) 204, 208–
    209
Black, Robin 52, 76, 97, 105, 113, 119,
    129, 139, 145, 157, 162, 187, 250, 251,
    317, 318

"Black and White Television" (song) 173, 175

Black Barn Studio 187

"Black Mamba" (song) 289, 291

Black Sabbath 38, 193

"Black Satin Dancer" (song) 105, 108, 170, 196, 199, 203, 213, 319

"Black Sunday" (song) 157, 158, 159, 165, 180, 184, 220, 229, 230, 246, 251

Blackmore, Ritchie 193

The Blades 25

Blennin, John 210

Blodwyn Pig 73, 218, 265, 269

The Blood of the British (TV series) 186, 198

Blood, Sweat and Tears 42, 270

Bloom, Michael 136, 140

"Blues Instrumental" (instrumental) 196, 199

"Blues Jam"(instrumental) 271, 272

Bolin, Tommy 157

Bonham, John 149, 248

Bord-du-Quai, Roland 295, 299

"Boris Dancing" (instrumental) 295–296, 301, 305

Boston Pops Orchestra 185

Boston Tea Party/Gardens 42, 96, 105, 285

"Bourée" (instrumental) 13, 44, 47–48, 53, 76, 78, 140, 142, 184, 185, 186, 195, 197, 213, 215, 229, 230, 237, 240, 241, 242, 246, 251, 265, 272, 282, 294, 318, 320, 321

Bowie, David 98, 171

Bozzio, Terry 157

Bradley, Bill 75

Britten, Benjamin 98

British Broadcasting Corporation (BBC) 127, 145–146, 181, 186, 197–198, 215, 219, 269, 271, 272

"Broadford Bazaar" (song) 137, 260, 264

"Broadsword" (song) 20, 162, 166, 169, 170, 171, 228, 246, 251, 263, 284, 320, 321

The Broadsword and the Beast (album) 19, 20, 162–172, 178, 192, 198, 199, 206, 207, 252, 253, 254, 263, 264, 278, 292

Brooker, Gary 171, 256, 270

Bruce, Ian 300

Bruce, Jack 175

Bruford, Bill 157

"Budapest" (song) 187, 188, 190, 191–192, 194, 203, 207, 212, 213, 215, 227, 228, 247, 254, 270, 320

Bundrick, John ("Rabbit") 223, 225, 260, 263

"Bungle in the Jungle" (song) 97, 101–102, 114, 161, 185, 186, 196, 199, 246, 250, 317, 318, 320, 321

Bunker, Clive 28–29, 30, 33, 35, 36, 38, 39, 42, 44, **46**, **51**, 52, **54**, 55, 56, 60, 61, 62, 66, 67, 72–73, 76, 77, 78, 79, 81, 179, 180, 195, 218, 245, 247, 249, 250, 251, 253, 258, 265, 269, 305, 315, 317, 318, 319, 320, 321; on other members of Jethro Tull 39

Bunting, Heather 16

Burdon, Eric 270

Burgess, Paul 171, 184, 185, 247, 315

Burkhardt, Gerd 6, 9, 234

Burns, Declan 289

Burns, John 62, 76, 317, 318

Burns, Robert 18, 66, 100, 122, 123, 132, 134, 141, 239

Bush, George (President of the United States) 213

Bush, Kate 171

Butler, Tony (a.k.a. "Geezer") 39

"By Kind Permission Of" (instrumental suite) 60, 76, 79, 85, 251

The Byrds 270

Cable News Network (CNN) 214, 287, 301

Caird Hall (Dundee) 215

Caldwell, Doug 244

Capercaillie 302

Capitol Theater (Aberdeen) 214

Captain Beefheart 74, 89, 230

Caraeff, Ed 76

Carlton, Larry 229

Carmen (band) 114, 153

Carnegie, Andrew 21, 22, 60

Carnegie Hall 60, 76, 77, 79, 84, 251

Carrey, Jonathon 273

Carroll, Lewis 95

Carthy, Martin 191

Casino Ballroom (Hampton Beach) 294

Caswell, Judson C. 56, 103–104, 123, 130

Catfish Rising (album) 6, 223–234, 251, 254, 262, 263, 264, 271, 272, 281

"Cat's Squirrel" (instrumental) 33, 37

CBS Studios 184

Central Intelligence Agency (CIA) 214

Centrum (Worcester) 194

Charles (Prince of Wales) 171, 288, 299

Charles I, King of England 21

Charles, Ray 28, 43

The Chase (band) 225

Chateau d'Herouville 92–93, 95, 97, 101, 102, 260, 261

"Chateau D'Isaster Tapes" (aborted album project) 92, 95, 100, 101, 196, 198, 260, 261–262

"Cheap Day Return" (song) 62, 67, 68, 180, 196, 199, 211, 213, 270

Checkerdome (St. Louis) 160

"Cheerio" (song) 162, 167, 215, 246, 251, 252, 284, 321

"The Chequered Flag (Dead or Alive)" (song) 113, 114, 117–118

Chicago Theatre 6, 306–307

The Chieftains 305

Chopin, Fredric 112

"A Christmas Song" (song) 45, 47, 76, 77, 125, 167, 207, 211, 215, 229, 237, 239, 320

Chrysalis Music 16, 20, 55, 61, 84, 153, 157, 158, 177, 188, 197, 229, 230, 234, 261

Cianci, Bubby 232

"Circular Breathing" (song) 295, 301

Citizen (Ottawa) 244

Civic Auditorium (Omaha) 151

Civic Centre (Orlando) 213

Clapton, Eric 31, 32, 37, 40, 78, 198, 244

The Clash 137, 244, 309

"Clasp" (song) 162, 165, 169, 171, 181, 196, 199

A Classic Case: The London Symphony Orchestra Plays the Music of Jethro Tull (album) 184–186, 219, 276

Cleese, John 98

"Clint Eastwood" (a.k.a. "Andy Gidding's Parrot") (instrumental) 265

Coates, Eric 45, 140, 142

Cobo Hall (Detroit) 104

Cockburn, Bob 169, 230

Cocker, Joe 50

The Cocktail Cowboy Goes It Alone (Dave Pegg album) 167

"Cold Wind to Valhalla" (song) 105, 108, 116, 195, 198, 213, 246, 250

Cole, Nat "King" 301

Collins, Michael (American astronaut) 55

Collins, Michael (Irish revolutionary) 55

Collins, Phil 171

Colston Hall (Bristol) 127

"Commons Brawl" (song) 260, 263

Conan Doyle, Sir Arthur 3

Concert Hall (Stockholm) 253

"Concerto for Two Violins in D Minor" (J. S. Bach) 184

Congress Centrum Halle (Hamburg) 170

"Conquistador" (Procul Harum song) 270

Constable, John 301

Continental Arena (New Jersey Meadowlands) 182

"Conundrum" (instrumental) 140, 142

Conway, Gerry 162, 163, **164**, 165, 166, 167, 171, 186, 187, 190, 195, 245, 247, 249, 258, 260, 263, 295, 298, 315, 319, 320, 321

Cooke, Brian 139

Cooper, Alice 89, 202

Cooper, Michael 289

Copland, Aaron 276

Cordier, Veronique 16

Cornick, Glenn 13, 15, 26–27, **26**, 33, 35, 39, 44, **46**, **51**, 52, **54**, 55, 62, 63, 67, 76, 77, 78, 89, 195, 198, 245, 247, 250, 253, 269, 315, 317, 318, 319, 320, 321; attitude toward drugs 57; on *Aqualung* 61; on *Benefit* 53–54, 55, 57, 58; on folk-rock music 50, 312; on his musical development 27; on his stage persona 51–52; on *J-Tull Dot Com* 294; on Jimi Hendrix 41; on leaving Jethro Tull 61; on "Living in the Past" 42; on other members of Jethro Tull 28–29, 36, 37, 38, 41–42, 45, 46, 54, 57, 58–59, 61, 65, 84, 155, 282, 305; on rock 'n' roll festivals 42–43, 60; on *Stand Up* 45, 46, 47–48, 49; on the early days of Jethro Tull 38; on the name "Jethro Toe" 29–30; on *The Rolling Stones Rock 'n' Roll Circus* 40; on *Thick as a Brick* 61; on *This Was* 34, 37; on touring 50, 51

"Coronach" (song) 186, 195, 198, 319

Cotier, James 129

Courage Shire Horse Centre 129

Craney, Mark 157–158, 159, 160, 245, 247, 249, 270, 315, 320; on favorite Jethro Tull songs 161; on other members of Jethro Tull 158, 161

"Crazed Institution" (song) 113, 115–116

Cream 37, 60

Crest of a Knave (album) 19, 186–193, 202, 206, 215, 254, 263, 281

"Crew Nights" (song) 260, 263

"Critique Oblique" (song) 260, 262

Cropper, Steve 229

Cropredy Festival 189, 192, 203, 277, 286, 307

Crosby, Bing 286
"Cross-Eyed Mary" (song) 3, 13, 62, 64, 67, 127, 140, 142, 246, 250, 271, 272, 318, 320
"Crossfire" (song) 157, 159, 160
"Crossword" (song) 148, 196, 198, 319
"Cup of Wonder" (song) 119, 124–125, 127
"The Curse" (song) 260, 263
Curtis, Rob 16, 182
Curved Air 157
Cutts, Neil 6, 172

Dade, Dave 219
Daily Post (Liverpool) 216
Dallas Morning News 257
Daltrey, Roger 103
"The Dambuster's March" (Coates) 140, 142
"Dangerous Veils" (song) 277, 280, 285
"Dark Ages" (song) 19, 145, 146, 147, 151, 207
Darwin, Charles 71
David I (King of Scotland) 21
Davis, Matthew 204
Dawson, Micheal P. 230
Debussy, Claude 85, 112
Delares, George 239
Delius, Frederick 74
Denny, Sandy 149, 163
de Whalley, Chas 241
Dharma, Ritchie 26
"Dharma for One" (song) 8, 33, 35, 36, 47, 49, 59, 60, 76, 77, 79, 85, 180, 251, 255, 270, 320
Dickens, Charles 81
"Different Germany" (song) 173, 175
Digance, Richard 153–154
Dire Straits 188–189, 190–191, 192, 282
Dirty Linen 302
"Dirty Linen" (Fairport Convention instrumental) 302
Disney Studios 275
Divinities—Twelve Dances with God (Ian Anderson album) 273–276, 278, 279, 281, 282, 286, 290, 296, 301, 303, 306
Dixon, Willie 270
Docherty, Bernard 150
"Dr. Bogenbroom" (song) 73, 76, 80–81
"Doctor to My Disease" (song) 223, 224, 227, 233, 264
"The Dog Ear Years" (song) 289, 291–292
"Dogs in the Midwinter" (song) 187, 191

Dolby, Thomas 178
Dominion Theatres (London) 171
Donohue, Jerry 163
Doolin, Jim 25
Dorothy Chandler Pavilion (Los Angeles) 127
"Dot Com" (song) 289, 290, 292
"Double Violin Concerto" (instrumental) 184
"Down at the End of Your Road" (song) 167, 192, 195, 198
Drake, Sir Francis 311
"Drive on the Young Side of Life" (song) 260, 263–264
"Driving Song" (song) 76, 77
"Drowsy Maggie" (instrumental) 213, 215
"Dun Ringill" (song) 145, 147–148, 151, 153, 154, 165, 196, 199, 215, 228, 319, 320
Duncan, James B. 22
Durngate (North Hampton) 286
The Dwellers 40
Dwyer, Michael 268
Dylan, Bob 8

The Eagles 89, 304
"Ears of Tin (Mainland Blues)" (song) 204, 206, 209
Eddows, Rita 105
Eden Court Theatre (Inverness) 210
Edwards, Elizabeth 105
El Cid (film) 275
"El Niño" (song) 289, 291
Eldridge, Roy 20, 82, 84
Electric Ladyland Studios 230
"Elegy" (instrumental) 144, 145, 146, 148, 151, 184, 185, 186
Elgar, Edward 87, 118, 160, 229, 253
Elizabeth I (Queen of England) 99
Elizabethan era 99, 103, 107, 122, 125, 130, 170, 209
Ellington, Duke 144, 243
Ellis, Terry 28, 29, 33, 34, 41, 44, 46, 52, 61, 62, 64, 75, 82, 84, 96, 97, 127, 154, 164, 317, 318; on *Under Wraps* 177
Emerson, Sam 76
Emerson, Lake and Palmer 285
Empire (Liverpool) 216
"En Afrique" (instrumental) 273, 275
"End Game" (song) 173, 175
Engels, Mike 271, 272
Entwhistle, John 30
Ephesus (Ismir) 221

"European Legacy" (song) 176, 178, 181, 220

Evans, John 4, 24, 25, **26**, 29, 30, 52, 53, **54**, 55, 58, 59, 60, 62, 66, 67, 68, 71, 73, 74, 76, 78, 79, 80, 81, 82, 84, 85, 86, 87, **90**, 91, 95, 97, 99, 105, 107, 113, 114, 117, 119, **123**, 129, 134, 135, 139, 142, 145, 150, 154, 195, 218, 235, 245, 247, 252, 258–259, 260, 261, 269, 305, 315, 317, 318, 319, 320, 321

Evening Chronicle (Newcastle) 210

Evening News (Manchester) 211

Fairport Convention 4, 5–6, 7, 9–10, 11, 13, 15, 50, 65, 148, 149, 150, 152, 160, 171, 183–184, 189, 192, 196, **200**, 203, 205, 212, 215, 225, 233, 235, 240, 241, 247, 251, 258, 265, 269, 277, 286, 302, 305, 307, 312

Faith, Adam 114

"Fallen on Hard Times" (song) 19, 162, 166, 171, 190, 196, 199

"Far Alaska" (song) 289, 291

"Farm on the Freeway" (song) 19, 187, 188, 190, 196, 199, 207, 212, 215, 233, 320

Farmyard Studios 172, 176, 187, 203, 223

Farrell, Michael 113

"Fat Man" (song) 44, 49, 195, 197, 201, 218, 227, 230, 293, 317

Feasby, Peter 210

Fig, Anton 229

Fillmore East (New York) 42, 50, 59, 180, 285

Fillmore West (San Francisco) 42, 43

"Fire at Midnight" (song) 119, 126–127, 147, 171, 292

"First Post" (instrumental) 260, 261

Fisher, Archie 191

Fisher, Matthew 256

Fitzgerald's Nightclub (Chicago) 13

Fleetwood Mac 37, 217

Fleming, Ian 25

Flint, Sir William Russell 298

"Flute Solo Improvisation" (instrumental) 140, 142, 263

"Fly by Night" (song) 173, 174, 185, 186, 298

"Flying Colours" (song) 162, 166, 167, 169

"Flying Dutchman" (song) 20, 145, 146, 148, 208, 276, 300, 303

Folk Roots 149

"For a Thousand Mothers" (song) 44, 49, 61, 246, 254, 305

"For Later" (instrumental) 73, 76, 81

"For Michael Collins, Jeffrey and Me" (song) 53, 55, 61

Forbes, Bryan 98

Forum (Livingstone) 216

Foster, Geoff 223

Fotheringay 163

"4.W.D. (Low Ratio)" (song) 157, 160

Fradley, John 216

Free 50

Freud, Sigmund 69

"From a Dead Beat to an Old Greaser" (song) 113, 115, 116, 237, 240

"From 21 Subtract" (song) 28

Fuel 2000 Records 289

Fussell, G. E. 17

The Future of an Illusion (Freud essay) 69

"Fylingdale Flyer" (song) 157, 159, 165, 320

Gabriel, Peter 265

Gaines, Steve 104

Gamm, Victor 33, 76

Gander, Sid 273

Garvin, Rex 28

Gazette (Montreal) 245

Gee, John 37

"General Crossing" (song) 176, 178

Generation X 137

Genesis (band) 175, 244

Gentle Giant 89

George, Lowell 5

Gershwin, George 85, 95, 275

Gethsemane (band) 41

Gibbons, Billy 228

Gibbons, David 113

Gibson, Jim 162, 203, 224

Giddings, Andrew (a.k.a. "Andy") 8, 9–10, 13–14, 15, 131, 223, 225, 226, 234–235, **236**, 237, 238, 245, 247, **248**, 251, 253, 254, **255**, **256**, 265, 268, 270, 273, 275, 276, 277, 279, 284, 289, 290, 291, 292, 294, 295, 297, 298, 300, 301, 303, 306, 315, 320, 321; on *Divinities* 274; on Ian Anderson's voice problems 242; on playing Jethro Tull music 235; on *Roots to Branches* 280–281; on touring 235, 293

"A Gift of Roses" (song) 289, 292

"The Girl from Ipanema" (Jobim song) 201

Glascock, Brian 139

Glascock, John 4, 113, 114, 116, 119, **124**, 125, 128, 129, 133, 139, 141, 142, 145,

146, 148, 155–156, 195, 199, 245, 253, 315, 318, 319, 320, 321; death of 153

Glascock, Walter 139

"Glory Row" (song) 318

"God Rest Ye Merry Gentlemen" (instrumental) 140, 142, 242, 244, 253

Goddard, Martyn 173, 237, 248, 255, 289

Godfrey, Andrew 16

Goldmine 230

"Gold-Tipped Boots, Black Jacket and Tie" (song) 224, 228, 231

Gordon, Dougie 129

Gore, Albert, Jr. (Vice-President of the United States) 258

Graber, Michael 76

"Grace" (song) 106, 110, 195, 198, 319

Grammy Awards 19, 202

The Grand Mothers of Invention 270

Grand Theatre (Clapham) 269–270

Grashow, Jimmy 44

The Grateful Dead 311

Great Woods (Mansfield, Massachusetts) 258

Greater London Radio 228

Greek Theatre (Los Angeles) 294

Greig, Gavin 22

Greslin, Nina 273

Griffin, Dale 219

Guest, Christopher 181

Guild Hall (Preston) 216

Guildford Festival 286

Guitar for the Practicing Musician 220–221

"Guitar Solo" (instrumental) 246, 251

Guitar World 244

Gumby, W. S. 16, 95, 264

Gurson, Ben 65, 68, 70, 87–88, 94

"Gutter Geese" (Maddy Prior song) 129

"The Habanero Reel" (song) 295, 300, 302, 305

Half Moon (Putney) 203

Hall, Daryl 217

Halling, Patrick 97, 105

Halpin, Geoff 224

Hamer, Paul 189

Hamer Guitar Company 189

Hammond, Jeffrey (a.k.a. "Hammond-Hammond") 24, 25, 36, 37, 47, 55, 61, 62, 63, 66, 74, 76, 80, 81, 82, 84, 86, 87, 90, 91, 94, 95, 97, 105, 107, 108, 109, 110, 148, 155, 195, 245, 247, 250, 258–259, 262, 269, 315, 317, 318, 319, 320, 321; on *A Passion Play* 92–93; on leaving Jethro Tull 111; on 1990 Jethro Tull Convention 218; on *Thick as a Brick* 93; on touring 72, 96; on *War Child* 104

"Happy Birthday" (traditional song) 184

"Hardliner" (song) 260, 264

Hardy, Oliver 6

Harper, Roy 65, 98, 270

Headline News (CNN) 214

Heart of the Lion (charity album) 284

"Heat" (song) 176, 178, 181

Heavy Horses (album) 3, 8, 17, 18, 20, 100, 128–138, 140, 142, 160, 163, 171, 174, 198, 199, 225, 292, 297–298, 302

"Heavy Horses" (song) 3, 18, 129, 130, 134–136, 139, 144, 146, 147, 151, 153, 161, 165, 180, 233, 246, 251, 254, 265, 271, 272, 276, 299, 306, 320, 321

"Heavy Water" (song) 204, 207

Help! (film) 152

Hendrix, Jimi 37, 41, 59, 230

Henry VIII (King of England) 151

Herald Examiner (Los Angeles) 202

Herman, Woody 43

Herman's Hermits 27

Heston, Charlton 275

Hilary, Sir Edmund 311

Hindle, Mark 244

Hippodrome (Golders Green) 127

Holden, Stephen 93–94

Holly, Buddy 27

Holst, Gustav 275

"The Holy Fair" (Robert Burns poem) 66

"Home" (song) 147, 151, 152

"Hoochie Coochie Man" (Willie Dixon song) 270

Hooker, John Lee 27

Horslips 58

"Hot Mango Flush" (song) 289, 291

"Hotel California" (Eagles song) 304

Howard, Keith 119

The Howard Stern Show (TV show) 194

Howlin' Wolf 24, 112, 224

Huddersfield School of Music 197

Hungerthon 1987 (United Nations) 194

"Hunt by Numbers" (song) 289, 290–291, 300, 305

Hunter, Scott 223, 227

"Hunting Girl" (song) 18, 119, 123, 125, 127, 135, 140, 142, 161, 184, 206, 219, 294

Huntley, Scott 16, 302–303

Hutchings, Ashley 149

"Hymn 43" (song) 55, 62, 70–71, 72, 76, 77, 80, 103

I Talk with the Spirits (Roland Kirk album) 31
Ian Anderson Group of Companies 16
Ian Campbell Folk Group 149
Ibanez (guitar company) 205
Ibirapuera Arena (São Paulo) 202
"I Don't Want to Be Me" (song) 228, 260, 264
"I Wonder Who" (song) 265
"I'm Your Gun" (song) 167, 195, 198
"In a Black Box" (instrumental) 273, 275
"In a Stone Circle" (instrumental) 273, 275
"In Defense of Faiths" (instrumental) 273, 275
"In Maternal Grace" (instrumental) 273, 275
In Real Time (Fairport Convention Album) 192
"In Sight of the Minaret" (instrumental) 273, 275
"In the Grip of Stronger Stuff" (instrumental) 273, 275, 295, 303, 306
"In the Moneylender's Temple" (instrumental) 273, 275
"In the Olive Garden" (instrumental) 273, 275
"In the Pay of Spain" (instrumental) 273, 275
"In the Times of India (Bombay Valentine)" (instrumental) 273, 275–276
"Inside" (song) 53, 54, 55, 76, 78
International Congress Centrum (Berlin) 184
"Invasion of Privacy" (song) 28
Iommi, Tony 38–40; on playing with Jethro Tull 39; on the members of Jethro Tull 247–248
Iron Maiden 307
Island Records 33, 34
Island Studios 62, 317
Isle of Wight Festival 59–60
"It All Trickles Down" (song) 292
"It's Breaking Me Up" (song) 33, 35, 36, 77

J-Tull Dot Com (album) 288–294, 298, 305
"Jack Frost and the Hooded Crow" (song) 167, 195, 198, 207
"Jack in the Green" (song) 18, 19, 119, 123, 124, 127, 130, 140, 141, 171, 215, 302, 307, 320
"Jack-a-Lynn" (song) 167, 196, 198–199,

212, 215, 229, 230, 242, 246, 252, 319, 320
Jackman, Paul 25
Jackson, David 145
Jackson, Michael 88, 311
Jackson, Steve 225
Jacobsen, Todd 4, 16
Jacques, Dominick 111
Jagger, Mick 40, 206, 298
James, Elmore 35
Jamieson, Andrew 187
"Jams O'Donnell's Jigs" (instrumental) 152
Jansch, Bert 65
"The Jasmine Corridor" (song) 295, 300, 302
Jazziz 276
Jefferson Starship 270
"Jeffrey Goes to Leicester Square" (song) 44, 47, 49, 294
Jethro Tull: Complete Lyrics (book) 284
Jethro Tull Convention: (1989) 218; (1992) 241; (1994) 268; (Germany, 1994) 265; (Germany, 1998) 287; (Italy, 2000) 305
Jethro Tull in Concert—At the Hammersmith Odeon 8th October 1991 (album) 271–272
"Jethro Tull Summer Raid" 186
Jethro Tull: 25th Anniversary (box set) 245–256, 285
Jethro Tull: 25th Anniversary (video) 94, 269
Jobim, Antonio Carlos 201
Jobson, Eddie 156, 157, 159–160, 161, 165, 171, 184, 245, 247, 315, 319
The Joey Bishop Show (TV show) 51
John, Elton 92, 248
"John Barleycorn" (song) 203, 237, 239
The John Evan Band 25–26, 27–28, 30, 73, 74
Johns, Andy 44, 76, 317, 318
Johns, Glyn 44
Jones Beach Theatre (Wantagh, New York) 294
"Journeyman" (song) 129, 133
Jubilee (Edmonton) 243
Jude 73
"Jump Start" (song) 19, 187, 190, 229, 271, 272, 320
"Just Trying to Be" (song) 76, 79
Jyllands-Posten (Allborg) 221

Kampert, Patrick 230
"Kashmir" (Led Zeppelin song) 291
Kaye, Don 194

KBCO radio (Boulder) 188
Keating, Viktoria Pratt 294
"Kelpie" (song) 144, 148, 196, 199, 239, 252, 272, 319
Kennedy-Fraser, Marjorie 22
Kenwright, Tony 216
Kerouac, Jack 116
Kerrang 213
Key, Trevor 176
KGB 222–223
Kilborn, Craig 297
King, B. B. 27
King Biscuit Flour Hour (radio show) 160
"King Henry's Madrigal" (instrumental) 151–152, 195, 198
Kings Theatre (Edinburgh) 144
Kirk, Rahsaan Roland 31, 36, 43
"Kissing Willie" (song) 6, 203, 206, 207, 210, 211, 214, 215, 226, 247, 254, 320
Klepacz, Marilyn 16
Knopfler, Mark 188–189, 192, 206, 207, 209, 228
Kristofferson, Kris 59
Kubes, Pavel 139
Kuti, Fela 175

L.A. Music Center 127
"Ladies" (song) 97
"Land of Hope and Glory" (instrumental) 247, 253
Landers, Tim 297
"Lap of Luxury" (song) 176, 177–178
The Late, Late Show with Craig Kilborn (TV show) 297
Late Night with David Letterman (TV show) 168, 229–230
The Late Show with David Letterman (TV show) 297
"Later That Same Evening" (song) 176, 178, 181, 219–220
Laurel, Stan 6
"Law of the Bungle" (instrumental) 260, 261
"Law of the Bungle, Part II" (instrumental) 260, 262
Lawrence, Derek 28, 29–30
Led Zeppelin 36, 37, 42, 50, 62, 66, 107, 111, 149, 202, 220, 287, 291, 297
Lee, Christopher 81
Lee, Jay L. 119
Lee, Will 229
"Left, Right" (song) 260, 262
Lennon, John 40
Leno, Jay 258

Lenoir, J. B. 112
Leslie, Chris 12, 15, 276
"Let's Spend the Night Together" (Rolling Stones song) 298
Letterman, David 168, 229–230, 297
Lewis, Grover 74
Lewis, Roger 273, 274
"Lick Your Fingers Clean" (song) 103, 196, 198, 319
Liege and Lief (Fairport Convention album) 50
"Life Is a Long Song" (song) 73, 80, 81, 137, 180, 196, 199, 237, 238, 246, 250, 265, 270, 318, 319, 320, 321
"Light and Dark Tour" 7, 241–245, 252, 254
"Lights Out" (song) 260, 264
"Like a Tall Thin Girl" (song) 224, 227, 230, 271, 272
Little Feat 5
"The Little Flower Girl" (song) 295, 298
A Little Light Music (album) 236–242, 251, 272, 320
Live at Hammersmith '84—The Friday Rock Show Sessions (album) 219
Live: Bursting Out (album) 139–142, 215, 242, 263, 320
Living in the Past (album) 58, 75–81, 85, 86, 141, 215, 234, 239, 250, 251, 298
"Living in the Past" (song) 42, 50, 72, 76, 77, 181, 184, 185, 186, 196, 199, 215, 219, 220, 237, 238, 246, 247, 250, 254, 258, 265, 292, 317, 318, 319, 320, 321
"Living in These Hard Times" (song) 137, 196, 199
Lloyd, A. L. 103
"Locomotive Breath" (song) 10, 63, 64, 71, 76, 80, 140, 142, 161, 165, 181, 182, 184, 185, 186, 196, 199, 211, 215, 219, 220, 229, 230, 231, 237, 238, 240, 247, 253, 265, 269, 270, 276, 305, 312, 317, 318, 319, 320, 321
Loew, Tony 76
London Symphony Orchestra 184–186
Long, Siobhan 259
"Look at the Animals" (song) 260, 261
"Look into the Sun" (song) 44, 48, 237, 239, 272
"Looking for Eden" (song) 173, 175
"The Lord's Prayer" 70
Los Angeles Philharmonic Orchestra 53
Los Angeles Sports Arena 161
Louis, Jeroen 99–100
Louis, Mark 16, 90, 96–97, 304

"Love Story" (song) 37, 76, 77, 195, 197, 215, 319
Lowry, L. S. 301
Luc-Ponty, Jean 157
Lucas, Trevor 163
Lunny, Manus 302
Lustig, Jo 150
Lynyrd Skynyrd 10

Mabe, Chauncey 209, 309
McCaig, Ian 162
McCarthy, Sissel 287
McCartney, Paul 38, 175
McCrea, Willie 128
McCrorie, Alan 215
McGee, Brownie 246, 251
McGregor's Engine 28
MacKinnon (Scottish clan) 147
McPherson, Robbie Ann 257
McTell, Ralph 151
"Made in England" (song) 173, 174
Madison Square Garden 75, 143–144, 151
Madonna 88, 311
Magritte, René 116
Maison Rouge Mobile Studio 105, 106, 113, 119, 139, 145, 157
Maison Rouge Studios 129, 145, 146, 150, 157, 162, 163, 172
Malcolm III (King of Scotland) 21
Mammoth Gardens (Denver) 59
"Man of Principle" (song) 260, 263
"The Man with the Weird Beard" (Ray Charles song) 28
Mancini, Henry 275
Mandoki, Leslie 270
Manfred Mann 73
"Mango Surprise" (song) 289, 291
Mantle, Leigh 145, 157, 162
"March the Mad Scientist" (song) 125, 195, 198, 319
Marillion 186
Marquee Club (London) 29, 30, 34, 37, 39, 285
Martin, George 64, 164
The Martin Barre Band 270
Maschwitz, Eric 301
Mathieson, Midge 7, 15, 293
Mattacks, David 7, 15, 149, 183, 189, **200**, 235, 236, 237, 238, 239, 240, 241, 247, 316, 320
"Matty Groves" (Fairport Convention song) 203
Matyear, Tim 6, 16, 187, 203, 223, 289
Maurstad, Tom 257

Mayall, John 27, 31, 36, 37, 40
"Mayhem, Maybe" (song) 167, 196, 199, 319
The Meeting (Martin Barre album) 282, 286
Mehta, Zubin 53
Melody Maker 154, 157, 163
Melrose Abbey 22
Memorial Auditorium (Dallas) 90
Metallica 202, 307
Metella, Ellen 243
MGM Records 29
Michelob Beer 231
The Midnight Special (TV show) 139
The Mike Douglas Show (TV show) 169
Miller, Brett 258
Miller, Glenn 25
Milton Keynes Bowl 186
Mineirinho Areana (Belo Horizonte) 201
Minstrel in the Gallery (album) 19, 71, 105–111, 115, 116, 135, 198, 203, 213, 239, 297, 298
"Minstrel in the Gallery" (song) 19, 105, 107–108, 127, 140, 142, 180, 195, 198, 246, 250, 271, 272, 306, 318, 320, 321
"Mr. Nareesh" 266–267
"Mr. Tambourine Man" (Bob Dylan song) 8
Mitchell, Douglas 273
"Montserrat" (song) 295, 298
Monty Python 88, 95, 98
Moon, Keith 40
Mooney, Darren 295, 301
Moonraker (novel) 25
The Moonrakers 40
Moore, Gary 193, 250
Morgan Studio 44, 52, 76, 77, 78, 91, 97, 119, 317
Moss, Thing 119
"Mother Goose" (song) 3, 67–68, 72, 211, 213, 215, 230, 265, 292, 320
"Moths" (song) 129, 136–137, 196, 199
"Motoreyes" (song) 167, 196, 199, 319
Mountain 62
"Mountain Men" (song) 19, 187, 192
"Move On Alone" (song) 33, 36, 270
MTV 182, 190, 237
M.U.: The Best of Jethro Tull (album) 317
Muir, Edwin 130
"My God" (song) 3, 59, 60, 62, 64, 69–70, 75, 89, 103, 146, 213, 215, 242, 244, 246, 247, 251, 252–253
"My Sunday Feeling" (song) 33, 36, 37, 48, 180, 242, 246, 250, 251, 265, 270

Nance, Donald Craig 7–8, 16
Nash, Joseph 105
National Stadium (Dublin) 259
"Nellie (The Revenge)" (instrumental) 215
A New Day 4, 16, 197, 202
"A New Day Yesterday" (song) 44, 47,
    140, 142, 195, 197, 237, 239, 242, 246,
    252, 271, 272, 318, 319, 320, 321
New York Symphony Orchestra 42
New York Yankees 258
Newman, Paul 231
Newport Jazz Festival 43
The Nice 34, 35, 38, 53
Nicol, Simon 12, 15, 149, 183, 189, **200,**
    247, 265
"Night in the Wilderness" (song) 229, 262
Nightcap: The Unreleased Masters (album)
    137, 167, 229, 259–264
"Ninth Symphony" (Beethoven) 118, 127,
    213
"No Lullaby" (song) 20, 129, 133, 139, 141
"No Rehearsal" (song) 196, 260, 262
"No Step" (song) 260, 263, 264
"Nobody's Car" (song) 176, 178, 247,
    253–254
Nollen, Harold 16
Nollen, Michelle 15, 16
Nollen, Shirley 13–14, 16
Nollen-Richter, Debra 3, 16
"North Sea Oil" (song) 18, 145, 146, 147
Noriega, Manuel Antonio 214
Nosotti, Fabio 240, 241
Nostel Priory 172
"Nothing @ All" (instrumental) 289, 290
"Nothing Is Easy" (song) 44, 48–49, 59,
    60, 213, 246, 247, 254, 305, 317, 320
"Nothing to Say" (song) 53, 55, 180
Now We Are Six (Steeleye Span album)
    98, 115
Noyce, Jonathan 13, 15, 276, 282–284,
    289, 290, 291, 294, 316
"Nursie" (song) 73, 76, 81, 196, 199, 215,
    237, 239, 319

Oates, John 217
O'Beirne, Gerry 301
"Occasional Demons" (song) 224, 226
Odeon (Hammersmith) 153, 181, 192,
    219, 232, 258, 271
"Old Ghosts" (song) 145, 147
O'List, Davy 38
O'Lochlainn, Jackie 76
O'Lochlainn, Ruan 52–53, 76, 139
Olson, Keith 162

Olympic Studios 48
O'Malley, Brian 7, 8–11, 13, 16
"On the 7th Side of 9" (song) 28
"Once in Royal David's City" (carol) 77
"One Brown Mouse" (song) 129, 132, 134,
    140, 141–142, 144, 171
"One for John Gee" (tune) 37, 195, 198
"One White Duck/0^{10}=Nothing at All"
    (song) 106, 109, 196, 199, 237, 239
"Only Solitaire" (song) 97, 102, 104, 196,
    199, 262
Ono, Yoko 40
Oral, Aykut 16, 304
Original Masters (album) 318
"Orion" (song) 145, 146, 147, 151
Orpheum (Boston) 284
Ostseehalle (Kiel) 105
"Out of the Noise" (song) 277, 279
Overall, Rick 244
"Overhang" (song) 167, 196, 199, 319

Page, Jimmy 36, 66–67
Palmer, David 4, 33, 36, 44, 45, 49, 62,
    67, 68, 71, 76, 77, 78, 82, 91, 97, 99, 105,
    108, 109, 110, 113, 115, 117, 119, 125, 127,
    129, 133, 134, 135, 139, 141, 142, 144,
    145, 147, 148, 150, 151–152, 153, 154,
    184–186, 195, 198, 219, 235, 239, 245,
    247, 253, 263, 276, 305, 316, 317, 318,
    319, 320, 321; on leaving Jethro Tull
    156; on 1989 Grammy Award 202–203;
    on *This Was* 45–46; on *War Child* 98;
    on *The Water's Edge* 144
"Pan Dance" (instrumental) 104, 125, 195,
    198
"Panama Freighter" (song) 295, 300, 303
Pan's People 104
"Paparazzi" (song) 176, 178
Paradise Lost (Milton) 93
"Paradise Steakhouse" (song) 260, 262
Parker, Charlie 116, 117
Parnell, Marc 268–269
Parrish, Michael 302
"Part of the Machine" (song) 19, 196, 199,
    201, 206, 209, 319
Pasche, John 173, 176, 187, 203, 224
"Passion Jig" (instrumental) 247, 254
A Passion Play (album) 17, 68, 91–96, 98,
    99, 100, 101, 103, 109, 135, 198, 242, 253,
    261, 262
"A Passion Play" (song/album excerpts)
    247, 253, 317, 318, 320
"Pastime with Good Company" (song)
    151, 198, 239

Paterson, Foss 223, 225, 228
Paterson, Rod 300
Pavilions (Plymouth) 286
Pegg, Albert 149
Pegg, Christine 5, 16, 149
Pegg, David (a.k.a. "Peggy") 4–13, 5, 15–16, 131, 148–153, 157, 160, **164**, 165, 166, 167, 170–171, 176, 178, 181, 183–184, 185, 186, 187, 189, 190, 192, 195, 196–197, 198, 199, **200**, 203, 205, 207, 210, 215, 219, 220, 223, 225, 226, 228, 232, **236**, 237, 238, 239, 241, 245, 247, **248**, 251, 252, 253, **255**, **256**, 258, 259, 263, 265, 269, 271, 272, 276, 279, 280, 282–284, 286, 307, 316, 319, 319, 320, 321; on *A* 158–159, 161; on *Catfish Rising* 233; on David Letterman 229–230; on Fairport Convention 192; on fans of Jethro Tull 313–314; on favorite Jethro Tull albums 163; on folk elements in Jethro Tull music 233; on Jethro Tull tour programs 234; on joining Jethro Tull 149–150; on leaving Jethro Tull 277–278; on 1989 Grammy Award 202, **212**; on other members of Jethro Tull 150–151, 152–153, 155, 161, 163–164, 171, 217, 218, 234, 239–240, 277–278; on playing Jethro Tull music 151; on smashing his bass 216; on *The Broadsword and the Beast* 162–163, 171; on touring 152, 217, 230, 234, 313–314; on *Under Wraps* 177
Pegg, Matthew 10, 223, 225, 226, 227, 255, 257, 259, 268–269, 270; on touring with Jethro Tull 258
"Peggy's Pub" (instrumental) 153
Pegrum, Nigel 98
Pentangle 65
Perry, Doane 4, 7, 8, 12–16, **14**, 187, 195, 197, 203, 213, 215, 219, 220, 225, 234, 235, **236**, 245, 247, **248**, 250, 252, 253, **255**, **256**, 260, 263, 269, 270, 271, 272, 273, 274, 275, 276, 277, 289, 290, 291, **293**, 294, 297, 305, 306, 307, 316, 319, 320; and spicy food/hot peppers 12, 13, 14, 265, 284; on British pop music 179; on *Catfish Rising* 227, 228; on *Crest of a Knave* 189–190, 192; on favorite Jethro Tull songs 180–181; on *Jethro Tull: 25th Anniversary* 251; on McDonald's 257; on other members of Jethro Tull 183, 194, 232–233, 249, 257, 282–284; on playing Jethro Tull music 179–180, 182–183, 205–206, 249, 283–284; on

Roots to Branches 278–279, 280, 281–282; on singing on stage 214; on the Rock and Roll Hall of Fame 310–311; on *The Secret Language of Birds* 302; on *This is Spinal Tap* 181–182; on touring 193, 194, 221, 232–233, 303, 310; on touring in India 265–268; on touring in the Eastern bloc 191, 222–223, 257; on touring with Procul Harum 255–257
Philamusica of London 97
Phillips, Leon 236, 246, 273
Phoenix House 60
"Pibroch (Cap in Hand)" (song) 119, 125–126, 133, 170, 196, 199, 215, 306, 319
"Piece of Cake" (song) 260, 262
"Pied Piper" (song) 113, 117
"The Pine Marten's Jig" (song) 157, 158, 160, 212, 215
Pinewood Studios 143
Pink Floyd 27, 30, 35
The Planets (Holst) 275
Plant, Robert 149, 248
"Play in Time" (song) 53, 58
Poe, Edgar Allan 87
"Pop Goes the Weasel" (tune) 142
"Post Last" (instrumental) 260, 262
"Postcard Day" (song) 295, 298, 302
"Prelude in G-Sharp Minor" (Rachmaninov) 60
Presley, Elvis 23, 27
Press Herald (Portland, Maine) 233
Presshouse Studios 223, 251
The Prince's Trust 171
Prior, Maddy 98, 113, 115, 129, 318
Procter, Bridget 105
Procul Harum 255–257, 270
Prokofiev, Sergei 74
Proops, Tony 118
"Protect and Survive" (song) 157, 159, 160, 246, 251, 252
Prown, Pete 220
Purcell, Henry 94
"Pussy Willow" (song) 162, 166, 171, 215, 219, 220, 237, 240, 247, 254, 255, 320
Puterbaugh, Parke 169
Putterford, Mark 213

Q 199, 209–210, 241, 276
"Quartet" (instrumental) 260, 263
"Quatrain" (instrumental) 140, 142
"Queen and Country" (song) 97, 99, 115
"Quizz Kid" (song) 113, 115, 320

Rabe, Brian 245
Rachmaninov, Sergei 60
"Radio Free Moscow" (song) 176, 178
Radio Monte Carlo 105, 113
R.A.F. (band) 163
Rainbow (band) 193
Rainbow (London) 104
"Rainbow Blues" (song) 185, 186, 317
"Raising Steam" (song) 187, 192
Ramey Communications 139
"Rare and Precious Chain" (song) 277, 278–279, 320
"The Rattle Snake Trail" (song) 203, 206
Ravinia Festival (Chicago) 13, 305–306
Raw Fruit Records 219
Reagan, Ronald 191
"Reasons for Waiting" (song) 44, 49, 60, 246, 254, 272
Record Collector 200–201
Red and Gold (Fairport Convention album) 5–6, 201, 203, 204
Red Rocks (Denver) 73–74
Redding, Dan 273
Redford, Robert 168
Redmond, Cindy 234
Reeday, Maggie 287
Rees, David 16, 197, 202
Regent's Theatre (Ipswich) 243–244
Reilly, Ken 53
Reiner, Rob 181
Renbourn, John 65
Renton, Robert 241
Repeat: The Best of Jethro Tull, Volume II (album) 318
Reprise Records 57
Requiem (band) 73
"Requiem" (song) 105, 108, 203, 213
Rhapsody in Blue (Gershwin) 275
"Rhythm in Gold" (song) 167, 196, 199
Richard, Cliff 27
Richards, Keith 244
Riley, Chris 26
"Ring Out, Solstice Bells" (song) 18, 119, 125, 152
Rivercity People 217
Riviera Nightclub (Chicago) 7, 8, 242, 254
Robert I (King of Scotland) (a.k.a. "Robert the Bruce") 21–22
Roberts, Keith 16
Robin Hood: A Cinematic History of the English Outlaw and His Scottish Counterparts (book) 12, 13, 15
Robson, Dave 29

Rock, Sheila 176
Rock Island (album) 5, 201, 203–214, 215, 226, 233, 254, 264, 280, 309
"Rock Island" (song) 204, 207, 215
Rockline (radio show) 169, 230, 231
"Rocks on the Road" (song) 224, 226, 229, 230, 237, 238–239, 271, 272, 281, 299
Rockwalk (Hollywood) 197
Rogers, Phil 224
Rogovoy, Seth 211
"Roll Yer Own" (song) 224, 226, 231
Rolling Stone 19, 65, 74, 87, 93, 94, 109, 136, 140, 143, 169–170, 181
The Rolling Stones 24, 40, 82, 107, 111, 137, 225, 272, 298, 309
The Rolling Stones Rock 'n' Roll Circus (TV show) 40
Roots to Branches (album) 276–285, 291, 298, 305
"Roots to Branches" (song) 277, 278, 306, 307, 321
"Rosa on the Factory Floor" (song) 229, 260, 263, 264
Rosenblatt, Amy 16, 294
Rosza, Miklos 275
"Round" (instrumental) 33, 37
"Rover" (song) 129, 133–134, 139
Roxy Music 157
Royal Academy of Music 45, 276
Royal Albert Hall 161
Royal Navy 99
Royal Philharmonic Orchestra 274
Royal Scottish Ballet 23, 144
R.P.I. Fieldhouse (Troy, New York) 211
Russell, Bertrand 63, 69
Ryan, Jerome 201–202

"Saboteur" (song) 176, 178
"Said She Was a Dancer" (song) 187, 190–191, 215, 281
"The Sailor's Alphabet" (Fairport Convention song) 9
St. Denis Theatre (Montreal) 245
"Salamander" (song) 113, 114, 116, 196, 199
Salt Palace (Salt Lake City) 73
Samwell-Smith, Paul 162, 164, 165
Sandbu, Dag 16
"Sanctuary" (song) 295, 299, 303
Sanders, Ric 12, 15, 184, 187, 189, 192, 200, 203, 247, 254, 265
Santana 53, 303
Sanville, Jim 233

"Saturation" (song) 196, 319
Savoy Brown 50
"Scenario" (song) 196, 260, 262
Scott, Sir Walter 122
Scottish Highland Hospice 284
Scottish Nationalist Party 128, 228
Sea Hawks 99
"Sea Lion" (song) 97, 100–101, 213
"Sea Lion II" (song) 260, 262
"Seal Driver" (song) 20, 162, 167, 170, 171, 247, 253, 254
Sebastian, John 59
The Secret Language of Birds (Ian Anderson album) 289, 292, 295–303, 305, 307, 312
"The Secret Language of Birds" (song) 289, 292, 295
"The Secret Language of Birds, Part II" (song) 295, 300–301
"Serenade to a Cuckoo" (instrumental) 33, 36, 184, 194, 215, 232, 294
Sergeant Pepper's Lonely Hearts Club Band (Beatles album) 88
"Set Me Up" (Fairport Convention song) 203
"Set-Aside" (song) 295, 299
Seven Nations 307
"Seventeen" (song) 195, 198
The Sex Pistols 137, 309
Shaffer, Paul 229, 297
Shakespeare, William 103
Shaw, John 157
Sheep and Fish and Rock 'n' Roll (TV show) 186
Sight and Sound in Concert (TV show) 127
"Silver River Turning" (song) 229, 260, 263
Silverman, Burton 62, 64
Sinatra, Frank 74, 301
"Singing All Day" (song) 76, 78
The Six and Violence 220
"Skating Away (on the Thin Ice of the New Day)" 97, 101, 127, 140, 141, 161, 192, 194, 302, 317, 318, 320
Skyrme, Martin 25
"Sleeping with the Dog" (song) 224, 228
Slinde, Wade 8–11, 16
"Slipstream" (song) 62, 71
Slipstream (video) 165, 190
"Slow Marching Band" (song) 162, 166, 207
"A Small Cigar" (song) 260, 263
Smejkai, Marek 236
Smith, Neil (a.k.a. "Chick Murray") 26, 28

Smith, Peter 113
"So Much Trouble" (song) 218, 246, 251, 265
"Sock It to 'Em, J.B." (Rex Garvin song) 28
"Solitaire" 260, 262
"Someday the Sun Won't Shine for You" (song) 33, 36, 218, 237, 238, 246, 251, 265
"Something's on the Move" (song) 145, 147, 151
"Son" (song) 53, 55, 71
"Sonata Number 8 in C-Flat" ("Pathé-tique") (Beethoven) 60
"A Song for Jeffrey" (song) 33, 37, 40, 60, 76, 77, 195, 197, 242, 246, 247, 250, 254, 320, 321
Songs from the Wood (album) 3, 17, 18, 81, 116, 119–128, 129, 130, 131, 135, 147, 160, 163, 169, 171, 174, 198, 232, 252, 253, 278, 292, 294, 297, 302
"Songs from the Wood" (song) 18, 119, 123–124, 127, 140, 142, 151, 161, 165, 180, 193, 196, 199, 246, 250–251, 254, 318, 320, 321
"Sossity: You're a Woman" (song) 53, 58, 60, 68, 246, 254, 255
Sound Techniques 73, 76, 80
Soundi 129
"Sparrow on the Schoolyard Wall" (song) 224
Spectrum (Philadelphia) 182
Spencer Davis Group 149
"Spiral" (song) 289, 290
Spooky Tooth 34, 50
Spreckels Theatre (San Diego) 243
Stand Up (album) 17, 43–51, 53, 54, 58, 64, 65, 77, 78, 88, 93, 140, 142, 186, 198, 213, 226, 231, 232, 239, 241, 251, 253, 254, 272, 285–286, 290, 303, 304, 305, 306
Status Quo 311
"Steel Monkey" (song) 19, 187, 188, 190, 192, 215, 320, 321
Steele, Davy 300
Steeleye Span 4, 98–99, 115, 129, 149, 203
Steinbrenner, George 258
Stenzel, Kurt 220
Stephens, Michael 24, 25
Stereo Review 205, 231
Stern, Howard 194
Stevens, Cat 92, 163
Stevenson, Robert Louis 68, 79, 86, 87, 109
Stewart, Andy M. 300, 301

"Still Loving You Tonight" (song) 224, 227, 247, 254, 271, 272, 320
"A Stitch in Time" (song) 19, 142, 195, 198
"The Stormont Shuffle" (instrumental) 295, 301–302
Stormwatch (album) 10, 18–19, 20, 99, 145–153, 155, 157, 159, 160, 169, 198, 199, 207, 225, 292, 298, 311, 313
"Stormy Monday Blues" (song) 37, 195, 197, 319
"Strange Avenues" (song) 204, 209, 211, 215
Strathaird 4, 128, 146, 169, 210, 264, 287–288
"Strip Cartoon" (song) 127, 195, 198
"Stuck (Out) in the August Rain" (song) 277, 281–282
"Such Sweet Thunder" (Ellington) 144
"Suite in E Minor for Lute" (J. S. Bach) 47
Summer Band (Martin Barre) 241, 287
"Summerday Sands" (song) 110, 195, 198, 319
Sun Sentinel (Fort Lauderdale) 209, 309
Sunbury Jazz and Blues Festival 31, 41
Sunday Sun (Ottawa) 244
Sunderland Echo 210
"Sunshine Day" (song) 30, 195, 198
Swan Lake (Tchaikovsky ballet) 103, 144
Swarbrick, David 149
"Sweet Dream" (song) 51, 76, 77, 78, 139, 141, 142, 146, 165, 196, 199, 246, 250, 307, 318, 320, 321
Swenson, John 143–144
"The Swirling Pit" (instrumental) 171
The Switched-On Symphony (TV show) 53
Symphony Number One (Elgar) 229

Taj Mahal 40
"Take the Easy Way" (song) 28
Tallinn Festival (Estonia) 222
Tarlair Festival (MacDuff, Scotland) 259
"Taxi Grab" (song) 113, 114, 116
Taylor, Ian 250, 251
Taylor, James 149
Taylor, Mick 40, 45
Taylor, Paul 211
Taylor, Stephen 187
Tchaikovsky, Pyotr Ilyich 24, 74, 95, 98
"Teacher" (song) 51, 53, 57–58, 76, 78, 185, 186, 196, 199, 246, 250, 319, 320
Ten Years After 43
"That Smell" (Lynyrd Skynyrd song) 10
Thatcher, Margaret 19, 165, 190, 191

Theakston Brewery 171–172
Theatre Royal (Glasgow) 144
Thick as a Brick (album) 3, 17, 19, 61, 77, 81–88, 92, 93, 95, 97, 109, 116, 135, 142, 174, 180, 182, 186, 215, 220, 234, 242, 272, 303
"Thick as a Brick" (song/album excerpts) 140, 142, 146, 185, 196, 199, 246, 252, 265, 271, 295, 317, 318, 320, 321
"Thinking Round Corners" (song) 224, 230, 231
"The Third Hoorah" (song) 97, 101, 102, 133, 180, 213
"This Free Will" (song) 277, 279–280
"This Is Not Love" (song) 223, 224, 225–226, 229, 237, 238, 271, 272, 320
This Is Spinal Tap (film) 181, 182
This Was (album) 33–38, 45, 47, 49, 65, 73, 77, 78, 117, 198, 225, 231, 232, 238, 242, 250, 251, 253, 254, 270, 305
Thomas, Craig 19–20, 35, 84, 130, 148
"Thomas the Rhymer" (Steeleye Span song) 98
Thomason, Neil R. 109
Thompson, Richard 65, 149, 191, 203, 205
Through the Years (album) 320
Thulborn, Katherine 105
"Tiger Toon" (instrumental) 260, 261
Time 109
"A Time for Everything?" (song) 53, 57
Titanic (ship) 148
"To a Mouse…" (Robert Burns poem) 134
"To Be Sad Is a Mad Way to Be" (song) 247, 253
"To Cry You a Song" (song) 53, 56, 57, 60, 73, 127, 246, 287, 293, 318, 320
"Toad in the Hole" (song) 173, 175
Toby, Lou 76, 250
Tommy (Who album) 88
The Tonight Show with Jay Leno (TV show) 258
"Too Many Too" (song) 167, 195, 198
Too Old to Rock 'n' Roll: Too Young to Die! (album) 3, 113–118, 159, 189, 232, 240, 263
"Too Old to Rock 'n' Roll: Too Young to Die" (song) 113, 114, 117, 140, 142, 165, 184, 185, 186, 198, 214, 215, 217, 219, 220, 237, 239, 246, 250, 254, 318, 320, 321
Top of the Pops (TV show) 50
Townshend, Pete 103, 171, 209
Traffic 239

"Trains" (song) 173, 175, 181
Treasure Island (Stevenson novel) 68
A Trick of Memory (Martin Barre album)
    270
Trower, Robin 73
"Truck Stop Runner" (song) 228, 260,
    262, 264
Tucker, Mark 203, 223
Tull, Jethro 18
"Tundra" (song) 176, 178
Tutbury Castle 269
20 Years of Jethro Tull (album) 319
20 Years of Jethro Tull (box set) 19, 80,
    110, 125, 137, 148, 152, 167, 186, 194–
    201, 262, 269, 270
20 Years of Jethro Tull (video) 201
"Two Fingers" (song) 97, 103, 198

U2 88
The Uglies 149
U.K. (band) 157
Under Wraps (album) 176–179, 181, 182,
    183, 188, 190, 191, 198, 199, 202, 219–
    220, 263
"Under Wraps #1" (song) 176, 178, 181,
    219
"Under Wraps #2" (song) 178, 181, 196,
    199, 237, 238, 319, 320
Underground Rumours (ballet) 144
"Undressed to Kill" (song) 204, 207, 226
Unhalfbricking (Fairport Convention
    album) 50
"Uniform" (song) 157, 160
United States Marine Corps 213–214
Universal Amphitheater (Los Angeles)
    284
"Up the 'Pool" (song) 73, 76, 80
"Up to Me" (song) 19, 62, 69
"User-Friendly" (song) 173, 175

Vai, Steve 229
Valentine, Neil (a.k.a. "Ranger") **26**
"Valley" (song) 277, 280
Valli, Frankie 42
Vanden, Mike 201, 204
Vanilla Fudge 42
Vantone Studio 42, 76, 317
"Velvet Green" (song) 18, 119, 123, 125,
    126, 127, 129, 195, 198, 206
The Ventures 27, 40
The Very Best of Jethro Tull (album) 306,
    321
Vettese, Peter-John 162, 163–164, **164**,
    165, 166, 168, 169, 171, 172, 173, 174,

175, 176, 178, 184, 192, 195, 203, 207,
    219, 220, 245, 247, 253, 260, 263, 264,
    298, 316, 319, 320, 321
VH1 1, 307
Victoria Hall (Hanley) 216
Vietnam War 52
The Village Voice 157, 179
Voorbij, Jan 16
Vormstein, Manfred 184
Vox 241

Wagg, Peter 145, 157
Waits, Tom 305
"The Waking Edge" (song) 187, 192
Walk into Light (Ian Anderson album)
    172–175, 176, 179, 181, 188, 263, 264,
    296, 298
"Walk into Light" (song) 173, 174–175
Walker, Don 219
Wallace, Ian 256
War Child (album) 19, 97–105, 114, 115,
    133, 161, 180, 198, 262
"War Child" (song) 97, 99, 185, 186, 318,
    320
Ward, Bo 26
Ward, Brian 33, 76, 91, 105
"Warm Sporran" (instrumental) 145, 147,
    152, 284, 302
"Watching Me, Watching You" (song)
    162, 166–167, 198
"The Water Carrier" (song) 295, 298,
    305
Waters, Muddy (McKinley Morganfield)
    24, 27, 112, 224
The Water's Edge (ballet) 144, 146
Watts, Charlie 40
Way, Darryl 129
"We Used to Know" (song) 44, 49, 59,
    60, 246, 286, 304, 305, 320
"Weathercock" (song) 129, 136, 171, 302
Webb, Martin 16, 197
Webb, Nick 295
Welch, Chris 175
Wembley Stadium (London) 217
Western Recorders 42, 76, 77
Westmorland Arms (London) 247, 269
Wetton, John 157
"The Whaler's Dues" (song) 204, 208,
    209, 211–212, 213
"When Jesus Came to Play" (song) 224,
    228, 230
"The Whistler" (song) 18, 119, 125, 127,
    232, 242, 247, 252, 320, 321
White, Trevor 113

White Bear 172
"White Innocence" (song) 224, 228, 233, 263, 264
"A Whiter Shade of Pale" (Procul Harum song) 270
The Who 30, 40, 50, 59, 107, 137, 202, 209
"Whole Lotta Love" (Led Zeppelin song) 297
Why I Am Not a Christian (Russell book) 69
"Wicked Windows" (song) 289, 290
Widdows, Philip 216
Wigs, Randy 273
Wild Turkey 61, 89
Wilkinson, Tony 26, 29
Williams, Tony 143, 155, 247, 316
Williamson, Sonny Boy 24, 35
Wilson, Francis 145, 154, 228
Wilson, Tim 269
Wilson, Tony 219
"Wind-Up" (song) 63, 71–72, 89, 247, 253, 320
Winwood, Steve 149
"Witch's Promise" (song) 51, 63, 76, 77, 78, 196, 199, 246, 250, 293, 318, 319, 321
"With You There to Help Me" (song) 53, 55, 59, 60, 180, 242, 246, 305
WMMR radio (Philadelphia) 230
WNEW radio (New York) 230
Woman in the Wings (Maddy Prior album) 129

"Wond'ring Again" (song) 63, 76, 79, 86
"Wond'ring Aloud" (song) 63, 68, 79, 107, 127, 181, 184, 196, 199, 215, 265, 270, 319
Wood, Gareth 273
Wong, Judy 52
Wood, John 76
Woodhouse, C. 293
Woodstock Festival 14, 43
Woodworm Records 167
Woodworm Studios 187, 203, 204, 223, 251
"Working John, Working Joe" (song) 157, 159, 160, 190
World Music Theatre (Chicago) 8
World War II 263
Woughton Centre (Milton Keynes) 218
"Wounded, Old and Treacherous" (song) 277, 281, 291
Wright, Chris 28, 29, 84, 177, 290
Wylie, Kenny 4, 12, 15, 158, 310

Yamaha (music company) 238
Yeltsin, Boris 296, 301
Yes 144
"You Got Me" (song) 28
Young Dubliners 13, 305

Zappa, Frank 157, 175, 281
Zarkowski, Bogdan 237, 246, 260, 273, 277, 289, 295
ZZ Top 188, 190, 192, 206, 227, 228, 229